JESUS
Then & Now

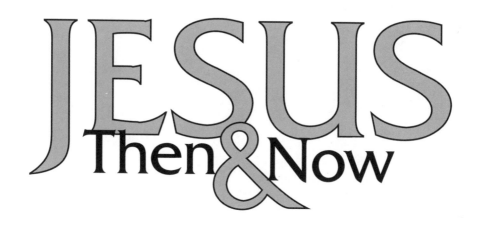

JESUS
Then & Now

Images of Jesus
in History
and Christology

Edited by
Marvin Meyer
and
Charles Hughes

TRINITY PRESS INTERNATIONAL
Harrisburg, Pennsylvania

#44932109

Trinity Press International, P.O. Box 1321, Harrisburg, PA 17105
Trinity Press International is a division of the Morehouse Group.

Cover art: *The Holy Face,* Georges Rouault, 1946, Musée du Vatican, Cat. de l'Oeuvre peint, vol. II no. 2388, © 2001 Artists Rights Society (ARS), New York/ ADAGP, Paris, and Scala/Art Resource, NY. Icon painting of Jesus Christ as Panto-crator, © 2001 Corbis, all rights reserved.

Cover design: Wesley Hoke

Library of Congress Cataloging-in-Publication Data

Jesus then and now : images of Jesus in history and Christology / edited by Marvin Meyer and Charles Hughes.
    p. cm.
    Includes bibliographical references and index.
    ISBN 1-56338-344-6 (alk. paper)
    1. Jesus Christ – Person and offices. I. Meyer, Marvin W. II. Hughes, Charles.
BT203 .J47 2001
232'.8 – dc21
                              00-064838

Printed in the United States of America

01   02   03   04   05   06   10 9 8 7 6 5 4 3 2 1

Contents

Part Three
IMAGES OF JESUS IN JUDAISM,
ISLAM, AND THE FUTURE

Abbreviations

AASOR	Annual of the American Schools of Oriental Research
AGJU	Arbeiten zur Geschichte des antiken Judentums und des Urchristentums
AnBib	Analecta Biblica
ANRW	*Aufstieg und Niedergang der römischen Welt: Geschichte und Kultur Roms im Spiegel der neueren Forschung.* Edited by H. Temporini and W. Haase. Berlin, 1972–
ASOR	American Schools of Oriental Research
BAGD	W. Bauer, W. F. Arndt, F. W. Gingrich, and F. W. Danker, *Greek English Lexicon of the New Testament and Other Early Christian Literature.* 2d ed. Chicago, 1979
BAR	*Biblical Archaeology Review*
BASOR	*Bulletin of the American Schools of Oriental Research*
BBR	*Bulletin for Biblical Research*
BETL	Bibliotheca Ephemeridum Theologicarum Lovaniensium
BZNW	Beihefte zur Zeitschrift für die neutestamentliche Wissenschaft
ETL	*Ephemerides Theologicae Lovanienses*
EvT	*Evangelische Theologie*
HTR	*Harvard Theological Review*
IEJ	*Israel Exploration Journal*
JAAR	*Journal of the American Academy of Religion*
JBL	*Journal of Biblical Literature*
JETS	*Journal of the Evangelical Theological Society*
JRS	*Journal of Roman Studies*
JSJ	*Journal of the Study of Judaism in the Persian, Hellenistic and Roman Period*

JSNT	*Journal for the Study of the New Testament*
JSNTSup	Journal for the Study of the New Testament Supplement Series
JSOT	*Journal for the Study of the Old Testament*
JSPSup	Journal for the Study of the Pseudepigrapha Supplement Series
LCL	Loeb Classical Library
NovT	*Novum Testamentum*
NovTSup	Novum Testamentum Supplements
NTOA	Novum Testamentum et Orbis Antiquus
NTS	*New Testament Studies*
NTTS	New Testament Tools and Studies
PEQ	*Palestine Exploration Quarterly*
SBLDS	Society of Biblical Literature Dissertation Series
SBLTT	Society of Biblical Literature Texts and Translations
SBT	Studies in Biblical Theology
SJLA	Studies in Judaism in Late Antiquity
SJT	*Scottish Journal of Theology*
SNTSMS	Society for the Study of the New Testament Monograph Series
WUNT	Wissenschaftliche Untersuchungen zum Neuen Testament
ZAW	*Zeitschrift für die alttestamentliche Wissenschaft*
ZNW	*Zeitschrift für die neutestamentliche Wissenschaft und die Kunde der älteren Kirche*
ZTK	*Zeitschrift für Theologie und Kirche*

Introduction

Marvin Meyer and Charles Hughes

At the beginning of the twentieth century, a century rich in its contributions to the study of Jesus, Albert Schweitzer observed in his *Quest of the Historical Jesus,* "The study of the life of Jesus has had a curious history" (399).[1] In the preceding pages of his book Schweitzer had examined a wide range of interpretations of the figure of Jesus, from Hermann Samuel Reimarus to William Wrede, in a bold, lucid, and engaging fashion. At the very opening of his final chapter, entitled "Results," he was led to conclude, "Those who are fond of talking about negative theology can find their account here. There is nothing more negative than the result of the critical study of the life of Jesus" (398).

Schweitzer proceeded to bury, in a manner of speaking, the historical Jesus of modern theology. The Jesus "designed by rationalism, endowed with life by liberalism, and clothed by modern theology in an historical garb" (398) never really existed, Schweitzer exclaimed. Rather, the Jesus of history is a stranger to our time and, in the memorable words of Schweitzer repeated often and even set to music, "He comes to us as one unknown, without a name, as of old, by the lake-side, he came to those men who knew him not" (403). Schweitzer emphasized, "the truth is, it is not Jesus as historically known, but Jesus as spiritually arisen within men, who is significant for our time and can help it. Not the historical Jesus, but the spirit which goes forth from him and in the spirits of men strives for new influence and rule, is that which overcomes the world" (401). Schweitzer's presentation of Jesus has had a profound impact upon subsequent contributions to the study of Jesus, and his concern for Jesus then and Jesus now still challenges us.

This challenge is the concern of the present volume, *Jesus Then and Now: Images of Jesus in History and Christology.* In this volume we present a wide variety of scholarly interpretations of the historical Jesus and Christ in christological formulations. In these scholarly essays Jesus comes to us as one known and unknown, one familiar and strange, and the interplay between the Jesus of history and Christology is often evident. In the variety of images of Jesus presented here, we propose, lies the richness of this volume.

The essays contained in this volume offer conclusions that are grounded in the conviction that historical and theological investigations can yield signifi-

1

cant insights about Jesus. Nevertheless, the authors of these essays frequently disagree with each other about what is known of Jesus as well as about what the historical and christological significance of that might be. There are many reasons for these disagreements, but the most fundamental basis for them is worth identifying.

The interpretive contexts that render each author's conclusions about Jesus both possible and plausible are based upon sets of fundamental philosophical, theological, and methodological assumptions typically described as "worldviews." Worldviews offer "big pictures" of reality that contain answers to the most basic and fundamental questions about existence. Thus many, but not all, of the disagreements among our contributors over philosophical, theological, and methodological ideas are traceable to differences in worldview. To illustrate this, reflect for a moment on the question of how Jesus of Nazareth is to be understood and interpreted from within the worldviews of theism, which claims that God exists, and naturalism, which claims that there is no God. From the standpoint of theism, Jesus could have performed miracles, could have been raised from the dead, and could have been the Jewish Messiah and even God incarnate, as traditional Christians claim. But from the standpoint of naturalism, miracles, messiahs, and God incarnate are ruled out from the beginning because there is no God or supernatural dimension to reality that could make such things possible. For this reason, a person's interpretive starting point, in terms of worldview and other important assumptions, plays a crucially important role in determining how that person can understand Jesus of Nazareth.

The essays in this volume are divided into three parts: (1) Images of Jesus in History, (2) Images of Jesus in Christology, and (3) Images of Jesus in Judaism, Islam, and the Future. While historical and christological issues emerge throughout the volume, and many essays address aspects of Jesus then and Jesus now, it is convenient to divide the essays in this manner.

In Part 1, Images of Jesus in History, seven essays offer interpretations of the historical, literary, and archaeological evidence concerning the historical Jesus. James M. Robinson assesses the present state of the scholarly study of Q, the synoptic sayings source, and sketches a portrait of the image of Jesus in Q. Robinson notes the radical message of Jesus in Q: "Jesus is not easy at all: One must lose one's life...take up one's cross...." Colin Brown reads what is most likely the earliest New Testament gospel, the Gospel of Mark, "with the grain" and "against the grain," as he puts it, and he judges that Mark presents the life of Jesus as a tragic-epic narrative in which Jesus is depicted as a second Joshua who seeks to deliver the people and land of Israel. N. T. Wright presents a study of Jesus and traditions of his resurrection, typically a difficult issue for historians to discuss. Wright asserts that "Christianity began as a resurrection movement," and he argues that an affirmation of the resurrection of Jesus best explains how Christianity arose. Marvin Meyer addresses the image of Jesus in another sayings gospel, the Gospel of Thomas, in which "the living Jesus," not the resurrected Christ, according to Meyer, speaks words that may impart life. John Dominic Crossan raises questions regarding eschatology and apocalyptic intended to "desimplify" the issue of an apocalyptic image of Jesus over against a nonapocalyptic image of Jesus. Jonathan Reed explores the archaeological evidence of Galilee in the first century and shows the implications for the study of Jesus of Nazareth. Robert Funk summarizes the collaborative work of the Jesus Seminar and the decisions it has reached. The conclusion of his essay provides a segue to discussions of Christology and faith in the second part of the volume: "The recovery of the historical figure of Jesus may well serve as that catalyst of a new beginning for the Christian movement as it enters the third millennium."

In Part 2, Images of Jesus in Christology, seven essays offer christological interpretations of the meaning and significance of Jesus. John Hick compares and assesses literal and metaphorical interpretations of Christology with respect to the doctrine of the incarnation. He concludes that a metaphorical understanding of Christology is both logically and religiously superior to the traditional literal understanding of divine incarnation. Charles T. Hughes compares and contrasts the simplicity and explanatory adequacy of John Hick's religious pluralism with Christian inclusivism, both of which are acknowledged as important theologies of the world's religions. Hughes argues that inclusivism, with its traditional Christology, offers a simpler and more adequate theology of the world's religions than does Hick's pluralism. Richard Swinburne presents evidence in favor of the view that Jesus Christ was God incarnate. He structures his argument according to the demands of the Bayesian probability calculus in order to justify formally the claim that the evidence makes it more probable than not that Jesus was God incarnate. Karen Torjesen identifies a wisdom Christology that was important for women prophets in the early church and that she believes holds new promise for contemporary feminists. She traces the implications of wisdom Christology for understanding both God and female authority in the church. Ronald L. Farmer sets out what he believes are three important contributions that process theology makes toward interpreting the nature and significance of Jesus of Nazareth. He provides a very helpful explication of the categories of process theology in order to show the context in which his christological proposals are both intelligible and plausible. Carter Heyward discusses how living a life committed to God in Christ helps one to identify and subvert traditional and unjust power relations that afflict both the church and society. She argues that Christology, motivated by faith, provides the ground for a "revolutionary spiritual struggle toward social change and personal transformation." Didier Pollefeyt develops a Catholic perspective about Christology in the aftermath of Auschwitz. He develops what he sees as the christological implications required to ground Jewish-Christian interfaith dialogue positively.

In Part 3, Images of Jesus in Judaism, Islam, and the Future, three essays discuss Jesus in Jewish and other contexts. S. David Sperling provides Jewish perspectives on Jesus from the Talmud as well as later Jewish traditions. Commenting on interfaith dialogue among Jewish and Christian scholars, Sperling observes, "If we can apply contextual historical scholarship to deepen our understanding of each other, and disseminate that knowledge on a popular but academically responsible level within our respective faith communities, it can only be to the good." F. E. Peters surveys the place of Jesus the prophet in Islam and stories about Jesus in the Qur'an, including stories about the annunciation, the virgin birth, the miracles or signs of Jesus, and the apparent death of Jesus. (Meyer discusses additional Islamic traditions about Jesus in his earlier essay.) Peters suggests that Muhammad got his information from Eastern monks "who have left behind no literary texts, churches, chapels, or shrines, but whose traces may still be preserved in the Qur'an, and through it have found their way deep into Muslim consciousness." Finally, Lloyd Geering traces three phases of cultural evolution—ethnic culture, transethnic culture, and global culture—and proposes that we now have entered the third, global phase of human history. The implications of globalization, Geering believes, are enormous, including implications for Christianity and the place of Jesus. Geering concludes, "It is the Jesus who could look both appreciatively and also critically at his cultural past, who can inspire us as we in turn look back to a receding Christian past and forward to an unknown global future. It is Jesus the teller of stories, which shocked people out of their traditional ways of thinking and behaving, who can free us from the mind-sets in which we become imprisoned. The Jesus most relevant to us is he who, far from providing ready-made answers, prompted people by his tantalizing parables to work out their own most appropriate answers to the problems of life."

The essays in this volume derive, in large part, from an international conference on "Images of Jesus" and several other special presentations at Chapman University in the autumn of 1999. These presentations have been revised for this volume, and to them have been added other invited essays. The events at Chapman University were made possible through the generous support of the Department of Religious Studies, the Francis Lectureship, the Griset Lectureship, the Huntington Lectureship, and the Rodgers Center for Holocaust Education. For this support we express our gratitude.

Note

1. Albert Schweitzer, *The Quest of the Historical Jesus: A Critical Examination of Its Progress from Reimarus to Wrede,* trans. W. Montgomery (Baltimore: Johns Hopkins University Press, 1998).

Part One

Images of Jesus
in History

The Image of Jesus in Q

James M. Robinson

The twentieth century began with the quest of the historical Jesus at its peak. But the first half of the century was largely devoted to dismantling that "assured result of critical scholarship," and only in the last half of the century has there been a series of efforts to return to the study of the historical Jesus. It is the contours of these developments that lead to the present status of the scholarly study of Jesus that I would like to summarize in this essay, as the context for the use of *The Critical Edition of Q*[1] for the study of Jesus today.

The Teachings of Jesus

At the opening of the twentieth century, it was Q to which critical scholarship had naturally turned in its quest of the historical Jesus. For it was upon the sayings of Jesus that Adolf Harnack had built his "essence of Christianity":

> If, however, we take a general view of Jesus' teaching, we shall see that it may be grouped under three heads. They are each of such a nature as to contain the whole, and hence it can be exhibited in its entirety under any one of them.
>
> *Firstly, the kingdom of God and its coming.*
>
> *Secondly, God the Father and the infinite value of the human soul.*
>
> *Thirdly, the higher righteousness and the commandment of love.*[2]
>
> But the fact that the whole of Jesus' message may be reduced to these two heads—God as the Father, and the human soul so ennobled that it can and does unite with Him—shows us that the Gospel is in no wise a positive religion like the rest; that it contains no statutory or particularistic elements; *that it is, therefore, religion itself.*[3]

This sublime picture of Jesus' teaching is no doubt responsible for the emphasis in American Protestantism throughout most of the twentieth century on "the teachings of Jesus." But one should not uncritically idealize

Q as a definitive ethical code. Jesus was not a theoretician in the field of ethics. Hence the sayings of Jesus in Q do not derive from reflection in the abstract, but from concrete situations. Jesus, as a person of his time, did not speak to all issues important in our time, nor did his conduct conform to all our ideals of today. "The peril of modernizing Jesus,"[4] inherent in ethical idealism's definition of the quintessence of religion, only aggravates the historian's recognition, for example, that the ideals of the Pauline church, "There is no longer Jew or Greek, there is no longer slave or free, there is no longer male and female . . . " (Gal. 3:28), are topics that for Q, and to this extent apparently for Jesus, were quiescent.

This first became apparent with regard to Gentiles. Q presents Jesus caring for the Centurion's sick boy (Q 7:1–10), but without risking defilement by coming under his gentile roof (Q 7:6), even though his faith exceeded any Jesus had found in Israel (Q 7:9). The Cornelius story of Acts 10–11 makes clear what was involved in such a major step, a step apparently taken only after Jesus' death. Jesus' first disciples, as documented in Q, consisted of a Jewish community, to which the gentile mission, led by Barnabas and Paul, was added rather independently, as an afterthought. At the Jerusalem Council, a mutually tolerant double mission was agreed on, which at times, such as the crisis in Antioch reflected in Gal. 2:11–14, tended to break down.

The *explicit* of Q (22:30) presents Jesus' followers as judging the twelve tribes of Israel.[5] This again recognizes the focus of Jesus on Israel, yet with the judgmental recognition that Israel did not produce the needed kind of faith (Q 7:9). Hence God would, as John said (Q 3:8), have to produce children to Abraham from the (gentile) stones. Gentiles will replace Abraham, Isaac, and Jacob's lineal descendents at the eschatological banquet (Q 13:29, 28). There are invidiously favorable sayings about biblical Gentiles (but not Jesus' gentile contemporaries): Sodom (Q 10:12), Tyre and Sidon (Q 10:14), the Queen of the South (Q 11:31), the Ninevites (Q 11:32). But they function in Q primarily as a foil to put to shame "this generation" (Q 7:31; 11:29 *bis*, 30, 31, 32, 50, 51), made up of the chosen people, Israel. There is no indication that uncircumcised Gentiles were part of the Q community.

Nor had "there is no longer slave or free" been adequately implemented. Q refers to slaves as part of the real world presupposed in parables (Q 7:8; 12:43–46; 14:21; 19:15–22), without using the occasion to condemn the inhumanity of slavery. Paul's Letter to Philemon shows that "no longer slave or free" had not been adequately addressed. The American experience in the "Bible Belt" surely shows how slavery remained unfinished business for the church down to modern times.

In a somewhat similar way the text of Q does not do justice to our modern feminist sensitivity as to the full equality of women. The most that one can say is that male-female pairs are present in Q, with which both men and women can hence identify. The male Ninevites are paired with the Queen of the South standing in judgment against Israel (Q 11:31–32); a man sowing a field with mustard seed (Q 13:18–19) is paired with a woman making bread out of yeast (Q 13:20–21); the shepherd seeking a lost sheep (Q 15:4–5a, 7) is paired with the woman seeking a lost coin (Q 15:8–10); two males on a couch (Q 17:34) are paired with two females grinding at a mill (Q 17:35). Pairings may be implicit, even if less visible, in such formulations as bread (baked by women) and fish (caught by fishermen) in Q 11:11–12, and ravens (in contrast to men working in the fields) and lilies (in contrast to women making cloth) in Q 12:24, 27–28. The Q movement's disruption of family ties between generations involves the women as well as the men (Q 12:53; 14:26). Though such pairings thus recognize women as well as men, no inclusive point is explicitly scored. The patriarchal culture is tacitly presupposed, in such formulations as "marrying and giving in marriage" (Q 17:27), and in addressing God as "Father" (Q 10:21 *bis;* 11:2; cf. 6:36; 10:22 *bis;* 11:13; 12:30).[6]

In sum, there are major ethical problems of society that Q, and hence presumably Jesus, did not adequately address. It is clear that the "teachings of Jesus" as reflected in Q do not present the "political correctness" of an ethical idealism for today.

Jesus the Apocalypticist

The central position that Q had attained in terms of ethical idealism a century ago did not go unchallenged at the time. It was Albert Schweitzer who carried to its ultimate consequences a dramatic renunciation of that quest of the historical Jesus, as a modernization of Jesus effected by projecting Protestant liberalism's ideology back on him.

Central to Schweitzer's own solution was his assumption that Q did not exist. For he preferred Ferdinand Christian Baur's prioritizing of Matthew rather than the development of the Q hypothesis from its discovery in 1838 by Christian Hermann Weisse to its definitive demonstration in 1863 by Heinrich Julius Holtzmann.

> Research was initially spared having to experience the problem in its whole weight, in that it, under the influence of Christian Hermann Weiße, *Die Evangelienfrage* (1856), and Heinrich Julius Holtzmann, *Die synoptischen Evangelien* (1863), gives up the view advocated by Ferdinand Christian Baur (1792–1860) and the Tübingen School, to the effect that the Gospel of Matthew is the oldest and most original, and regards the Gospel of Mark to be this. The preference for the shorter Gospel made it possible for it to evaluate the significant material that Matthew offers over and beyond that of Mark as not fully valid. And it is precisely this that contains the discourses and reports in which Jesus' thought world is shown to belong to that of late Jewish eschatology. It is especially the Sermon on the Mount (Matthew 5–7), the great discourse at the sending forth of the disciples (Matthew 10),

the inquiry of the Baptist and the statements of Jesus it called forth (Matthew 11), the discourse on the coming of the Son of Man and the judgment he will hold (Matthew 25)....

For the quest of the historical Jesus, the point is not which of the two oldest Gospels could be a little bit older than the other. Incidentally, this literary question will hardly ever be solved. With the fragmentary report of Mark, the historical problem of the life of Jesus could not be resolved, indeed would not even come in view. The reports of the two oldest Gospels are in their way of equal value. That of Matthew is, however, as the more complete, of more value. In substance, Ferdinand Christian Baur and his school, in preferring it, are still right.[7]

Though Schweitzer was guarded in his statements (Holtzmann had, after all, been his professor in Strassburg), the position that he took on the sources only makes sense if he considered the canonical Gospel of Matthew to be the product of an eyewitness, which amounts to treating it as a definitive work of the apostle Matthew, the prevalent precritical view ever since Papias. He simply dismissed, as absurd, efforts to dismantle into its sources Matthew's Mission Instructions, whose detailed historicity was decisive for his own interpretation of Jesus' public ministry. Whereas one maintained, then and now, that material from the Markan apocalypse was interpolated by Matthew into the Mission Instructions of Mark and Q, which were conflated both with each other and with other Q and special Matthean material, Schweitzer maintained:

Thus this discourse [Matt. 10] is historical as a whole and down to the smallest detail precisely because, according to the view of modern theology, it must be judged unhistorical....

That being so, we may judge with what right the modern psychological theology dismisses the great Matthean discourses off-hand as mere "composite structures." Just let any one try to show how the Evangelist when he was racking his brains over the task of making a "discourse at the sending forth of the disciples," half by the method of piecing it together out of traditional sayings and "primitive theology," and half by inventing it, lighted on the curious idea of making Jesus speak entirely of inopportune and unpractical matters; and of then going on to provide the evidence that they never happened.[8]

He remained completely unaware of how form and redaction criticism would show the Gospels to be mirrors of the intervening time of the church in their portrayal of Jesus' time. Hence he could hang his whole thesis on Matt. 10:23, "...you will not have gone through all the towns of Israel before the Son of Man comes," which is a bit of special Matthean material absent both from the Mission Discourse of Q and from the Mission

Discourse of Mark, reflecting no doubt only the history of the Matthean community.

The result was Schweitzer's own bizarre "life of Jesus," with which his *Quest of the Historical Jesus* concluded. His point of departure was Jesus' fascination with parables of harvest:

> If this genuinely "historical" interpretation of the mystery of the Kingdom of God is correct, Jesus must have expected the coming of the Kingdom at harvest time. And that is just what He did expect. It is for that reason that He sends out His disciples to make known in Israel, as speedily as may be, what is about to happen.[9]

The Mission of the Twelve was to be Jesus' final act before the end:

> He tells them in plain words (Matt. x. 23), that He does not expect to see them back in the present age. The Parousia of the Son of Man, [359] which is logically and temporally identical with the dawn of the kingdom, will take place before they shall have completed a hasty journey through the cities of Israel to announce it.[10]

Schweitzer described "the significance of the sending forth of the disciples and the discourse which Jesus uttered upon that occasion" as follows:

> Jesus' purpose is to set in motion the eschatological development of history, to let loose the final woes, the confusion and strife, from which shall issue the Parousia, and so to introduce the supra-mundane phase of the eschatological drama.[11]

He was convinced that "at the time of their mission," Jesus "did not expect them to return before the Parousia."[12] But that is in fact just what happened:

> There followed neither the sufferings, nor the outpouring of the Spirit, nor the Parousia of the Son of Man. The disciples returned safe and sound and full of a proud satisfaction; for one promise had been realized—the power which had been given them over the demons.[13]

Schweitzer drew the inevitable consequence:

> It is equally clear, and here the dogmatic considerations which guided the resolutions of Jesus become still more prominent, that this prediction was not fulfilled. The disciples returned to Him; and the appearing of the Son of Man had not taken place. The actual history disavowed the dogmatic history on which the action of Jesus had been based. An event of supernatural history which must take place, and must take place at that particular point of time, failed to come about. That was for Jesus, who lived wholly in the dogmatic history, the first "historical" occurrence, the central event which closed the former period of His activity and gave the coming period a new character.[14]

The failure of the apocalyptic end to come before the end of the mission must have been a terrible letdown for Jesus, to such an extent that he felt compelled to change his strategy:

> This change was due to the non-fulfillment of the promises made in the discourse at the sending forth of the Twelve. He had thought then to let loose the final tribulation and so compel the coming of the Kingdom. And the cataclysm had not occurred. He had expected it also after the return of the disciples....
>
> In leaving Galilee He abandoned the hope that the final tribulation would begin of itself. If it delays, that means that there is still something to be done, and yet another of the violent must lay violent hands upon the Kingdom of God. The movement of repentance had not been sufficient. When, in accordance with His commission, by sending forth the disciples with their message, he hurled the fire-brand which should kindle the fiery trials of the Last Time, the flame went out.[15]

So Jesus determined to go to Jerusalem for Passover, in order to provoke there his own martyrdom as an alternate way to compel God to bring in the end:

> ...His death must at last compel the Coming of the Kingdom....
>
> The new thought of His own passion has its basis therefore in the authority with which Jesus was armed to bring about the beginning of the final tribulation.... For now He identifies his condemnation and execution, which are to take place on natural lines, with the predicted pre-Messianic tribulations. This imperious forcing of eschatology into history is also its destruction; its assertion and abandonment at the same time.[16]

This heroic resolve ended in a second, even more painful encounter with actual history, leading to his last anguished cry: "My God, my God, why have you abandoned me?" In summary:

> The Baptist appears, and cries: "Repent, for the Kingdom of Heaven is at hand." Soon after that comes Jesus, and in the knowledge that He is the coming Son of Man lays hold of the wheel of the world to set it moving on that last revolution which is to bring all ordinary history to a close. It refuses to turn, and He throws Himself upon it. Then it does turn; and crushes Him. Instead of bringing in the eschatological conditions, He has destroyed them. The wheel rolls onward, and the mangled body of the one immeasurably great Man, who was strong enough to think of Himself as the spiritual ruler of mankind and to bend history to His purpose, is hanging upon it still. That is His victory and His reign.[17]

Q or the Kerygma

Between the two world wars, the focus of attention moved to the oral transmission of traditions under the influence of their social settings, thus shifting away from the social setting in the public ministry of Jesus to social settings in the primitive church, and shifting away from written sources embedded in the Gospels to oral material the Evangelists collected.

Though the form critics Rudolf Bultmann and Martin Dibelius both assumed the existence of Q, their point of departure was more nearly the Q of Julius Wellhausen[18] than that of Adolf Harnack. For it was Wellhausen who had anticipated the new kerygmatic orientation.[19]

> It is as the crucified, resurrected and returning one that Jesus is the Christian Messiah, not as religious teacher. The apostolic gospel, which preaches faith in the Christ, is the real one, and not the gospel of Jesus which prescribes to the church its moral. . . . And the expression purportedly committed by Harnack, "not the Son, but only the Father belongs in the Gospel," is basically false, if it is intended to claim a fact and not merely to express a postulate.[20]

Harnack had indeed said: *"The Gospel, as Jesus proclaimed it, has to do with the Father only and not with the Son."*[21] Wellhausen, apparently quoting from hearsay, left out the decisive *"as Jesus proclaimed it."*[22] The "Gospel" that Wellhausen has in view is of course that of the church, i.e., the kerygma, which became more nearly what one could refer to as "the essence of Christianity" down through the history of the church, e.g., in the form of the *Apostolicum* and subsequent creeds, whereas Jesus' message was largely overlooked, though occasionally rediscovered, as by Francis of Assisi.

This debate between Wellhausen and Harnack was to a remarkable extent repeated in 1923 in a debate between Karl Barth and Harnack. Here it is quite clear that dialectic theology created a theological climate in which Wellhausen's position regarding the relative unimportance, not to say illegitimacy, of Q would have the ascendancy.[23]

Harnack spoke of "the close connection, even equating, of love for God and love for one's neighbor which constitutes the heart of the gospel,"[24] to which Barth replied:

> Does anything show more clearly than this "heart" (not of the gospel, but of the law), that God does not make alive unless he first slays?[25]

Thus the central sayings of Jesus (Mark 12:28–34; Matt. 22:34–40; Luke 10:25–28) that Harnack hailed as "gospel" were for Barth "law," over against which he appealed to the "gospel" of God granting life only in death.

It was primarily in terms of the history of religions that Wellhausen had made it clear that "Jesus was no Christian, but rather a Jew."[26] This was echoed by Bultmann:

> I am further attacked because in my book *Primitive Christianity* I have not described Jesus' preaching in the chapter on "Primitive Christianity," but rather in the chapter on "Judaism," and hence have conceived of Jesus as a Jew. Similarly, the objection has been raised that in my *Theology of the New Testament* I have stated that Jesus' preaching belongs to the presuppositions of New Testament theology. Over against the reproach that I conceive of Jesus as a Jew and assign him to the sphere of Judaism I must first of all simply ask: Was Jesus—the historical Jesus!—a Christian? Certainly not, if Christian faith is faith in him as the Christ. And even if he should have known that he was the Christ ("Messiah") and should actually have demanded faith in himself as the Christ, then he would still not have been a Christian and ought not to be described as the subject of Christian faith, though he is nevertheless its object.[27]

Yet the implication of this history-of-religions classification of Jesus as Jew by Wellhausen and Bultmann was heard theologically by Barth as the dialectic of law and gospel, in which sense Q is by definition not gospel, but law.

Whereas Q uses the verb that etymologically corresponds to the noun "gospel" to refer to its sayings as "evangelizing the poor" (Q 7:22), Paul makes clear that any other "gospel" than his kerygma, even if it were to come from an angel, is anathema (Gal. 1:8–9). This tension persists down to the present, as the theological background of the discussion as to whether Sayings Gospels such as Q and the Gospel of Thomas should be called Gospels at all.[28]

There were many Gospels circulating in early Christianity. Even those that the early church did not canonize were nonetheless called Gospels, and so they are still called Gospels. But they were declassified in the nineteenth century, by inserting the pejorative adjective "apocryphal" ("hidden"), and by assigning them to the postapostolic age. Yet this reasoning does not function in the case of Q, which is older than the canonical Gospels, and is no longer hidden, but rather has resurfaced, visible in Matthew and Luke, and thus indirectly in the canon. And Q texts have, down through the ages, in their Matthean and Lukan form, been the basis for preaching, which was originally the function the designation *canonical* had in view. Furthermore, since Q consists of sayings ascribed to Jesus, it is ultimately based on his Galilean disciples—their memory, reformulation, and reuse of what Jesus had said. On the other hand, none of the canonical Gospels was written by an apostle or eyewitness. Hence the relative appropriateness of calling Q also a Gospel should not be underestimated.

The Image of Jesus in Q

Albert Schweitzer resolved to move beyond Johannes Weiss's limitation to the eschatological sayings of Jesus,[29] in order to present the resultant eschatological "conduct and action" of Jesus:

> Johannes Weiß demonstrates the thoroughly eschatological character of Jesus' proclamation of the kingdom of God. My contribution consists primarily in that I proceed to make comprehensible not only his proclamation but also his conduct and action as conditioned by the eschatological expectation.[30]

But Schweitzer's presentation of Jesus as a deluded fanatic had such disastrous results that subsequent scholarship has in all timidity retreated to Weiss's limitation to the sayings of Jesus. This is exemplified perhaps most clearly in Bultmann's *Jesus and the Word*.[31] Yet Schweitzer was in a sense correct, that Jesus' message must have meant something in Jesus' actual practice. If Schweitzer found the key in Matthew's redactional Mission Instructions, which he took to be historically factual down to the last detail, and as a result depicted a "public ministry" that in fact never took place, perhaps the archaic Mission Instructions of Q can provide a more solid foundation for what actually went on during Jesus' Galilean ministry.

The best that the Synoptic Gospels could do by way of presenting Jesus' Galilean ministry was to assemble disparate anecdotes that produced portrayals of Jesus wandering rather aimlessly from place to place, until they have Jesus steadfastly turn to Jerusalem to die, with a bee-line, purposeful itinerary based on the kerygma. But it is more reasonable to assume that Jesus did in fact have something in mind for his Galilean ministry. His plan of action may be relatively accurately reflected in the Mission Instructions of Q. For Gerd Theissen is probably right that "the earliest Christian itinerant charismatics continued the preaching and life-style of Jesus."[32] Hence, if one uses the archaic sayings collections to interpret the oldest layer of the Mission Instructions, one has a relatively solid basis for understanding what went on in Jesus' Galilean ministry.

After being baptized by John (Q 3:21–22), Jesus apparently went back to Nazara (Q 4:16) only long enough to break with his past and to move to Capernaum (Q 7:1), as the base camp of a circuit that initially may have comprised Capernaum well below sea level on the northern tip of the Sea of Galilee, Chorazin in the mountains behind it, and Bethsaida just across the Jordan to the east, in the safer territory of Philip (Q 10:13–15).

What did he do on such a circuit? He set out without any human security. He had no backpack for provisions, no money at all, no sandals, no stick—helpless and defenseless (Q 10:4). This hardly makes sense in terms of the history of religions. His was neither the getup of his precursor John the Baptist, nor a Cynic garb.[33] But it does make sense in terms of his message, as echoed in the other archaic Q collections:[34] One is not anxiety-laden about food and clothing, any more than the ravens and lilies would seem to be (Q 12:22b–30). Rather, one orients oneself exclusively to God reigning (Q 12:31). One prays to God to reign, and thus to provide bread (Q 11:2b–3). One trusts God as a benevolent Father to know one's needs for bread and fish and to provide them (Q 11:9–10), trusting that God will not instead give a stone or snake, but will in fact, in this regard as in others, reign as a benevolent Father (Q 11:11–13). That kind of message of radical trust calls for that kind of radical lack of physical security, if it is to be validated as credible in actual reality.

In the case of the Mission Instructions, it is striking that Jesus did not advocate going to the local synagogue, which would at the time seem to have been rather nonexistent in Galilee in terms of architecture, nor address masses on a Mount or on a Plain or by the seaside. No location is given for the Inaugural Sermon, Q 6:20–49, which in fact seems less meant as an actual scene than as the basic core collection of the sayings of Jesus.[35] Rather, the Mission Instructions were oriented to houses (Q 10:5, 7).[36] One walked from farm to farm, from hamlet to hamlet, from house to house, and there knocked at the door to bring attention to one's presence. To gain admission, one called out: Shalom! (Q 10:5b) If admitted by the head of the household, and thereby accorded the normal hospitality, one designated him as "son of peace" (Q 10:6a), since God's peace had been bestowed as "performative language" in the shalom of the opening greeting. If turned away at the door, God's peace left along with Jesus or his disciple (Q 10:6b), to be offered again at the next house where one knocked. But what took place in a house that did take one in was understood as God reigning. This was in fact expressly said to the household while in their home: "The kingdom of God has reached unto you" (Q 10:9b).

God's reign involved the hospitality itself. Food was accepted at face value as God's gift, and eaten as offered, without ascetic dietary restrictions such as John and other "holy men" practiced at that time. This makes it clear that the drastic absence of gear for the journey was not due to an ascetic ideology, but rather was meant as demonstrative documentation for one's trust exclusively in God for such human needs. For, as the other archaic collections make clear, the food offered and eaten in the house was in reality God already knowing one's need and providing for it, as God does for the ravens; it was the answer to prayer for God to reign by giving a day's ration of bread and not a stone.

The needs of the household itself are comparably met. The sick are healed, with the explanation that this is in turn God's reign reaching even to them (Q 10:9). For the healing is done by God's finger, which is God reigning (Q 11:20), irrespective of whether the human involved is Jesus or someone else (Q 11:19). For it was understood not as human action, but as God's action.

All of this must have been explained by means of such sayings, and by means of the Prayer itself (Q 11:2b–4). In this way "workers" were enlisted for the mission (Q 10:2), and in the process of time such "worthy" houses (Matt. 10:13) might well become "safe houses," where workers knew they would be taken in. Indeed they might well develop into what Paul called "house churches" (Rom. 16:5; 1 Cor. 16:19; Philem. 1–2; Col. 4:15). The itinerant "worker" (Q 10:2, 7) and the sedentary "son of peace" (Q 10:6a) would be primitive designations for what might evolve from their functions into what we today would call church offices.

The decision of a member of such a household to become an itinerant worker might well not take place easily. Not only did Jesus leave home, Nazara, and in Q had no further relations with his family. There are even sayings explicitly calling for the disruption of family ties: Jesus came to divide son against father, daughter against her mother, and daughter-in-law against her mother-in-law (Q 12:53). To become a disciple, one must hate father and mother, son and daughter (Q 14:26).

What could be more drastic than to hate one's family and love one's enemies? Even if this "hating" was understood euphemistically as "loving" Jesus more than family members (Matt. 10:37), in any case it meant abandoning the family and one's responsibilities at home. Central to the way of life that Jesus envisaged was indeed to love one's enemies (Q 6:27). For this, amplified by praying for one's persecutors (Q 6:28), is accorded the supreme value of being what makes one a child of God, God-like, since God raises his sun and showers his rain on the bad as well as on the good (Q 6:35). The title "son of God" did not begin just as a christological title but, like the title "son of peace," began as a designation for those involved in the Jesus movement. This was not just a pious well-wishing sentiment, but meant in practice turning the other cheek, giving the shirt off one's back, going the second mile, lending without ever asking for it back (Q 6:29–30). It was living the Golden Rule even though faced with opposition (Q 6:31).

Jesus was not easy at all; one must lose one's life (Q 17:33), take up one's cross (Q 14:27). It is not surprising that in such a movement the salt of resolve lost its strength and had to be thrown out (Q 14:34–35). Enlistments must have been rare, and the dropout rate must have been devastating. For all practical purposes, the Q movement did die out. But its remnant merged with the gentile Christian church under the leadership of the Evangelist "Matthew," whereby its text, the Sayings Gospel Q, was rescued, and with it the most reliable information we have about the image of Jesus, who clearly gave his life for his cause (Q 11:47–51; 12:4–5; 13:34–35).

Notes

1. James M. Robinson, Paul Hoffmann, and John S. Kloppenborg, eds., *The Critical Edition of Q: Synopsis including the Gospels of Matthew and Luke, Mark and Thomas with English, German, and French Translations of Q and Thomas* (Leuven: Peeters and Minneapolis: Fortress, 2000). The present essay is based on this publication.

2. Adolf Harnack, *Das Wesen des Christentums: 16 Vorlesungen vor Studieren-den aller Fakultäten im Wintersemester 1899/1900 an der Universität Berlin* (Leipzig: Hinrichs'sche Buchhandlung, 1900) 33. A student, Walther Becker, took down the lectures in shorthand, which Harnack edited for publication. It was an immediate best-seller: 1900, 3d ed. (11 to 15 thousand [quoted here]), 45 to 50 thousand 1903, 56 to 60 thousand 1908, 70 thousand 1925; more recent reprints: Adolf von Harnack, *Das Wesen des Christentums:* Neuauflage zum fünfzigsten Jahrestag des ersten Erscheinens mit einem Geleitwort von Rudolf Bultmann (Stuttgart: Klotz, 1950); Adolf von Harnack, *Das Wesen des Christentums:* Mit einem Geleitwort von Wolfgang Trillhaas, Gütersloher Taschenbücher/Siebenstern 227 (Gütersloh: Gütersloher Verlagshaus Mohn, 1985); Adolf von Harnack, *Das Wesen des Chris-tentums: Herausgegeben und kommentiert von Trutz Rendtorff* (Gütersloh: Chr. Kaiser/Gütersloher Verlagshaus, 1999) 33 (1900), 40 (1985), and 87 (1999):

> Überschauen wir aber die Predigt Jesu, so können wir drei Kreise aus ihr gestal-ten. Jeder Kreis ist so geartet, dass er die *ganze* Verkündigung enthält; in jedem kann sie daher vollständig zur Darstellung gebracht werden:
>
> *Erstlich, das Reich Gottes und sein Kommen,*
> *Zweitens, Gott der Vater und der unendliche Wert der Menschenseele,*
> *Drittens, die bessere Gerechtigkeit und das Gebot der Liebe.*

English Translation: *What Is Christianity* (London, Edinburgh, Oxford: Williams and Norgate, and New York: Putnam, 1901, 3d revised edition [quoted here] 1904) 52.

3. Harnack, *Das Wesen des Christentums*, 41 (1900), 47 (1985), and 96 (1999):

> Indem man aber die ganze Verkündigung Jesu auf diese beiden Stücke zurück-führen kann—Gott als der Vater, und die menschliche Seele so geadelt, dass sie sich mit ihm zusammenzuschließen vermag und zusammenschließt—, zeigt es sich, dass das Evangelium überhaupt keine positive Religion ist wie die anderen, dass es nichts Statuarisches und Partikularistisches hat, *dass es also die Religion selbst ist.*

English Translation: *What Is Christianity,* 65.

4. Henry J. Cadbury, *The Peril of Modernizing Jesus* (New York: Macmillan, 1937).

5. Richard A. Horsley's repeated argument, most recently in Richard A. Horsley with Jonathan A. Draper, *Whoever Hears You Hears Me: Prophets, Performance, and Tradition in Q* (Harrisburg, Pa.: Trinity Press International, 1999) 261–63: 263, understanding Q's *explicit* to have "the highly positive sense of liberating/delivering/ saving/effecting justice for," as the basis for the thesis "that the context of those discourses and of Q as a whole was the renewal of Israel (movement) underway"

has been already adequately refuted by John S. Kloppenborg, "The Sayings Gospel Q and the Quest of the Historical Jesus," *HTR* 89 (1996) 307–44: 327–28.

6. Luise Schottroff, *Itinerant Prophetesses: A Feminist Analysis of the Sayings Source Q*, Occasional Papers 21 (Claremont, Calif.: Institute for Antiquity and Christianity, 1991); Schottroff, "Wanderprophetinnen: Eine feministische Analyse der Logienquelle," *EvT* 51 (1991) 332–44. Helga Melzer-Keller, *Jesus und die Frauen: Eine Verhältnisbestimmung nach den synoptischen Überlieferungen,* Herders biblische Studien 14 (Freiburg: Herder, 1997), Teil IV: "Jesus und die Frauen in der Logienquelle," 330–53; Melzer-Keller, "Frauen in der Logienquelle und ihrem Trägerkreis: Ist Q das Zeugnis einer patriarchatskritischen, egalitären Bewegung?" in *Wenn Drei das Gleiche sagen...Studien zu den ersten drei Evangelien,* ed. Stefan H. Brandenburger and Thomas Hieke, Theologie 14 (Münster: Lit, 1998) 37–62; Melzer-Keller, "Wie frauenfreundlich ist die Logienquelle?" *BiKi* 54 (1999) 89–92.

7. Albert Schweitzer, *Von Reimarus zu Wrede: Die Geschichte der Leben-Jesu-Forschung* (Tübingen: Mohr-Siebeck, 1906). The second edition, entitled only *Die Geschichte der Leben-Jesu-Forschung* (Tübingen: Mohr-Siebeck, 1913), is considerably revised, especially in the concluding sections under discussion here. The quotations are from the first edition, with the pagination in the second edition, when parallel (though, even then, copyedited to produce a smoother text), given in parentheses, both according to 1951, 6th ed., and the republication (for which I wrote the Einführung) as Siebenstern-Taschenbuch 77/78, Munich, 1966. A retrospective "Vorrede" dated 1950, included only in the German editions, beginning with 1951, 6th ed., is quoted here, vi, xii (1951) and 30, 36 (1966):

Das Problem in seiner ganzen Schwere erfahren zu müssen bleibt der Forschung vorerst dadurch erspart, daß sie unter dem Einfluß von Christian Hermann Weißes "Die Evangelienfrage" (1856) und Heinrich Julius Holtzmanns "Die synoptischen Evangelien" (1863) die von Ferdinand Christian Baur (1792–1860) und der Tübingerschule vertretene Ansicht, daß das Matthäusevangelium das älteste und ursprünglichste sei, aufgibt und als solches das Markusevangelium ansieht. Die Bevorzugung dieses kürzeren Evangeliums erlaubt es ihr, das bedeutende Material, das Matthäus über das des Markus hinaus bietet, nicht als ganz vollgültig zu bewerten. Und gerade dieses enthält die Reden und Berichte, in denen sich die Zugehörigkeit der Gedankenwelt Jesu zu der spätjüdischen Eschatologie bekundet. Vornehmlich sind dies die Bergpredigt (Mt 5–7), die große Rede bei der Aussendung der Jünger (Mt 10), die Anfrage des Täufers und die durch sie veranlaßten Äusserungen Jesu (Mt 11), die Rede vom Kommen des Menschensohnes und des von ihm abzuhaltenden Gerichts (Mt 25)....

Für die Leben-Jesu-Forschung kommt es nicht darauf an, welches der beiden ältesten Evangelien ein klein wenig älter sein könnte als das andere. Diese literarische Frage wird sich überdies kaum je entscheiden lassen. Mit dem lückenhaften Bericht des Markus wäre das historische Problem des Lebens Jesu nicht zu lösen, ja nicht einmal zu erkennen gewesen. Die Berichte der beiden ältesten Evangelien sind ihrer Art nach gleichwertig. Das des Matthäus ist aber als das vollständigere das wertvollere. Sachlich haben Ferdinand Christian Baur und seine Schüler mit ihrer Bevorzugung desselben Recht behalten.

(In the 1951 edition Baur's last name is omitted, but is added in the 1966 edition.) ET: *The Quest of the Historical Jesus: A Critical Study of Its Progress from Reimarus to Wrede* (New York: Macmillan, 1910). Even the paperback edition of 1961 (for which I wrote the Introduction) and its reprints—ninth printing 1975—lack this "Vorrede" of 1950.

8. Schweitzer, *Von Reimarus zu Wrede*, 360 (*Die Geschichte der Leben-Jesu-Forschung*, 410 [1951] and 420 [1966]):

So ist die Aussendungsrede als Ganzes und bis in das kleinste Detail geschichtlich, gerade weil sie nach der Auffassung der modernen Theologie als ungeschichtlich erfunden werden muß....

Danach beurteile man, mit welchem Recht die modern-psychologische Theologie die großen matthäischen Reden kurzerhand als "Redekompositionen" hinstellt. Man beweise doch einmal, wie der Evangelist, der an seiner Feder saugte, um eine Aussendungsrede aus überlieferten Sprüchen und aus der "Gemeindetheologie" halb zusammenzustellen, halb zu erfinden, auf den seltsamen Gedanken kommen konnte, Jesum von lauter unzeitgemäßen und unsachlichen Dingen reden zu lassen und nachher selber zu konstatieren, daß sie nicht in Erfüllung gingen.

ET: *The Quest of the Historical Jesus*, 363.

9. Schweitzer, *Von Reimarus zu Wrede*, 355 (*Die Geschichte der Leben-Jesu-Forschung*, 405 [1951] and 415 [1966]):

Ist diese in Wahrheit "historische" Deutung des Geheimnisses des Reiches Gottes richtig, so muß Jesus zur Erntezeit den Anbruch des Reiches Gottes erwartet haben. Das hat er wirklich getan. Darum sendet er ja die Jünger aus, damit sie eilend in Israel verkünden, was kommen soll.

ET: *The Quest of the Historical Jesus*, 358.

10. Schweitzer, *Von Reimarus zu Wrede*, 355 (*Die Geschichte der Leben-Jesu-Forschung*, 405 [1951] and 416 [1966]):

Jesus sagt den Jüngern in dürren Worten, Mt 10 23, daß er sie in diesem Äon nicht mehr zurückerwartet. Die Parusie des Menschensohnes, die mit dem Einbruch des Reiches logisch und zeitlich identisch ist, wird stattfinden, ehe sie mit ihrer Verkündigung die Städte Israels durcheilt haben.

ET: *The Quest of the Historical Jesus*, 358–59.

11. Schweitzer, *Von Reimarus zu Wrede*, 367:

Diese Erwägungen über den besonderen Charakter der synoptischen Eschatologie waren notwendig, um die Bedeutung der Aussendung und der sie begleitenden Rede zu verstehen. Jesus will die eschatologische Geschichte in Gang bringen, die Enddrangsal, die Verwirrung und den Aufruhr, aus denen die Parusie hervorgehen soll, entfesseln und die überirdische Phase des eschatologischen Dramas einleiten.

ET: *The Quest of the Historical Jesus*, 371.

12. Schweitzer, *Von Reimarus zu Wrede,* 383: "...zur Zeit der Aussendung, als er sie vor der Parusie nicht mehr zurückerwartete...." ET: *The Quest of the Historical Jesus,* 386.

13. Schweitzer, *Von Reimarus zu Wrede,* 360 (*Die Geschichte der Leben-Jesu-Forschung,* 411 [1951] and 421 [1966]):

Es traf aber weder das Leiden, noch die Geistesausgießung, noch die Parusie des Menschensohnes ein, sondern gesund und frisch, voll stolzer Genugtuung kehrten die Jünger zum Herrn zurück. Eine Verheißung war real geworden: die Vollmacht, die er ihnen über die Dämonen gegeben.

ET: *The Quest of the Historical Jesus,* 364. Schweitzer did not point out that this anticlimactic return of the disciples from their mission is not mentioned in Matthew 10, but only in Mark 6:30 and Luke 10:17–20. Indeed the "proud satisfaction" in "the power which had been given them over the demons" is only in Luke, although Schweitzer had confidence primarily in Matthew, and to a lesser extent in Mark, and even less in Luke.

14. Schweitzer, *Von Reimarus zu Wrede,* 355 (*Die Geschichte der Leben-Jesu-Forschung,* 406 [1951] and 416 [1966]):

Ebenso klar ist aber, und hier tritt das Dogmatische der Entschließungen Jesu noch stärker hervor, daß diese Weissagung nicht in Erfüllung ging. Die Jünger kehrten zu ihm zurück und die Erscheinung des Menschensohnes fand nicht statt. Die natürliche Geschichte desavouierte die dogmatische, nach welcher Jesus gehandelt hatte. Ein Ereignis der übernatürlichen Geschichte, welches stattfinden mußte, in jenem Zeitpunkte stattfinden mußte, blieb aus. Das war für Jesus, der einzig in der dogmatischen Geschichte lebte, das erste "geschichtliche" Ereignis, das Zentralereignis, welches seine öffentliche Tätigkeit nach rückwärts abschließt, nach vorn neu orientiert.

ET: *The Quest of the Historical Jesus,* 359.

15. Schweitzer, *Von Reimarus zu Wrede,* 385–86:

Die Wandlung beruht auf dem Nichteintreten der Verheißungen der Aussendungsrede. Er hatte damals die Enddrangsal zu entfachen gemeint, um damit das Reich herbeizuzwingen. Und der Aufruhr war ausgeblieben. Er hatte ihn auch nach der Rückkehr der Jünger noch erwartet.... [386]

Mit dem Verlassen des Bodens Galiläas gibt er die Hoffnung auf, daß sich die Drangsal von sich aus einstellen werde. Wenn sie ausbleibt, will dies besagen, daß noch eine Leistung fehlt und noch ein Gewalttätiger zu den Vergewaltigern des Reiches Gottes hinzutreten müsse. Die Bußbewegung hatte nicht ausgereicht. Als er seiner Vollmacht gemäß bei der Aussendung den Feuerbrand, der die Drangsal zum Auslodern bringen sollte, in die Welt schleuderte, erlosch er.

ET: *The Quest of the Historical Jesus,* 389.

16. Schweitzer, *Von Reimarus zu Wrede,* 387, 388:

...sein Tod—endlich—das Reich herbeizwingt... [388]

Der neue Leidensgedanke ist also seinem Wesen nach begründet in der auf das Heraufführen der Drangsal gehenden Vollmacht, mit welcher Jesus in der Welt auftritt. . . . Denn jetzt identifiziert er seine natürliche Verurteilung und Hinrichtung mit der geweissagten vormessianischen Drangsal. Dieses gewaltsame Hineinzerren der Eschatologie in die Geschichte ist zugleich ihre Aufhebung; ein Bejahen und Preisgeben zugleich.

ET: *The Quest of the Historical Jesus,* 390–91.

17. Schweitzer, *Von Reimarus zu Wrede,* 367:

> Da erscheint der Täufer und ruft: Tuet Buße! das Reich Gottes ist nahe herbeigekommen! Kurz darauf greift Jesus, als der, welcher sich als den kommenden Menschensohn weiß, in die Speichen des Weltrades, daß es in Bewegung komme, die letzte Drehung mache und die natürliche Geschichte der Welt zu Ende bringe. Da es nicht geht, hängt er sich dran. Es dreht sich und zermalmt ihn. Statt die Eschatologie zu bringen, hat er sie vernichtet. Das Weltrad dreht sich weiter und die Fetzen des Leichnams des einzig unermeßlich großen Menschen, der gewaltig genug war, um sich als den geistigen Herrscher der Menschheit zu erfassen und die Geschichte zu vergewaltigen, hängen noch immer daran. Das ist sein Siegen und Herrschen.

ET: *The Quest of the Historical Jesus,* 370–71.

18. Bultmann's only essay on Q, written before World War I, came only two years after Wellhausen's second edition, and built explicitly on him rather than on Harnack: "Was läßt die Spruchquelle über die Urgemeinde erkennen?" *Oldenburgisches Kirchenblatt* 19 (1913) 35–37, 41–44: 35:

> Den folgenden Ausführungen liegt also eine bestimmte Auffassung der synoptischen Frage zu Grunde, die ich natürlich hier nicht näher entwickeln kann. Ich verweise auf B. Weiß, A. Jülicher und J. Wellhausen.

ET: "What the Sayings Source Reveals about the Early Church," *The Shape of Q: Signal Essays on the Sayings Gospel,* ed. John S. Kloppenborg (Minneapolis: Fortress, 1994) 23–34: 23, n. 1:

> The following explication presupposes a definite solution to the Synoptic problem, which obviously I cannot pursue in more detail here. I refer the reader to B. Weiss 1908; Jülicher 1904; and Wellhausen 1905, 1911.

Rudolf Bultmann, *Jesus,* 1926, 18 (reprint 1951, Tübingen: Mohr-Siebeck, 16): "Die Übersetzung der evangelischen Texte schließt sich oft an die von J. Wellhausen an." ET: "The translation of the Gospel texts often makes use of that of J. Wellhausen." Martin Dibelius, *Die Formgeschichte des Evangeliums* (Tübingen: Mohr-Siebeck, 1919, revised 1933, 2d ed., 1966, 5th ed., ed. Günther Bornkamm [quoted here]) 236, n. 1. ET: *From Tradition to Gospel,* trans. Bertram Lee Woolf (New York: Scribners, n.d.), 235, n. 1, appeals to the first edition of Julius Wellhausen, *Einleitung in die drei ersten Evangelien* (Berlin: Reimer, 1905, 1st ed., 1911, 2d ed.) 66–67, for his own skepticism (quoted below) regarding Q.

19. The second revised edition of Julius Wellhausen, *Einleitung in die drei ersten Evangelien,* was reprinted with the same pagination in Wellhausen's *Evangelienkommentare* (Berlin and New York: de Gruyter, 1987), with an "Einleitung" by Martin Hengel, who commented, vi–vii: "Er endet mit einer harschen Kritik der Leben-Jesu-Forschung des 19. Jh.s, die wesentlich über die A. Schweitzers, mit dem er

sich kritisch auseinandersetzt, hinausgeht und die sich in manchen Punkten mit Martin Kähler und der frühen dialektischen Theologie K. [vii] Barths und R. Bultmanns berührt. In der dadurch befruchteten kritischen Evangelienforschung zwischen den beiden Weltkriegen wird die Wirkung des Neutestamentlers Wellhausen am ehesten sichtbar."

20. Wellhausen, *Evangelienkommentare*, 153, also quoted by Hengel, "Einleitung," vii:

> Als der Gekreuzigte, Auferstandene und Wiederkommende ist Jesus der christliche Messias, nicht als Religionslehrer. Das apostolische Evangelium, welches den Glauben an den Christus predigt, ist das eigentliche, und nicht das Evangelium Jesu, welches der Kirche ihre Moral vorschreibt.... Und der angeblich von Harnack getane Ausspruch: "nicht der Sohn, sondern nur der Vater gehört ins Evangelium" ist grundfalsch, wenn damit ein Faktum behauptet und nicht nur ein Postulat ausgesprochen werden soll.

Hengel, vi, inaccurately states that chapter 17 of the second edition ("Das Evangelium und das Christentum," 147–53) corresponds to chapter 12 of the first edition, which, however, in fact corresponds to chapter 10 of the second ("Das Evangelium und Jesus von Nazareth," 98–104). There is in the first edition no chapter equivalent to chapter 17 of the second edition. Hence the quotation is not in the first edition at all.

21. Harnack, *Das Wesen des Christentums*, 91 (1900) and 90 (1985): "*Nicht der Sohn, sondern allein der Vater gehört in das Evangelium, wie es Jesus verkündigt hat, hinein.*" ET: *What Is Christianity*, 147.

22. Harnack, *Das Wesen des Christentums*, in the endnotes added to the 1908 edition (56th to 60th thousand), drew attention to this omission as distorting his position (on p. 183 of the 1950 edition and pp. 154–55, n. 22, of the 1999 edition):

> Dieses Wort ist von vielen Seiten aufs schärfste bekämpft, aber nicht widerlegt worden. Ich habe nichts an ihm zu ändern. Nur sind die Worte: "Wie es Jesus verkündigt hat," hier kursiv gesetzt worden, weil sie von vielen Gegnern übersehen worden sind. Dass Jesus in das Evangelium, wie es Paulus und die Evangelisten verkündigt haben, nicht nur hineingehört, sondern den eigentlichen Inhalt dieses Evangeliums bildet, braucht nicht erst gesagt zu werden.

23. This exchange was published in *Die christliche Welt*, 1923, as follows: Harnack: "Fünfzehn Fragen an die Verächter der wissenschaftlichen Theologie unter den Theologen," 6–8; Barth: "Fünfzehn Antworten an Herrn Professor von Harnack," 89–91; Harnack: "Offener Brief an Herrn Professor K. Barth," 142–44; Barth: "Antwort auf Herrn Professor von Harnacks offenen Brief," 244–52; and Harnack: "Nachwort zu meinem offenen Brief an Herrn Professor Karl Barth," 305–6. This debate has been republished in Barth's *Gesammelte Vorträge*, vol. 3: *Theologische Fragen und Antworten* (Zollikon: Evangelischer Verlag, 1957) 7–31: 7–9, 9–13, 13–17, 18–30, 30–31 (quoted here). ET in *The Beginnings of Dialectic Theology*, vol. 1, ed. James M. Robinson (Richmond, Va.: John Knox, 1968); Harnack: "Fifteen Questions to Those Among the Theologians Who Are Contemptuous of the Scientific Theology," 165–66; Barth: "Fifteen Answers to Professor von

Harnack," 167–70; Harnack: "An Open Letter to Professor Karl Barth," 171–74; Barth: "An Answer to Professor von Harnack's Open Letter," 175–85; and Harnack: "Postscript to My Open Letter to Professor Karl Barth," 186–87.

24. Harnack, "Fünfzehn Fragen," 8: "... die enge Verbindung, ja Gleichsetzung der Gottes- und Nächstenliebe, welche den Kern des Evangeliums bildet,... " ET: "Fifteen Questions," 165.

25. Barth, "Fünfzehn Antworten," 11: "Was zeigt deutlicher als dieser 'Kern' (nicht des Evangeliums, aber des Gesetzes), daß Gott nicht lebendig macht, er töte denn zuvor?" ET: "Fifteen Answers," 168.

26. Wellhausen, *Einleitung in die drei ersten Evangelien* (Berlin: Georg Reimer, 1905, 1st ed., 1911, 2d ed., *Nachdruck* of the second edition, *Evangelienkommentare;* Berlin: Walter de Gruyter, 1987) 1905, 1st ed., 113; 1911, 2d ed., 102: "Jesus war kein Christ, sondern Jude."

27. Rudolf Bultmann, "Das Verhältnis der urchristlichen Christusbotschaft zum historischen Jesus," SHAW.PH, Jg. 1960, Abh. 3 (Heidelberg: Winter, 1960, 1st ed., 1962, 3d ed.) 8:

> Nun werde ich ferner angegriffen, weil ich in meinem Buch "Das Urchristen-tum im Rahmen der antiken Religionen" die Verkündigung Jesu nicht in dem Kap. "Das Urchristentum," sondern im Kapitel "Das Judentum" dargestellt, Jesus also als Juden aufgefaßt habe. Im gleichen Sinne hat man beanstandet, daß ich in meiner "Theologie des Neuen Testaments" gesagt habe, die Verkündigung Jesu gehöre zu den *Voraussetzungen* der Neutestamentlichen Theologie. Gegenüber dem Vorwurf, daß ich Jesus als Juden verstehe und ihn in den Bereich des Judentums rechne, habe ich zunächst einfach zu fragen: war Jesus—der historische Jesus!—denn ein Christ? Nun, wenn christlicher Glaube der Glaube an ihn als den Christus ist, doch gewiß nicht, und selbst wenn er sich als den Christus ('Messias') gewußt haben und gar den Glauben an sich als den Christus gefordert haben sollte, so wäre er immer noch kein Christ und nicht als Subjekt des christlichen Glaubens, dessen Objekt er doch ist, zu bezeichnen.

ET: "The Primitive Christian Kerygma and the Historical Jesus," in *The Histori-cal Jesus and the Kerygmatic Christ,* ed. Carl E. Braaten and Roy A. Harrisville (Nashville: Abingdon, 1964) 15–42: 19.

28. For the resultant discussion about the legitimacy of calling Q a "Sayings Gospel," see Frans Neirynck, "Q: From Source to Gospel," *ETL* 71 (1995) 421–34.

29. Weiss, *Die Predigt Jesu vom Reiche Gottes* (Göttingen: Vandenhoeck & Ruprecht, 1892). ET: *Jesus' Proclamation of the Kingdom of God* (Philadelphia: Fortress, 1971).

30. Schweitzer, *Die Geschichte der Leben-Jesu-Forschung,* "Vorrede zur sechsten Auflage," viii [1951] and 32 [1966]:

> Johannes Weiß weist den durchaus eschatologischen Charakter der Verkün-digung Jesu vom Reiche Gottes nach. Mein Beitrag besteht hauptsächlich darin, daß ich dazu fortschreite, nicht nur seine Verkündigung sondern auch sein Verhalten und Handeln als durch die eschatologische Erwartung bedingt begreiflich zu machen.

31. Rudolf Bultmann, *Jesus*, Die Unsterblichen: Die geistigen Heroen der Menschheit in ihrem Leben und Wirken mit zahlreichen Illustrationen, 1 (Berlin: Deutsche Bibliothek, n.d. [1926]). ET: *Jesus and the Word* (New York: Scribner's Sons, 1934). In the "Translators' Preface to the New Edition" of 1958, Louise Pettibone Smith and Erminie Huntress Latero explain the enlarged title: "It was felt by both publishers and translators that the title, *Jesus and the Word*, would convey a more definite idea of the content and viewpoint of the book than the original title, *Jesus*. This change was made with the approval of the author."

32. Theissen and Merz, *Der historische Jesus*, 28: "Urchristliche Wandercharismatiker führten den Predigt- und Lebensstil Jesu weiter." ET: *The Historical Jesus*, 10. The footnote refers to Theissen's basic essay in this regard, "Wanderradikalismus: Literatursoziologische Aspekte der Überlieferung von Worten Jesu im Urchristentum," *ZTK* 70 (1973) 245–71, reprinted in: Theissen, *Studien zur Soziologie des Urchristentums*, WUNT 19 (Tübingen: Mohr-Siebeck, 1979, 1st ed., 1989, 3d ed.) 79–105, and his monograph *Soziologie der Jesusbewegung: Ein Beitrag zur Entstehungsgeschichte des Urchristentums* (TEH.NF 194 = KT 34; Munich: Kaiser, 1977, 1st ed., 1991, 6th ed.). ET: "Itinerant Radicalism. The Tradition of Jesus' Sayings from the Perspective of the Sociology of Literature," an abbreviation in *The Bible and Liberation: A Radical Religion Reader*, ed. Antoinette Wire (Berkeley, Calif.: Graduate Theological Union, 1976) 84–93; "The Wandering Radicals: Light Shed by the Sociology of Literature on the Early Transmission of the Jesus Sayings," in Theissen, *Social Reality and the Early Christians: Theology, Ethics, and the World of the New Testament* (Minneapolis: Fortress, 1992; Edinburgh: T. & T. Clark, 1993) 33–59, and abbreviated as "The Role of the Wandering Charismatics," 3–16, in his monograph *The First Followers of Jesus: A Sociological Analysis of the Earliest Christianity* (London: SCM, 1978), American title *The Sociology of the Earliest Jesus Movement* (Philadelphia: Fortress, 1978).

33. James M. Robinson, "Building Blocks in the Social History of Q," in *Reimagining Christian Origins: A Colloquium Honoring Burton L. Mack*, ed. Elizabeth A. Castelli and Hal Taussig (Valley Forge, Pa.: Trinity Press International, 1996) 87–112: 87–90.

34. James M. Robinson, "*Galilean Upstarts*: A Sot's Cynical Disciples?" in *Sayings of Jesus: Canonical and Non-Canonical: Essays in Honour of Tjitze Baarda*, ed. William L. Petersen, Johan S. Vos, and Henk J. de Jonge, NovTSup 89 (Leiden, New York, Cologne: Brill, 1997) 223–49: 243–49.

35. It is a remarkable attestation for Matthew's familiarity with the tradition in which he obviously stood that he knew to build into the core collection of the Inaugural Sermon other archaic collections that comprise the core of Q, so as to produce the Sermon on the Mount, with the exception of the Mission Instructions themselves, which did not fit the setting of the Sermon on the Mount. It is thus appropriate that the Sermon on the Mount has been sensed as this core from time to time, beginning with Francis of Assisi, and re-emerging in Tolstoy, Gandhi, and Martin Luther King.

36. James M. Robinson, "From Safe House to House Church: From Q to Matthew," in *Das Ende der Tage und die Gegenwart des Heils. Begegnungen mit dem Neuen Testament und seiner Umwelt: Festschrift für Heinz-Wolfgang Kuhn zum 65. Geburtstag*, ed. Michael Becker and Wolfgang Fenske, AGJU 44 (Leiden: Brill, 1999) 183–99.

The Jesus of Mark's Gospel

Colin Brown

Any attempt to recover the historical Jesus must address two issues. It must locate Jesus in the religious, political, and economic world of Second-Temple Judaism, and it must examine the genre of its sources. With this in mind I wish to offer some thoughts on the following:

1. Factors That Throw Light on Mark's Jesus

2. The Genre of Mark

3. Mark's Presentation of Jesus

4. Implications

Factors That Throw Light on Mark's Jesus

Purity

The political world of Jesus has received careful social analysis in recent years.[1] The situation of Judea and Galilee with client rulers subject to Rome is rendered complex by a variety of religious factors. Among them is the importance of purity. The main biblical laws are found in Leviticus 11–17 and Numbers 19. Impurity is hateful to God, and the unclean are excluded from God's presence (Lev. 11:43–47). It was therefore necessary to separate from whatever defiled God's dwelling place (Lev. 15:31; Ezek. 11:21–23). Jacob Neusner observes: "The land is holy, therefore must be kept clean. It may be profaned by becoming unclean."[2]

Mark's Jesus repeatedly appears to cross the boundaries of purity.[3] Actions like touching a leper, a woman with a flow of blood, and the corpse of a girl, healing on the Sabbath, consorting with tax collectors and sinners, and challenging dietary laws appear as threats to the religious system centered on the Temple.[4] Marcus J. Borg sees the difference between Jesus and his adversaries as one of orthopraxis. For the Pharisees, the dominant paradigm was holiness. For Jesus, it was justice, mercy, and faithfulness.[5] Klaus Berger traces the root of the conflict to different conceptions of purity.[6] The Pharisees had a "defensive" attitude, which avoided contact with whatever defiled, and followed prescribed rituals when contact was unavoidable.

Jesus' disregard of "defensive" purity violated Pharisaic practice. His practice of "offensive" holiness conveyed purity to the unclean in virtue of his anointing by the Spirit.[7] Mark's Jesus makes the impure pure, the common holy, and includes the excluded.[8] Berger's view puts purity at center stage. While it brings Jesus into conflict with tradition, it accords with the Torah's underlying concept of holiness, which (in the words of Jacob Milgrom) "represents the forces of life."[9] The common factor underlying impurity is *death*. Mark's narrative is about the conflict between the forces of life and death.

Exile Theology

To many Jews, although they were living in the Promised Land with an embellished Temple, the conditions were tantamount to living in exile. Mark gives some indication of this situation in his description of John the Baptist and the intertextual echoes of return from exile in the opening of his Gospel (1:2–3; cf. Mal. 3:1 and Isa. 40:3).[10] John is the messenger sent to prepare the way of the Lord. If the Lord's way needs to be prepared, the Lord is no longer or not yet in the land. There is reason to think that Jesus understood his message and activity in terms of restoration from exile.[11] Mark views Jesus' activity as healer, exorcist, and teacher as part of his program to purify and restore Israel.

Expectation of the Spirit and Cleansing

The coming of the Spirit, as the means of cleansing and establishing righteousness, is widely attested in prophecy.[12] Some passages speak of the outpouring of the Spirit upon the nation, as God's servant, while others suggest that the servant anointed by the Spirit of God is an individual (Isa. 42:1; 61:1). Such passages form the subtext for Mark's portrait of Jesus as the Spirit-anointed Christ. Malachi prophesied the return of the Lord to his Temple to purify it (Mal. 3:1–5). Mark identifies Malachi's prophecy of God's messenger with John the Baptist (1:2). He is the Elijah come to restore all things (Mal. 4:5; Mark 9:12).

Magic

John Dominic Crossan has painted a portrait of the historical Jesus as "a peasant Jewish Cynic" who sought to subvert the brokered economic and political system imposed by Rome through "magic and meal."[13] Crossan seeks to disarm criticism by observing that "The title *magician* is not used here as a pejorative word but describes one who can make divine power present *directly through personal miracle* rather than *indirectly through communal ritual*."[14] He distances himself from Morton Smith who saw Jesus in a more sinister light. In *Jesus the Magician* Smith sought to show magic was the key to Jesus' activity and the authorities' rejection of him.[15]

Smith's charge has been examined in detail.[16] For now we may observe that the magician in the ancient world was not the harmless, eccentric figure found at Disneyland. Jonathan Z. Smith contends that "the one, universal characteristic of magic" in the Greco-Roman world was its illegality, which carried penalties of death or deportation.[17] In the Jewish world practitioners were to be put to death so that the land may be purged of evil (Exod. 22:18; Lev. 19:26, 31; 20:6, 27; Deut. 13:1–11; 18:9–14). There is a trajectory of tradition in patristic and Jewish sources that Jesus was perceived as a magician and deceiver.[18]

Christian scholarship has brushed aside this tradition too lightly. It provides a vital clue to understanding Jesus and his world. In this regard Jesus has been compared with figures like Honi the Circle Drawer and Hanina ben Dosa who have been variously described as holy men and magicians.[19] Rabbinic tradition displays a tendency to credit them with being holy men (*hasidim*) and/or rabbis, and to turn their activities into stories of piety and answered prayer. There is an important difference between them and Jesus. It is illustrated by the story of a healing performed at a distance by Hanina ben Dosa (Berakhot 34b). The holy man disclaimed being a prophet, and insisted that he was favored as a man of prayer. By contrast, it was the *combination* of healing/exorcism *with* unorthodox teaching and practice that made Jesus offensive.

The Genre of Mark

Two Theses

Mark is a work of Christian apologetics, and in order to lay bare the basic building blocks we need to engage in a modest exercise in deconstruction. It takes the form of two conflicting theses. It involves reading Mark *with the grain* to determine what Mark wants us to see, and reading Mark *against the grain* to discover the standpoint of Jesus' adversaries. The exercise will lead us into the realm of intertextuality and the investigation of prior bodies of discourse, sign-systems, and values without which texts are unintelligible. Put concretely, Jesus' adversaries viewed him in light of their understanding of the Torah, while Jesus' followers saw him as the fulfiller of prophecy. Both sides viewed Jesus in light of their belief systems based on prior sacred texts. We might even say that the key issue in Mark is a question of hermeneutics.

Thesis A represents the viewpoint of the evangelist. It argues that in giving prominence to the prophecy of John the Baptist (1:8), Mark intends us to understand that the prophecy was fulfilled in the activity of Jesus.[20] Mark's version reads: "I have baptized you with water; but he will baptize you with the Holy Spirit." Christian tradition has treated it as a prophecy of Pentecost and the gift of the Spirit to the church (cf. Acts 1:5; 11:16). In so doing it has failed to notice that the prophecy is addressed not to disciples but to the crowds that have come to John for baptism. It has turned Jesus' activity into an interlude prior to the prophecy's posthumous fulfillment. As such, John's prophecy has no direct relevance to Mark's narrative. My counterproposal argues that the prophecy provides an important key. Baptism is a rite of purification and consecration. The activities of Mark's Jesus were directed at the purification and consecration of Israel through "baptism" with the Holy Spirit.

Thesis B represents the viewpoint of Jesus' adversaries. It argues that when they saw Jesus violating sabbath and purity laws, propounding deviant teaching, and gaining a following through his healings, they sought guidance from the Torah. In light of instructions concerning prophets who perform signs and wonders in order to lead astray (Deut. 13:1–18; 18:20–22), those who serve other gods (Deut. 17:2–7), magicians (Lev. 19:31; 20:6; Deut. 18:10), and "the stubborn and rebellious son" (Deut. 21:18–21), they concluded that they had no alternative but to "purge the evil" from their midst lest the land be defiled.[21]

Mark's Tragic-Epic Life of Jesus

My view of Mark breaks with the conventional wisdom inherited from Rudolf Bultmann that Mark was merely a collector of random stories.[22] It also breaks with the simple analysis that divides Mark into two: activity in Galilee and activity in Jerusalem linked by a travel narrative. Mark is a form of ancient biography, an apocalyptic apology, written to be declaimed in accordance with the canons of tragic-epic narrative, in vindication of Jesus.

The claim that the gospels were not biographies has been a mantra among scholars.[23] Certainly they do not provide the kind of information regarding background, influences, formation, and psychological speculation that characterize modern biography. But a growing number of scholars see similarities with ancient biography.[24] Richard A. Burridge concludes that, "the four canonical gospels and Graeco-Roman *bios* [life] exhibit a clear family resemblance."[25] David E. Aune draws a distinction between the conscious and unconscious functions of biography. The former includes strategies to persuade people to make decisions about past events. The latter gives historical legitimation of a social belief or value system personified in the subject of the biography.[26] Jonathan Z. Smith observes that every major religious biography in the ancient world is characterized by a "double defense against the charge of magic—against the calumny of outsiders and the sincere misunderstanding of admirers."[27] Mark also draws upon apocalyptic. N. T. Wright observes that not only Mark 13, but the entire Gospel, is apocalyptic in the sense of belonging to a genre which is "a way of investing space-time events with their theological significance."[28]

Numerous studies analyze Mark in terms of modern literary theory.[29] Others suggest that Mark constructed his narrative in a manner comparable with the canons of tragedy and epic described by Aristotle.[30] Aristotle viewed epic and tragedy as an "imitation" of life.[31] They differed in that tragedy was acted, but in other respects the rules were the same.[32] Their aim was to arouse pity and fear in order to produce a catharsis.[33] Whereas the poet describes "a kind of thing that might happen," the historian describes "the thing that has been."[34] Pity and fear have their greatest effect when incidents "occur unexpectedly and at the same time in consequence of one another."[35] Tragedy has three main parts: prologue, episode (the development of the plot), and the exode or catastrophic ending.[36] It is characterized by three elements: "discovery" or "recognition," "reversal," and "suffering." "The finest form of discovery is one attended by reversal,"[37] especially when it is directly connected with the plot.

Mark is a story told from the standpoint of a narrator. The action moves forward by means of a succession of scenes. It was probably declaimed, like other dramatic works in the Roman world in Mark's day.[38] Perhaps this is the reason why the Gospel of Mark lends itself so well to public performance today.[39] Stylistic features like Mark's use of the historic present tense may be explained by the desire to create dramatic movement. Frequent use of "and immediately" (110 times) serves as markers of new scenes. Recent study identifies careful rhetorical structure.[40] It would seem that Mark was adopting Greco-Roman conventions in order to present his "life" of Jesus in a world where Judaism and Hellenism intersected. If one looks for a context in the life of the church where Mark might be declaimed, the answer may lie in the celebration of baptism and eucharist. Jesus' question, "Are you able to drink the cup that I drink, or be baptized with the baptism that I am baptized with?" (10:38), appears to be directed beyond the Twelve to later would-be disciples.

Whereas Aristotle held that the basic form of tragedy consisted of prologue, episode, and exode, by the time of Horace (65–8 B.C.E.) the five-act form was widely recognized.[41] This appears to be the case in Mark, where the five "Acts" are separated by four teaching sections that function like a chorus giving comment on what has happened and linkage with what is to come.[42] The "tragedy" proper ends with the death of Jesus (15:39). The epilogue transforms tragedy into triumph. What drives the entire work forward is the tension set up by the clash of forces that I have sought to identify with my Thesis A and Thesis B. I offer the following analysis:

Prologue (1:1–13)

Act 1. The Beginnings of Conflict (1:14–4:34)

Act 2. The Conflict Spreads (4:35–7:23)

Act 3. The Climax (7:24–10:45)

Act 4. The Dénouement (10:46–13:37)

Act 5. The Catastrophe (14:1–15:39)

Epilogue (15:40–16:8)

Mark's Presentation of Jesus

Prologue (1:1–13)

Mark opens with the words: "The beginning [*arche*] of the Gospel of Jesus Christ, the Son of God" (1:1). In Aristotle *arche* denotes the beginning of a tragic plot from which the action happens as a natural result.[43] Mark's Prologue fits this definition. In contrast to the main action, that of the Prologue and Epilogue takes place *off stage* as it were, in locations alien to normal life.

The Prologue introduces a name and two titles, which play a crucial part in the narrative. We are apt to take the name Jesus for granted. It derives from the Latin *Jesus*, which translates and contextualizes the name for the Roman world and its heirs. However, the Greek *Iesous* is itself a translation of the Hebrew *Yeshu* or *Yehoshua*, i.e., Joshua.[44] The Latin contextualization has the effect of obscuring the *Jewishness* of Jesus. It also obscures allusions to Joshua, the son of Nun, who was "full of the spirit of wisdom" (Deut. 34:9) and who led the people of Israel into the Promised Land. The significance of the point emerges in Act 2 with the hint that Jesus' actions are those of *a new Joshua* who is about to reclaim the land for a purified people.

In the Prologue Christ is treated virtually as a surname. But it is actually a title, which lies at the heart of the conflict. Jesus Christ is a contraction for Jesus *the* Christ. Christ (Greek *christos*; Hebrew *mashiach*, i.e., Messiah) means "anointed." It raises the question: "Anointed by whom?" Mark gives his answer in his account of the Spirit's descent upon Jesus after receiving the baptism of John (1:10), when he is also identified as Son of God by the "voice from heaven" (1:11).[45] In view of the diversity of messianic beliefs in Judaism,[46] we should beware of preconceptions. I share the view that the original application of the title to Jesus may simply have meant "the anointed one" without further connotations.[47] It has a double reference, pointing to Jesus as "the anointed one" and to the Spirit as the agent of the anointing.

The Prologue contains three sets of prophecy. The first two identify John as the messenger preparing the way of Yahweh (1:2–3). The third is John's prophecy: "I have baptized you with water; but he will baptize you with the Holy Spirit [*en pneumati hagio*]" (1:8). Mark's version differs from Matthew and Luke, who add "and with fire" (Matt. 3:11; Luke 3:16). James D. G. Dunn concludes that in the Q source which supplies the material common to Matthew and Luke, the prophecy "must have been a metaphor of judgment" by which the impenitent would be destroyed and the penitent purged.[48] If we ask why Mark omits the reference to fire, the reply must be that prophecy rarely has exact, literal fulfillment. Subsequent reality modifies and defines the way in which it is fulfilled. Mark omitted the words "and fire" because he saw *the primary fulfillment* of the prophecy in Jesus' endeavor to purify and renew the people of Israel. Only when it failed did judgment come to the fore in the form of the events predicted in Mark 13, Jesus' reply to the high priest (14:62), and the symbolic rending of the temple veil (15:38).

The Prologue concludes with the forty days of testing in the wilderness (1:12–13). To Susan R. Garrett, the incident epitomizes the theme of testing that runs throughout the Gospel. It corresponds to the traditional model of declared divine approval followed by Satanic testing, and the testing of Israel. It is a test of whether Jesus will walk in the way of Yahweh, or whether he will succumb to the ways of Satan—to which he was believed to have succumbed according to Thesis B. It is part of Mark's "apocalyptic epistemology."[49] *In the apocalyptic view, events transpiring on the earthly plane are merely the reflection or outworking of events happening on a higher unseen plane.*[50]

Act 1. The Beginnings of Conflict (1:14–4:34)

Following John's arrest Jesus returns to Galilee, proclaiming the imminent Kingdom of God (1:14–15) and calling the Twelve. Then follows what appears to be a motley collection of healings and strained encounters with the authorities. On closer inspection they form a pattern that illustrates my twin theses regarding the conflicting ways of viewing Jesus.

Thesis A argues that the activities of Mark's Jesus were directed at the purification and consecration of Israel through "baptism" with the Holy Spirit. Jesus' first public act occurs in the synagogue at Capernaum on the sabbath, where he is accosted by a man with an unclean spirit (1:21–28). There is an implicit contrast between the Holy Spirit and the unclean spirit which is reflected in the terminology: "with the Holy Spirit [*en pneumati hagio*]" (1:8) and "with an unclean spirit [*en pneumati akatharto*]" (1:23). The phrase is repeated in the description of "Legion" (5:2). The theme of conflicting spirits finds later echoes (3:22; 11:28–29, 33). Mark's stress on time and place—the Sabbath and the synagogue—gives symbolic emphasis to the pollution and danger on the holy day and in the holy place, and to Jesus' unique authority. Typically the acknowledgment of Jesus as "the Holy One of God" (1:24) is taken as recognition of his identity. But here it is a form of self-defense in an attempt to gain power over Jesus by declaring his name.[51] By commanding the spirit to be silent and depart, Jesus has demonstrated his superior power. By making the man clean, Jesus has taken the first step towards fulfilling the Baptist's prophecy that "he will baptize you with the Holy Spirit."

The episode may be read on two levels. Paul W. Hollenbach's social historical approach sees such instances of possession as the outcome of colonial oppression.[52] Peter G. Bolt argues that Mark's hearers would have understood demons as the spirits of the departed, and Jesus' action as the initial skirmish with the powers of death.[53] While the episode exemplifies Thesis A, the response of the onlookers adumbrates Thesis B with their question:

"What is this? A new teaching—with authority! He commands even the unclean spirits, and they obey him" (1:27). The link between teaching and an
event that could be construed as a sign or wonder raises the question of
whether Jesus might be the kind of prophet described in Deuteronomy 13.

The remainder of Mark 1 is taken up with accounts of healing and exorcism, beginning with Simon's mother-in-law (1:29–31). That evening at
sundown, i.e., when the Sabbath was over, "they brought him all who were
sick or possessed with demons" (1:32). The climax is the healing of the leper,
where the motif of cleansing is stressed (1:40–45). Jesus' act of touching the
leper (1:41) goes beyond Elisha's treatment of Naaman (2 Kings 5), for physical contact would have made Jesus himself unclean. Jesus makes clean by
his touch and his word. Jesus' command to the leper to show himself to the
priest follows the instructions of the Torah, but the failure to heed Jesus'
injunction sows the seeds of Jesus' estrangement from the authorities.

With the healing of the paralytic (2:1–12) we are introduced to another
aspect of cleansing: the forgiveness of sin. It also brings into the open the
opposition I have sought to identify with Thesis B. Jesus' pronouncement,
"My son, your sins are forgiven" (1:5), prompts the question, "Why does
this man speak thus? It is blasphemy! Who can forgive sins but God alone?"
(2:7). Abuse of the divine name was punishable by death (Lev. 24:10–11,
14–16, 23; Sanhedrin 7:5). But Jesus does not invoke the divine name. He
pronounces forgiveness, employing the *theological passive*. The blasphemy
would seem to consist in the presumption of acting as God's agent. The
charge anticipates the charge on which Jesus will be eventually condemned
(14:64).

Tension continues over Jesus' eating with sinners and tax collectors (1:15–
17) and condoning his disciples plucking corn on the sabbath (2:23–28).
E. P. Sanders questions the authenticity of the account on the grounds that
the Pharisees, who rarely left Jerusalem, did not spend their Sabbaths in
Galilean cornfields in the hope of catching transgressors.[54] The narrative is
put in a different light, if with Ethelbert Stauffer we see Jesus as someone
who is already under suspicion of leading astray and a delegation has been
sent to check the evidence.[55] Events reach breaking point with the healing
of the man with the withered hand which again takes place in sacred space
on a sacred day (3:1–6). The episode closes on a note of irony. The man's
hand is *restored*, and the Pharisees hold counsel with the Herodians how
they might *destroy* Jesus (3:6).

Jesus' apparent success (3:7–8) is reversed by the growing alienation of his
family (3:20–21, 31–35) and the charge by the delegation of Torah lawyers
from Jerusalem that Jesus was casting out demons by Beelzebul (3:20–32).
Mark shows Jesus as a master of riposte. It leads to the saying "whoever
blasphemes against the Holy Spirit never has forgiveness, but is guilty of
an eternal sin" (3:29). Mark's comment points up its significance: "for they
had said, 'He has an unclean spirit'" (3:30). With this comment my two

theses come together. Mark intends his readers to understand that Jesus is empowered by the Holy Spirit (Thesis A). The construction placed on Jesus' activity by the scribes from Jerusalem represents the opposite (Thesis B). It implies that the spirit that has come upon Jesus is an alien deity—Beelzebul— and that he is leading the people astray (Deut. 13:1–18; 17:2–7; Lev. 20:27; Damascus Document 12:1–3). The penalty for such a charge was death so that evil may be purged from the land and its people.

Act 1 closes with the response of Jesus' mother and brothers (3:31). Their action implies dissociation, suggesting perhaps that he was a stubborn and rebellious son (Deut. 21:18–21). Jesus reciprocates by disowning his family. "And looking at those who sat around him, he said, 'Here are my mother and brothers! Whoever does the will of God is my brother and sister and mother'" (3:34–35).

The parables of Mark 4 give comment on the reception of Jesus and anticipation of what is to come. They speak of the varied reception given to the Kingdom and the word, and the activity of Satan in taking it away. The Kingdom of God is set over against the kingdom of Satan. God's Kingdom is present in Jesus' activity. As Joachim Jeremias observed: "All the Gospel parables are a defence of the Good News. The actual proclamation of the Good News to sinners took a different form: in the offer of forgiveness, in Jesus' invitation to the guilty to taste his hospitality, in his call to follow him."[56]

Act 2. The Conflict Spreads (4:35–7:23)

Act 2 begins and ends with sea crossings. The first (the stilling of the storm) is a tactical retreat; the second (Jesus' walking on the sea) marks the beginning of a new conquest. The themes of Thesis A and Thesis B are further developed. The concluding controversy with the Pharisees highlights fundamental differences over purity.

The decision to cross to the other side of the lake of Galilee is made in light of the events that conclude Act 1. The stilling of the storm (4:35–5:1) is generally seen as a nature or rescue miracle.[57] Several layers of Scripture appear to form the subtext. They include allusions to Psalms 104:7, 106:9, 107:28–30, and echoes of Jonah. Like Jonah, Jesus was asleep, and like the crew in Jonah the disciples fear for their lives. The parallels are not merely linguistic and formal. Jesus was—like Jonah—a prophet under judgment. Mark's version is not (as in Matthew and Luke, who detach it from the Beelzebul charge) essentially a story of providential care. It is linked to the charges at the end of Act 1 and thus reprises the theme of Thesis B. If the boat had sunk, it would have been seen as a judgment. Jesus' rebuke of the storm is a repudiation of its demonic assault.[58] The response of fear (4:41), which constitutes a leitmotiv (5:15; 6:50; 16:8), suggests links with Aristotle's view of the purpose of tragedy and also the role of fear in the Hebrew Scriptures.

Three stories develop the theme of purity. That of "Legion" (5:2–20) is located in the Decapolis, a Roman foundation. The herd of pigs indicates gentile ownership. Political and religious motifs are intertwined. The tenth legion, stationed in Syria since 6 c.e., had an image of a boar on its standards and shields.[59] In this light the story of driving the pigs into the sea would appeal to Jewish hearers. Pigs were sacrificial animals in Greece and Rome.[60] From the standpoint of the Torah, anything idolatrous should be devoted to destruction (Deut. 13:17–18). For these various reasons the destruction of the pigs would have been a gain in Jewish eyes. For the inhabitants of the Decapolis, Jesus poses a threat, and is begged to leave. The story combines two aspects of demon possession noted earlier: political servitude and unclean spirits as the spirits of the departed. The former is indicated by the allusion to "Legion," and the latter by the fact that the man lived among the tombs (5:3–5).

The stories of Jairus's daughter (5:21–24, 35–43) and the woman with the flow of blood (5:25–34) are characterized by the question of uncleanness.[61] Like the preceding story, they show Jesus crossing boundary lines as the agent of purity. All three stories are linked with death, and physical contact would have brought defilement. Instead of being defiled, Jesus bestows purity and life.

The feeding of the five thousand (6:32–44) is replete with echoes of provision narratives.[62] Barnabas Lindars[63] and John P. Meier[64] locate the story in the Elisha tradition, the latter also seeing influence of the Christian eucharist. Others see Jesus as a new Moses.[65] J. D. M. Derrett[66] sees a connection with Joshua, and in my view this is correct. The textual paradigms are woven into a tapestry, which depicts Jesus as the *new Joshua* provisioning his followers for *a new conquest* of the land of Israel. A clue is given by the incidental remark that "he had compassion for them, because they were like sheep without a shepherd" (6:34). The subtext is Numbers 27:17, where Moses, envisaging his own death, asks God to appoint his successor, so that Israel may not be "like sheep without a shepherd." Whereupon God directs Moses to Joshua, "a man in whom is the spirit," as the man to whom Moses' authority is to be given. It scarcely needs to be added that the name of Jesus was *Joshua*, and that the Spirit had come upon him after his baptism. Three candidates might qualify to be the shepherd of Israel. Herod Antipas belongs to the category of shepherd condemned by 1 Kings 22:17 and Ezekiel 34:5. John the Baptist might have become the shepherd of Israel, had he not been executed by the wicked shepherd (6:14–29). The remaining candidate is Jesus/Joshua, who proceeds to feed the sheep.

The feeding of the five thousand is followed by what is frequently referred to as Jesus walking on water. The more correct designation is "walking on the sea" (6:45–52). The obvious difficulties presented by the idea of walking on water have prompted suggestions that it is a displaced resurrection narrative[67] or an epiphany.[68] "He meant to pass them by" (6:48) is the language of epiphanies (Exod. 33:19, 22; 34:6; 1 Kings 19:11). J. D. M. Derrett's provocative article, "Why and How Jesus Walked on the Sea,"[69] offers a more down-to-earth explanation.

In answer to the question "Why?" Derrett suggests Jesus was reenacting the crossing of the Jordan in order to embark on a new conquest. In answer to "How?" Derrett observes that the location at the mouth of the Jordan as it enters the Sea of Galilee is at times shallow enough to ford.[70] Just as Joshua sanctified himself and communed with Yahweh before the crossing of the Jordan, so Jesus went up the mountain to pray alone (6:46–47; cf. Josh. 3:5, 7). Jesus then made his way along the edge of the shelf across the lake in order to stand like Joshua with his feet in the Jordan (6:48; cf. Josh. 3:8) before joining the disciples in the boat and crossing to Gennesaret on the west bank (6:53).

The teaching section that follows brings into focus the question of purity as the issue that divides Jesus and the Pharisees.[71] From the perspective of Thesis B, Jesus is a subverter of the law in his disregard of ritual purity. The passage takes up the language of baptism in the parenthetical description that Mark provides for his gentile audience noting the importance of washing (*baptisontai*) before eating and "the washing [*baptismous*] of cups, pots, and bronze kettles" (7:4).[72] Mark's Jesus insists that what defiles is not what enters the stomach but what comes out of the heart. Mark draws the implication: "Thus he declared all foods clean" (7:19).

Act 3. The Climax (7:24–10:5)

Like the previous act, Act 3 begins with a tactical retreat and an exorcism. Seeking secrecy Jesus moves to the region of Tyre. David Rhoads observes: "Mark's story of the Syrophoenician woman [7:24–30] functioned much like the story of the Ninevites who repented to Jonah's reluctant preaching or like the parable about the (oxymoronic) good Samaritan. The story challenges the audience not to set limits on the universality of the good news of the kingdom of God. The whole first part of Mark's story prepares the hearer to go with Jesus across this final boundary to Gentile territory."[73]

A generation ago Austin Farrer drew attention to other aspects of Mark's symbolism.[74] Mark describes the healing of twelve Israelites plus one Gentile, corresponding to the twelve tribes of Israel plus a representative of the gentile world. The number also corresponds to the number of the disciples, plus the tax collector Levi. They form a kind of composite of the human body, afflicted by typical ailments of the day: the unclean spirit (1:25), Simon's mother-in-law's fever (1:31), leprosy (1:41), paralysis (2:11), the withered hand (3:5), Legion (5:8), a dead girl (5:23), the unclean woman (5:29), the deaf mute (7:34), the blind Bethsaidan (8:25), the epileptic boy (9:25), blind Bartimaeus (10:52), and the possessed Syro-phoenician girl (7:29).

The feeding of the four thousand (8:1–10) is widely regarded as a doublet of the earlier feeding.[75] It appears to be set in predominantly gentile Decapolis (7:31). If the boy was a local Gentile, Jesus was apparently willing to share his non-kosher food. His action was thus an instance of imparting purity. Derrett again links the narrative with the Joshua tradition.[76] By taking gentile food, Jesus in effect enters into a relationship with the Gentiles (cf. Jos. 9:31–15). The story is thus a counterpart to the importunity of the Syro-phoenician woman. Gentiles are enlisted in his cause through Jesus' act of taking their food.

The Pharisees' request for "a sign from heaven" (8:11) is typically taken as a request for evidence. But in the nature of the case, it is difficult to see how any sign could pass such a test. The Torah's teaching regarding prophets who perform signs and wonders extends from Deuteronomy 13:1–11 through writings of the Second-Temple period into the rabbinic tradition. No sign whatever should be accepted, if it was linked with teaching that led astray. Such signs were to be seen as tests from God (Deut. 13:3). In light of the conviction that Jesus was possessed by Beelzebul (3:22), the performance of a sign like the one just described could only be construed as a Satanic miracle.

Peter's confession marks the climax and turning point of the narrative. Jesus is in the region of Caesarea Philippi, some twenty-five miles north of the Sea of Galilee at the foot of Mount Hermon. The choice of location may seem strange on account of the city's dedication to Caesar and its famous grotto dedicated to Pan. On the other hand, it would be an ideal location from which to challenge the authority of Caesar and the power of pagan religion, especially since it was located close to Dan, and the reputed source of the Jordan. As such it could be the starting point for a new conquest from north to south, as in the traditional phrase, "from Dan to Beersheba."

It would be anachronistic to read into Peter's confession the theology of the ecumenical councils. In the context of Mark, "You are the Christ [*su ei ho christos*]" (8:29) means that Jesus is anointed by the Spirit and is doing the work of the Lord's Anointed (Thesis A), in contrast with the people's surmise that one of the prophets has returned, Herod's suspicion of necromancy (6:14), and the scribes' accusation of possession by Beelzebul (Thesis B). This new insight leads to an unexpected "reversal" and further "discovery." Instead of publicizing Jesus, the disciples are ordered not to tell anyone about him (8:30).[77] Even more ominous is the new turn in Jesus' teaching: "[T]he Son of Man must undergo great suffering, and be rejected by the elders, the chief priests, and the scribes, and be killed, and after three days rise again" (8:31). It is the first of three predictions (8:31–33; 9:30–32; 10:31–34). Jesus is set on a collision course. The way is now prepared for the dénouement and catastrophe in Jerusalem.[78]

The teaching at the conclusion of Act 3 (9:35–10:45) focuses on the way of the Son of Man and that of would-be disciples. It touches on the whole range of life: children, marriage, property and wealth, discipleship. In each case the purity that Jesus calls for goes beyond convention. At its heart is the concept of agency noted earlier: "Whoever welcomes one such child in my name welcomes me, and whoever welcomes me welcomes not me but the one who sent me" (9:37). Two issues call for comment.

The first, which again is posed by the Pharisees, has to do with divorce (10:1–12). On the surface, it looks like an academic question of whether Jesus agrees with the stricter school of Shammai or with the less rigid of Hillel. In contrast with modern Western society, the Torah viewed divorce as a matter of purity (Deut. 24:1–4). But the Pharisees' question has a political dimension. Jesus is now "beyond the Jordan," in other words, in territory governed by Herod Antipas. Herod had arrested John the Baptist for denouncing Herod's divorce of his wife in order to marry the divorced Herodias (6:17–18, 22–29; cf. Josephus, *Antiquities* 18.110–11, 136). If Jesus were to adopt the same stance as John, he would run the risk of inviting the same fate. If he were to repudiate John, he would in effect repudiate his baptism, and with it the prophecy that he would baptize with the Holy Spirit. Jesus' masterful reply goes beyond Moses to creation (10:6–9; Gen. 2:24).

The second observation has to do with Jesus' puzzling question: "Are you able to drink the cup that I drink, or to be baptized with the baptism that I am baptized with?" Had he not been baptized already? The cup that Jesus was about to drink (10:38; 14:23–25, 36) was the cup of wrath and judgment (Isa. 51:17–22; Jer. 25:15; Ezek. 23:31–33; Hab. 2:16). From the standpoint of Thesis B, Jesus' death would be an act of judgment and cleansing. As such, it would be a "baptism." From the standpoint of Thesis A, Jesus' death would be "a ransom for many" (10:45).[79]

Act 4. The Dénouement (10:46–13:37)

The dénouement centers on Jesus' Temple action. Act 4 begins with Jesus' final healing act as he leaves Jericho with its ancient memories of the conquest under Joshua. The story of the blind beggar Bartimaeus (10:46–52) contrasts with the hostility of the Jerusalem hierarchy. Two comments are in order. The first has to do with the exclusion of the blind from the Temple on the grounds of impurity.[80] Jesus' healing of Bartimaeus would purify him and qualify him to enter the Temple. The second observation has to do with Bartimaeus's cry "Son of David, have mercy on me!" (10:47). The cry gains new meaning in light of David's reputed attitude to the blind (1 Sam. 5:8). But "Son of David" has messianic kingly implications, and also connotations of gifts of healing in light of traditions concerning David and Solomon.[81]

It is widely agreed that Jesus performed some drastic action in the Temple, which led to his death. E. P. Sanders regards it as "the surest starting point" for the investigation of the historical Jesus.[82] Sanders rejects the common view that it was in some sense a "cleansing" of the temple directed at "external" religion. He concludes that it was a symbolic act indicating expectation of the eschaton and with it a new Temple given from heaven.[83] By contrast, Bruce Chilton contends that Jesus' action was designed to ensure that Israel's offerings would indeed be owned by the people prior to sacrifice, and not bought within the Temple precincts.[84] However, the sayings of 11:17 are not protest about improper provision and mode of sacrifice, but condemnation of the Temple's failure to fulfill its function.[85]

In light of my twin theses, Jesus' action in the Temple appears as the climactic act of his program of purification. When asked about his authority for acting as he did (11:27–33), Jesus asks an apparently evasive counter-question: "Did the baptism of John come from heaven, or was it of human origin? Answer me" (11:30). The authorities rightly perceive that, if they were to acknowledge that John's baptism was from God, the next question would be, "Why then did you not believe him?" But what had been the burden of John's message? He had proclaimed a baptism of repentance for the forgiveness of sins. But this was only preparatory to another baptism. "I have baptized you with water; but he will baptize you with the Holy Spirit" (1:8). In this light, Jesus' action in the Temple could be described as *the baptism of the Temple*. His authority was given by the Spirit, which came upon Jesus at his baptism. But the authorities see Jesus as an impostor whose actions merit the death penalty (11:18; 12:12). In this way Thesis A and Thesis B converge in presenting the actions and teaching of Jesus from opposing perspectives.

The encounters that follow—questions about tribute to Caesar, marriage and resurrection, the first commandment, Jesus' question about the Messiah, his warnings about the scribes, and the widow casting her two copper coins—all have to do with orthodoxy and pure religion. Jesus' identification of Deuteronomy 6:4–5 as the first commandment indicates his fundamental commitment to the monotheistic orthodoxy of the Torah. His addition of a second commandment, "You shall love your neighbor as yourself" (12:31; cf. Lev. 19:18), evinces the acknowledgment that he had answered truly. The scribe's comment that the two commandments are "much more important than burnt offerings and sacrifices" (11:33; cf. 1 Sam. 15:22; Hos. 6:6; Mic. 6:6–8) has the effect of relativizing the Temple. It functions like the comment on the dietary laws in 7:19.

The so-called "apocalyptic discourse" has provoked a welter of conflicting interpretations.[86] I see it as a prophetic-apocalyptic oracle concerning the judgment that would occur within the span of "this generation" (13:30). Like the teaching that follows the previous Acts, Mark 13 relates to what has just occurred. The "desolating sacrilege" (13:14; cf. 1 Macc. 1:54; Dan. 9:27; 11:31; 12:11) alludes to the desecration of the temple.[87] The warnings about messiahs and false prophets (13:22), which echo the language of Deuteronomy 13, find fulfillment in the sign-prophets in the period leading up to the war with Rome.[88] The cosmic language is not to be seen as predictions of unprecedented astronomical events. It is the prophetic language of judgment used to denote the divine dimension of this-worldly events.[89] Some of the phenomena described in Mark 13 occur already in Mark 14–16.[90]

The coming of the Son of Man in clouds is, as in Daniel 7:13–14, a coming to the Ancient of Days.[91] The events on earth will be the sign of Jesus' vindication in heaven. In the words of G. B. Caird, "Jesus believed that Israel was called by God to be the agent of His purpose, and that he himself had been sent to bring about its reformation without which Israel could not fulfill its national destiny. If the nation, so far from accepting that calling, rejected God's messenger and persecuted those who responded to his preaching, how could the assertion of God's sovereignty fail to include an open demonstration that Jesus was right and the nation was wrong?"[92]

Act 5. The Catastrophe (14:1–15:39)

The final Act begins with the decision to arrest Jesus and ends with his death. It includes the story of the anointing, the Passover meal with the Twelve, and Jesus' arrest in Gethsemane. Jesus' appearance before the Sanhedrin (14:53–63) was not a formal trial, but a hearing or interrogation.[93] Despite claims that the condemnation of Jesus was politically motivated, religious factors are also evident. Both Pharisees and Sadducees were represented in the Sanhedrin.[94] Otto Betz observes: "The Sadducees who were charged with political responsibility for law and order were more sensitive towards a prophetic criticism of the political and moral state of Israel, delivered in the spirit of Holy Scripture.... They too applied the criteria of Deut. 13 and in addition 21:22–23 to the actions and claims of Jesus, according to which false messianic claims which endangered the people, the city, and the temple constituted a blasphemy against God."[95] August Strobel likewise sees the teaching of Deuteronomy 13 regarding a prophet who leads others astray as the key factor.[96]

Testimony that Jesus intended to destroy the Temple and build another "not made with hands" (14:56–57) fits Thesis B, in that it involves both prophecy and a miraculous sign. But the contradictions of the witnesses and the silence of Jesus produce a stalemate, which is broken by the high priest's question and Jesus' answer. The question, "Are you the Christ? [*su ei ho christos*]," is verbally identical in Greek with Peter's confession (14:61; cf. 8:29). This fact may be ascribed to the dramatic powers of the evangelist. At the same time it plausibly represents the issue at stake: Is Jesus the Lord's Anointed? In dramatic terms, Jesus' reply provides the high point of "recognition" and "reversal." "I am; and 'you will see the Son of Man seated at the right hand of the Power,' and 'coming with the clouds of heaven' " (14:62). In a symbolic act on hearing blasphemy the high priest tears his clothes (Sanhedrin 7:5) and asks, " 'Why do we still need witnesses? You have heard his blasphemy! What is your decision?' All of them condemned him as deserving of death" (14:63–64). Thus, Jesus is condemned for blasphemy—a charge that was laid against him at the outset of his public activity (2:7).

The blasphemy appears to have several facets,[97] but the common factor is Jesus' claim to be God's Anointed, and as such would give a sign. The blasphemy could be construed as reviling the high priest, the appointed leader of the people (Exod. 22:28; Deut. 17:12; cf. Josephus, *Against Apion* 2.193–95).[98] It implied that Jesus would assume the high priest's place in judgment. Jesus' language appropriates Psalm 110 and Daniel 7:13, making him equal with God riding the clouds (Exod. 14:20; Num. 10:34; Psalm 104:3; Isa. 19:1). The blasphemy is even more acute if the Holy of Holies in the Temple were a model of heaven representing the place of God's presence to which only the high priest had access (Lev. 16). It implies not only that Jesus had access to the Holy of Holies, but that a second throne would be placed by God's throne for Jesus.[99]

The motif of Jesus as a sign-working false prophet is maintained in the incidents of the blindfold and taunts to prophesy (14:65; cf. Isa. 11:3–4),[100] the challenge to come down from the cross (15:29–32), and the assumed call to Elijah (15:35–36). Alongside are the political motifs. Helen K. Bond sums up Pilate's situation: "Far from being a tool in the hands of the chief priests and crowd...Pilate is very much in control. He recognizes the self-interest in the actions of the chief priests [cf. 15:10] but also realizes that Jesus is a potential threat to law and order."[101] In Mark Pilate is not the weak governor who bows to pressure, but the political manipulator who makes others take responsibility (15:6–15). The *titulus* inscription "King of the Jews" (15:26; cf. 15:2, 9, 12, 18, 26, 32) betrays the mockery of the gentile prefect, as does the soldiers' mock homage (15:16–19). The events narrated in 15:16–39 are presented like a Roman triumphal march in which the conquered are led in procession through the streets as they go to their place of execution.[102]

The tradition regarding the Temple veil (15:38) has suggested to some that the Holy Place was thereby opened to all. But as Raymond E. Brown observes, the function of the veil was to *separate* the holy place from the profane, and thus the rending of the veil left the sanctuary vulnerable to the invasion of the profane. "Against the background of the sanctuary as a divine dwelling place—an idea shared by pagans and Jews alike—rending the veil could mean that the deity or deity's presence had left."[103] Van Iersel relates the rending of the veil to the prophecy of John the Baptist that "he will baptize you with the Holy Spirit" (1:8).[104] In death, the Spirit that had come upon Jesus at his baptism left him to become the breath of divine judgment (cf. Isa. 11:4; 27:8; Job 4:9; Wisd. of Sol. 11:20). On this view, the rending of the Temple veil was *a sign from heaven* that prompted the centurion's admission, "Truly this man was God's Son!" (15:39). The comment forms a counterpart to 1:11, bringing Mark's narrative full circle. The words are not a confession of faith but of defeat.[105]

Epilogue (15:40–16:8)

Mark's Epilogue transforms tragedy into triumph. But it presents notorious problems.[106] The best manuscript tradition ends with the words *ephobounto gar*, "for they were afraid" (16:8). The existence of different manuscript traditions is itself testimony to early sentiment that such an abrupt ending was unsatisfactory. More recently scholars have surmised that the original ending was lost or that Mark was prevented from concluding his narrative. This conclusion is reinforced by belief that to end a work with *gar* ("for") is ungrammatical if not impossible. In response it may be pointed out that clauses and sentences ending with *gar* are well attested.[107] Moreover, fear is a major motif in Aristotle's concept of tragedy and also in biblical religion, as the most appropriate response to divine acts (Deut. 5:29; 13:4; 31:12–13; Ps. 2:11; Prov. 1:7).

The question of the empty tomb still excites debate about its historical value. Gerd Lüdemann links it to "apologetic legend."[108] Stephen T. Davis sees it as "a necessary but not sufficient condition for the bodily resurrection of Jesus."[109] While not dismissing this argument, it seems to me that perhaps we have failed to see the forest for the trees. As elsewhere in Mark, what is important lies in what is not said.[110] The tacit element in the story is the question of purity and impurity. There is a young man in the tomb clothed in "a white robe" (16:5), reminiscent of Jesus' transfiguration (9:3). Evidently the young man, an angel, is not defiled. Nor are the women. But in Jewish tradition corpses and graves defile.[111] The implication is there for those who will grasp it. Jesus has cleansed the grave from its defiling power. The ancient prayer used in the office of Compline speaks of Jesus Christ, who at the hour of Compline rested in the sepulchre, and "didst thereby sanctify the grave to be a bed of hope to thy people."[112] Far from being an anticlimax, Mark's narrative of the angel and the women in the tomb is the climax of the Gospel. What has taken place is the ultimate act of cleansing, the climax of the series of cleansing acts which began with the cleansing of the man with the unclean spirit. If, as was argued in the discussion of 1:21–28, the "unclean spirit" was a ghost, an emissary of death, Mark's narrative has moved from the conquest of individual spirits to the conquest of death itself.

In this way, my two theses converge for the final time. Thesis B is indicated by the fact that Joseph of Arimathea obtained from Pilate the corpse of the executed blasphemer, and had it hastily buried in a makeshift tomb of a kind reserved for criminals.[113] But the thesis is countered by the story of what is misleadingly called the *empty* tomb. It was empty of Jesus' body, but the presence of the angel is an indication that the tomb had been cleansed. It points us to the answer contained in Thesis A, carrying with it the implication that what has happened is the ultimate fulfillment of John the Baptist's prophecy, that "he will baptize you with the Holy Spirit."

Implications

Mark's Christology

I have tried to read Mark *with the grain* and *against the grain*. The result is my two theses. Together they raise the question: "What spirit had gotten into Jesus?" Thesis A replies that it was the Spirit of God. Thesis B replies that it was the devil that got into him, and that he was a deceiver who was rightly purged. In the end, it is a matter of hermeneutics. How we read Mark's Jesus depends on the values, codes, belief-systems, and texts that we bring to Mark's narrative, and on how we respond to the Jesus whom Mark presents.

If you ask me "Who did Mark's Jesus think that he was?" my reply is "Joshua." Or rather, he acts like a second Joshua who sought to reclaim the people of Israel and the land for God. The Kingdom of God proclaimed by Jesus is God's presence in power and purity, in contrast to the kingdom of Satan (3:24) and the kingdoms of this world (6:23; 13:8).[114] Unlike a modern biographer, Mark shows little interest in the personality of Jesus— or for that matter, in the personalities of those whom Jesus healed and of the disciples who followed him. He appears as a master of riposte (bested only by the Syro-phoenician woman, 7:28–29), and on occasion as entering into altered states of consciousness. But personality is subordinate to Jesus' vocation to be the agent of the purifying, life-giving Spirit of God.

In this regard I find myself at odds with Dominic Crossan and his contention that Jesus' itinerant activities were "a symbolic representation of unbrokered egalitarianism" in the service of "unmediated physical and spiritual contact with God."[115] From first to last Mark's Jesus acts like God's agent—his *shaliach,* to use the rabbinic term—acting with the authority of God, which derived from the Spirit that came upon him at his baptism, and which left him only as he expired. It was the Spirit that made him the Christ. Mark presents what I call "an up-front Spirit Christology." But there is also a developing "word Christology," insofar as Jesus speaks God's word "with authority." He is the sower who sows the word of the Kingdom. There is even a hint of a "wisdom Christology" in the question, "Where did this man get all this? What is this wisdom that has been given him? What deeds of power are being done by his hands!" (6:2). But for a developed "wisdom Christology" we have to turn to Matthew and Luke.

Mark's Jesus and the Historical Jesus

If my reading of Mark is anything like correct, we cannot treat his narrative as straightforward eyewitness reporting. It is shot through with symbolism in both the incidents related and in the manner of narrating them. Sayings, episodes, and titles are replete with echoes of earlier texts. They prompt the question whether D. F. Strauss was right after all in his charge that the Gospels were pervaded by myth and were thus virtually worthless as historical records.[116] In response I would say that a lot depends on what one means by myth. If myth is an extended metaphor or series of metaphors, I would say that one cannot get to a nonmetaphorical reality, as if the language of realism and the language of metaphor belong to separate realms.[117] If we define myth as "the false attribution of reality to a suggestive metaphor,"[118] we shall at least be alerted to the dangers of reifying metaphorical language. Even so, I do not think that we can know the Jesus of history by any other route than through the texts that have come down to us.

My account of Mark raises other questions. If Mark has shaped his life of Jesus in the form of a tragic-epic narrative, could it be that formal requirements have influenced his selection and arrangement of events?[119] The answer has to be "Yes." It sets a question mark against using Mark's framework as if it provided the definitive chronology. But in so doing, it opens the door to John's claims that Jesus paid more than one visit to Jerusalem, and to recognition of teaching and events found in other strands of tradition. The shape of Mark's narrative and the material that he included were determined by the apologetic factors in his "life" of Jesus.

Can we have confidence that we may encounter the Jesus of history through Mark's Jesus? My answer is "Yes." There are several avenues that may be explored. One is to look at other sources. Here I would discount the now discredited Secret Mark.[120] On the other hand, one can compare Mark with other traditions like the Q tradition, and find not only points of convergence but supplementary traditions. Another approach is to compare Mark, as Maurice Casey has done, with a reconstruction of his Aramaic sources.[121] Casey, who is not known for credulity, has reconstructed several passages into Second-Temple Aramaic (2:23–3:6; 9:11–13; 10:35–45; 14:12–26) and concluded a date c. 40 c.e. for Mark's Aramaic sources.

Finally, we may note the resurgence of interest in the question of criteria in historical Jesus studies.[122] The days are long past since the criterion of dissimilarity reigned supreme. (For a saying or event to be deemed historical, it had to be dissimilar to Judaism and dissimilar to the life setting of the early church.) Instead, scholars now talk about *contextual plausibility,* asking how any given Jesus tradition relates to its Jewish context, and *impact plausibility,* which seeks to interpret sources as the outworking of the history to which they testify. It is questions such as these that we should put to Mark's Gospel. And it is along these lines, I believe, that historical Jesus research will proceed in the new century.

Notes

1. See, e.g., Richard A. Horsley, *Jesus and the Spiral of Violence: Popular Resistance in Roman Palestine* (San Francisco: HarperSanFrancisco, 1987); John Dominic Crossan, *The Historical Jesus: The Life of a Mediterranean Jewish Peasant* (San Francisco: HarperSanFrancisco, 1991); Ekkehard W. Stegemann and Wolfgang Stegemann, *The Jesus Movement: A Social History of Its First Century* (Minneapolis: Fortress Press, 1999).

2. Jacob Neusner, *The Idea of Purity in Ancient Judaism*, SJLA 1 (Leiden: Brill, 1973) 108; cf. Hannah K. Harrington, *The Impurity Systems of Qumran and the Rabbis: Biblical Foundations*, SBLDS 143 (Atlanta, 1993); Paula Fredriksen, *Jesus of Nazareth, King of the Jews: A Jewish Life and the Emergence of Christianity* (New York: Knopf, 2000) 52–54, 65–70, 197–214.

3. David Rhoads, "Social Criticism: Crossing Boundaries," in *Mark and Method*, ed. Janice Capel Anderson and Stephen D. Moore (Minneapolis: Fortress Press, 1992) 135–61.

4. James D. G. Dunn, "Jesus and the Temple," in *The Partings of the Ways: Between Christianity and Judaism and their Significance for the Character of Christianity* (London: SCM, and Philadelphia: Trinity Press International, 1991) 37–56.

5. Marcus J. Borg, *Conflict, Holiness, and Politics in the Teachings of Jesus* (Harrisburg, Pa.: Trinity Press International, [1984] 1998) 116.

6. Klaus Berger, "Jesus als Pharisäer und frühe Christen als Pharisäer," *NovT* 30 (1988) 231–62; cf. Jerome H. Neyrey, "The Idea of Purity in Mark's Gospel," *Semeia* 35 (1986) 91–128.

7. Klaus Berger, *NovT* 30 (1988) 247.

8. On the exclusion of the lame, blind, deaf, and blemished, see Num. 5:2–3; Lev. 21:17–24; 2 Sam. 5:6–8; Isa. 52:1; Joel 3:17; 1Q28a 2:3–10; 11QTemple 45:12–14; Kelim 1:1–9.

9. Jacob Milgrom, *Leviticus 1–16*, Anchor Bible (New York: Doubleday, 1991) 1003.

10. Colin Brown, "What Was John the Baptist Doing?" *BBR* 7 (1997) 37–50.

11. Craig A. Evans, "Aspects of Exile and Restoration in the Proclamation of Jesus and the Gospels," in *Exile: Old Testament, Jewish and Christian Conceptions*, ed. James M. Scott, Supplements to the Journal for the Study of Judaism 56 (Leiden, New York, Cologne: Brill, 1997) 299–328; Evans, "Jesus and the Continuing Exile of Israel," in *Jesus and the Restoration of Israel: A Critical Assessment of N. T. Wright's* Jesus and the Victory of God, ed. Carey C. Newman (Downers Grove, Ill.: InterVarsity Press, 1999) 77–100.

12. James D. G. Dunn, *Christology in the Making: An Inquiry into the Origins of the Doctrine of Incarnation*, 2d ed. (London: SCM, 1989) 132–36.

13. J. Dominic Crossan, *The Historical Jesus*, 303–53; cf. David E. Aune, "Magic in Early Christianity," *ANRW* 2.23.2 (1980) 1507–57.

14. Crossan, Ibid., 138.

15. Morton Smith, *Jesus the Magician* (New York: Harper & Row, 1978).

16. Edwin M. Yamauchi, "Magic or Miracle? Disease, Demons and Exorcisms," in *The Miracles of Jesus*, ed. David Wenham and Craig Blomberg, Gospel Perspectives 6 (Sheffield: JSOT Press, 1986) 89–185; cf. Wendy Cotter, *Miracles in Greco-Roman*

Antiquity: A Sourcebook (London and New York: Routledge, 1999) 175–247; Barry L. Blackburn, "The Miracles of Jesus," in *Studying the Historical Jesus: Evaluations of the State of Current Research,* ed. Bruce Chilton and Craig A. Evans, NTTS 19 (Leiden, New York, Cologne: Brill, 1994) 353–94; Graham H. Twelftree, *Jesus the Miracle Worker: A Historical and Theological Study* (Downers Grove, Ill.: InterVarsity Press, 1999); John Pilch, *Healing in the New Testament: Insights from Medical and Mediterranean Anthropology* (Minneapolis: Fortress Press, 1999).

17. Jonathan Z. Smith, "Good News Is No News: Aretalogy and Gospel," in *Christianity, Judaism and Other Greco-Roman Cults: Studies for Morton Smith at Sixty,* ed. Jacob Neusner, SJLA 12 (Leiden: Brill, 1975) 23.

18. Justin, *Dialogue with Trypho* 69, 102, 106–7; *First Apology* 30; Origen, *Contra Celsum* 1.38; Eusebius, *Demonstration of the Gospel* 3; Acts of Thomas 96; Sanhedrin 43a; cf. Graham N. Stanton, "Jesus of Nazareth: A Magician and a False Prophet Who Deceived God's People?" in *Jesus of Nazareth, Lord and Christ: Essays on the Historical Jesus and New Testament Christology,* ed. Joel B. Green and Max Turner (Grand Rapids, Mich.: Eerdmans, 1994) 164–80; Eugene V. Gallagher, *Divine Man or Magician? Celsus and Origen on Jesus,* SBLDS 64 (Chico, Calif.: Scholars Press, 1982); Harold Remus, *Pagan-Christian Conflict over Miracle in the Second Century,* Patristic Monograph Series 10 (Cambridge, Mass.: Philadelphia Patristic Foundation, 1983); Frederic W. Norris, "Eusebius on Jesus as Deceiver and Sorcerer," in *Eusebius, Christianity and Judaism,* ed. Harold W. Attridge and Gohei Hata (Detroit: Wayne State University Press; Leiden: Brill, 1992) 523–40.

19. G. Vermes, "Hanina ben Dosa" in *Post-Biblical Jewish Studies,* SJLA 8 (Leiden: Brill, 1975) 178–214; William Scott Green, "Palestinian Holy Men: Charismatic Leadership and Rabbinic Tradition," *ANRW* (1979) 2.19.2: 619–47; Crossan, *The Historical Jesus,* 137–67; Craig A. Evans, "Jesus and Jewish Miracle Stories," in *Jesus and His Contemporaries: Comparative Studies,* AGJU 25 (Leiden, New York, Cologne: Brill, 1995) 213–43.

20. I first presented my two-part thesis in "Synoptic Miracle Stories: A Jewish Religious and Social Setting," *Foundations and Facets Forum* 2/4 (1986) 55–76.

21. Cf. Ethelbert Stauffer, *Jerusalem und Rom im Zeitalter Jesu* (Berne: Francke Verlag, 1957); Stauffer, *Jesus and His Story* (New York: Alfred A. Knopf, 1960); August Strobel, *Die Stunde der Wahrheit. Untersuchungen zum Strafverfahren gegen Jesus,* WUNT 21 (Tübingen: Mohr-Siebeck, 1980); Otto Betz, "Probleme des Prozesses Jesu," *ANRW* 25.1 (1982) 566–647; J. Duncan M. Derrett, "Jesus as a Seducer (ΠΛΑΝΟΣ=ΜΑΤ'ΕΗ)," *Bijdragen* 55 (1994) 43–55.

22. Rudolf Bultmann, *The History of the Synoptic Tradition* (Oxford: Blackwell, 1963) 350.

23. See Peter Stuhlmacher, ed., *The Gospel and the Gospels* (Grand Rapids, Mich.: Eerdmans, 1983).

24. Graham N. Stanton, *Jesus of Nazareth in New Testament Preaching,* SNTSMS 27 (Cambridge: Cambridge University Press, 1974) 117–36; David E. Aune, *The New Testament and its Literary Environment* (Philadelphia: Westminster Press, 1987) 17–76; Richard A. Burridge, *What Are the Gospels? A Comparison with Graeco-Roman Biography,* SNTSMS 70 (Cambridge: Cambridge University Press, [1992] 1995); Dirk Frickenschmidt, *Evangelium als Biographie. Die vier Evangelien im Rahmen antiker Erzählerkunst* (Tübingen: Francke, 1997).

25. Burridge, *What Are the Gospels?* 258.

26. Aune, *The New Testament in its Literary Environment,* 35.

27. Neusner, ed., *Christianity, Judaism and Other Greco-Roman Cults,* 1:25.

28. N. T. Wright, *The New Testament and the People of God* (Minneapolis: Fortress Press, 1992) 392.

29. Anderson and Moore, *Mark and Method;* W. R. Telford, *Mark* (Sheffield: Sheffield Academic Press, 1995) 86–119; David Rhoads, Joanna Dewey, and Donald Michie, *Mark as Story: An Introduction to the Narrative of a Gospel* (Minneapolis: Fortress Press, 1999).

30. Gilbert G. Bilezikian, *The Liberated Gospel: A Comparison of the Gospel of Mark and Greek Tragedy* (Grand Rapids, Mich.: Baker Book House, 1977); Friedrich Gustav Lang, "Kompositionsanalyse des Markusevangeliums," *ZTK* 74 (1977) 1–24; Benoît Standaert, *L'Évangile selon Marc. Composition et genre littéraire* (Nijmegen: Stichting Studenpers, 1978; reprint Brugge: Zevenkerken, 1984); Martin Hengel, *Studies in the Gospel of Mark* (Philadelphia: Fortress Press, 1985) 34–37; Mary Ann Beavis, *Mark's Audience: The Literary and Social Setting of Mark 4:11–12,* JSNTSup 33 (Sheffield: Sheffield Academic Press, 1989); Morna D. Hooker, *Beginnings: Keys That Open the Gospels* (Harrisburg, Pa.: Trinity Press International, 1998) 1–22.

31. *Poetics* 1447a 14–17. For the *Poetics* see Jonathan Barnes, ed., *The Complete Works of Aristotle* (Princeton, N.J.: Princeton University Press, 1984) 2:2316–40.

32. *Poetics* 1449b 18–20.

33. *Poetics* 1449b 25–28.

34. *Poetics* 1451a 38–1451b 5.

35. *Poetics* 1452a 3–5.

36. *Poetics* 1452b 15–21.

37. *Poetics* 1452a 33.

38. See the discussion of Seneca's tragedies by C. J. Herrington in *The Cambridge History of Classical Literature,* ed. E. J. Kenney, vol. 2, *Latin Literature* (Cambridge: Cambridge University Press, 1982) 519–30. J. D. M. Derrett thinks that Mark was composed to be recited from memory (*The Making of Mark: The Scriptural Bases of the Earliest Gospel* [Shipston-on-Stour: P. Drinkwater, 1985] 1:33).

39. Alec McGowen, *Personal Mark: An Actor's Proclamation of St. Mark's Gospel* (New York: Crossroad, 1985); David Rhoads, "Performing the Gospel of Mark," in *Body and Bible: Interpreting and Experiencing Biblical Narratives,* ed. Björn Krondorfer (Philadelphia: Trinity Press International, 1992) 102–19.

40. Joanna Dewey, *Markan Public Debate: Literary Technique, Concentric Structure, and Theology in Mark 2:1–3:6,* SBLDS 48 (Chico, Calif.: Scholars Press, 1980); Mary Ann Tolbert, *Sowing the Gospel: Mark's World in Literary-Historical Perspective* (Minneapolis: Fortress Press, 1989); John G. Cook, *The Structure and Persuasive Power of Mark: A Linguistic Approach* (Atlanta: Scholars Press, 1995); Bas M. F. van Iersel, *Mark: A Reader Response Commentary,* JSNTSup 164 (Sheffield: Sheffield Academic Press, 1998).

41. Horace, *Ars Poetica* 189.

42. Mary Ann Beavis, *Mark's Audience,* 126–30.

43. *Poetics* 1450b 27–28.

44. John P. Meier, *A Marginal Jew: Rethinking the Historical Jesus* (New York: Doubleday, 1991) 1:205–8.

45. The subtext for the oracle is provided by Ps. 2:7, 2 Sam. 7:14, and Isa. 42:1, applying the ancient title of divine sonship to Jesus' messianic kingship (Joel Marcus, *The Way of the Lord: Christological Exegesis of the Old Testament in the Gospel of Mark* [Louisville: Westminster John Knox Press, 1992] 70–71).

46. Jacob Neusner, William S. Green, and Ernest Frerichs, eds., *Judaisms and Their Messiahs at the Turn of the Christian Era* (Cambridge: Cambridge University Press, 1987); James H. Charlesworth, ed., *The Messiah: Developments in Earliest Judaism and Christianity* (Minneapolis: Fortress Press, 1992); John J. Collins, *The Scepter and the Star: The Messiahs of the Dead Sea Scrolls and Other Ancient Literature* (New York: Doubleday, 1995); Gerbern S. Oegema, *The Anointed and his People: Messianic Expectations from the Maccabees to Bar Kochba*, JSPSup 27 (Sheffield: Sheffield Academic Press, 1998).

47. Anthony Harvey, *Jesus and the Constraints of History*, Bampton Lectures 1980 (Philadelphia: Westminster Press, 1982) 80–82, 139–43, 149–53.

48. James D. G. Dunn, *The Christ and the Spirit*, 2, *Pneumatology* (Grand Rapids, Mich.: Eerdmans, 1998) 105.

49. Susan R. Garrett, *The Temptations of Jesus in Mark's Gospel* (Grand Rapids, Mich.: Eerdmans, 1998) 63.

50. Garrett, Ibid., 53 (Garrett's italics).

51. Graham H. Twelftree, *Jesus the Exorcist*, WUNT 54 (Tübingen: Mohr-Siebeck, 1993) 53–71.

52. Paul W. Hollenbach, "Jesus, Demoniacs, and Public Authorities: A Socio-Historical Study," *JAAR* 49 (1981) 567–88; Hollenbach, "Recent Historical Jesus Studies and the Social Sciences," *SBL 1983 Seminar Papers* (Chico, Calif.: Scholars Press, 1983) 61–78; Hollenbach, "Help for Interpreting Jesus' Exorcisms," *SBL 1993 Seminar Papers* (Atlanta: Scholars Press, 1993) 119–28.

53. Peter G. Bolt, "Jesus, the Daimons and the Dead," in *The Unseen World: Christian Reflections on Angels, Demons and the Heavenly Realm*, ed. Anthony N. S. Lane (Grand Rapids, Mich.: Baker Book House, 1996) 75–102.

54. E. P. Sanders, *Jesus and Judaism* (Philadelphia: Fortress Press, 1985) 265.

55. Stauffer, *Jesus and His Story*, 84–88. Josephus tells of a delegation that included Pharisees, which was sent to Galilee to investigate him (*Life*, 197–98).

56. Joachim Jeremias, *The Parables of Jesus*, rev. ed. (London: SCM, 1963) 145.

57. Gerd Theissen, *The Miracle Stories of Early Christian Tradition* (Philadelphia: Fortress Press, 1983) 99–103; John P. Meier, *A Marginal Jew*, 2:924–33.

58. The same wording—"rebuke" (*epitimao*), "be silent" (*siapao*)—occurs in 1:25 and 4:39; cf. 9:35.

59. Gerd Theissen, *The Gospels in Context: Social and Political History in the Synoptic Tradition* (Minneapolis: Fortress Press, 1991) 110.

60. J. D. M. Derrett, "Legend and Event: The Gerasene Demoniac: An Inquest into History and Liturgical Projection" (*Studies in the New Testament* [Leiden: Brill, 1982] 3:47–58). Cicero observed that "places of burial do not really become graves until the proper rites are performed and the pig is slain" (*Laws* 2.22.57).

61. Craig A. Evans, "'Who Touched Me?' Jesus and the Ritually Impure," in

Jesus in Context: Temple, Purity, and Restoration, ed. Bruce Chilton and Craig A. Evans, AGJU 39 (Leiden, New York, Cologne: Brill, 1997) 353–76.

62. Ernst Bammel, "The Feeding of the Multitude," in *Jesus and the Politics of His Day*, ed. Ernst Bammel and C. F. D. Moule (Cambridge: Cambridge University Press, 1984) 211–40; Robert M. Fowler, *Loaves and Fishes: The Function of the Feeding Stories in the Gospel of Mark*, SBLDS 54 (Chico, Calif.: Scholars Press, 1981); J. D. M. Derrett, "Crumbs in Mark," in *Studies in the New Testament* (Leiden: Brill, 1986) 4:82–91; Joseph A. Grassi, *Loaves and Fishes: The Gospel Feeding Narratives* (Collegeville, Minn.: Liturgical Press, 1991).

63. Barnabas Lindars, "Elijah, Elisha and the Gospel Miracles," in *Miracles: Cambridge Studies in Their Philosophy and History*, ed. C. F. D. Moule (London: A. R. Mowbray, 1965) 61–79.

64. Meier, *A Marginal Jew*, 2:960–63.

65. Grassi, *Loaves and Fishes*, 29–35; Dale C. Allison, Jr., *The New Moses: A Matthean Typology* (Minneapolis: Fortress Press, 1993) 238–42.

66. Derrett, "Crumbs in Mark," *Studies in the New Testament* 4:82–91.

67. Patrick J. Madden, *Jesus' Walking on the Sea: An Investigation of the Origin of the Narrative Account*, BZNW 81 (Berlin, New York: De Gruyter, 1997).

68. J. P. Heil, *Jesus Walking on the Sea: Meaning and Gospel Functions of Matt. 14:22–33, Mark 6:45–52 and John 6:15–21*, AnBib 87 (Rome: Biblical Institute Press, 1981) 67–75; Gerd Theissen, *The Miracle Stories*, 186–87; Robert A. Guelich, *Mark* (Dallas: Word, 1989) 1:350–54; Barry Blackburn, *Theios Aner and the Markan Miracle Traditions*, WUNT 40 (Tübingen: Mohr-Siebeck, 1991) 145–52.

69. J. D. M. Derrett, "Why and How Jesus Walked on the Sea," *Studies in the New Testament* 4:92–111.

70. *Studies in the New Testament* 4:95–97. Derrett's account of geological formation is confirmed by Richard Cleave, ed., *The Holy Land Satellite Atlas* (Nicosia: Rohr Productions, 1994), which gives images taken by NASA Landsat 5 on January 18, 1987. The shallow shelf described by Derrett appears clearly on pp. 24–25 and 34–45.

71. On the question of the historical Pharisees see Anthony J. Saldarini, *Pharisees, Scribes and Sadducees in Palestinian Society: A Sociological Approach* (Wilmington, Del.: Michael Glazier, 1988); Roland Deines, *Die Pharisäer. Ihr Verständnis im Spiegel der christlichen und jüdischen Forschung seit Wellhausen und Graez*, WUNT 101 (Tübingen: Mohr-Siebeck, 1997); J. Sievers, "Who Were the Pharisees?" in *Hillel and Jesus: Comparative Studies of Two Major Religious Leaders*, ed. James H. Charlesworth and Loren L. Johns (Minneapolis: Fortress Press, 1997) 137–55.

72. On this passage see Roger P. Booth, *Jesus and the Laws of Purity: Tradition History and Legal History in Mark*, JSNTSup 13 (Sheffield: JSOT Press, 1986); James D. G. Dunn, "Jesus and Ritual Purity: A Study of the Tradition-History of Mark 7:15," in *Jesus, Paul, and the Law: Studies in Mark and Galatians* (Louisville: Westminster John Knox Press, 1990) 37–60.

73. David Rhoads, "Jesus and the Syrophoenician Woman in Mark: A Narrative-Critical Study," *JAAR* 72 (1994) 370.

74. Austin Farrer, *St. Matthew and St. Mark* (London: A. & C. Black, Dacre Press, 1954) 23.

75. Robert M. Fowler argues that the feeding of the four thousand is traditional, and the feeding of the five thousand a Markan composition (*Loaves and Fishes*, 181).

76. J. D. M. Derrett, "Crumbs in Mark," *Studies in the New Testament* 4: 82–91.

77. For interpretations of the so-called "messianic secret" see Christopher Tuckett, ed., *The Messianic Secret* (London: SPCK, and Philadelphia: Fortress Press, 1983); Heikki Räisänen, *The 'Messianic Secret' in Mark's Gospel* (Edinburgh: T. & T. Clark, 1990). In light of my two theses, I suggest that Jesus' order not to tell others about himself was bound up with a desire to avoid actions which would implicate himself or others with the charges associated with Thesis B.

78. John J. Pilch suggests that the transfiguration be viewed in terms of psychological anthropology, where the etic represents the outsiders' perception of an altered state of consciousness and the emic the insider's perception ("The Transfiguration of Jesus: An Experience of Alternate Reality," in *Modelling Early Christianity: Social-Scientific Studies of the New Testament in Its Context*, ed. Philip F. Esler [London and New York: Routledge, 1995] 47–64).

79. The question of whether 10:45 refers to the suffering servant of Isa. 53 or whether it alludes to the Maccabean martyrs, whose deaths were held to have atoning significance (2 Macc. 6:27–29; 7:37; 4 Macc. 17:22; 18:4), is keenly debated. I see allusions to both. See William H. Bellinger, Jr., and William R. Farmer, eds., *Jesus and the Suffering Servant: Isaiah 53 and Christian Origins* (Harrisburg, Pa.: Trinity Press International, 1998).

80. See n. 8.

81. 1 Sam. 16:13–23; cf. Josephus, *Antiquities* 6.166–69; 8.42–49. The wisdom of David's son, Solomon, included gifts of healing. Cf. Dennis Duling, "Solomon, Exorcism, and the Son of David," *Harvard Theological Review* 68 (1975) 235–52; Duling, "The Promises to David and Their Entrance into Christianity—Nailing Down a Likely Hypothesis," *NTS* 20 (1974–75): 55–77; L. R. Fisher, "Can This Be the Son of David?" in *Jesus and the Historian*, ed. F. T. Trotter (Philadelphia: Westminster Press, 1968) 82–97; David E. Aune, *ANRW* 2.23.2 (1980) 1526; Bruce Chilton, "Jesus *ben David:* Reflections on the *Davidssohnfrage*," *JSNT* 14 (1982) 88–112.

82. Sanders, *Jesus and Judaism*, 61.

83. Ibid., 75.

84. Bruce Chilton, *The Temple of Jesus: His Sacrificial Program Within a Cultural History of Sacrifice* (University Park, Pa.: The Pennsylvania State University Press, 1992) 155.

85. Craig A. Evans, "From 'House of Prayer' to 'Cave of Robbers': Jesus' Prophetic Criticism of the Temple Establishment," in *The Quest for Context and Meaning: Studies in Biblical Intertextuality in Honor of James A. Sanders*, ed. Craig A. Evans and Shemaryahu Talmon (Leiden, New York, Cologne: Brill, 1997) 417–42.

86. George R. Beasley-Murray, *Jesus and the Last Days: The Interpretation of the Olivet Discourse* (Peabody, Mass.: Hendrickson, 1993).

87. E. Nestle, "Der Greuel der Verwüstung," *ZAW* 4 (1884) 248; Beasley-Murray, *Jesus and the Last Days*, 408–16.

88. Josephus, *War* 2.258–64; *Antiquities* 20.97–98, 168–72; cf. Rebecca Gray,

Prophetic Figures in Late Second-Temple Jewish Palestine: The Evidence from Josephus (New York and Oxford: Oxford University Press, 1993).

89. Cf. 13:24 with Isa. 13:10; Ezek. 32:7; Amos 8:9; Joel 2:10; cf. 13:31 with Isa. 34:4 and Acts 2:17–21.

90. Dale C. Allison, Jr., *The End of the Ages Has Come: An Early Interpretation of the Passion and Resurrection of Jesus* (Philadelphia: Fortress Press, 1985) 36–38; John T. Carrol and Joel B. Green with Robert Van Voorst, Joel Marcus, and Donald Senior, *The Death of Jesus in Early Christianity* (Peabody, Mass.: Hendrickson, 1995) 36–37.

91. G. B. Caird, *Jesus and the Jewish Nation* (London: University of London, Athlone Press, 1965) 20; N. T. Wright, *Jesus and the Victory of God* (Minneapolis: Fortress Press, 1996) 339–43.

92. G. B. Caird, *New Testament Theology*, completed and edited by L. D. Hurst (Oxford: Clarendon Press, 1995) 365–66.

93. For literature and discussion see Ernst Bammel, ed., *The Trial of Jesus: Cambridge Studies in Honour of C. F. D. Moule*, SBT Second Series, 13 (London: SCM, 1970); David R. Catchpole, *The Trial of Jesus: A Study in the Gospels and Jewish Historiography from 1770 to the Present Day*, StPB 18 (Leiden: Brill, 1971); August Strobel, *Die Stunde der Wahrheit. Untersuchungen zum Strafverfahren gegen Jesu*, WUNT 21 (Tübingen: Mohr-Siebeck, 1980); Otto Betz, "Probleme des Prozesses Jesu," in *ANRW* 2.25.1 (1982) 565–647; Raymond E. Brown, *The Death of the Messiah: From Gethsemane to the Grave* (New York: Doubleday, 1994) 1:315–560; Richard A. Horsley, "The Death of Jesus," in *Studying the Historical Jesus*, ed. Chilton and Evans, 395–422.

94. Emil Schürer, *The History of the Jewish People*, 2d edition. Edited by Geza Vermes, Fergus Millar and Matthew Black (Edinburgh: T. & T. Clark, 1979) 2:213.

95. *ANRW* 2.25.1: 595 (author's translation).

96. Strobel, *Die Stunde der Wahrheit*, 81–86.

97. Otto Betz, *ANRW* 2.25.1:595; Strobel, *Die Stunde der Wahrheit*, 81–86; Darrell L. Bock, "The Son of Man Seated at God's Right Hand and the Debate over Jesus' 'Blasphemy,' " in Joel B. Green and Max Turner, eds., *Jesus of Nazareth, Lord and Christ*, 181–91; Bock, *Blasphemy and Exaltation in Judaism and the Final Examination of Jesus: A Philological-Historical Study of the Key Jewish Themes Impacting Mark 14:61–64*, WUNT 106 (Tübingen: Mohr-Siebeck, 1998).

98. Bock, *Blasphemy and Exaltation*, 206–9.

99. On the offense of Rabbi Aqiba's suggestion that Dan. 7 implied a throne for the Son of David see Hagigah 14a; Sanhedrin 38b (Bock, *Blasphemy and Exaltation*, 98–99, 145–46).

100. Joachim Jeremias, *New Testament Theology* (London: SCM, 1971) 1:78; W. C. van Unnik, "Jesu Verhöhnung vor dem Synedrium (Mc xiv 65 par.)," *Sparsa Collecta: The Collected Essays of W. C. Van Unnik*, NovTSup 29 (Leiden: Brill, 1973) 1:3–5; *ANRW* 2.25.1: 638.

101. Helen K. Bond, *Pontius Pilate in History and Interpretation*, SNTSMS 100 (Cambridge: Cambridge University Press, 1998) 111.

102. Thomas Schmidt, "Mark 15:16–32: The Crucifixion Narrative and the Roman Triumphal Procession," *NTS* 41 (1995) 1–18; Schmidt, "Jesus' Triumphal

March to Crucifixion: The Sacred Way as Roman Procession," *Bible Review* 13, no. 1 (1997) 30–37.

103. Brown, *The Death of the Messiah*, 2:1101.

104. B. M. F. van Iersel, "He Will Baptize You with the Holy Spirit: The Time Perspective of *baptisei*," in *Text and Testimony: Essays on New Testament and Apocryphal Literature in Honour of A. F. J. Klijn*, T. Baarda, A. Hilhorst, G. P. Luttikhuizen, and A. S. van der Woude (Kampen: J. H. Kok, 1988) 132–41.

105. John Pobee, "The Cry of the Centurion—A Cry of Defeat," in Bammel, *The Trial of Jesus*, 91–102.

106. Bruce M. Metzger, *A Textual Commentary on the Greek New Testament* (London, New York: United Bible Societies, 1971) 122–26; W. R. Farmer, *The Last Twelve Verses of Mark*, SNTSMS 25 (Cambridge: Cambridge University Press, 1974); R. H. Gundry, *Mark: A Commentary on his Apology for the Cross* (Grand Rapids, Mich.: Eerdmans, 1993) 1012–21; Joel F. Williams, "Literary Approaches to the End of Mark's Gospel," *JETS* 42, no. 1 (1999) 21–25.

107. LXX examples are Gen. 18:15; 45:3; cf. BAGD 151, 862; Thomas E. Boomershine and Gilbert L. Bartholomew, "The Narrative Technique of Mark 16:8," *JBL* 100 (1981) 213–23; Thomas E. Boomershine, "Mark 16:8 and the Apostolic Commission," *JBL* 100 (1981) 225–39.

108. Gerd Lüdemann, *The Resurrection of Jesus: History, Experience, Theology* (Minneapolis: Fortress Press, 1994) 121.

109. Stephen T. Davis, *Risen Indeed: Making Sense of the Resurrection* (Grand Rapids, Mich.: Eerdmans, 1993) 84; cf. Davis, Daniel Kendall, and Gerald O'Collins, eds., *The Resurrection: An Interdisciplinary Symposium on the Resurrection of Jesus* (Oxford and New York: Oxford University Press, 1997).

110. Julius Wellhausen, *Das Evangelium Marci*, 2d ed. (Berlin: Georg Reimer, 1909) 137; reprinted in *Evangelienkommentare*, Mit einer Einleitung von Martin Hengel (Berlin, New York: De Gruyter, 1987).

111. Num. 6:6; 19:14–22; Lev. 21:1–2, 12; Mishnah Ohalot. Graves were to be marked to avoid causing defilement (Matt. 23:27; Luke 11:44; Mishnah Sheqalim 1:1).

112. Quoted from the Church of England proposed 1928 *Book of Common Prayer*.

113. Byron R. McCane, " 'Where No One Had Yet Been Laid': The Shame of Jesus' Burial," in *Authenticating the Activities of Jesus*, ed. Bruce Chilton and Craig A. Evans, NTTS 28,2 (Leiden, Boston, Cologne: Brill, 1999) 431–52.

114. 1:15; 4:11, 26, 30; 9:1; 10:14–15, 23–25; 11:10; 12:34; 14:25; 15:43; cf. Joel Marcus, *The Mystery of the Kingdom of God*, SBLDS 90 (Atlanta: Scholars Press, 1986); Bruce Chilton, *God in Strength: Jesus' Announcement of the Kingdom* (Sheffield: JSOT Press, 1987); Chilton, *Pure Kingdom: Jesus' Vision of God* (Grand Rapids, Mich.: Eerdmans, 1996).

115. Crossan, *The Historical Jesus*, 346, 421–22.

116. D. F. Strauss, *The Life of Jesus Critically Examined* (Tübingen: C. F. Osiander, 1835), trans. George Eliot, new edition edited by Peter C. Hodgson (London: SCM, 1973); cf. Colin Brown, *Jesus in European Protestant Thought, 1778–1860* (Durham, N.C.: Labyrinth Press, 1985) 183–204.

117. Cf. Janet Martin Soskice, *Metaphor and Religious Language* (Oxford: Clarendon Press, 1985).

118. Earl R. MacCormac, *Metaphor and Myth in Science and Religion* (Durham, N.C.: Duke University Press, 1976) viii.

119. Dennis R. MacDonald suggests that Mark was composing a prose anti-epic modeled after but superior to Greek heroes (*The Homeric Epics and the Gospel of Mark* [New Haven and London: Yale University Press, 2000]). His work compares numerous incidents from Homeric literature, whereas I have sought to examine Mark in light of the subtexts of the Hebrew Scriptures.

120. Morton Smith, *Clement of Alexandria and a Secret Gospel of Mark* (Cambridge, Mass.: Harvard University Press, 1973); Smith, *The Secret Gospel: the Discovery and Interpretation of the Secret Gospel According to Mark* (New York: Harper & Row, 1973); cf. Gundry, *Mark*, 603–23, and the comments of Jacob Neusner in Birger Gerhardsson, *Memory and Manuscript with Tradition and Transmission in Early Christianity* (Grand Rapids, Mich.: Eerdmans, 1998) xxvi–xxvii.

121. Maurice Casey, *Aramaic Sources of Mark's Gospel*, SNTSMS 102 (Cambridge: Cambridge University Press, 1998). See also the review of external evidence in E. Earle Ellis, *The Making of the New Testament Documents*, Biblical Interpretation Series 39 (Leiden, Boston, Cologne: Brill, 1999) 357–76.

122. William Telford, "Major Trends and Interpretative Issues in the Study of Jesus," in *Studying the Historical Jesus*, ed. Chilton and Evans, 33–74; Gerd Theissen, "Historical Scepticism and the Criteria of Jesus Research, or My Attempt to Leap Across Lessing's Yawning Gulf," *SJT* 49 (1996) 147–76; Gerd Theissen and Dagmar Winter, *Die Kriterienfrage in der Jesusforschung. Vom Differenzkriterium zum Plausibilitätskriterium*, NTOA 34 (Freiburg, Switzerland: Universitätsverlag; Göttingen: Vandenhoeck & Ruprecht, 1997); Gerd Theissen and Annette Merz, *The Historical Jesus: A Comprehensive Guide* (Minneapolis: Fortress Press, 1998) 114–18; Bruce Chilton and Craig A. Evans, eds., *Authenticating the Words of Jesus*, NTTS 28,1, and *Authenticating the Activities of Jesus*, NTTS 28,2 (Leiden, Boston, Cologne: Brill, 1999).

3

Jesus and the Resurrection

N. T. Wright

Introduction:
Resurrection in Some Recent Writing

In this essay, I will explore some questions that have arisen in my own work in dialogue with a new wave of books that have been appearing on Christian origins, not least on the resurrection. I have three in mind out of the dozen or so we might pick: J. Dominic Crossan, *The Birth of Christianity;*[1] Gregory J. Riley, *Resurrection Reconsidered: Thomas and John in Controversy;*[2] and A. J. M. Wedderburn, *Beyond Resurrection.*[3] I shall briefly summarize what each says about the Resurrection, and then, by way of challenging the adequacy of their accounts, develop an argument of my own about what the early Christians meant when they said that Jesus of Nazareth had been raised from the dead, and what as historians we should say by way of comment. I am very much aware of the philosophical and theological issues that I am keeping offstage in this essay, and I apologize to those for whom these are the primary questions. It hardly needs saying that every statement in this essay could be amplified and developed at much greater length.[4]

The subtitle of Crossan's book is "Discovering What Happened in the Years Immediately after the Execution of Jesus." The book is, of course, a tour de force, for several reasons, of which I highlight one: there is almost no discussion of the Resurrection, which many will suppose to be among the most important things, from the early Christian viewpoint, that happened after the execution of Jesus.[5] To this extent I am cheating somewhat, introducing this book into a discussion of resurrection, except that it shows the extent to which a major portion of the discipline has gone down the road of assuming that whatever resurrection language is about it isn't about an event that happened once, shortly after Jesus' execution, and that had a cataclysmic effect on his followers.

Crossan's very brief treatment is mostly contained in his prologue.[6] Borrowing from Riley, Crossan states that, within the pagan world, visions of those who had died were very common. People were always coming back from the dead in one way or another:

That the dead could return and interact with the living was a common-place of the Greco-Roman world, and neither pagans nor Jews would have asserted that it could not happen. That such interaction could generate important processes and events, as with Hector saving Aeneas to found the Roman people and the Julian ascendancy, was also a commonplace.[7]

With visions and resurrections apparently happening all over the place, we should, Crossan says, abandon the sterile debate between rationalist secularists who said Resurrection couldn't happen and rationalist fundamentalists who said that it did, just that once. He notes at once that Paul poses a problem for this reading, since he sees Jesus' resurrection as the beginning of a larger event, the general resurrection of which Jesus' is the beginning. Why, Crossan asks, is Paul not content to suppose that Jesus' resurrection was like Elijah's going up to heaven in a whirlwind? Why should it have cosmic and apocalyptic connotations? Why should it mean that the general resurrection has begun? After all, he says, there are strong indications that the resurrection stories in the gospels were not originally literal or historical accounts; they were symbolic and theological, "more about establishing an authority than about receiving an apparition," as Crossan states.

There are many things that could be said about this account. I choose one for my focus here: Crossan seems to me to be eliding several different experiences into one general category. He lumps together visions, apparitions, and various forms of contact with the dead; and he calls them all "resurrection." In the one later discussion of the Resurrection he adds to these a further element: the sense in the early church of the "presence" of Jesus.[8] What happened, according to Crossan, is that the "female lament tradition," in which the women closest to Jesus were lamenting his death in standard Jewish fashion, transformed the "male exegetical tradition" in which the men around Jesus were searching the scriptures, "into a passion-resurrection story once and for all forever."[9] The stories we now have, in other words, are theological, symbolic fictions which grew out of those early communal practices.

Whatever we say about the early Christian claim that Jesus was raised from the dead, it was always much more specific than that. For them it did indeed involve something happening to Jesus which had happened to nobody else ever before, or in their own day ever again. The complex and highly ingenious reconstruction offered by Crossan would seem, to all the early Christians for whom we have actual evidence, quite unnecessary. Why would one travel from San Francisco to Los Angeles via New York? They knew a shorter way.

Crossan drew, as I said, on the work of Gregory Riley. He represents what has come to be in some circles a new critical orthodoxy: the view that the bodily resurrection of Jesus entered Christianity as a late development, a re-

Judaizing of a tradition that had initially been innocent of any such thing.[10] Crucial here, of course, is the reading of Paul, especially 1 Corinthians 15, to which we shall return. But Riley provides the apparently solid backbone for the arguments of Crossan and others, that the initial belief of the early church that many had seen Jesus alive again is to be located within the wider world of pagan apparition stories. The dead, he says, were quite widely held to be able to eat and drink with the living.

His presentation of the evidence, on closer examination, seems to me unperceptive and unpersuasive. I think any early Christian would have given Riley short shrift on being told that libations poured down a funnel onto a corpse, meaning that the dead were in some sense sharing a meal with the living, was the same sort of thing as the incidents described in Luke 24 and John 21.[11] And the stories from Homer, Hesiod, Herodotus, Virgil, and Lucian do not seem to me in any meaningful sense parallel with the Gospel resurrection accounts, or the belief that, as we shall see, characterized the early church at large. We have witnessed in the last few years, I believe, an interesting turn of events in New Testament scholarship in this area; over against the modernist denial that anything remotely like resurrection could ever occur, we now have a classic postmodern acceptance of all kinds of stories about dead people doing things, which are all to be celebrated as the experience of some community or other, without making much distinction between them.[12] But can the historian really be satisfied with that? What Riley builds on this foundation, like Crossan only more so, is a theory about controversy in the early church: the story of Thomas in John 20 reflects a polemic between Johannine Christians, who wanted to promote the newly invented, re-Judaized, bodily-resurrection idea, over against the Thomas Christians, represented of course in the Gospel of Thomas, for whom Jesus was in some sense alive but as a spiritual being, not a physical one.[13]

So to a very different work, Wedderburn's *Beyond Resurrection*. The thesis of this book is quite simply stated.[14] The traditions concerning Jesus' resurrection are so contradictory that, though Wedderburn argues that something must have happened to explain the rise of early Christianity and the stories it told, we can only remain agnostic about what that actually was. The concept of individual survival of death is itself philosophically problematic anyway; so our best course is to move "beyond resurrection and a faith bewitched by that concept to a faith that is thoroughly this-worldly" (p. 167). Wedderburn angrily rejects the notion of a sovereign and omnipotent God who, by intervening in the world, provides what he calls a "cozy familiarity" on the basis of an "easy anthropomorphism."[15] Another classic postmodern move; at least the question of God is back on the agenda, though perhaps not raised in the most helpful fashion.

There are many points one could debate with Wedderburn, and I only pick one. At several points he makes a nod in the direction of Paul's Jewish context, but he never takes seriously the question of what a first-century Pharisee might have believed, and how he might have used key terms like *resurrection*. The closest he comes to this is when he dismisses some of Paul's thinking, precisely at those points, as simply the hangover from his previous life, from which we, with the aid of the blessed tool *Sachkritik,* thinking Paul's thoughts better than he did himself, can free him, like a psychotherapist freeing a client from the constraints of an unfortunate buried memory. Wedderburn has not, for all his massive learning, attempted the most basic task of all, which is to ask: what did the early Christians mean when they used the word and concept *resurrection* to speak of what had happened to Jesus and to explain why that had started them off in a whole new direction? To that task I now turn.

One preliminary remark. My reading of recent literature leads me to guess that much revisionist material grows in a soil where a very low-grade view of Jesus' resurrection has been the norm. At a popular level, I discover that a lot of people, including many Christians, use the word *resurrection* to mean simply "life after death" and, since they think of "life after death" as a vague and disembodied existence in some quite non-earthly sphere, they think that predicating resurrection of Jesus is simply a way of saying that he somehow "went to heaven when he died." This is such a huge misunderstanding that we can hardly begin to address it now, but it affects many presentations, even at a scholarly level, that seem to assume that the only meaning bodily resurrection could then have would be that God can do spectacular miracles or that Jesus is somehow specially favored. This, as I hope will become obvious, simply doesn't begin to do justice to the evidence. *Resurrection* is precisely not about the survival of death, but about the gift of a new bodily life following death.

The Second-Temple Jewish Context

There is no space here for a survey of the material about life after death in the ancient world and particularly in Judaism. I content myself with two theses about the non-Jewish world and three about the Jewish, each of which could be expounded and defended at length.

a. The Greco-Roman world was familiar with, and developed multiple views about and practices in connection with, the survival of death. These cover a spectrum from the murky existence of shades to the blessed life in the Elysian fields, with even apotheosis available in certain cases.

b. But these views regularly and specifically ruled out resurrection, the idea of a new bodily life. This is stated explicitly as early as Aeschylus and repeated thereafter by many classical writers. The ancients, in other words, knew a clear distinction between nonbodily survival and bodily resurrection; broadly, they affirmed the first and denied the second.

c. Quite a wide spectrum of belief about life after death is evidenced in Second-Temple Judaism. Some believed in a postmortem permanent disembodied immortality; some, namely the Sadducees, seem to have denied all postmortem life. But where belief in resurrection occurs, it is always one point on that spectrum, never a term for life after death in general.

d. Resurrection seems to have entered Jewish thinking as a metaphor for the restoration of Israel, the great return from exile, that many still expected in Jesus' day. It demonstrably retained that metaphorical meaning into early Christianity.

e. But, from at least Daniel and 2 Maccabees on into Rabbinic thought, the resurrection of the dead, meaning precisely not "survival" but the new embodiment of the righteous dead, and sometimes the unrighteous as well, became one element within that larger hope. "The resurrection" thus functioned both as metaphor and metonymy: an image of the great hope, and one specific literal element within it. This is not to establish, as has been suggested, an island of literalness in the sea of metaphoricity,[16] but to recognize that those Jews who believed in the resurrection came to the point, ultimately, on the basis of creation-theology. Israel's God was the good creator, who intended, and was capable of, new creation.

This is the world within which the early Christians used resurrection language, not just to reminisce about Jesus but to explain their own existence. What then did they mean, and what can we say about that meaning?

The Rise of Christianity

My argument now shares the outline shape of the well-known line of thought expounded by C. F. D. Moule over thirty years ago, often ignored and never, to my knowledge, satisfactorily answered.[17] But the content that I put into that form is significantly different from Moule's.

I take this in three stages. Christianity began as a Kingdom-of-God movement, as a Messianic movement, and as a resurrection movement. In each case, this poses a puzzle for the historian. In each case, my argument falls into three steps. First, I shall examine the way in which Christianity began as a movement of the type in question. Second, I shall revisit Judaism to enquire what such movements looked like and what they hoped for. Third, I shall show that the striking differences between the relevant movements in Judaism and the apparently equivalent movement in Christianity call for a particular sort of explanation, and that the early Christians supply one and only one, namely the bodily resurrection of Jesus.

A Kingdom-of-God Movement

First, then, early Christianity thought of itself as a Kingdom-of-God movement. Already by the time of Paul the phrase "Kingdom of God" and its equivalents had become more or less a shorthand for the movement, its way of life, and its raison d'être. It is already woven into the structure of early Christian thinking. In Romans 14, Paul uses it to summarize the entire essence of Christianity, giving as its meaning a quick summary of one of the central paragraphs of the letter.[18] In 1 Corinthians 6:9–10, Paul speaks of those who will and who won't inherit the Kingdom of God, assuming his hearers know well enough what this means. In 1 Corinthians 15:20–28, he spells out the coming of the Kingdom in a way which should leave no doubt that he is referring to it in a thoroughly Jewish, apocalyptic, and eschatological sense; that is, that the decisive victory has been won over the powers of evil that have oppressed God's people, inaugurating the new age that will end with the defeat of death itself.

Of course, some have recently argued that the phrase "Kingdom of God" meant, for Jesus and the earliest Christians, a new personal or spiritual experience, rather than a Jewish-style movement designed to establish the rule of God in the world. I have discussed this proposal in detail elsewhere.[19] But the actual evidence we have, as opposed to the reconstructed evidence based on hypothetical early documents—I don't mean Q itself, I mean the earlier strata which some have discovered behind it and other sources—indicates to the contrary.[20] As I have argued elsewhere, if Jesus' movement was a counter-Temple movement, early Christianity was a counter-Empire movement. When Paul said "Jesus is Lord," it is clear that he meant that Caesar is not. This was neither Cynic-style countercultural aphoristic teaching, nor yet incipient Gnosticism. It was Jewish-style Kingdom-of-God theology, with Jesus in the middle of it.

This theology was born within, and was sustained by, not a group of Gnostic-style conventicles, but a Jewish-style new-covenant community. The early Christians told the story of the Kingdom as their own story. They reordered their lives, in the case of ex-pagans, quite drastically, around the new symbolic universe in which the Jewish hope that there would be "no king but God" had come true in Jesus the Messiah. They engaged in praxis which affirmed that there was a different way of being human, a way that answered to the claims of this kingdom. Christianity was indeed, in the Jewish sense, a Kingdom-of-God movement. This is the first step of this first stage in my argument.

The second step, then, is to glance at what "Kingdom of God" meant in Judaism. Within Judaism the coming Kingdom of God meant the end of Israel's exile; the overthrow of pagan empire and the exaltation of Israel; the return of YHWH to Zion to judge and save. These motifs emerge from that great kingdom-prophecy, Isaiah 40–55, and from numerous psalms and other parts of the Hebrew scriptures.[21] And, as Josephus makes clear, in Jesus' day it was in particular the slogan of the revolutionaries. Judas the Galilean, he says, was a *sophistes* who led his rebellion (the revolt of 6 C.E., which ended with the crucifixion of Judas and thousands of others) not just because they did not want the new Roman rule and its attendant taxes, but because they believed there should be "no King but God."

For the Second-Temple Jew, then, the coming of the Kingdom was not about a private existentialist or spiritual experience, but about public events. At its narrowest, it was about the liberation of Israel. At its broadest, it was about the coming of God's justice and liberation for the whole cosmos. Thus, if you had said to a first-century Jew "The Kingdom of God is here," and had explained yourself by speaking of a new spiritual experience, a new sense of forgiveness, or an exciting reordering of your private religious interiority, he or she might well have said that they were glad you had had this experience, but why did you refer to it as the Kingdom of God? This, then, is the second step of this first stage in the argument.

The third step puts these two together, and observes the contrast. Whatever the early Christians said, the Kingdom of God had not come in the way that first-century Jews had been imagining. Israel was not liberated; the Temple was not rebuilt; evil, injustice, pain, and death were still on the rampage. The question presses, then: why did the early Christians say that the Kingdom of God had come?

One answer could be: because they changed the meaning of the phrase radically, so that it now referred not to a political state of affairs but to an internal or spiritual one. They had taken the apocalyptic meaning current in their world, and had demythologized, de-Judaized, spiritualized, or hellenized it, possibly all four. But this is simply untrue to early Christianity. In the first written exposition of Christian Kingdom theology, which significantly enough is in the same chapter as the first written exposition of the Resurrection (1 Cor. 15), Paul explains the new Christian perspective: the Kingdom is coming in a two-stage process, so that the Jewish hope, for God to be all in all, will be realized fully in the future, following its decisive inauguration in the events concerning Jesus. The early Christians, in fact, not only used the phrase "Kingdom of God"[22] but they reordered their symbolic world, their storytelling world, their habitual praxis, around it. They acted, in other words, as if the Jewish-style Kingdom of God was really present; they organized their life as if they really were the returned-from-exile people, the people of the new covenant. What is more, they did indeed speak of a new state of affairs at the internal or spiritual level; but for this they used, not the language of the Kingdom of God, but the language of the new heart, the indwelling of the spirit, and so forth.[23]

The historical question is therefore posed: what on earth would have caused them to act, speak, and think this way? Why, indeed, did they not continue the sort of Kingdom revolution they had imagined Jesus was going to lead? How do we explain the fact that early Christianity was neither a nationalist Jewish movement nor a private existential or spiritual experience? How do we explain the fact that it asserted, from within the Jewish worldview, that the eschaton had arrived, even though it did not look like they had imagined it would? The early Christian answer was, of course, that Jesus had been bodily raised from the dead. That was why they said that the Kingdom had come, that the new age had dawned.

This brings us to the second stage in the argument.

A Messianic Movement

I have argued elsewhere that Christianity was from the first a messianic movement. The earliest Christian sources that we possess speak of Jesus as Messiah. According to Acts 2.36, the decisive point of the early proclamation was that God had made Jesus "Lord and Christ." This, you say, might just be later Lukan theology. Very well: what about Paul? I have argued elsewhere that Jesus' messiahship remained central and explicit for Paul; that is, I do not share the opinion of those who think that the word *Christos* became for him a mere proper name, devoid of its Jewish and royal connotations.[24] But even if you are not convinced that by the time of Paul the word *Christos* has become simply a proper name with a few distant messianic memories attached to it, it is hard to evade the conclusion that if the ex-Pharisee Paul, within thirty years of Jesus' death, was referring to Jesus as *Christos,* especially if he was doing so without giving a thought to the Jewish meaning of that word, that only goes to show how firmly within the earliest tradition the idea of Jesus' messiahship had taken hold. Of course, since several of the phrases in which Paul calls Jesus *Christos* arguably are or contain very early fragments of tradition, obvious examples being 1 Corinthians 15:3–5 and Romans 1:3–4, it becomes much easier historically to agree that the early Christians intended to designate Jesus as Messiah, and that Paul thoroughly agreed with them. How do we explain all this? Why did they say he was Messiah?

Nils Dahl argued a generation ago that the Resurrection alone cannot explain why the early Christians thought of Jesus as Messiah. If someone else other than Jesus had been raised from the dead, there is no reason to suppose that their contemporaries would have thought him or her to be the Messiah. Dahl postulated, therefore, that we must seek the reason in Jesus' messianic execution, crucified as he was with the words "King of the Jews" above his head. I have argued that this, in turn, forces us to look further back, and to see some of Jesus' key symbolic actions, notably his action in the Temple, and some of his key riddles and parables, as both implicitly and explicitly messianic.[25] Once again, let me stress that in Second-Temple Judaism the word *Messiah* carried no connotations of what we would call "divinity." Again, even if you disagree with Dahl, or with me, and insist that Jesus only came to be thought of as Messiah at his resurrection, that, if anything, tightens the screw of my argument even tighter.

Because, to move to the second step in this second stage, a first-century Jew, faced with the crucifixion of a would-be Messiah, or even of a prophet who had led a significant following, would not conclude that this person was the Messiah and that the kingdom had come. He or she would conclude that he wasn't, and that it hadn't. There were, to be sure, several variations on Jewish messianic belief in this period. None of them envisaged a Messiah who would die at the hands of the pagans.

On the contrary: where Jewish expectations of a Messiah did exist, they regularly possessed a dual focus. In a line of tradition stretching from David to Bar-Kochba, including the Maccabees and Herod along with it, we find that the Messiah would have to defeat the pagans, and that he would have to rebuild the Temple, or at least cleanse it. The two would of course go together; as long as the pagans remained undefeated, YHWH had not returned to Zion, presumably because his house was not ready. If a Messiah was killed by the pagans, especially if he had not rebuilt the Temple or liberated Israel, that was the surest sign that he was another in the long line of false Messiahs.

It is surely clear what follows from this. If the Messiah you had been following was killed by the pagans, you were faced with a choice. You could give up the revolution, the dream of liberation. Some went that route: notably, of course, the rabbinic movement as a whole after 135 C.E. Or you could find yourself a new Messiah, if possible from the same family as the late lamented one. Some went that route: witness the continuing movement that ran from Judas the Galilean in 6 C.E.[26] to his sons or grandsons in the 50s, to another descendant, Menahem, during the war of 66–70, and to another descendent, Eleazar, who was the leader of the ill-fated Sicarii on Masada in 73.

Once again, let us be clear. If, after the death of Simon Bar-Giora in Titus's triumph in Rome, or if, after the death of Simeon Ben-Kosiba in 135, you had claimed that Simon, or Simeon, really was the Messiah, you would have invited a fairly sharp response from the average first-century Jew. If, by way of explanation, you said that you had had a strong sense of Simon, or Simeon, as still being with you, still supporting and leading you, the kindest response you might expect would be that their angel or spirit was still communicating with you, not that he had been raised from the dead and that he really was the Messiah after all. So far as we know, the followers of all the first-century messianic or quasi-messianic movements were fanatically committed to the cause. They, if anybody, might be expected to suffer from cognitive dissonance after the death of their great leader.[27] But in no other case, right across the century before Jesus and the century after him, do we hear of any Jewish group saying that their executed leader had been raised again from the dead.

So, the third step in the second stage of my argument: granted that Jesus of Nazareth was certainly crucified as a rebel king, it is extremely strange that the early Christians not only insisted that he was actually the Messiah, but reordered their worldview, their praxis, their stories, symbols, and theology around this belief.

They had the two normal options open to them. They could simply have gone back to their fishing, glad to have escaped Jerusalem with their lives. They could have switched to a different tack, given up messianism (like the post-135 rabbis), and gone in for some form of private religion instead, whether of intensified Torah observance, private gnosis, or something else. They clearly did not do that; anything less like a private religion than going around the pagan world saying that Jesus was the *kyrios kosmou,* the Lord of the World, it would be hard to imagine. Equally, and most interestingly, they could have found themselves a new Messiah from among Jesus' blood relatives. This is not, I think, normally considered. It deserves to be.

We know from various sources that Jesus' relatives were important, and well known, within the early church.[28] Jesus' own brother James, though not part of the movement during Jesus' lifetime, became the anchorman in Jerusalem while Peter and Paul went off around the world. Yet, and this is a vital clue, like Sherlock Holmes's dog that didn't bark in the night, nobody in early Christianity ever dreamed of saying that James was the Messiah. Nothing would have been more natural, especially on the analogy of the family of Judas the Galilean. Yet James was simply known as "the brother of the Lord." Even Josephus, who has no idea why this strange movement continued to exist, simply refers to him, when telling of his murder in 62, as "the brother of the so-called Messiah."[29] The historian is faced with a double problem. Why did James become a Christian after Jesus' death? And why did the others not regard him as Messiah?

Why, then, did this group of first-century Jews, who had cherished messianic hopes and focused them on Jesus of Nazareth, not only continue to believe that he was the Messiah despite his execution, but actively announce him as such in the pagan as well as the Jewish world, cheerfully redrawing the picture of messiahship around him but refusing to abandon it? Their own answer, consistently throughout the evidence we possess, was that Jesus, following his execution on a charge of being a would-be Messiah, had been raised from the dead. They cannot have meant by this that he had in some sense survived death and was now alive in a different sphere. That is not only not what *resurrection* meant; it is insufficient as a historical explanation of the rise of this movement. They must have meant that an event had occurred of such striking significance as to reverse all the normal reactions to Jesus' crucifixion.

This brings us to the third, and perhaps the most important, stage within this present argument.

A Resurrection Movement

Christianity began as a resurrection movement. As I have already remarked, there is no evidence for a form of early Christianity in which the Resurrection was not a central belief. Nor was this belief, as it were, bolted on to Christianity at the edge. It was the central driving force, informing the whole movement.

In particular, we can see woven into the earliest Christian theology we possess—that of Paul, of course—the belief that the resurrection had in principle occurred, and that the followers of Jesus had to reorder their lives, their narratives, their symbols, and their praxis accordingly.

There are two points to be made here. First, the Resurrection, as something that has already happened to Jesus and as something that characterizes both the present experience and the future hope of those who belong to him, is a central strand within all early Christianity for which we have solid textual evidence. You cannot remove it without doing serious damage to the entire structure. Second, this thinking about the resurrection has a remarkable precision and consistency. Unlike the Jewish beliefs about bodily resurrection, which are important but by no means very specific, from the very beginning it is astonishingly free of vague and generalized speculation. It is crisp and clear; resurrection means that after death one is given a new life, out the other side. This is in fact the new life God had promised to Israel. Christianity, then, began as a resurrection movement. I have no space to discuss the views of Paul, which I think have often been misunderstood on the basis of a wrong reading of the *soma pneumatikon*, the so-called "spiritual body," in 1 Corinthians 15:44, 46. The whole chapter, the whole letter, and the parallel passages elsewhere, for instance in Romans 8 and 2 Corinthians 5, are emphatic that what Paul believed was new life for dead bodies, not the survival of an immortal spirit or soul.[30] That is the first step of this third stage in my argument.

The second step refers to what I said above. The resurrection of the dead was a symbol for the coming of the new age and itself, taken literally, one central element in the package. It was both metaphor and metonymy. Where Second-Temple Jews believed in resurrection, then, that belief had to do, on the one hand, with the reembodiment of formerly dead human beings and, on the other, with the inauguration of the new age, the new covenant, in which all the righteous dead would be raised simultaneously.

If, therefore, you had said to a first-century Jew "The resurrection has occurred" at any time in this period, you would have received the puzzled response that it obviously hadn't, since the patriarchs, prophets, and martyrs were not walking around alive again, and since the restoration spoken of by Ezekiel 37 had clearly not occurred either, not to mention the great prophecies of Isaiah and the rest. And if, by way of explanation, you had said that you meant that, rather, you had had a wonderful new sense of divine healing and forgiveness, or that you believed the former leader of your movement was alive in the presence of God following his shameful torture and death, or that you had a sense of the presence of Jesus in the worshiping life of your community, your interlocutor might have congratulated you on having such an experience, and discussed with you such a belief. But he or she would still have been puzzled as to why you would use the phrase "the resurrection of the dead" to describe either of these things. That simply wasn't what the words meant.

But, and this is the third step in this third stage of the argument, as we have stressed before, the new age had not dawned in the way that first-century Jews imagined. Nor had the resurrection of all God's people of old taken place.[31] And yet the very earliest church declared roundly not only that Jesus was raised from the dead but that "the resurrection of the dead" had already occurred.[32] What is more, they redesigned their whole worldview— their characteristic praxis, their controlling stories, their symbolic universe, and their basic theology—around this new fixed point. They behaved, in other words, as though the new age had already arrived. That was the inner logic of the gentile mission; since God had now done for Israel what God was going to do for Israel, the Gentiles would at last share the blessing. The early Christians did not behave as though they had had a new sort of religious experience, or as if their former leader was (as the followers of the Maccabaean martyrs would no doubt have said of their heroes) alive and well in the presence of God, whether as an angel, a soul, or a spirit. The only explanation for their behavior, their stories, their symbols, and their theology is that they really believed that Jesus had been reembodied, had been bodily raised from the dead.

We must, therefore, as historians, enquire whether we have any better alternative to offer, or whether in fact the early church was right. We must postulate something that will account for this group of first-century Jews, including a well-educated Pharisee like Paul, coming so swiftly and so strongly to the conclusion that, against their expectations of all the righteous being raised to life at the end of the present age, one person had been raised to life in the middle of the present age. And we must postulate something that would transform the wide-ranging Jewish speculations about the resurrection which were current at the time into something as sharp and definite as we find already within very early Christian thinking.

The Question and the Options

The historian is faced with the question of why early Christianity began in the first place, and why it took the shape it did. I am aware that many of my colleagues in the guild have offered sophisticated and nuanced answers to this question, and I apologize that I have no space to reply to these accounts in detail.

Most of the answers offered within the world of New Testament scholarship in the last half-century have been variations on the theme of Rudolf Bultmann that Easter language describes, not an event which took place involving Jesus' body, but the rise of faith in the early church. Jesus rose into the church's kerygma. My whole argument thus far tells very heavily against this suggestion. If we are to think in first-century Jewish terms, it is impossible to conceive what sort of religious or spiritual experience someone could have which would make them say that the Kingdom of God had arrived when it clearly hadn't, that a crucified leader was the Messiah when he obviously wasn't, or that the resurrection occurred last week or last month when it obviously didn't. We may comment that even if the disciples had had a very vivid sense, which they interpreted as God-given, that Jesus' cause was secure with Israel's God, that his life and proclamation had been on the right lines and would eventually be vindicated, or even that his death had functioned as a lightning conductor through which the pagan hostility against Israel might be drawn away from the rest of the nation—in other words, if in their love, devotion, and continuing faith they gave to his life, his sufferings, and his death some kind of Second-Temple atoning significance—they would still not have said he had been raised from the dead. They would have written a new version of 2 Maccabees 7, which embodies most of what I have just described. They might well have suggested that Jesus had predicted his own resurrection; they would not have said that it had actually happened yet.[33] Once we think in resolutely Second-Temple Jewish terms, instead of projecting post-Enlightenment concepts of faith and religious experience back on to the first century, Bultmann's suggestion, and all similar ones, simply will not work.[34]

A further twist has been given to Bultmann's hypothesis by Gerd Lüdemann.[35] He suggests that Peter was so deeply grieved over Jesus' death that he experienced what people in such a state often report: a sense of the loving presence of the recently deceased person, perhaps even a sense of him speaking and reassuring him. Peter then, so Lüdemann asks us to believe, communicated this experience to the others, who were spontaneously filled with joy at the thought that Jesus was still alive. Meanwhile Paul underwent the opposite sort of hallucination; having been vehemently opposed to the new movement, he was overcome by guilt and experienced a guilt-induced fantasy that he, too, was able to share with others to remarkably powerful effect. My response to this proposal is (1) that it requires enormous credulity to suppose that, even allowing Peter and Paul to have had such fantasies or hallucinations, they would have generated more than a passing comment of sympathy among their colleagues or contemporaries; (2) that psychological theories of this sort, about people two thousand years ago in a different culture, are at best unprovable and at worst wildly fantastic in their own turn. But, most important, (3) the proposal simply does not make sense within the world of first-century Judaism. There are three points here that I judge to be of considerable importance.

First, as we can see not least in Acts 12, first-century Jews knew about postmortem visitations from recently deceased friends, and they already had language systems for speaking of such phenomena. "It must be his angel," they said when they thought they were having a visit of just this sort from Peter. They would not say that Peter had been raised from the dead. If we suppose ourselves for a moment in that group in Acts 12, and if they were aware of a recently executed Petrine angel as a ghostly or spiritual presence with them, they would conclude that he was now alive with God and that he would be raised, along with the rest of God's people, at the last day. This is also, we must conclude, what the early Christians would have said if what they had had were "luminous" postmortem visions of Jesus.

Second, to broaden this point, it would have been very natural for first-century Jews, especially if they had belonged to a Kingdom-of-God movement already, to say, of a leader who had paid the ultimate penalty at the hands of the authorities, that his soul was in the hands of God, that he was alive to God, that he had been exalted to paradise, that he was among the righteous who, as in Wisdom of Solomon 2 and 3, had been unjustly put to death but who would shine forth and rule the world in God's good time. If Jesus' followers had had a sense that he was alive in a nonphysical sense, even that he was still with them in some way, this is the language that they, as first-century Jews, would have most naturally reached for. But, in doing so, they would not suppose that the eschaton, the Kingdom of God, had now arrived; they would not say that he was the Messiah; they would not say that he had been raised from the dead, or indeed that the resurrection from the dead had now occurred. They must have thought that something else had happened, something which would make all these things suddenly not just appropriate but mandatory.

Third, we have no reason to suppose that after the crucifixion of a would-be Messiah anyone would suppose that he had been exalted to a place either of world rulership or divine equality. Nobody, so far as we know, suggested that this had happened after the death of Judas the Galilean, or Simon Bar-Giora, or Simeon Ben-Kosiba. Indeed, the suggestion is almost laughable; their failure to lead a successful messianic movement debars them from further consideration as candidates for such a position. But, even if someone had made such a suggestion, they would not then go on to say that this person had been raised from the dead. Belief in exaltation simply would not lead, in the world of first-century Judaism, to belief that resurrection had already occurred. However, if we suppose that the followers of a crucified would-be Messiah came to believe that he had been bodily raised from the dead, we can trace a clear line by which they would then come to believe that he was indeed the Messiah and, if the Messiah, then the world ruler promised in Psalm 89 and Daniel 7; and thus that he was exalted over the world, and so on. Our primary sources suggest that this train of thought was exactly what the early Christians followed.

I have only dealt, obviously, with a tiny fraction of the theories that have been advanced as to what happened at Easter. But I hope I have said enough to show that any theory which wants to say that what the early Christians meant by speaking of the resurrection of Jesus was that his body was still in the tomb while his spirit was present with them has a formidable task ahead of it, simply in terms of first-century history. What we find, rather, is the universal early Christian claim that Jesus had gone, as it were, through death and out the other side; that he was not just in some intermediate state, some disembodied existence—he had not simply "survived"—but that his body had been transformed in a way for which they, his followers, had been quite unprepared but with which they had had to come to terms.

This, though I have had no space to develop it here, is both the substance of the Johannine and Lukan resurrection accounts, and the center of Paul's in 1 Corinthians 15. In all three cases what we find is a body that has neither been abandoned in the tomb, nor merely resuscitated into the same kind of life as before, but transformed into a new sort of body for which there was no precedent and of which there remains no subsequent example. Despite a long scholarly tradition, we cannot play off Paul against Luke and John. Paul, in fact, provides the theological and exegetical underpinning for the re-markably unexegetical accounts the gospels give of Jesus' appearances. And where we find, as in the Valentinian and similar texts, the use of resurrection language in a transferred sense that actually rules out what Second-Temple Jews meant by the term, it is far easier to explain this as a derivation from, and a polemical turn against, an earlier Jewish-style Christian view than as a parallel development, alongside that view, of a primitive belief that underlies both equally.[36]

What then can the historian say by way of comment on the belief of the earliest Christians? Three things, by way of very brief concluding statements of a case that could be argued at much greater length.

First, the historian must claim the right to speak of unique events. Indeed, this is what historians, precisely unlike scientists, do all the time. The rise of early Christianity is itself such a unique event, unlike the rise of any other movement before or since, and my argument has been that precisely as such it demands an explanation. Nor should the historian be frightened off by theologians declaring that since the Resurrection, if it oc-curred, would be an eschatological or theological event it cannot be spoken of. Indeed, it is precisely because the historian observes the early Christians drawing eschatological and theological conclusions that she or he wants to know why.

Second, I agree with Crossan that we must avoid the sterile antithesis between rationalist modernism, denying that resurrection can take place, and rationalist fundamentalism, declaring that it did, just this once. But similar denials, and similar affirmations, antedate modernist rationalism by well over a millennium. Just because the debate has been badly conducted in the last two centuries, that doesn't mean there isn't a real debate asking to take place. I am, therefore, wary of the philosophers who seek as it were to create space for the bodily resurrection by arguing that a supernaturalist worldview is just as rational as a naturalist one; I regard those categories themselves as more than a little flawed.[37] I prefer the Jewish ones that speak of the one God as the creator, sustainer, and recreator of the entire cosmos, in both its interlocking parts, i.e., heaven and earth.

Third, when we raise the question in these terms, I am convinced that all the evidence points in one direction. Of course, if you begin with the large a priori assumption that amounts, more or less, to a restatement of what Aeschylus has Apollo say in the *Eumenides,* or what "the wicked" say in Wisdom of Solomon 2, then you will continue to search for explanations of Christian origins elsewhere.[38] Having reviewed the attempts, I have to say that they strike me as remarkably unsatisfying historically, to say nothing of the theological problems they create. Unless we grasp the nettle here, we will have a long journey through the thorns and thistles of improbable historiography. I propose that, when faced with the historical problem of the resurrection of Jesus and the rise of Christianity, the only way forward is to grasp the nettle, to recognize that history drives us to the borders of language, of philosophy, of theology, and of history itself, and to point out as best we can that the only explanation that will fit all the evidence available is that Jesus of Nazareth was indeed bodily raised from the dead on Easter morning. This and only this enables us to answer our initial question, why Christianity arose and why it took the shape it did. This and only this offers a convincing reason why the message of the early church was not just good advice but Good News.

Of course, grasping this nettle raises huge questions of epistemology and indeed of worldview. But if at this moment of history, when the Western world faces the crisis of postmodernity, we are to rule out all such questions and retreat either into the barren wastelands of modernity or the sterile quicksands of postmodernity, we are indeed of all people the most to be pitied. On the contrary: as far as this historian is concerned, the line that begins with the historical Jesus and the historical resurrection moves forward into the historical present and future, offering as much of a challenge to the world of the twenty-first century as it did to the world of Second-Temple Judaism and the early Roman empire. But that is another story, for another day.

Notes

1. J. Dominic Crossan, *The Birth of Christianity* (San Francisco: Harper-SanFrancisco, 1998). See my review in *Scottish Journal of Theology* 53 (2000) 72–91.

2. Gregory J. Riley, *Resurrection Reconsidered: Thomas and John in Controversy* (Minneapolis: Fortress, 1995).

3. A. J. M. Wedderburn, *Beyond Resurrection* (London: SCM, 1999).

4. See my forthcoming book, *The Resurrection of the Son of God* (Minneapolis: Fortress). The present essay stands in a complex redactional relationship to ch. 7 of N. T. Wright and Marcus J. Borg, *The Meaning of Jesus: Two Visions* (San Francisco: HarperSanFrancisco, 1999); and to ch. 6 of N. T. Wright, *The Challenge of Jesus* (Downers Grove, Ill.: InterVarsity Press, 1999); and, at a further remove, to N. T. Wright, "The Resurrection of the Messiah," *Sewanee Theological Review* 41 (1998) 107–56.

5. More detailed discussion of the whole book can be found in my review in *Scottish Journal of Theology* 53 (2000) 72–91.

6. Crossan, *Birth of Christianity*, xiii–xx.

7. Ibid., xvi.

8. Ibid., 423, 546–73, drawing on an article by H. Koester, "Jesus' Presence in the Early Church," in *Cristianesimo nella Storia* 15 (1994) 541–57.

9. Ibid., 573.

10. This view was classically expressed by James M. Robinson in his 1981 Society of Biblical Literature presidential address ("Jesus from Easter to Valentinus [or to the Apostles' Creed]," *JBL* 101 [1982] 5–37).

11. Riley, *Resurrection Reconsidered*, 48.

12. Dominic Crossan has rightly pointed out that invoking pagan stories about contact with the dead goes back to the second century at least. But my point remains, I think, valid: modernism was characterized not least by its rationalism, denying that anything like a resurrection could have occurred; postmodernism is characterized not least by its openness to experiences of all sorts. That this particular postmodern viewpoint has earlier antecedents is neither here nor there.

13. Riley argues from later centuries' interpretation of Paul that the *soma pneumatikon* could just as easily be seen not as any sort of physical body, but as identical with the normal Greco-Roman view of the soul.

14. Wedderburn, *Beyond Resurrection*, 167.

15. Ibid., 218.

16. J. D. Crossan, "What Victory? What God?" *Scottish Journal of Theology* 50 (1997) 345–58, at 353.

17. C. F. D. Moule, *The Phenomenon of the New Testament: An Inquiry into the Implications of Certain Features of the New Testament* (London: SCM, 1967).

18. 14:17: " . . . the Kingdom of God is . . . righteousness and peace and joy in the Holy Spirit," summarizing 5:1–5 and indeed 5:1–2.

19. See N. T. Wright, *Jesus and the Victory of God* (Minneapolis: Fortress, 1996) ch. 6; and, e.g., my review of Crossan's *The Birth of Christianity* (n. 1 above).

20. Though the point remains very controversial, I have argued that even Q, if indeed it existed, probably presupposed belief in Jesus' resurrection: N. T. Wright, "Resurrection in Q?" in *Christology, Controversy, and Community: New Testament*

Essays in Honour of David R. Catchpole, ed. D. G. Howell and C. M. Tuckett (Leiden: Brill, 2000) 85–97.

21. See again Wright, *Jesus and the Victory,* ch. 6.

22. The early Christians used the phrase "Kingdom of God" so clearly, indeed, that when the early Gnostics wanted to produce their own new religion they borrowed the phrase even though it didn't mean anything like what they were offering.

23. Luke 17:21 is not an exception to this; cf. Wright, *Jesus and the Victory,* 469.

24. See N. T. Wright, *The Climax of the Covenant* (Edinburgh: T. & T. Clark, 1991; Minneapolis: Fortress, 1992) chs. 2, 3.

25. On all this, see Wright, *Jesus and the Victory,* ch. 11. Dahl's discussion is in N. A. Dahl, *The Crucified Messiah and Other Essays* (Minneapolis: Augsburg, 1974) 10–36 (originally published in 1960).

26. And possibly his father, if he was the same as the other Judas. On this point, and these movements in general, cf. N. T. Wright, *The New Testament and the People of God* (Minneapolis: Fortress, 1992) 177–81.

27. On "cognitive dissonance," a phrase, and a theory, more popular a generation ago than today, see above all L. Festinger, *A Theory of Cognitive Dissonance* (Stanford, Calif.: Stanford University Press, 1957).

28. See particularly R. J. Bauckham, *Jude and the Relatives of Jesus in the Early Church* (Edinburgh: T. & T. Clark, 1990).

29. *Antiquities* 20.200–3; cf. Wright, *New Testament,* 353f.

30. For a good brief discussion see R. B. Hays, *First Corinthians* (Louisville: John Knox Press, 1997) 271–74.

31. Though Matthew implies, in a very strange passage (27:51–54), which seems to be closely dependent on Ezekiel 37, that something like a foretaste of this happened after the crucifixion.

32. E.g., Acts 4:2.

33. Against, e.g., S. J. Patterson, *The God of Jesus: The Historical Jesus and the Search for Meaning* (Harrisburg, Pa.: Trinity Press International, 1998), ch. 7.

34. Similar comments could be made about, e.g., E. Schillebeeckx, *Jesus. An Experiment in Christology* (London: SCM, 1979) 516–58.

35. G. Lüdemann, *The Resurrection of Jesus: History, Experience, Theology* (London: SCM, 1994). Idem (in collaboration with A. Ötzen), *What Really Happened to Jesus: A Historical Approach to the Resurrection* (Louisville: Westminster John Knox, 1995) 34.

36. Against, e.g., Robinson, "Jesus from Easter to Valentinus"; this is the barest outline of an argument that could be made at this point.

37. I have in mind, e.g., S. Davis, *Risen Indeed: Making Sense of the Resurrection* (Grand Rapids, Mich.: Eerdmans, 1993), though this single comment scarcely does justice to the range and sophistication of the wider argument there presented.

38. Cf. Aeschylus, *Eumenides,* 647–8: "Once a man has died and the dust has soaked up his blood, there is no resurrection"; Wisd. of Sol. 2.1: "...no one has been known to return from Hades"; 2.5: "...there is no return from our death, because it is sealed up and no one turns back."

4

Albert Schweitzer
and the Image of Jesus
in the Gospel of Thomas

Marvin Meyer

I know of no evidence that Albert Schweitzer, the theologian, philosopher, musician, and medical doctor, knew about or commented on the Gospel of Thomas, though he might have done so late in his life.[1] It is my conceit to suspect that if he had commented on it, he would have agreed that the Gospel of Thomas is a valuable text for our knowledge of the Jesus tradition. After all, Schweitzer based his research on the historical Jesus upon the Gospel of Matthew as well as the Gospel of Mark, and that may have been his way of incorporating Matthean sayings material, from what we now prefer to designate the sayings gospel Q, into his portrait of Jesus.[2] Schweitzer's profound interest in the Sermon on the Mount shows how he valued sayings of Jesus, and this interest led him to declare that the teachings of Jesus on love may be equated with Schweitzer's own ethic of reverence for life, now widened, he states, into a universal concern for the will to live of humans, animals, and plants.[3] In 1905, in a sermon he preached on November 19 in St. Nicolai's church, Schweitzer anticipated the Gospel of Thomas, particularly in its opening, with its presentation of the living Jesus who lives through his sayings. Schweitzer's words from that sermon call out powerfully over the years and remind us of "the hidden sayings that the living Jesus spoke," according to Thomas: "What kind of a living person is Jesus? Don't search for formulas to describe him, even if they be hallowed by centuries. I almost got angry the other day when a religious person said to me that only someone who believes in the resurrection of the body and in the glorified body of the risen Christ can believe in the living Jesus. . . . Let me explain it in my way. The glorified body of Jesus is to be found in his sayings."[4]

So I affirm my conviction concerning the significance of the image of Jesus in the Gospel of Thomas for our knowledge of Jesus traditions and our investigation of the historical Jesus. As I do so, I wish to advance three suggestions that will guide this discussion of the Gospel of Thomas.

Three Initial Suggestions

1. I suggest that a very reasonable though probably not compelling case can be made for a first-century date for a version of the Gospel of Thomas.[5] The manuscript evidence for the Gospel of Thomas includes the Coptic text of the Gospel of Thomas (almost certainly from a Greek original) in the fourth-century Nag Hammadi library, and three Greek Oxyrhynchus papyrus fragments (1, 654, 655) now housed at Oxford, the British Library, and Harvard. These Greek fragments have been dated, most recently by Harold W. Attridge, to just after 200, around 250, and between 200 and 250, respectively, dates that correspond fairly well to the dates assigned by Grenfell and Hunt.[6] Recall that they calculated that the original document, which was composed not in Egypt but in Syria, must be dated at least half a century earlier, and so they placed the *terminus ad quem,* or latest date of composition, at 140.[7] Gospel of Thomas materials are also cited in the church fathers, especially in the account of the Naassene Gnostics in Hippolytus of Rome (early third century).[8] The manuscript tradition for the Gospel of Thomas thus rivals that of any other gospel, including the canonical gospels. Furthermore, the Gospel of Thomas illustrates features that we commonly identify with first-century issues—quarrels over apostleship, uncertainty about James the righteous, the brother of Jesus, use of sayings collections, and so on. Some aspects of Thomas and the forms of sayings in Thomas seem clearly to antedate the canonical gospels—for example, the use of parables without allegorical amplification, as we shall note below. Gospel of Thomas saying 17 presents a saying of Jesus—"I shall give you what no eye has seen, what no ear has heard, what no hand has touched, what has not arisen in the human heart"—which sounds strikingly like Paul's characterization of the wisdom Christians with whom he disagrees in Corinth in the mid-first century.[9]

2. I suggest that we do well to think of multiple editions of the Gospel of Thomas, even Gospels of Thomas, rather than a single Gospel of Thomas. In the pre-Gutenberg world of antiquity, texts typically went through substantial changes and modifications as they were copied and recopied. In a way, each copy of a text was a new edition. Helmut Koester has shown how different editions of the Gospel of Mark (including Secret Mark, canonical Mark, Matthew, Luke, and Carpocratian Mark) may represent a continuously developing Markan tradition.[10] Such may also be said of editions of the Gospel of Thomas. The Coptic text, Greek fragments, and testimonies of the church fathers all differ from one another and may represent different versions of the Gospel of Thomas. The fluidity of the textual tradition of the Gospel of Thomas may be more pronounced on account of its genre as a sayings gospel. As a collection of sayings, the Gospel of Thomas was open to easy modification. We may dub the Gospel of Thomas a loose-leaf text in which sayings might be added, deleted, or rearranged with little dif-

ficulty, particularly since no overall organizational scheme seems operative in the Gospel of Thomas,[11] but only specific points of linkage supplied by *Stichwörter* (catchwords) and small subcollections of parables and other sayings.[12] The limited evidence of the Coptic manuscript and the Oxyrhynchus papyrus fragments supports these possibilities of modification.

3. If there were different editions of the Gospel, or Gospels, of Thomas, then I suggest we shall need to address the likelihood of multiple editors with different perspectives, points of view, literary styles, and theologies in the versions of the Gospel of Thomas. It has sometimes been popular to delineate the theology of the Gospel of Thomas.[13] We may be forced to abandon such naiveté, and instead acknowledge multiple theological perspectives in a gospel text that was subjected to editorial modification as it was copied and translated. I do not hesitate, therefore, to identify very early Jesus traditions and much later Gnosticizing elements in the same Coptic text.

With these three suggestions in mind, let us begin to explore the image, or, perhaps, the images, of Jesus in the Gospel of Thomas.

Jesus the Jewish Sage

We begin our quest for the Jesus of Thomas by observing what is most prominent regarding Thomas's Jesus. In the Gospel of Thomas Jesus is a Jewish sage, a wise fellow who utters sayings that are described as hidden or secret sayings. The gospel of Thomas is thus a sayings gospel, with little narrative but numerous sayings presented as life-giving sayings of the sagacious Jesus. In the words of the unnamed speaker of saying 1, most likely Jesus, but possibly his twin Judas Thomas, "Whoever discovers the interpretation of these sayings will not taste death." As a sayings source, the Gospel of Thomas has much in common, in terms of form and content, with the synoptic sayings source Q, and it also recalls another possible text that is sometimes connected with Q, Papias's logia of the master compiled in Aramaic, according to Papias, by Matthew.[14] In this regard we should also mention the parable and sayings collection in Mark, the sayings of Jesus in the Didache, and other extracanonical sayings of Jesus, sometimes called *agrapha*.[15] Within the early decades of the Jesus movement there was an expressed interest in *mnemoneuein ton logon tou kuriou Iesou*, as the Acts of the Apostles and 1 Clement put it, "remembering the sayings of the master Jesus."[16] Or, as James in the Secret Book of James imagines the scene, "The twelve followers [were] all sitting together, recalling what the savior had said to each of them, whether in a hidden or an open manner, and organizing it in books. [And] I was writing what is in [my book]"—a Hebrew book in fact, the text maintains.[17]

Early in the Jesus movement there is this special interest in sayings of Jesus and sayings gospels, but this interest is also to be found much later, in a world of religious thought too often neglected by scholars of early

Christianity, the world of Islam.[18] In Muslim sources Jesus ('Isa in Arabic) is portrayed as a prophet of God, the messiah and servant and spirit and word of God, the son of Mary, who spoke words of wisdom, performed mighty deeds, and died—if in fact he truly died; perhaps he only seemed to die—at the end of a remarkable human life. In the Qur'an there are relatively few sayings of Jesus, but in other Islamic sources Jesus is featured as preeminently a teacher of wisdom. One Muslim author who collected and edited sayings of Jesus is Abu Hamid Muhammad al-Ghazali. Al-Ghazali was an eleventh and twelfth century Muslim professor, theologian, and mystic who wrote voluminously, and the greatest of his books is *Ihya' 'ulum al-din, The Revival of the Religious Sciences*. In this book al-Ghazali presents Jesus as a sage whose sayings often recall sayings of Jesus in Q, the New Testament gospels, and the Gospel of Thomas. Thus, in al-Ghazali Jesus says, "Whoever knows and does and teaches will be called great in heaven's Kingdom." In a manner that recalls Jewish and Christian wisdom and a passage in Mark, and its parallels, this Jesus says, "Do not offer wisdom to those who are not worthy of it, or you might harm it, and do not withhold it from those who are worthy of it, or you might harm them. Be like a gentle doctor who puts medicine on the diseased spot." In a manner reminiscent of Q and the Gospel of Thomas and one of Aesop's fables, Jesus says, "Evil scholars are like a rock that has fallen at the mouth of a brook: it does not drink the water, nor does it let the water flow to the plants. And evil scholars are like the drainpipe of a latrine that is plastered outside but filthy inside; or like graves that are decorated outside but contain dead people's bones inside." As in Q and Thomas, Jesus in al-Ghazali contrasts his lot in life with that of a wild beast so as to indicate that he himself, unlike the beast, has no resting place. Jesus offers his *as-salaam 'alaykum* to a pig so that his tongue will not grow accustomed to speaking evil, and when his followers express disgust about the stinking carcass of a dog, Jesus replies, "How white are its teeth!"[19]

A Gospel of Wisdom

The Gospel of Thomas, like these other sources, offers an image of Jesus as a Jewish sage. I hesitate to call him a teacher of wisdom here, since Jesus explicitly denies being a teacher in saying 13, but more on that saying below. The portrait of Jesus the sage in Thomas is a remarkable portrait, with stunning differences from the portraits of Jesus in other gospels, especially New Testament gospels. I reiterate what I have written elsewhere: Jesus in the Gospel of Thomas performs no physical miracles, reveals no fulfillment of prophecy, announces no apocalyptic Kingdom about to disrupt the world order, and dies for no one's sins.[20]

Jesus in the Gospel of Thomas is not named the Christ or the messiah, he is not acclaimed master or lord, and when he refers to himself as the son of man, or the child of humankind, once in the gospel, he does so in the generic sense of referring to any person or simply to himself. This is in saying 86, a saying paralleled, as we have noted, in al-Ghazali: "[Foxes have] their dens and birds have their nests, but the child of humankind has no place to lay his head and rest." And if in the Gospel of Thomas Jesus is a child of humankind, so are other people called the children of humankind.[21] Jesus in the Gospel of Thomas is not presented as the incarnate and unique son of God, and nothing is said of a remarkable birth. The only saying that might conceivably refer to his birth at all is something of a scandal. Thomas 105 reads, "Jesus said, 'Whoever knows the father and the mother will be called the child of a whore,'" and it is possible (though not certain) that this might be an oblique reference to the tradition, known from Celsus in Origen and other sources, that Jesus' mother was seduced or raped by a Roman soldier named Pantera.[22] Recent speculation in this regard has focused upon the gravestone of a Sidonian archer named Tiberias Julius Abdes Pantera, who was stationed in Palestine around the time of the birth of Jesus.[23] In the Gospel of Thomas Jesus has nothing remarkable recorded about his childhood. Of course, except for a single legend in the Gospel of Luke about young Jesus in the temple, no early gospel discusses the young life of Jesus.[24] This point should be mentioned here, however, because later the Infancy Gospel of Thomas seems to pick up themes from the Gospel of Thomas—for example, the old person asking a little child about life in saying 4—and creates stories about young Jesus. The Infancy Gospel of Thomas has Zacchaeus the teacher say about his young pupil Jesus, "Friends, I think on my shame that I, an old man, have been overcome by a child."[25]

In the Gospel of Thomas a cross is mentioned only one time, in saying 55, and in what seems to be a metaphorical manner, having to do with bearing a burden and maintaining a commitment against all odds. The saying echoes what we know from Q and the synoptic Gospels: "Jesus said, 'Whoever does not hate father and mother cannot be a follower of me, and whoever does not hate brothers and sisters and bear the cross as I do will not be worthy of me.'"[26] In any case, there is no thought of a cross with saving significance here. In the Gospel of Thomas there is no empty tomb—there is no tomb at all—and Jesus is nowhere portrayed as having risen from the dead. In Oxyrhynchus Papyrus 654 there is a clause about what is buried being raised that is not a part of the Coptic text of Gospel of Thomas saying 5. It might refer to what is hidden away being uncovered, but it should be noted that this statement about being raised is also preserved on a Christian burial shroud from Oxyrhynchus.[27] In Thomas Jesus is called "the living Jesus," *Iesous etonh,* but if Jesus is a living one, so is God, and so are the followers of Jesus.[28] It is most likely meant that the living Jesus of the Gospel of Thomas lives through his sayings—even as Albert Schweitzer proclaimed in Alsace many centuries after the Gospel of Thomas.

What sort of a portrait of Jesus the Jewish sage do we find, then, in the Gospel of Thomas? Here I wish to highlight, in more positive terms, five distinctive features of Jesus that will help to clarify the image of Jesus in the Gospel of Thomas.

Seeking and Finding

First, in Thomas Jesus encourages people to seek and find, to search and discover: *shine auo tetnacine,* "Seek and you will find." This encouragement is given in different forms throughout the Gospel of Thomas,[29] but it is presented in a programmatic way in saying 2: "Jesus said, 'Let one who seeks not stop seeking until one finds. When one finds, one will be troubled. When one is troubled, one will marvel and will rule over all.' " Versions of this familiar saying are also known from the Gospel of the Hebrews and the Book of Thomas; Oxyrhynchus Papyrus 654 adds an additional stage in the program of seeking and finding: "and having ruled, one will rest."[30] The stages enumerated for seeking and finding illumine what it means to discover and learn, and this description of the learning process rings true to the present day. Seeking, searching, learning, the Gospel of Thomas suggests, is to be undertaken with commitment, and while the way to discovery may be upsetting, it is also marvelous, and people will attain the end of their journey—here identified as the reign and rest of God—if only they persevere. Jesus' words to his followers on seeking and finding are partially paralleled in Q, the synoptic Gospels, and the Gospel of John, as an essay in the volume *From Quest to Q* discusses,[31] but this saying has a particular focus, prominence, and even urgency in the Gospel of Thomas. In Thomas the exhortation to seek and find sets the tone for the entire gospel, which is a gospel of wisdom that may be comprehended by those who seek and find.

What is to be sought and found? This question is not easily answered, and Jesus in Thomas may seem at times to assume only a general posture of recommending seeking and finding. The end of the search in the particular saying under scrutiny is the reign and rest of God, the Kingdom of God. The following saying, saying 3, goes on to discuss the reign or Kingdom of God with a couple of Jesus jokes, in reference to the Delphic maxim *gnothi sauton,* "know yourself," and a declaration that the Kingdom is within and without but is not to be localized in heaven or in the underworld: "Jesus said, 'If your leaders say to you "Look, the Kingdom is in heaven," then the birds of heaven will precede you. If they say to you, "It is in the sea" [the Greek has "under the earth"], then the fish will precede you. Rather the Kingdom is inside you and it is outside you. When you know yourselves, then you will be known, and you will understand that you are children of the living father. But if you do not know yourselves, then you dwell in poverty, and you are poverty.' " Yet, while such may be the goal of the quest, what is specifically to be sought and discovered is clarified in saying 1: "Whoever discovers the interpretation (*hermeneia*) of these sayings will not taste death." The Jesus of Thomas asks his followers, his students, to seek the interpretation of his sayings, to complete his thoughts, and in this search for meaning life is to be found.

In his recent study on the Gospel of Thomas, Richard Valantasis appears to me to be in the right track when he recognizes the need for hearers or readers of Jesus' hidden sayings to encounter the sayings creatively and to add their our interpretive meaning to the sayings.[32] Valantasis calls the theology of the Gospel of Thomas "a performative theology," and he asserts that "the theology emerges from the readers' and the hearers' responses to the sayings and their sequence and their variety."[33] Again, "The readers and the interpreters of sayings . . . construct their own narrative and theology linking the individual sayings into a cohesive text. In that strategy, the readers mirror the activity of the recorder of the sayings who has already constructed a meaningful meta-text of collected individual sayings. The recorder has also constructed a voice for the meta-text and described that voice as the 'living Jesus' whose speaking conveys life, meaning, knowledge, immortality, and all the riches of the Kingdom."[34]

Seek and you will find, says Jesus in Thomas and in other gospels. I suggest that the oftentimes elusive Jesus of Thomas in not remarkably different from the oftentimes elusive Jesus of Q and the New Testament gospels—though, as we shall observe, some sayings of Jesus in Thomas are certainly more cryptic and riddle-like. I also suggest that the Jesus of Thomas, like the Jesus of Q and some portions of the New Testament gospels, invites his followers and his listeners to engage his sayings, to find their meaning, and to think his thoughts after him. To this extent, like the Buddha in Theravada Buddhism, Jesus points the way, but it is up to us to labor at the interpretive task.

Telling Stories about the Kingdom

Second, in Thomas Jesus tells stories or parables that have an ambiguous quality but that are narrated to help explain, among other things, the Kingdom.[35] As in Q and the synoptic gospels, Jesus in Thomas is wonderfully vague in his references to the Kingdom or reign of God and refers to the Kingdom in aphorisms and metaphors. According to the Gospel of Thomas, Jesus says that the Kingdom is within and without; people who are like nursing babies will attain the Kingdom, when they are transformed, and children will know the Kingdom, but businesspeople and merchants will not get in; women can get in—that's the good news—if they become male—that's the bad news; the Kingdom is not an apocalyptic phenomenon, but rather it is spread out upon the earth and people do not see it; and, Jesus says, in a saying also given elsewhere and now known, in a slightly different form, in the so-called Gospel of the Savior, "Whoever is near me is near the fire, and whoever is far from me is far from the Kingdom."[36] Jesus is vague in these statements, but he describes the Kingdom more vividly when he employs the techniques of a story-teller. There are also some stories or parables in

Thomas that are not told with the Kingdom specifically in mind; for example, saying 8, the story of the smart fisherman who keeps the big one but throws the small fry back, is said to be about humankind, in Coptic *prome*.

Thus Jesus tells his illustrative stories in Thomas. Some are familiar, some are not. Heaven's Kingdom "is like a mustard seed. <It> is the smallest of all seeds, but when it falls on prepared soil, it produces a large plant and becomes a shelter for birds of heaven" (saying 20). "The father's Kingdom is like a person who had [good] seed. His enemy came at night and sowed weeds among the good seed. The person did not let them pull up the weeds, but said to them, 'No, or you might go to pull up the weeds and pull up the wheat along with them.' For on the day of the harvest the weeds will be conspicuous and will be pulled up and burned" (saying 57). "The father's Kingdom is like a merchant who had a supply of merchandise and then found a pearl. That merchant was prudent; he sold the merchandise and bought the single pearl for himself" (saying 76). "The Kingdom is like a shepherd who had a hundred sheep. One of them, the largest, went astray. He left the ninety-nine and sought the one until he found it. After he had gone to this trouble, he said to the sheep, 'I love you more than the ninety-nine'" (saying 107). "The Kingdom is like a person who had a treasure hidden in his field but did not know it. And [when] he died, he left it to his [son]. The son [did] not know (about it). He took over the field and sold it. The buyer went plowing, [discovered] the treasure, and began to lend money at interest to whomever he wished" (saying 109). "The father's Kingdom is like [a] woman. She took a little yeast, [hid] it in dough, and made it into large loaves of bread" (saying 96). "The [father's] Kingdom is like a woman who was carrying a [jar] full of meal. While she was walking along [a] distant road, the handle of the jar broke, and the meal spilled behind her [along] the road. She did not know it; she had not noticed a problem. When she reached her house, she put the jar down and discovered that it was empty" (saying 97). "The father's Kingdom is like a person who wanted to put someone powerful to death. While at home he drew his sword and thrust it into the wall to find out whether his hand would go in. Then he killed the powerful one" (saying 98). And that is what the Kingdom is like.

A few observations should be made about these Kingdom stories of Jesus in the Gospel of Thomas. They are stories that compare the Kingdom to features of everyday life in Palestine, stories about the Kingdom... and seeds and weeds, and farming and herding and buying and selling, and discovering hidden treasure out in a field, and carrying meal and baking bread and assassinating the strong man. Often they are stories with a surprising twist, or even godly foolishness, as with the merchant who cashes in his or her entire inventory for a single pricey stone, or the shepherd who abandons his or her entire flock for a single recalcitrant sheep. In Thomas, as elsewhere, Jesus intimates that God's reign is to be recognized in the events, at time the surprising events, of everyday life happening all around us. Unlike some parables of Jesus in the synoptic Gospels, Thomas's stories do not have allegorical interpretations added to them, and it is not clear that these stories themselves have the sorts of allegorical elements within the stories that we may identify in the synoptic versions. Consider Gospel of Thomas sayings 64 and 65, for instance, the stories of the feast to which people are eventually invited off the street and the vineyard that becomes a site of murder and mayhem.[37] Further, unlike some parables of Jesus in the synoptic Gospels, Thomas's parables do not have overtly apocalyptic elements, and as Stephen Patterson rightly reminds us, "one must be careful not to read into Thomas a note of apocalypticism based upon sayings whose synoptic parallels are given an apocalyptic interpretation in the synoptic tradition."[38] Such is the case in the story of the planted weeds, as we have just read it. In that story the place of God's Kingdom around us is uncertain and unclear, but the growth of wheat and weeds will elucidate what is good and what belongs to God, and that will triumph.

Living an Alternative Lifestyle

Third, in Thomas Jesus advocates a radical lifestyle, an alternative lifestyle that actively questions the polite amenities, political loyalties, and religious observance of ordinary folks. In saying 42 Jesus says, "Be passersby," *shope etetenerparage,* apparently advocating a homeless life of wandering.[39] The closest parallel I know to this saying is a saying of Jesus in an inscription from a mosque at Fatehpur-Sikri, India: "This world is a bridge. Pass over it, but do not build your dwelling there." The same basic saying is cited by the medieval author Petrus Alphonsi.[40] In saying 86, quoted above, Jesus observes that he, unlike some animals, has no den or nest or place to rest and call home. In saying 14 Jesus similarly assumes an itinerant, wandering life for his followers, and he advises that they eat whatever is served and return whatever act of gratitude they can provide to those who are kind enough to take them in for the night: "When you go into any region and walk through the countryside, when people receive you, eat what they serve you and heal the sick among them. For what goes into your mouth will not defile you; rather it is what comes out of your mouth that will defile you."[41] The aphoristic saying on what goes in and what goes out is Thomas's version of a well-known saying. However, the gospel writers could not seem to figure out precisely what bodily exit Jesus had in mind as the one that can make you dirty, and Mark has Jesus simply say that what comes out of a person will defile him. My guess is that Jesus, with a twinkle in his eye, might have kept it ambiguous, leaving it to the people around to contemplate their orifices.

In Thomas Jesus tells his followers to reject mundane family ties and family values and identify with a new order of family. This new family of Jesus consists of the women and men together who are followers of Jesus, with no special twelve singled out for apostolic attention—"Those here who do the will of my father are my brothers and my mother. They are the ones who will enter my father's Kingdom" (saying 99). These people are the poor, and they are declared fortunate for being poor. They are the beggars who, when they get some money, give it away. Jesus himself may demand his due too, as a panhandler, if Patterson is correct in his understanding of Thomas 100, where Jesus says, "Give Caesar the things that are Caesar's, give God the things that are God's, and give me what is mine."[42] These people of Jesus do not worry about food or fashion, for what is truly necessary will be provided. As Jesus puts it in saying 36, in words that remind us of Q, "Do not worry, from morning to evening and from evening to morning, about what you will wear." Or, in the Greek version, "[Do not worry] from morning [to evening nor] from evening [to] morning, either [about] your [food], what [you will] eat, [or] about [your clothing], what you [will] wear. [You are much] better than the lilies, which do not card or [spin]. As for you, when you have no garment, what [will you put] on? Who might add to your stature? That is the one who will give you your garment."[43] These people, the poor ones of Jesus, are declared fortunate for their concern to feed the hungry: "Fortunate are they who are hungry, that the stomach of the person in want may be filled" (saying 69). They are not impressed with the rich and the powerful, and they are not impressed by religious observance. In Thomas Jesus has nothing good to say about fasting, praying, tithing, and observing food laws or getting circumcised—if circumcision were really important, would not baby boys be born circumcised, Jesus asks—except that Jesus suggests a more symbolic or spiritual observance: fasting from the world, keeping the Sabbath as a Sabbath, being circumcised in spirit.[44] Most important, Jesus maintains, is integrity, honesty, authenticity: "Do not lie, and do not do what you hate, because all things are disclosed before heaven" (saying 6). "Do not do what you hate" is the negative formulation of the golden rule, the ethical principle of reciprocity, which Schweitzer used as the basis of his ethic of reverence for life. This saying in Thomas may be compared to the command to love one's neighbor, given in a distinctive form in Thomas 25: "Love your brother [*pekson;* or, your brother and sister, your sibling] like your soul [*tekpsyche;* or, your life, yourself], protect that person like the pupil of your eye." Show reverence and respect and love for another life, said Schweitzer, just as you show reverence and respect and love for your own life.[45]

These sayings promoting an alternative lifestyle cannot easily be spiritualized away under the assumption that the author or authors and the readers of the Gospel of Thomas were people who cared not for lifestyle but only for mental and spiritual reflection and meditation. Rather, today we might say that the Gospel of Thomas portrays Jesus and his followers as street people, people like those invited off the street to the feast in Jesus' parable, with a rejection of everyday mores and a fresh sense of a community of love and mutuality. We might further say that Jesus resembles a Jewish street preacher, a peasant preacher whose insights and stories provide a glimpse of a dramatically different way of living together in God's reign.

Being Transformed

Fourth, in Thomas Jesus announces that the wholeness to be experienced by those who find the meaning or interpretation of the sayings promises transformation. One of the most common verbs employed in the Gospel of Thomas is *shope*, "become," and this verb (and other grammatical constructions) may be used to describe the transformation of those who respond to and follow Jesus. Thus Jesus says that the followers become a single one (*oua ouot*), and they stand alone (*monachos*), with a Greek word, used as a loan word in the Coptic, which eventually takes on the meaning of "monk."[46] This word must in fact have been understood in precisely this way by the fourth-century Pachomian monks, at Pabau, who copied and stored the Gospel of Thomas in their library. Jesus says that the lion that people eat becomes human.[47] Jesus says that once people became two, but now they may become one again.[48] The followers of Jesus may enter the Kingdom when they are completely transformed: "When you make the two into one, and when you make the inner like the outer and the outer like the inner, and the upper like the lower, and when you make male and female into a single one, so that the male will not be male nor the female be female, when you make eyes in place of an eye, a hand in place of a hand, a foot in place of a foot, an image in place of an image, then you will enter [the Kingdom]" (saying 22). Mary of Magdala, and any female for that matter, may be transformed and become a living spirit when she makes herself male (saying 114). This statement of transformation, put in strikingly misogynist terms, most likely uses common sexist symbolism from antiquity to depict what is heavenly and imperishable as male and what is earthly and perishable as female. Parallels to this saying are numerous in the literature of antiquity and late antiquity; the parallels in the Hellenistic Jewish thinker Philo of Alexandria are particularly noteworthy. We still sometimes use this symbolism to the present day in speaking of God as the father who is in heaven and of the earth as mother earth or mother nature. We can guess the sort of interpretive spin those Pachomian monks reading the Gospel of Thomas may have put on this saying. And some women who chose the ascetic life of self-denial took these symbols of gender quite seriously, and assumed the trappings of maleness by cutting their hair, putting on men's clothing, and looking like males.[49]

An additional kind of transformation is described in the Gospel of Thomas 108. Jesus says, "Whoever drinks from my mouth will become like me; I myself shall become that person, and the hidden things will be revealed to that person." In this saying Jesus announces mystical transformation: one will become like Jesus, and Jesus will become that one. The reference to drinking from the mouth of Jesus recalls the imagery of drinking from divine wisdom in Jewish wisdom literature and the Odes of Solomon.[50] Elsewhere in the Gospel of Thomas, in saying 13, Jesus also alludes to drinking: "I am not your teacher [he says to Thomas]. Because you have drunk, you have become intoxicated from the bubbling spring that I have tended." Jesus denies that he is a teacher, because his followers must take the initiative and drink for themselves—compare what we observed above about seeking and finding. He is the tender of the spring, the bartender who tends the bubbling spring of wisdom and dispenses the intoxicating spiritual brew. When Jesus goes on to tell Thomas three things, to speak three sayings to Thomas, those three sayings are never disclosed—a coy but effective way of reiterating the need for the reader to seek and find.[51]

One more statement of transformation is of interest in this regard. In Gospel of Thomas saying 77 Jesus articulates a vision of a transformed cosmos. All comes from Jesus, all attains to Jesus, and Jesus is all and in all. Here Jesus is made to speak in "I am" statements, aretalogical self-predications, so that he sounds like the voice of the divine; and he uses language that is pantheistic or panentheistic: "I am the light that is over all things. I am all: from me all has come forth, and to me all has reached. Split a piece of wood; I am there. Lift up the stone, and you will find me there." In the Greek Oxyrhynchus fragment 1 this saying is combined with a version of another, nearly inscrutable saying: "Where there are [three], they are without God, and where there is only one, I say, I am with that one."[52] While this powerful statement is at home with the description of wisdom, in the Wisdom of Solomon, which permeates and penetrates and renews everything, it is also similar to Johannine and Pauline formulations, and later this sort of saying seems to find a natural form of expression in Gnostic and Manichaean mystical texts.[53]

Speaking in Cryptic Sayings

Fifth, in Thomas Jesus speaks in hidden sayings throughout the gospel, but some of the sayings are particularly cryptic, riddle-like, and esoteric. Bentley Layton describes all the sayings of Jesus in Thomas as obscure, and writes, "Without recognition of their hidden meaning, Jesus' sayings are merely 'obscure.'"[54] He is right, but some of Jesus' sayings are more obscure than others. Consider the following: "Jesus said, 'This heaven will pass away, and the one above it will pass away. The dead are not alive, and the living will not die. During the days when you ate what is dead, you made it alive. When you are in the light, what will you do? On the day when you were one, you became two. But when you become two, what will you do?'" (saying 11). "The followers said to Jesus, 'Tell us how our end will be?' Jesus said, 'Have you discovered the beginning, then, so that you are seeking the end? For where the beginning is the end will be. Fortunate is one who stands at the beginning: that one will know the end and will not taste death'" (saying 18). "Jesus said, 'Fortunate is one who came into being before coming into being.

If you become my followers and listen to my sayings, these stones will serve you. For there are five trees in paradise for you; they do not change, summer or winter, and their leaves do not fall. Whoever knows them will not taste death' " (saying 19). "Jesus said, 'If they say to you, "Where have you came from?" say to them, "We have come from the light, from the place where the light came into being by itself, established [itself], and appeared in their image." If they say to you, "Is it you?" say, "We are its children, and we are the chosen of the living father." If they say to you, "What is the evidence of your father in you?" say to them, "It is motion and rest" ' " (saying 50).

How may these and other esoteric sayings in the Gospel of Thomas be understood? Stevan Davies sees these sorts of sayings in the Gospel of Thomas in the general context of ancient wisdom traditions, and there is good evidence to support his perspective.[55] In this essay we have seen that Jesus is a Jewish sage in Thomas, and that traditions placed on his lips are often quite similar to what may be read in other Jewish, Hellenistic Jewish, and Christian wisdom texts. Bentley Layton, conversely, sees the key to understanding these sayings in the ancient myth of the soul, *psyche,* often depicted as a female entity whose career is tied up with the vicissitudes of the human experience. As Layton reminds us, a version of the myth of the soul is to be found prominently in the Thomas tradition in the "Song of the Pearl" within the Acts of Thomas.[56] Other scholarly commentators on the Gospel of Thomas seek the meaning of the obscure sayings in Gnostic mythology, for example the Gnostic myth presented in a famous document of Sethian Gnostic spirituality, the Apocryphon or Secret Book of John. In the case of the last saying cited above, saying 50, the destiny of the people of the light may be paralleled, it is said, in the Gnostic concern for the origin of Gnostics in the light and their return to the light, which becomes manifest in this world in the image of the divine, and is empowered to move and is destined to rest.[57] I myself doubt whether there is necessarily a single, comprehensive explanatory key that may unlock the meaning of all the sayings in a text like the Gospel of Thomas, which was subject to editorial changes and modifications as it went through multiple editions.

Jesus, Thomas, and Schweitzer

If these are five of the leading features of Jesus in the Gospel of Thomas, what may we conclude about the image of Jesus in this text? I propose three conclusions.

1. The image of Jesus in the Gospel of Thomas presents us with an alternative kerygma to the proclamation that dominates the New Testament Gospels. This alternative kerygma is simply another among the several kerygmata that characterized the diversity of proclamation in early Christianity. In this alternative proclamation Thomas resembles Q to an extent. Like Q, the Gospel of Thomas is not a gospel of the cross. Thomas proclaims a nonapocalyptic Jesus who utters life-giving words, and those who

follow Jesus and respond to his words will not taste death. Thomas's Jesus is not the incarnate son of God, he is not the sacrifice for sin, he is not the firstfruits of the Resurrection, he is not the Messiah, the Christ, the anointed one of God. Whether the Gospel of Thomas should even be considered a specifically Christian text remains a question—the same question we have with Q—but chiefly a scholarly question about taxonomy. Whether this sort of gospel of wisdom remains a viable gospel for today and for the future also remains a question, but a much more interesting question to consider.

2. As we have seen, the image of Jesus in the Coptic Gospel of Thomas from the Nag Hammadi library contains not only early Jesus traditions but also other themes, probably later themes, that are more developed, more esoteric, more riddle-like. These more esoteric themes have prompted some scholars to classify the Gospel of Thomas as a Gnostic gospel, and this classification sometimes has been used polemically in order to marginalize the gospel. I am not convinced by those who wish to classify Thomas as a Gnostic gospel. To begin with, we scholars continue to struggle with what Gnosticism actually was, and to this day there is no consensus whatsoever. Michael Williams proposes that we dismantle the category of Gnosticism altogether, a category that he considers dubious, and he suggests that we contemplate replacing it with what he calls "biblical demiurgical traditions."[58] Besides, the Gospel of Thomas rarely uses the word *gnosis* (only once, in saying 39, and then negatively in the context of the Pharisees), and when it reflects upon knowing oneself, it is indebted to discussions of the Delphic maxim (as in, for instance, saying 3). Unlike the Secret Book of John and other Gnostic or biblical demiurgical texts, the Gospel of Thomas presents no narrative of the biblical creation story in order to show the origin of mystical insight and enlightenment in the face of the megalomaniacal creator of the world. Indeed, the Gospel of Thomas contains very little that ancient heresiologists and modern scholars are inclined to consider Gnostic in some specific sense of the word.

For these reasons many scholars, and I am one of them, do not classify the Gospel of Thomas as a Gnostic gospel without considerable qualification. The Coptic version of the gospel is an esoteric piece of wisdom, to be sure, but many of us tend to resort to qualifying adjectives to describe the Coptic Gospel of Thomas. We call it Gnosticizing or proto-Gnostic, we identify Gnostic proclivities, and we find other subtle ways to nuance our words. The fact is that the Coptic Gospel of Thomas contains elements that illustrate how primitive first-century Jesus traditions, with a wisdom orientation, could be read and revised in a second- and third-century early Christian world that was exploring new ways of wisdom and new ideas of gnosis. Here the work of Helmut Koester and James Robinson is helpful, especially Robinson's essay "LOGOI SOPHON," which traces the trajectory from Jewish wisdom literature to Q and Thomas and to Gnostic discourses of the risen Lord with his followers.[59] The Coptic Gospel of Thomas may not fit neatly into our scholarly categories. And if that calls into question our scholarly categories and our reconstructions, so much the better.

3. I propose that the image of Jesus in the Gospel of Thomas contains primitive Jesus traditions that may bring us a bit closer to the historical Jesus. In Thomas Jesus is a Jewish sage, who uses stories, aphorisms, and other utterances to tell of God's presence and God's reign. The manifestation of God's presence may not be readily apparent but it is all around, and sometimes it startles and surprises. Those who seek to respond to Jesus and his sayings may adopt a counterculture lifestyle that embodies the life of love and mutuality. It is, in a way, a secular life, not a life of religious piety, but while it is in the world, it is not worldly. It is a life that runs counter to the world and the ways of the world. And it is a life that transforms.

With this image of Jesus the Gospel of Thomas may bring us close to aspects of the historical Jesus. Thomas may, in significant respects, have gotten it right.

Which brings us back, at last, to Albert Schweitzer. As we all know, Schweitzer emphasized that Jesus was a Jewish apocalyptic figure who was profoundly committed to his vision but was fundamentally mistaken. Jesus' was a thoroughgoing eschatology. Jesus finally throws himself upon the wheel of the world, but he is crushed, mangled, destroyed.[60] Yet Schweitzer was also deeply interested in the sayings of Jesus, as we noted at the opening of this study, and this interest impacted his thinking, his preaching, and his life. In his 1950 preface to *The Quest of the Historical Jesus*, Schweitzer goes so far as to suggest that Jesus' sayings and his teachings on love may actually have transformed and overcome the apocalyptic vision. He writes, "It was Jesus who began to spiritualize the idea of God's Kingdom and the messiah. He introduced into the late-Jewish conception of the Kingdom his strong ethical emphasis upon love, making this, and the consistent practice of it, the indispensable condition of entrance. By so doing he charged the late-Jewish idea of God's Kingdom with ethical forces, which transformed it into the spiritual and ethical reality with which we are familiar."[61] Finally, then, Schweitzer may look, with us, to Jesus the Jewish sage, the Jesus we identify in the Sermon on the Mount, Q, and Thomas, as the Jesus whose words and sayings may impart life.

Notes

1. On Albert Schweitzer, Jesus, and reverence for life, see my essay, "Affirming Reverence for Life," in *Albert Schweitzer for the Twenty-First Century: The Ethics of Reverence for Life,* ed. Marvin Meyer and Kurt Bergel (Syracuse: Syracuse University Press, 2001 [in press]). On Schweitzer and Jesus, see also the essay by James M. Robinson, "The Image of Jesus in Q," in the present volume.

2. Albert Schweitzer, *The Quest of the Historical Jesus: A Critical Examination of Its Progress from Reimarus to Wrede,* trans. W. Montgomery (Baltimore: Johns Hopkins University Press, 1998).

3. Albert Schweitzer, *Out of My Life and Thought: An Autobiography,* trans. Antje Bultmann Lemke (Baltimore: Johns Hopkins University Press, 1998) 235.

4. Albert Schweitzer, *Reverence for Life,* trans. Reginald H. Fuller (New York: Irvington/Harper & Row, 1969) 65 (slightly revised).

5. Compare Stephen J. Patterson, *The Gospel of Thomas and Jesus,* Foundations and Facets (Sonoma, Calif.: Polebridge, 1993) 113–20; Stephen J. Patterson, "Understanding the *Gospel of Thomas* Today," 40–45 in Stephen J. Patterson, James M. Robinson, and Hans-Gebhard Bethge, *The Fifth Gospel: The Gospel of Thomas Comes of Age* (Harrisburg, Pa.: Trinity Press International, 1998).

6. Harold W. Attridge, "The Greek Fragments," 95–128 in vol. 1 of Bentley Layton, ed., *Nag Hammadi Codex II,2–7 Together with XIII,2*, Brit. Lib. Or. 4926(1), and P. Oxy. 1, 654, 655,* Nag Hammadi Studies 20 (Leiden: E. J. Brill, 1989). See n. 7 for Grenfell and Hunt.

7. B. P. Grenfell and A. S. Hunt, *Logia Iesou: Sayings of Our Lord* (London: Henry Frowde, 1897) 16. Now Søren Giversen, "The Palaeography of Oxyrhynchus Papyri 1 and 654–655" (paper given at the Society of Biblical Literature Annual Meeting, Boston, Mass., November 1999), suggests earlier dates for the Oxyrhynchus papyrus fragments on palaeographical grounds.

8. Hippolytus, *Refutatio omnium haeresium* 5.7.20–21; 5.8.32.

9. 1 Cor. 2:9. The translation of this and other sayings in the Gospel of Thomas is taken from Marvin Meyer, *The Gospel of Thomas: The Hidden Sayings of Jesus* (San Francisco: HarperSanFrancisco, 1992). For parallels to this saying, see Meyer, *The Gospel of Thomas,* 76; Michael E. Stone and John Strugnell, trans., *The Books of Elijah: Parts 1–2,* SBLTT 18, Pseudepigrapha 8 (Missoula, Mont.: Scholars, 1979) 41–73.

10. Helmut Koester, "History and Development of Mark's Gospel (From Mark to Secret Mark and 'Canonical' Mark)," 35–57 in Bruce Corley, ed., *Colloquy on New Testament Studies: A Time for Reappraisal and Fresh Approaches* (Macon, Ga.: Mercer University Press, 1983).

11. Note the efforts of Stevan L. Davies, *The Gospel of Thomas and Christian Wisdom* (New York: Seabury, 1983); also John Dart, *The Jesus of Heresy and History: The Discovery and Meaning of the Nag Hammadi Gnostic Library* (San Francisco: Harper & Row, 1988). Elaine H. Pagels, "Exegesis of Genesis 1 in the Gospels of Thomas and John," *JBL* 118 (1999) 481–82, suggests seeking and finding as the organizational principle upon which the Gospel of Thomas is based—on which principle I elaborate below.

12. Compare Patterson, *The Gospel of Thomas and Jesus,* 94–110.

13. For example, Bertil Gaertner, *The Theology of the Gospel of Thomas*, trans. Eric J. Sharpe (London: Collins; New York: Harper, 1961).

14. In Eusebius, *Historia Ecclesiastica*, 3.39.16.

15. On the *agrapha* see Alfred Resch, ed., *Agrapha: Aussercanonische Schriftfragmente* (2d ed., Texte und Untersuchungen zur Geschichte der altchristlichen Literatur 15,3–4; Leipzig: J. C. Hinrichs; Darmstadt: Wissenschaftliche Buchgesellschaft, 1967); Marvin Meyer, *The Unknown Sayings of Jesus* (San Francisco: HarperSanFrancisco, 1998).

16. Acts 20:35; 1 Clement 13:1–2; 46:7– 8.

17. Secret Book of James (Nag Hammadi Codex I, 2), 2, 8–16; the reference to the Hebrew letters (-*hebraiois*) occurs at 1,16.

18. Compare Geoffrey Parrinder, *Jesus in the Qur'an* (New York: Oxford University Press, 1977); Marvin Meyer, "Did Jesus Drink from a Cup? The Equipment of Jesus and His Followers in Q and al-Ghazzali," 143–56 in *From Quest to Q: Festschrift James M. Robinson*, ed. Jon Ma. Asgeirsson, Kristin de Troyer, and Marvin W. Meyer, BETL 146 (Leuven: Peeters/Leuven University Press, 1999).

19. These quotations are taken from Meyer, *The Unknown Sayings of Jesus* (San Francisco: HarperSanFrancisco, 1998) 144–56.

20. Meyer, *The Gospel of Thomas*, 10.

21. Gospel of Thomas sayings 28, 106.

22. Origen, *Contra Celsum*, 1.28; 32; also rabbinic traditions on Ben Panthera/Pantera/Pandera and Ben Stada.

23. Compare John J. Rousseau and Rami Arav, *Jesus and His World: An Archaeological and Cultural Dictionary* (Minneapolis: Fortress, 1995) 223–25.

24. Luke 2:41–52.

25. Infancy Gospel of Thomas 7:3.

26. Compare Matt. 10:37–38 (Q); Luke 14:26–27 (Q); Matt. 16:24; Mark 8:34; Luke 9:23. Other parallels are known from Gospel of Thomas saying 101; Manichaean Psalm Book 175,25–30; Liber Graduum 3.5.

27. Meyer, *The Unknown Sayings of Jesus*, 139.

28. Gospel of Thomas prologue, sayings 3, 11, 37, 50, 52, 59, 111, 114.

29. Gospel of Thomas sayings 2, 18, 24, 38, 76, 92, 94.

30. Gospel of the Hebrews 4a, 4b; Book of Thomas (Nag Hammadi Codex II, 7) 140,40–141,2; 145,8–16; Papyrus Oxyrhynchus 654.5–9.

31. Harold W. Attridge, " 'Seeking' and 'Asking' in Q, *Thomas*, and John," 295–302 in *From Quest to Q* (see n. 18).

32. Richard Valantasis, *The Gospel of Thomas*, New Testament Readings (London and New York: Routledge, 1997); compare also John Kloppenborg, *The Formation of Q: Trajectories in Ancient Wisdom Collections*, Studies in Antiquity and Christianity (Philadelphia: Fortress, 1987) 305–6, on Pythagorean sayings.

33. Valantasis, *The Gospel of Thomas*, 7.

34. Ibid., 196.

35. Compare Karen L. King, "Kingdom in the Gospel of Thomas," *Foundations and Facets Forum* 3 (1987) 48–97.

36. Gospel of Thomas saying 82. See Marvin Meyer, *Gospel of Thomas*, 99–100; Charles W. Hedrick and Paul A. Mirecki, *Gospel of the Savior: A New Ancient*

Gospel, California Classical Library (Santa Rosa, Calif.: Polebridge, 1999) 40–41 (in the Gospel of the Savior the saying ends "is far from life").

37. Compare Matt. 22:1–10 (Q); Luke 14:16–24 (Q); Matt. 21:33–41; Mark 12:1–9; Luke 20:9–16. In the parable of the vineyard (saying 65) the owner of the vineyard may be identified as "a [good] person" or "a creditor," depending on the restoration of the Coptic. In the first instance a good person may be interpreted as the victim of violent tenant farmers; in the second an abusive creditor may be understood as opposed by the victimized poor.

38. Patterson, *The Gospel of Thomas and Jesus,* 230 n. 57.

39. Saying 42 may also be translated "Be wanderers." Less likely translations include "Come into being as you pass away" and "Be Hebrews," that is, "migrants."

40. See Meyer, *The Gospel of Thomas,* 87; on the inscription from Fatehpur-Sikri, see also Meyer, *The Unknown Sayings of Jesus,* 178

41. Compare Matt. 10:8 (Q); Luke 10:8–9 (Q); 1 Cor. 10:27; Matt. 15:11; Mark 7:15.

42. Patterson, *The Gospel of Thomas and Jesus,* 68–69, 137–38, 236.

43. Oxyrhynchus Papyrus 655 col. i.1–17. Compare Matt. 6:25–33 (Q), 34; Luke 12:22–31 (Q), 32; al-Ghazali, *Revival of the Religious Sciences* 4.190: "Consider the birds: they do not sow or reap or gather into barns, yet God sustains them day by day. If, however, you say, 'But we have a bigger belly than they have,' then I say to you, consider the cattle, how God has provided their sustenance for them" (in Meyer, *The Unknown Sayings of Jesus,* 159).

44. Sayings 27, 53.

45. See Albert Schweitzer, *The Philosophy of Civilization,* trans. C. T. Campion (Buffalo: Prometheus, 1987) 307–29, on reverence for life ("Ethics consist, therefore, in my experiencing the compulsion to show to all will-to-live the same reverence as I do to my own," 309).

46. Compare Aelred Baker, "Fasting to the World," *JBL* 84 (1965) 291–94; M. Harl, "A propos des Logia de Jésus: Le sens du mot *monachos,*" *Revue des études grecques* 73 (1960) 464–74; A. F. J. Klijn, "The 'Single One' in the Gospel of Thomas," *JBL* 81 (1962) 271–78.

47. Gospel of Thomas saying 7; Howard M. Jackson, *The Lion Becomes Man: The Gnostic Leontomorphic Creator and the Platonic Tradition* (Society of Biblical Literature Dissertation Series 81; Atlanta: Scholars, 1985).

48. Sayings 4, 11, 22, 23, 48, 106.

49. See Marvin Meyer, "Making Mary Male: The Categories 'Male' and 'Female' in the Gospel of Thomas," *New Testament Studies* 31 (1985) 554–70.

50. Sirach 24:21; Odes of Solomon 30: 1, 5.

51. On some of the efforts—most likely misguided—to find a specific identification of the three sayings or words, see Meyer, *The Gospel of Thomas,* 74–75.

52. Oxyrhynchus Papyrus 1 (horiz.).23–27 (reconstruction by Harold W. Attridge); compare Gospel of Thomas saying 30.

53. Wisd. of Sol. 7:24–30; John 8:12; Rom. 11:36; 1 Cor. 8:6; Manichaean Psalm Book 54,19–30.

54. Bentley Layton, *The Gnostic Scriptures* (Garden City, N.Y.: Doubleday, 1987) 376.

55. Davies, *The Gospel of Thomas and Christian Wisdom.*

56. Layton, *The Gnostic Scriptures,* 359–79; also see Gilles Quispel, *Makarius, das Thomasevangelium und das Lied von der Perle,* Novum Testamentum, Supplement 15 (Leiden: E. J. Brill, 1967).

57. Patterson, *The Gospel of Thomas and Jesus,* 200; Ernst Haenchen, *Die Botschaft des Thomas-Evangeliums,* Theologische Bibliothek Töpelmann 6 (Berlin: Töpelmann, 1961) 39–41, 44; compare Meyer, *The Gospel of Thomas,* 89–90.

58. Michael Allen Williams, *Rethinking "Gnosticism": An Argument for Dismantling a Dubious Category* (Princeton: Princeton University Press, 1996) 51–53, 263–66.

59. James M. Robinson, "LOGOI SOPHON: On the Gattung of Q," 71–113 in James M. Robinson and Helmut Koester, *Trajectories Through Early Christianity* (Philadelphia: Fortress, 1971).

60. Schweitzer, *The Quest of the Historical Jesus,* 370–71.

61. Cited in Henry Clark, *The Ethical Mysticism of Albert Schweitzer: A Study of the Sources and Significance of Schweitzer's Philosophy of Civilization* (Boston: Beacon, 1962) 88–89 (slightly revised).

• 5 •

Eschatology, Apocalypticism, and the Historical Jesus

John Dominic Crossan

The question I ask in this essay concerns, immediately and proximately, two books at either end of the twentieth century and also, distantly but more importantly, the historical Jesus and early Christianity in that first century two thousand years ago. It is this: How do you get an absolute out of an error, an imperious command out of a mistaken message?

Preamble

For the purposes of this essay, I bracket four claims made in *The Birth of Christianity*.[1] I do not in any way diminish or deny those four claims but neither do I intend to debate them against their opposites here and now in this essay. Instead, I wish to debate inside and within rather than outside and against apocalyptic eschatology and/or apocalypticism and/or eschatology with those various terms taken as basically equivalent for the present discussion. That is, of course, *dato non concesso* all over the place. I leave aside, then, these four consecutive and linked positions.

First, I proposed that to make sense of current terminology, eschatology must be taken as a genus-level term and apocalyptic as one of its several species-level subdivisions. Thus we speak of thoroughgoing eschatology or realized eschatology. In that understanding, apocalyptic should not be privileged as if it were synonymous with eschatology but taken always as but one of its possible investments. When apocalyptic and eschatology are used as equivalent terms, a species equals its genus, an adjective equals its noun, and confusion reigns within scholarly discourse.

Second, I defined eschatology as "one of the great and fundamental options of the human spirit. It is a profoundly explicit 'No' to the profoundly implicit 'Yes' by which we usually accept life's normalcies, culture's presuppositions, and civilization's discontents. It is a basic and unusual world-negation or rejection as opposed to an equally basic but more usual world-affirmation or acceptance." You will notice, for example, how Schweitzer's peroration shifted from his usual terms, eschatological or non-eschatological, which were synonymous with apocalyptic or nonapocalyptic to different terms, namely, "world-negating" and "world-affirming."[2] I deliberately adopted those terminal and climactic expressions to interpret the meaning of "eschatological" and "non-eschatological."

Third, I understood eschatology as having two basic components. The first component was "a vision and/or program which is radical, countercultural, utopian, or this-world-negating. It presumes that there is something fundamentally wrong with the way of the world, not something that could easily be fixed, changed, or improved, but something so profoundly and radically wrong that only something profoundly and radically opposite could remedy it." The second component is that "the mandate of that vision and/or program is taken to be divine, transcendental, supernatural, that is, it does not simply derive from natural or human forces or ideas. Eschatology is, as it were, a divinely mandated utopia, a divine radicality."

Fourth, depending on why one announces that radical and cosmic "No" and how one intends to live out that "No" in a fundamentally negated world, there were various types and modes of the eschatological challenge. Those latter were species of that genus-level term, eschatology or world negation. It was also necessary, I suggested, to delineate those diverse species as clearly as possible and to distinguish them as precisely as possible.

A Tale of Two Books

The first book is the one just mentioned by Albert Schweitzer. I am not presently concerned with his criticism of previous scholarship but with his own reconstruction of the historical Jesus.

Eschatological Mistake

First, for Schweitzer, Jesus was simply wrong or even seriously deranged. Jesus was quite wrong about the imminent end of the world and was quite mistaken in his attempt to force the hand of God by going deliberately toward martyrdom in Jerusalem. This is his description of that delusion. "There is silence all around. The Baptist appears, and cries: 'Repent, for the Kingdom of Heaven is at hand.' Soon after that comes Jesus, and in the knowledge that He is the coming Son of Man lays hold of the wheel of the world to set it moving on that last revolution which is to bring all ordinary history to a close. It refuses to turn, and He throws Himself upon it. Then it does turn; and crushes Him. Instead of bringing in the eschatological conditions, He has destroyed them. The wheel rolls onward, and the mangled body of the one immeasurably great Man, who was strong enough to think of Himself as the spiritual ruler of mankind and to bend history to His purpose, is hanging upon it still. That is His victory and His reign."[3]

Eschatological Command

Second, as everyone knows, despite that understanding of Jesus, Schweitzer ended his book with this very famous peroration: "He comes to us as One unknown, without a name, as of old, by the lake-side, He came to those men who knew Him not. He speaks to us the same word: 'Follow thou me!' and sets us to the tasks which He has to fulfill for our time. He commands. And to those who obey Him, whether they be wise or simple, He will reveal Himself in the toils, the conflicts, the sufferings which they shall pass through in His fellowship, and, as an ineffable mystery, they shall learn in their own experience Who He is."[4] We cannot simply dismiss that conclusion as climactic sentimentality because of Schweitzer's own life. Jesus was wrong but, instead of leaving the Christian Church for atheism, Schweitzer left Imperial Europe for Africa. He did it, as he said, at the command of that same Jesus. I asked in *The Birth of Christianity:* "What type of eschatology is both inaccurate and imperative, both misguided and mandatory, both wrong and right at the same time?"[5]

The second and much later book has intensified that question for me. It is Dale Allison's study, *Jesus of Nazareth: Millenarian Prophet.*[6] It may never attain the classic status of its famous predecessor, but it makes exactly the same judgment about the message of Jesus. Indeed, if anything, it delivers it much more clearly, openly, and brutally. Allison makes four major points.

Apocalyptic Matrix

Allison locates what biblical scholars term apocalypticism within the wider cross-cultural phenomenon known to comparative religion as millenarianism, a phenomenon often independent of Jewish or Christian sources.[7] I agree with him, of course, on the validity of that wider matrix.

Apocalyptic Continuity

Allison uses the following general argument which, while not absolutely logical, is surely persuasively commonsensical. There was apocalypticism before Jesus in John the Baptist, there was apocalypticism after Jesus in Paul, Q, and Mark. Furthermore, we find apocalyptic warnings on Jesus' own lips all over the synoptic Gospels. It is, therefore, at least most likely that Jesus was an apocalyptic visionary, a millenarian ascetic, an eschatological prophet.[8]

Apocalyptic Language

Allison argues for apocalyptic language as primarily if not exclusively literal in its own intentionality.[9] It is accepted metaphorically or at least with increasing metaphoricity only after its literal expectations falter and fail. He considers such metaphoricity as apologetical damage control. We should, he says, accept apocalypticism literally "even if this puts us in the disagreeable company of modern fundamentalists."[10] We should not translate it meta-phorically "like others who have offered us a more theologically convenient Jesus."[11] That last statement, by the way, is one of the few cheap shots in an otherwise extremely fair book.

Apocalyptic Command

Finally, on his last pages, Allison terminates with a peroration remarkably similar to that of Schweitzer. First, he had admitted at the very start of his book that Jesus and all other millenarian prophets were essentially irrational: "Surely if Jesus was, as so many have held, an eschatological prophet who lived in the imaginative world of the apocalypses, we should not expect much consistency from him, for the *essential irrationality* of apocalyptic is manifest from the history of messianic and millenarian movements."[12] Second, he repeats that inaugural statement in concluding that Jesus was wrong: "Jesus the millenarian prophet, like all millenarian prophets, was *wrong:* reality has taken no notice of his imagination."[13] Finally, he says this: "And yet, despite everything, for those who have ears to hear, Jesus, the millenarian herald of judgment and salvation, says the only things worth saying, for *his dream is the only one worth dreaming....* If in the end there is no good God to calm this sea of troubles, to raise the dead, and to give good news to the poor, then this is indeed a tale told by an idiot, signifying nothing."[14]

The starkness of Allison's judgment is not obfuscated, as Schweitzer's so often was, by ecstatic romanticism, mystical enthusiasm, and rhetorical brilliance. Not, at least, until those final few lines. For Schweitzer, Jesus *was* wrong and deluded but his call is the only one worth following. For Allison, Jesus *was* wrong and irrational but his dream is the only one worth having. With all due respect to both writers, we have had enough of prophets who were wrong, leaders who were deluded, and dreams that were irrational in this century alone, to make such perorations too dangerous for comfort. I therefore repeat my question to those twentieth-century writers but I intend it primarily for first-century speakers: How do you get an absolute out of an error, an imperious command out of a mistaken message?

Facing the Problem

At this point I bracket completely my own four previously cited positions on eschatology to move exclusively within Allison's own position on the apocalyptic Jesus. I accept it for here and now as fully and accurately as I can. This is not some sort of devious strategy but an attempt to see what is most fundamentally at stake in our disagreement. I want to know especially how that apocalyptic tradition from the Baptist to Mark was increasingly able to convince others of its veracity and validity, was increasingly able to convert others to dream its irrational dream. How is it, in summary, that the wronger they were, the stronger they were?

Accepting Allison's position and working absolutely within it, I have the following immediate problem. He asserts very clearly and very honestly that "Jesus the millenarian prophet, like all millenarian prophets, was wrong."[15] He uses no subterfuge that, for example, by "imminent" or "within this generation" he or they meant sometime within some generation maybe even two thousand years from then. But, for Jesus-based earliest Christianity, as I said aphoristically above, the longer they were wrong, the longer they got strong. That is my problem: longer, wronger, stronger. Why? As the decades of the first hundred years passed without millenarian consummation, tiny ripples of surprise appear on the surface of the tradition, but I see no evidence of profound doubt or massive loss of faith. I do not find what I might have expected: profound defensive strategies, desperate explanatory interpretations but, despite them, slow and steady attrition in faith. I would have expected, in other words, a steadily decreasing number of converts and communities and I find instead a steadily increasing number of both converts and communities.

I am not making any cryptic claim for the uniqueness of either historical Jesus or earliest Christianity. A careful study of Allison's cross-cultural millenarian parallels might indicate why, how, where, and when such movements survive, grow, and eventually develop into worldwide religions. Lacking that for the moment, I simply note that because of or despite being "wrong," Jesus-based earliest Christianity was increasingly successful in its missionary movement. Taking Allison's position seriously and arguing intrinsically with it precludes certain easy answers.

First, I do not suggest that the apocalyptic historical Jesus was millenarian and therefore wrong but that, having recognized the problem, earliest Christianity changed, became nonapocalyptic, and was right. That would deny his argument for fundamental apocalyptic continuity across most of Christianity's first century. Second, respecting his literal apocalyptic language claims, I do not suggest that metaphorical continuity solves the problem. Besides, even or especially a metaphor must be a metaphor for something. So we would still have to ask, what is that something? Finally, I cannot simply say that Jesus' resurrection explains it all, that Jesus' resurrection is what made, and even alone what made, Christianity a successful missionary religion. In *Jesus and the Victory of God,* for example, Tom Wright makes that claim by answering his own question "Why then did people go on talking about Jesus of Nazareth, except as a remarkable but tragic memory?" by saying that "Jesus was raised from the dead."[16] Allison never makes that claim and, as far as I can see, he would not and could not do so. One reason is that, having said that Jesus and all other millenarian prophets were wrong (so far), he could hardly claim that God raised Jesus from the dead to prove he alone was transcendentally wrong. Another and less facetious reason is this: resurrection is part and parcel of apocalypticism and stands or falls with it. Wrong on apocalyptic vision, wrong on resurrection faith.

Wrong, at least, on what those earliest Christians meant by both of those phenomena. Everything in 1 Corinthians 15 and the gospels' final chapters could still be taken literally (if one wished), but they would be describing Elijah-like exaltation, a very special privilege for Jesus himself but not the start of the general resurrection and the end of the world. You might, then, for example, still have Philippians 2:6–11, but that is sublime exaltation, not necessarily apocalyptic resurrection. If Jesus' announcement of apocalyptic consummation was wrong, then earliest Christianity's announcement of Jesus' resurrection was likewise wrong. Indeed, since resurrection could only intensify apocalyptic expectation (the general resurrection had actually begun!), it could but increase that wrongness. I do not use, in honor of Allison's own honesty, the solution that all of this was not about an imminent moment in the first century but about an imminent moment in the twenty-first century. In any case, resurrection cannot compensate for being wrong when it itself is included in that wrongness.

A Preliminary Example

Before proceeding, I cite here a single apocalypse as an example of what is under discussion. I use it because Allison did. I use it because of its date. The unified book of Sibylline Oracles 1–2 "consists of an original Jewish oracle and an extensive Christian redaction" and "the original Jewish oracle probably carried its review of history no later than the time of Augustus, and so the dating suggested by Kurfess [*ZNW* 40 (1941) 151–65], about the turn of the era, is most likely correct."[17] I use it because it is so complete, with very full details and very many possible elements included. I ask you to keep it at the back of your mind as I continue.

I distinguish, for my later purpose, between what I term material and social elements in this (or any other) apocalypse. By material elements I intend both heavenly and earthly events. Heavenly material events involve a darkened sun, lightless moon, stars falling. By earthly material events I intend catastrophe and cataclysm as well as extraordinary fertility and laborless prosperity. Those, of course, slide rather easily into social events. By social events I intend punishments for evil and rewards for good, equality, justice, and peace for all. My reason for those somewhat unnecessary distinctions will be clear under my second distinction (Material and Social Apocalypse) below.

For example, in the apocalyptic consummation of Sibylline Oracles 2, there are heavenly material events: "the heavenly luminaries will crash together" and "all the stars will fall together from heaven on the sea" (2:200–2). There are also earthly material events (sliding into social ones): there is "life without care," in "three springs of wine, honey, and milk," on an earth that "will then bear more abundant fruits spontaneously," and in a world with "no spring, no summer, no winter, no autumn" (2:316, 318, 321–22, 328). But there are also these very emphasized social events.

After the punishment of the unjust, this is the reward of those who "were concerned with justice and noble deeds" (2:319–20, 321–24):

The earth will belong equally to all, undivided by walls or fences....
Lives will be in common and wealth will have no division.
For there will be no poor man there, no rich, and no tyrant, no slave.
Further, no one will be either great or small anymore.
No kings, no leaders. All will be on a par together.

John Collins, whose translation I am gratefully using, notes that "most scholars incline to the opinion that such passages were taken over as part of the Jewish original" into their later Christian adaptation and usage.[18] Here is how that apocalyptic vision concludes (2:330–35):

To these pious ones imperishable God, the universal ruler,
will also give another thing.
Whenever they ask the imperishable God
to save men from the raging fire and deathless gnashing
he will grant it, and he will do this.
For he will pick them out again from the undying fire
and set them elsewhere and send them on account of his own people.

Collins footnotes that one Christian-edited manuscript family inserted a refutation of that gracious conclusion: "Plainly false. For the fire which tortures the condemned will never cease. Even I would pray that this be so, though I am marked with very great scars of faults, which have need of very great mercy. But let babbling Origen be ashamed of saying that there is a limit to punishment."[19] A Christian scribe rejects the mercy of the Jewish original.

Five Necessary Distinctions

My challenge is twofold in content and also twofold in claim. The content challenge is to make the following five distinctions and then to choose the second option in each case. The claim challenge is that we must do that as credible historians and/or as ethical humans. I think that those suggested distinctions and chosen options are necessary to explain what actually happened across that first Christian century among at least some Christians—for example, the inclusion of pagans and Jews in equal fellowship, the consistent refusal of violent resistance even when faced with martyrdom, and the continuation of apocalyptic assertion despite, as we might think, the failure of apocalyptic consummation. I also think that those distinctions and options are moral imperatives. We are now finally out of a terrible century, a century of world wide killing fields, a century worse by execution if not by intention than any in our past. At such a moment, our very humanity demands that we reject definitively the lure of a violent ultimacy, a violent transcendence, or a violent God. If, on the other hand, we sincerely believe in a violent God, we must surely follow openly the advice of Mrs. Job: Curse God and die.

First Distinction: Destructive or Transformative Apocalypse

Allison and I are in complete and actual agreement (*dato et concesso*) on the necessary and very important distinction between divine destruction of the material earth (creation repealed) and divine transformation of the unjust world (evil repulsed). Millenarianists or apocalypticists usually want only the latter event and, even if the former is ever envisaged, it is only as a subordinate part or necessary concomitant to that latter event. In any case, it is that latter event which is primarily or exclusively in focus. (I abstract here from contemporary apocalyptic nihilism or modern terroristic millenarianism where cosmic destruction may be exactly and exclusively in mind.) Cosmic catastrophe or material cataclysm, no matter how terrible or total, is not the same as millenarian consummation. I agree with Allison, therefore, that "most millenarian movements, whether ancient, medieval, or modern, have expected not the utter destruction and replacement of this world but rather a revolutionary change" and, so, for Jesus, " 'Heaven on earth,' we might say."[20] That is exactly the same phrase I used for apocalypticism in *The Historical Jesus:* "The everlasting Kingdom is apocalyptic, however, not in the sense of a destroyed earth and an evacuation heavenward for the elect, but rather of something like a heaven on earth."[21] It is, I think, necessary to emphasize this both in current scholarship and in contemporary popularization much more now than ever before. Hollywood's *Armageddon* is not the Bible's Armageddon. Hollywood's *Deep Impact* is not the Bible's divine justice. I do not think that we scholars, even or especially in our debates on an apocalyptic versus a nonapocalyptic Jesus, have insisted enough on that fundamental distinction between an ending of material earth and an ending of human injustice, between the amorality and secularity of current millenarianism and the morality and divinity of ancient millenarianism. But, granted our agreement on that understanding of millenarian or apocalyptic hope, I want to press Allison to probe more deeply the lineaments of such revolutionary changes promising a heaven on earth. I propose, therefore, a second distinction, but now within that latter understanding of transformative apocalypse as the elimination of earthly injustice, as the process of bringing the world to its knees before God.

Second Distinction: Material or Social Apocalypse

I fine-focus here on Allison's argument that apocalyptic language is to be taken literally and not metaphorically. Two asides. One: is he just being therapeutically provocative here? Was Virgil's *Fourth Eclogue* being literal with an imminent golden age not needing dye-works as lambs would be born already hued to purple, saffron, and scarlet? Two: even if that is metaphorical, one must still ask, metaphorical of what? Is it of imperial peace established by the Roman God of power or of cosmic equality established by the Jewish God of justice?

My point here is not to argue for metaphoricity but, working within Allison's own argument, to consider ancient priorities in such an allegedly literal totality. I am avoiding a division in apocalyptic language between what is literal and what is metaphorical by asking a different question. Within that language, what is necessary, nonnegotiable, and essential; what is unnecessary, negotiable, and unessential? I am raising a very general question about Jewish and/or Christian apocalypticism within cross-cultural millenarianism. I am afraid that a debate on what is metaphorical and what is literal in apocalyptic language may take us down a blind alley and miss more fundamental points worthier of debate.

Allison mentions celestial inversions such as darkened sun, shrouded moon, falling stars, and shaken celestial powers. He concludes that "maybe Mk 13:24 should be taken to mean what it says, just like *Sib. Or.* 2:200–2."[22] But why would anyone have wanted that celestial inversion effect in which the unusual arrival of darkness replaced the usual normalcy of light unless it was accompanied by a terrestrial inversion effect in which the unusual arrival of justice replaced the usual normalcy of injustice? Granted, for here and now, that one is neither metaphorical nor metonymical of the other, what about priorities within that double inversion? On the one hand, would it be apocalyptically adequate to get justice without darkness? On the other, would it be apocalyptically adequate to get darkness without justice? If millenarians could not have both, which would they have chosen? What was, if one had to choose, essential, what unessential?

Recall that distinction of material and social elements from above. Granted that millenarians thought of them as one undifferentiated package, what would they say if confronted with this choice? You can have the social without the material or you can have the material without the social elements? They would surely have opted for social above all others and that has to do with priority of the social even if not the metaphoricity of the material.

In terms of Sibylline Oracles 2, what if ancients, or moderns, had to make this choice. Which do you want: the no-fences world without the no-stars or the no-stars without the no-fences world? Which do you want: the all-on-a-par world without the abundant-fruits-spontaneously or the abundant-fruits-spontaneously without the all-on-a-par world? Granted, they might like it all as a total package deal but, absent any metaphoricity, were all apocalyptic details on the same level of importance or were there clear priorities in everyone's mind?

I think that must be emphasized even if one argues, as Allison does, that all apocalypticism is more or less equally literal. My counter is that, whether those material elements were metaphors, metonyms, enthusiastic hyperboles, exaggerated emphases, or literal expectations, they were nothing without the social elements. But, on the other hand, those social elements alone and by themselves could have been millennium enough, apocalypse now. My next two distinctions, therefore, focus more acutely on those social elements in terms of the just and righteous as against the unjust and unrighteous.

Third Distinction: Primary or Secondary Apocalypse

This distinction occurred to me in thinking about an article by John Kloppenborg, but he should not be held responsible for my reformulation and may not even agree with its content. He distinguished between apocalyptic eschatology and what he termed symbolic eschatology. His point was that while "it is difficult to miss the pervasive eschatological tenor" of even the sapiential elements in the Q Gospel, "it is another question whether the term apocalyptic is an accurate characterization for the redeployment of these wisdom materials."[23] In other words, "it is important to ask whether the presence of an eschatological horizon justifies the label 'apocalyptic.'"[24] He concluded that the Q Gospel used apocalyptic language "creatively to dramatize the transfiguration of the present: apocalyptic symbols lend their force both negatively, by the subverting of confidence in the everydayness of existence, and positively, by buttressing a vision of rich and empowered existence based on the instruction of Jesus."[25] That instruction (better, for me, that lifestyle) was "Q's advocacy of an ethic characterized by nonviolence (Q 6:27–28), refusal to participate in normative means of preserving honor through resort to courts or to retaliation (Q 6:29), and the idealization of poverty (6:20b; 12:33–34; 16:13), detachment (14:26–27), and homelessness (9:57–58; 10:4–10)."[26]

I rephrase and generalize Kloppenborg's distinction as follows, with appropriate apologies to its author. Primary apocalypticism or millenarianism demands immediate actions or extraordinary ethics because of the expectation of imminent consummation. You must give everything away, cease all family relations, retire to the desert, and wait in prayer and fasting for the coming end. The ethical slogan, in other words, is *interim,* and those ethics may be sensible only as such. Maybe they might survive being wrong but their future, granted failure, is very precarious. Secondary apocalypticism or millenarianism demands immediate actions or extraordinary ethics because of the permanent character and abiding revelation of God. This is how one should be living and what one should be doing here and now in any case and apocalyptic imminence is sanction rather than cause. This is what God demands and you better pay attention because the end is near. That is what Kloppenborg sees in the Q Gospel. I too see it there and also in the Didache. I think that Didache 16, whether imminent or distant, whether always expected or quietly postponed, is the sanction rather than the basis for Didache 1–15. The failure of Didache 16 to happen will not necessarily destroy that community because its truth is experienced in the success of its lifestyle in imitation of the *tropoi* of the Lord (Jesus/God). The ethical slogan there is *semper interim.*

Compare the following two general admonitions and focus, for example, on their divergent advice about an unmarried virgin woman. First, as an example of primary apocalypticism, think of Paul's advice, not demand, about marriage in 1 Corinthians 7, an advice perfectly reasonable in terms of the approaching end. Celibacy is better, wiser, more appropriate: "I wish that all were as I myself am.... I think that, in view of the impending crisis, it is well for you [virgins] to remain as you are.... [T]he appointed time has grown short; from now on, let even those who have wives be as though they had none... and those who deal with the world as though they had no dealings with it. For the present form of this world is passing away" (7:7, 26, 29, 31). Second, as a counterexample of secondary apocalypticism, think about this demand, not advice, from the *Damascus Document:* "And this is the rule of the Many, to provide for all their needs: the salary of two days each month at least. They shall place it in the hand of the Inspector and of the judges. From it they shall give to the orphans and with it they shall strengthen the hand of the needy and the poor, and to the elder who [is dy]ing, and to the vagabond, and to the prisoner of a foreign people, and to the girl who has no protector, and to the unma[rried woman] who has no suitor; and for all the works of the company, and [the house of the company shall not be deprived of its means]" (CD-A, col. XIV).[27]

I confess for myself, by the way, that falling stars, laborless fertility, and the panoply of most apocalyptic scenarios are far easier to imagine or expect than to imagine, let alone expect, a nonviolent world or a nonviolent God. That absolutely staggers my imagination. I also confess that sustained and nonviolent resistance to the cosmic normalcy of structural injustice strikes me as impossible without transcendental sources for such conviction, courage, and continuance.

I do not find that secondary apocalypticism usually insists on basic ethics because of the impending consummation, insisting, for example, that you'd better observe the Ten Commandments because of imminent judgment. It is usually much more radical ethics that is in question. That is not, however, because they are special, extraordinary, interim ethics. It is because the very awareness of distributive injustice, systemic evil, and normal violence that generates an opposing hope for imminent divine justice, goodness, and nonviolence so emphasizes the character of God that participation, imitation, and union with such a God necessitates the most radical morality imaginable.

Fourth Distinction: Negative or Positive Apocalypse

I also took this distinction from another scholar and, although I am not reformulating or renaming it as I did the preceding one, its author should not be held responsible for my present use. Paula Fredriksen asked this question:

"The twelve tribes are restored, the people gathered back to the Land, the Temple and Jerusalem are renewed and made splendid, the Davidic monarch restored: God's Kingdom is established. What place, if any, do Gentiles have in such a kingdom?" She responds: "We can cluster the material around two poles. At the negative extreme, the nations are destroyed, defeated, or in some way subjected to Israel.... At the positive extreme, the nations participate in Israel's redemption. The nations will stream to Jerusalem and worship the God of Jacob together with Israel."[28] Both results are present side by side in Micah, for example. The negative pole is in 5:15 as God warns that "in anger and wrath I will execute vengeance on the nations that did not obey." The positive pole is in 4:1–4. "In days to come the mountain of the Lord's house shall be established as the highest of the mountains, and shall be raised up above the hills. Peoples shall stream to it, and many nations shall come and say: 'Come, let us go up to the mountain of the LORD, to the house of the God of Jacob; that he may teach us his ways and that we may walk in his paths.' For out of Zion shall go forth instruction, and the word of the LORD from Jerusalem. He shall judge between many peoples, and shall arbitrate between strong nations far away; they shall beat their swords into plowshares, and their spears into pruning hooks; nation shall not lift up sword against nation, neither shall they learn war any more; but they shall all sit under their own vines and under their own fig trees, and no one shall make them afraid; for the mouth of the LORD of hosts has spoken."

First, Gentiles are not exterminated because they are Gentiles but because Gentiles had increasingly oppressed Israel ever since she became a colony of successive imperial conquerors. Second, they are not converted to become ethnically Jews but, while remaining Gentiles (for example, males would not be circumcised), they are converted to the justice and righteousness, morality and ethics of the Jewish God. I agree with Fredriksen on that last point. "Eschatological Gentiles... those who would gain admission to the Kingdom once it was established, would enter as Gentiles. They would worship and eat together with Israel, in Jerusalem, at the Temple. The God they worship, the God of Israel, will have redeemed them from the error of idolatry: he will have saved them—to phrase this in slightly different idiom—graciously, apart from the works of the Law."[29] That choice between, in Fredriksen's terms, negative or positive extremes, is also, in my terms, the choice between human extermination or human conversion, between divine vengeance or divine justice and, ultimately, between transcendental violence or transcendental nonviolence. It is a question whether God's final solution of evil is the genocidal slaughter of all evil-doers. It is a question about transcendental eth(n)ic cleansing. It is a question for both Jews and Christians.

Fifth Distinction: Violent or Nonviolent Apocalypse

This is actually not just one more distinction but is, for me, a basis, summary, and climax of those preceding four ones. Was apocalyptic consummation as allegedly imagined by both the historical Jesus and early Christianity one of violent vengeance or one of nonviolent justice? I reject absolutely any hint that the Old Testament has a God of vengeance and the New Testament has a God of love. That is simply untrue. There is, however, a dialectic of vengeance and justice running across both Testaments from one end to the other. What do our early Christian texts do with that ambivalence: Do they equate them, succeed them, or choose one over the other?

Options. First, I find an equation of nonviolence and violence, vengeance and justice, in the last book of the Christian Bible. In Revelation 14:19–20 "... the angel swung his sickle over the earth and gathered the vintage of the earth, and he threw it into the great wine press of the wrath of God. And the wine press was trodden outside the city, and blood flowed from the wine press, as high as a horse's bridle, for a distance of about two hundred miles." I take that to be a description of violence rather than of nonviolence, and I presume that here, vengeance and justice are simply equated. In any case, it is the selection of violence rather than nonviolence as the final solution to evil and injustice.

Second, I find a succession of those two reactions in Paul's letter to the Romans, first justice but then vengeance. He says in Romans 12:14–21, "Bless those who persecute you; bless and do not curse them.... Do not repay anyone evil for evil.... [N]ever avenge yourselves, but leave room for the wrath of God; for it is written, 'Vengeance is mine, I will repay, says the Lord.' No [as the Old Testament's Proverbs 25:21 says], 'if your enemies are hungry, feed them; if they are thirsty, give them something to drink; for by doing this you will heap burning coals on their heads.' Do not be overcome by evil, but overcome evil with good." I read that as saying: take no vengeance now, God will do a much better job of it later on. And it is not at all clear what "coals of fire" mean. Does the metaphor mean your nonviolent goodness will vastly increase their future punishment or it will convert them from their violent evil? In any case, succession would mean that nonviolence is offered first and, thereafter, for those who refuse it, only violence is left.

Third, I find a selection, a choice of nonviolence over violence, of justice (slow, merciful, nonviolent) over vengeance (swift, merciless, violent) as another solution to that dichotomy. I understand this to mean nonviolent resistance to injustice which is undertaken not as a political tactic or a safer strategy, but in imitation of and union with God's own character.

Examples. There is, for example, as suggested in *The Birth of Christianity,* a radical mini-catechism found independently in both the Q Gospel at Matthew 5:39–48; 7:12 = Luke 6:27–36 and in the Didache at 1:2–5. I understand that as a nonviolent interpretation of the Golden Rule (since you do not want to be attacked, do not attack back even to defend yourself), adopted in imitation of God, and derived by those texts from a very early written source.[30] There is another example in that highly polemical and completely unhistorical scene from the *Clementine Recognitions* 1.71.1–2 when "a certain hostile man," presumably Paul, has just killed James of Jerusalem. The Latin text reads as follows, with the Syriac very similar, "But our colleagues lifted him up, for they were both more in number and greater in strength than the others. But because of their fear of God, they allowed themselves to be slain by the few rather than slay others."[31] Finally, I do not know a single early Christian text that suggests violent resistance even to protect oneself, one's family, or one's community from martyrdom.

Parallels. I emphatically do not suggest that the historical Jesus invented this position of nonviolent resistance to structural injustice even unto martyrdom. I already see it clearly present in two major collective incidents, one from a few years before his death, the other from a few years afterwards, incidents recorded by both Philo and Josephus.[32]

The first incident may date to 26–27 C.E., on the presumption that it would have happened very early in Pilate's administration (*Jewish War* 2.169–74 = *Jewish Antiquities* 18.55–59). His troops carried standards with images of Caesar into Jerusalem. The result was that "the indignation of the townspeople stirred the country-folk, who flocked together in crowds. Hastening after Pilate to Caesarea, the Jews implored him to remove the standards from Jerusalem and to uphold the laws of their ancestors. When Pilate refused, they fell prostrate around his house and for five whole days and nights remained motionless in that position" (2.170–71 = 18.57). Pilate eventually surrounded them with armed soldiers and warned them to submit. "Thereupon the Jews, *as by concerted action*, flung themselves in a body on the ground, extended their necks, and exclaimed that they were ready rather to die than to transgress the law. Overcome with astonishment at such intense religious zeal, Pilate gave orders for the immediate removal of the standards from Jerusalem" (2.174 = 18.59, italics added). I consider it most likely that this is the same incident narrated in Philo, *On the Embassy to Gaius* 299–305. Apart from minor differences, the major one is that instead of popular nonviolent protest backed up by a willingness for mass martyrdom he has "the people putting forward the four sons of the king . . . his other descendants, and those magistrates who were among them at the time" to entreat Pilate. From that start to the concluding reprimand of Tiberius, Philo is simply adapting the case of Pilate, the Jews of Jerusalem, and Tiberius (positively) to his own situation involving Flaccus, the Jews of Alexandria, and Caligula (negatively).

The second incident dates to Caligula's attempt to put his statue in the Temple of Jerusalem (*Jewish War* 2.185–203 = *Jewish Antiquities* 18.261–309). As Petronius comes south from Antioch a popular nonviolent protest greets him at Ptolemais ("many tens of thousands of Jews" in 18.263) and Tiberias ("many tens of thousands" in 18.270). Their nonviolence is emphasized as "the Jews assembled with their wives and children" (2.192) and assured him that "if he wished to set up these statues, he must first sacrifice the entire Jewish nation; and that they presented themselves, their wives and their children, ready for the slaughter" (2.197). The other version echoes the Pilate situation as "falling on their faces and baring their throats, they declared that they were ready to be slain" (18.271). The people would not give in but Petronius recognized "that the country was in danger of remaining unsown—for it was seed-time and the people had spent fifty days idly waiting upon him" (2.200), so he relented and returned to Antioch with his legions. That nonviolent resistance is backed up not only with a willingness for martyrdom but with, in effect, an agricultural strike.

Philo recounts this same incident in his work, *On the Embassy to Gaius* 203–336. I leave aside differences between his account and that of Josephus, differences such as the role of Herod Agrippa I or the fact that an agricultural strike at sowing time becomes an arson danger at reaping time. What is more significant is that, if anything, Philo emphasizes even more than does Josephus both the nonviolence of the resistance and the willingness for martyrdom. Here are the key sentences in that portion of his account (225, 227, 229, 233, italics added):

> But when the inhabitants of the holy city and of all the region round about heard of the design which was in agitation, they all arrayed themselves together *as if at a concerted signal,* their common misery having given them the word, and went forth in a body, and leaving their cities and their villages and their houses empty, they hastened with one accord into Phoenicia, for Petronius happened to be in that country at the moment. . . . And the multitude was divided into six companies, one of old men, one of young men, one of boys; and again in their turn one band of aged matrons, one of women in the prime of life, and one of virgins. . . . "We are, as you see, without any arms . . . [and we are] offering our bodies freely an easy aim to any one who desires to put us to death. We have brought unto you our wives, and our children, and our whole families, and in your person we will prostrate ourselves before Gaius, having left not one single person at home, that you may either preserve us all, or destroy us all together by one general and complete destruction. . . . And if we cannot prevail with you in this, then we offer up ourselves for destruction, that we may not live to behold a calamity more terrible and grievous than death. . . . We willingly and readily submit ourselves to be put to death."

That long citation underlines its importance for my argument. If only Josephus described such nonviolent resistance backed by a willingness for martyrdom, it might be dismissed as propaganda, as his wish for what might have been in the past or his example of what should be for the future. But, in this case at least, Philo agrees with Josephus and, even allowing for rhetorical transports, they agree on the major points.

Leaders? In citing those cases concerning Pilate and Petronius, I insist on one element. Such large-scale public demonstrations involved carefully controlled nonviolent protest and carefully prepared willingness for martyrdom. They therefore involved theoretical plans, practical controls, permanent leaders, and consistent managers. They did not simply happen ("as if at a concerted signal," say Josephus and Philo). Who organized those protests? Who exercised crowd-control on those resisters? The following is my best guess but, if it is not acceptable, the question still stands. Who invented, organized, and controlled these public demonstrations of nonviolent resistance and protest?

First, Steve Mason has argued that "Josephus's tendency is to *lament* the popularity and influence of the Pharisees. But this ongoing lament over Pharisaic predominance would be unnecessary—indeed it would make no sense—if the Pharisees did not hold a dominant position in pre-70 Palestine. Josephus has no discernible reason to invent this popularity, since he regarded it as an unpleasant fact of life." He concludes that in pre-70 Palestine "the Pharisees enjoyed the steady and eager support of the ordinary people."[33] Second, Tom Wright has made the following three points: (1) The pre-70 Pharisees were not just involved in exegetico-legal debates but also in politico-religious activities, that is, their piety and politics were always but two sides of the same coin. (2) The Shammaites, ascendant before 70, involved a "severe" and zealous thrust toward revolution. (3) The opposite position, ascendant after 70, "the 'live and let live' party were the 'lenient' Hillelites."[34] But, if Wright is correct about the Shammaites, the religio-political position of the Hillelites must surely have been as divinely interpreted and theologically profound as was that of their opponents. This, then, is my suggestion. If, the Shammaites proposed violent resistance in the name of God, the Hillelites proposed nonviolent resistance in the name of that same God. It was, in other words, the Hillelites who invented, organized, controlled, and led those demonstrations with mass martyrdom as their ultimate fallback position.

Objections. There are three objections to that distinction between violent and nonviolent apocalypse and I consider them here in order of increasing importance.

The first objection claims that any talk of nonviolent resistance against distributive injustice or nonviolent protest against systemic evil or nonviolent demonstration against imperial normalcy is simply an invalid retrojection of Gandhi and King from this century back into the first century. But against the charge of anachronism, I counter with the charge of condescension. We have not quite invented everything in the twentieth century. The Jewish homeland invented quite a few extremely creative responses to Greek cultural internationalism and Roman military imperialism in that first century. Think of the Sicarii as one example from the other end of the religio-political spectrum. First, they invented not just conspiratorial assassination but urban terrorism. Not only did they kill high-placed Jewish collaborators with Roman rule, they did it surreptitiously in the midst of urban crowds, so that "the panic created was more alarming than the calamity itself" (*Jewish War* 2.256; see also *Jewish Antiquities* 7.254–55). Second, before media coverage was available, "the festivals were their special seasons" not only for protection within the crowds but also for the maximum public awareness of their activities (*Jewish War* 2.255). Third, they invented kidnapping for prisoner-exchange purposes: "[they] kidnapped the secretary of the captain [of the Temple] Eleazar—he was the son of Ananias the high priest—and led him off in bonds. They then sent to Ananias saying that they would release the secretary to him if he would induce Albinus to release ten of their number who had been taken prisoner" (*Jewish Antiquities* 20.208–9). Fourth, that initial success led to the inevitable result of "greater troubles" as the Sicarii continued regular high-profile kidnappings for successive prisoner releases (*Jewish Antiquities* 20.210). Would we have imagined those tactics in the first-century Jewish homeland without Josephus's precise descriptions? None of that proves Hillelite-led nonviolent resistance backed by martyrdom. It just warns us that we did not invent everything either good or bad in this century.

The second objection claims that not all early Christians accepted a posture of nonviolence especially when under direct aggression. Notice, however, that in the following texts those who disagree are disagreeing precisely with such a posture. In other words, disagreement over nonviolence by some Christians proves that posture's presence for other Christians. I consider this objection under two rubrics, the staff and the sword.

Staff. There is a record of Jesus sending out his companions to live and act as he did in both the Q Gospel and in Mark 6:6b–13. In accepting those twin sources, Matthew conflates them into 10:1, 7–11, 14 but Luke keeps them relatively separate in his 9:1–6 (from Mark) and 10:1–11 (from the Q Gospel). One of their and our major problems in following both is that, as best we can reconstruct it, the Q Gospel had a list made up consistently of prohibitions (*no to*: purse, bag, sandals, staff) but Mark had two exceptions to such a list (*no to*: bread, bag, money, tunics; *yes to*: sandals, staff). These are the texts in question (watch italics):

Q Gospel (from Luke 10:4): Carry no purse, no bag, no sandals; and greet no one on the road.

Mark 6:8: He ordered them to take nothing for their journey *except a staff*; no bread, no bag, no money in their belts; but to wear sandals and not to put on two tunics.

Luke 9:3 (from Mark + Q Gospel): He said to them, "Take nothing for your journey, *no staff*, nor bag, nor bread, nor money—not even an extra tunic.

Matt. 10:9–10a (from Mark + Q Gospel): Take *no* gold, or silver, or copper in your belts, no bag for your journey, or two tunics, or sandals, or a *staff.*

Notice that in combining their twin sources both Matthew and Luke, independently of one another, allow the Q Gospel's prohibition of sandals and staff to override Mark's permission. I presume that the sequence there was *no/yes* rather than *yes/no* since permission for two such standard items as sandals and staff would hardly have been necessary if their prohibition had not come first. The staff was the basic and ubiquitous defensive weapon against dogs and thieves and one would not have been expected to travel anywhere without it. Even if one were guaranteed food and lodging on the way, the staff was minimal defensive equipment. Recall, for example, what Josephus says about communal hospitality for Essene travelers: "Consequently, they carry nothing whatever with them on their journeys, except arms as a protection against brigands" (*Jewish War* 2.125). I consider, therefore, that the change from prohibited staff in the Q Gospel to permitted staff in Mark is a change from absolutely no protection to normally basic protection, from absolute nonviolence to minimal defensive violence.

Sword. This is even more complicated than the preceding example. First, notice the way Luke mentioned only three prohibitions (omitting staff) in giving his version of the Q Gospel in 10:4 and how he alone has Jesus revoke those prohibitions on the night of his arrest:

Luke 22:35–38: He said to them, "When I sent you out without a purse, bag, or sandals, did you lack anything?" They said, "No, not a thing." He said to them, "But now, the one who has a purse must take it, and likewise a bag. And the one who has no sword must sell his cloak and buy one. For I tell you, this scripture must be fulfilled in me, 'And he was counted among the lawless'; and indeed what is written about me is being fulfilled." They said, "Lord, look, here are two swords." He replied, "It is enough."

I do not read that as an historical incident from the life of Jesus and neither do I take it as irony or sarcasm on the part of Luke. He is literally negating those earlier "mission" prohibitions and he gives no indication that, while the first half of that conversation is to be taken literally, the latter half is to be taken ironically (swords are impossible!) or metaphorically (swords are spiritual!). I read that unit as Luke's permission for the defensive sword from now on. In any case, no matter how I take it, and no matter whether Luke is affirming or denying its validity, somebody is proposing it and that is what is behind that unit.

That text in Luke seems intended as a prologue to what happens later that same night. A rather laconic comment in Mark begets a stream of tradition that is extremely difficult to determine. Is the defensive sword forbidden in this one case but allowed in other cases? Is it always forbidden and, if so, why? Here are the texts and notice their differences:

Mark 14:47: But one of those who stood near drew his sword and struck the slave of the high priest, cutting off his ear.

Matthew 26:51–54: Suddenly, one of those with Jesus put his hand on his sword, drew it, and struck the slave of the high priest, cutting off his ear. Then Jesus said to him, "Put your sword back into its place; for all who take the sword will perish by the sword. Do you think that I cannot appeal to my Father, and he will at once send me more than twelve legions of angels? But how then would the scriptures be fulfilled, which say it must happen in this way?"

Luke 22:49–51: When those who were around him saw what was coming, they asked, "Lord, should we strike with the sword?" Then one of them struck the slave of the high priest and cut off his right ear. But Jesus said, "No more of this!" And he touched his ear and healed him.

John 18:10–11: Then Simon Peter, who had a sword, drew it, struck the high priest's slave, and cut off his right ear. The slave's name was Malchus. Jesus said to Peter, "Put your sword back into its sheath. Am I not to drink the cup that the Father has given me?"

Once again, I do not read those texts as historical records and, by the way, John's inclusion of names does not impress me at all. Mark has no judgment on the event. All the rest offer negative judgments on it but from different angles. Only Matthew offers a universal one and it is almost more humanly practical than divinely theoretical. I take only one relatively secure conclusion from those texts. Behind them, there must be some sort of discussion about the defensive sword. To use or not to use? Ever or never?

In summary, then, those somewhat cryptic discussions of staff or no staff and sword or no sword indicate for me that the positions of defensive nonviolence or defensive violence were both present in early Christianity. But, as far as I can see, no-staff preceded staff, no-sword preceded sword, and those earlier and continuing positions had to be repealed by later and opposing ones.

The third objection is much more significant and it may even negate everything proposed in this fifth distinction. Is the very idea of end a violent idea? Even if one does not imagine divine or human eth(n)ic cleansing, is the very presumption of ending itself a violent concept, hope, wish, or plan? On the one hand, how can we not at least hope that evil and injustice will somehow and sometime be ended and justice and peace reign upon a transformed earth? On the other hand, is that simply our own way projected irrelevantly onto our own God? I first thought about this in considering the title of Tom

Wright's book *Jesus and the Victory of God*. Of course we all want the ultimate victory of good over evil, the final triumph of justice over injustice. But
what if God has already settled for a draw? And what if, far from achieving
that draw, we are losing out to evil and injustice not least because we are
imaging an ending or a victory already infected by their violence. Some of
us imagine heaven and hell as future locations, in the next life, somewhere
above. Others, myself included, see them as present options, in this life,
here below. After that last century in which we enthusiastically developed
and populated hell, does not a draw with heaven seem even beyond our
wildest dreams, our fondest hopes?

Conclusion

I have taken Allison here as a specific representative for all those who
interpret the historical Jesus and/or early Christianity in an eschatological-
as-apocalyptic understanding. He himself takes Jesus and early Christianity
in apocalyptic continuity within the matrix of millenarian expectation or eschatological hope. He says, and I am grateful for his honesty and accuracy,
that, like all such prophets, they were not only "wrong" but "essentially
irrational."[35] Granted that position, he must explain why, even within the
period of that irrational error, their message and mission did not slowly
decline and steadily disappear. My suggestion, working within his own thesis, postulates the necessity of qualifying their eschatological/apocalyptic/
millenarian expectation not only as transformative rather than destructive
(we agree there), but also as social rather than material, as secondary rather
than primary, as positive rather than negative, and, above all else, as nonviolent rather than violent. There are fleeting, all too fleeting, hints of those
latter distinctions in his text. For example, he asks: "Did [Jesus] live with
the expectation that not just dispersed Israel but righteous Gentiles would
go up to Zion," but he declines "to fill out the details of Jesus' eschatological vision."[36] But, maybe, God is in the details, the end is about means. Or
again, but only in a footnote, he notes that "Jesus seems to have muted the
element of vengeance in his eschatological language."[37] I find that terribly
weak, especially in terms of, first, his proposed apocalyptic continuity and,
second, the earliest and pre-Pauline attitude of Jesus' companions to gentile
converts.

It is necessary, I suggest, to desimplify the current easy confrontation of
apocalyptic versus nonapocalyptic Jesus. In my own case, for instance, an
apocalyptic Jesus and/or earliest Christianity where the emphasis is on transformative, social, secondary, positive, and nonviolent apocalyptic rather
than on destructive, material, primary, negative, and violent apocalyptic is
so close to what I have termed ethical eschatology or the radicality of divine
ethics, in *The Birth of Christianity*,[38] that I am not certain what would still
be worth a continuing argument. In any case, what makes such an apoca-

lyptic Jesus persuasive is not that it agrees with me but that it explains what actually happened to the Kingdom movement across its first hundred years.

Notes

1. John Dominic Crossan, *The Birth of Christianity* (San Francisco: Harper-SanFrancisco, 1998) 257–89. My citations are from 259–60.

2. Albert Schweitzer, *The Quest of the Historical Jesus. A Critical Study of Its Progress from Reimarus to Wrede*. Trans. William Montgomery. Intro. James M. Robinson (New York: Macmillan, [1906] 1969) 402.

3. Schweitzer, *Quest*, 370–71.

4. Ibid., 402.

5. Crossan, *Birth*, 274.

6. Dale C. Allison, *Jesus of Nazareth: Millenarian Prophet* (Minneapolis: Fortress Press, 1998).

7. Ibid., 78–94.

8. Ibid., 39–44.

9. Ibid., 152–69 especially.

10. Ibid., 164.

11. Ibid., 166.

12. Ibid., 4, my italics.

13. Ibid., 218, my italics.

14. Ibid., 219, my italics.

15. Ibid., 218.

16. Nicholas Thomas Wright, *Jesus and the Victory of God*. Vol. 2 of *Christian Origins and the Question of God* (Minneapolis: Fortress Press, 1997) 658–59.

17. John J. Collins, "Sibylline Oracles: A New Translation and Introduction," 317–72 in *The Old Testament Pseudepigrapha*, 2 vols. Ed. James H. Charlesworth (Garden City, N.Y.: Doubleday, 1983–85) 1:330–31.

18. Ibid., 330.

19. Ibid., 353, n. c3.

20. Ibid., 156.

21. John Dominic Crossan, *The Historical Jesus: The Life of a Mediterranean Jewish Peasant* (San Francisco, Calif.: HarperSanFrancisco, 1991) 285.

22. Allison, *Jesus*, 161.

23. John S. Kloppenborg, "Symbolic Eschatology and the Apocalypticism of Q," *Harvard Theological Review* 80 (1987) 287–306. Citation is from 291.

24. Ibid., 292.

25. Ibid., 304.

26. Ibid., 305.

27. Florentino Garcia Martinez, *The Dead Sea Scrolls Translated. The Qumran Texts in English*, trans. Wilfred G. E. Watson. 2d ed. (Brill: Leiden and Grand Rapids, Mich.: Eerdmans, 1996) 44.

28. Paula Fredriksen, "Judaism, The Circumcision of Gentiles, and Apocalyptic Hope: Another Look at Galatians 1 and 2," *Journal of Theological Studies* 42 (1991) 532–64. Citation is from 544–45.

29. Ibid., 548.

30. Crossan, *Birth*, 387–93. Note switch between singular and plural "you" in Greek.

31. Robert E. Van Voorst, *The Ascents of James: History and Theology of a Jewish-Christian Community,* SBLDS 112 (Atlanta: Scholars Press, 1989) 74.

32. Citations of Josephus are from Henry St. John Thackeray, Ralph Marcus, Allen Wikgren, & Louis H. Feldman, *Josephus.* 10 vols. LCL. Cambridge: Harvard University Press, 1926–65. Citations of Philo are from C. D. Yonge, *The Works of Philo,* New Updated Edition (Peabody, Mass.: Hendrickson, 1993). See also Mary Smallwood, "Philo and Josephus as Historians of the Same Events," 114–29 in *Josephus, Judaism, and Christianity,* ed. Louis H. Feldman and Gohei Hata (Detroit: Wayne State University Press, 1987).

33. Steve Mason, *Flavius Josephus on the Pharisees: A Composition-Critical Study,* Studia Post Biblica 39 (Leiden: Brill, 1991) 373, 375.

34. Wright, *Victory,* 379. See also 384–85 and 549. Those conclusions are based on his earlier volume, *The New Testament and the People of God.* Vol. 1 of *Christian Origins and the Question of God* (Minneapolis: Fortress Press, 1992) 186–99.

35. Allison, *Jesus,* 218 and 4.

36. Ibid., 152.

37. Ibid., 171 n. 285.

38. Crossan, *Birth,* 273–89.

· 6 ·

Galilean Archaeology and
the Historical Jesus

Jonathan L. Reed

The quest for the historical Jesus has been a literary venture and text-centered and, until recently, most attempts to integrate the archaeological record have been misguided. For the most part, appeals to archaeology have been in the tradition of hunting for relics or locating holy sites. Items Jesus might have seen or places he might have visited have merited the most attention.

Determining the real site of his burial—whether the traditional Holy Sepulchre or the Garden Tomb in Jerusalem—or authenticating the insula sacra at Capernaum as the house of Saint Peter were seen as archaeology's chief contribution.[1] Archaeology was a means to verify the Christian faith.[2] For the better part of the last century, "biblical archaeologists," under the legacy of William Foxwell Albright and his students, excavated and marshaled the results of excavations to situate the biblical narratives in history.[3] The underlying goal was to root these stories in history as opposed to viewing them in any way as myths.[4] Predictably, "New Testament archaeology" dwarfed in comparison to "Old Testament archaeology," since Jesus and his followers left behind neither building projects nor inscriptions, as did the ancient monarchies, nor did any New Testament event result in datable destruction layers, as did the Iron Age campaigns of the Hebrew Bible.

Nevertheless, "New Testament archaeologists" misused archaeology more subtly by displaying artifacts or sites as visual aids serving as latent proof that the stories of the New Testament occurred in history and were, by implication, "true." A frequently illustrated item was the first-century plaque from Caesarea Maritima inscribed by Pontius Pilate, displayed as confirmation of the historicity of the Gospels.[5] Other finds were noted by New Testament scholars as well, such as the first-century "Jesus" boat found protruding from the mud in the Sea of Galilee, which tantalized exegetes with its capacity of twelve.[6] Other discoveries were tied to Jesus in the most tenuous fashion, such as the theater at Sepphoris, some five kilometers from Nazareth; perhaps, it was suggested, Jesus had visited the site and adopted the term *hypocrite*—

113

Greek for "stage actor"—after visits to the theater.[7] In short, archaeology was eagerly pursued for tangible links to Jesus, and artifacts were sought as verification that the Gospel stories really did happen.[8]

But short of visual aids or direct links to Jesus, questers made little use of archaeology as a whole.[9] In recent years, however, as the number of excavations in Palestine and the volume of artifacts from the Roman Period have increased dramatically, historical Jesus research has began to take account of them. The import of these for historical Jesus research is not simply the amassing of more artifacts potentially relating to Jesus. Instead, their importance lies in providing a critical mass of evidence in which patterns are discernible, patterns that provide insights into the religious, cultural, social, and economic contours of the world of Jesus.[10]

Instead of mining the archaeological record for a few illustrations relating to Jesus, and extracting them from their stratigraphic and regional contexts, historical Jesus researchers have begun to appreciate the archaeological record in its totality, and incorporate it as a source from which the world of Jesus can be reconstructed.[11] Much of the data, however, is considerably more mundane, consisting of thousands of pottery sherds, as well as lamp fragments, loom weights, grinding stones, coins, metal, and detritus with faunal and botanical remains, and involves plodding through archaeological reports' top plans, section drawings, and locus sheets to understand the stratigraphy of walls and floors. From the patterns in such excavated artifacts, portions of Galilee at the time of Jesus can be reconstructed. From household artifacts, much about Jewish religion and ethnicity can be deduced, and the extent to which Galilee was Jewish or gentile can be gauged. Surveys and excavations help assess demographic issues, including the extent of Galilee's population and its distribution among cities and villages. With population estimates, land-holding patterns, and the extent of urban architecture in Galilee, socioeconomic forces at work in Galilee can be detected, giving some indication of class distribution and the social scale. Epigraphic evidence and the presence of religious structures—whether synagogues or temples—indicate the extent of religious diversity in Galilee and the extent of its hellenization. In short, the archaeological record furnishes the material for a thick description of ethnicity, religion, economics, and social class in Galilee at the time of Jesus.

Historical Jesus research is of necessity bifocal. It must focus both on investigating Jesus' life and teachings in early Christian texts and, at the same time, piece together the environment in which he lived. Any interpretation of Jesus must plausibly fit in his particular environment. Reconstructions of his Galilean milieu are thus as critical as reconstructions of his teachings, and must integrate the archaeological record as a whole, not merely select artifacts as illustrations.[12]

Characterizations of Jesus' environment have relied primarily on literary evidence, but the proliferation of archaeological excavations and surveys in

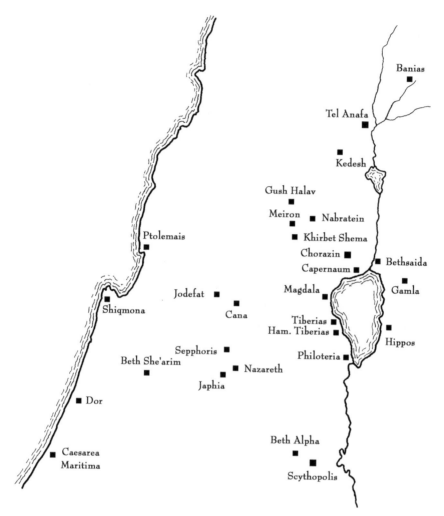

Figure 1. Excavations in and around Galilee

Galilee has invigorated the debate. The sites of Nazareth and Capernaum have stood exposed for some time, as have the Jewish necropolis at Beth She'arim and the synagogue at Hammath Tiberias.[13] The pace of excavations picked up in the mid-seventies, led by the Meiron Excavation Project under the direction of Eric Meyers and James F. Strange, who dug the villages of Meiron, Gush Halav, Nabratein, and Khirbet Shema' in Upper Galilee.[14] More recently, the spade has been put in Galilee to the pottery production site of Kefar Ḥananya,[15] the town of Yodefat which Josephus fortified,[16] Gamla in the Golan which was destroyed by the Romans in 67 c.e.,[17] Cana of the Galilee, and the cities of Sepphoris and Tiberias, its former capitals.[18]

Excavations outside Galilee reveal general trends in first-century Palestine, and underline Galilee's regional distinctness. Archaeological work at the Decapolis city of Scythopolis/Beth-Shean, just south of Galilee, paints a picture of a thriving Greco-Roman polis.[19] Northeast of Galilee, in the area inherited by Herod's son Philip, both the pagan cult city of Caesarea Philippi and the town of Bethsaïda/Julias have been uncovered.[20] Around the Huleh Valley to the north, the Syro-Phoenician village of Tel Anafa was excavated, and just recently expeditions have been undertaken at the village of Kedesh, with ruins of a Roman-style temple nearby, and at the temple complex of Umm Reit.[21] In the northern Golan, surveys and small-scale excavations have clarified the material culture of the Itureans, a pastoral people who moved into the region from Lebanon.[22] Herod the Great's many and massive building projects along the coast and in Judea have been subject to considerable archaeological inquiry. Underwater and shoreside excavations have revealed the magnificence and splendor of his port city of Caesarea Maritima, and his exquisite palaces have been uncovered at Masada, Jericho, and the mausoleum-fortress at Herodion.[23] Excavations around Jerusalem's Temple have exposed the colossal stature of his construction projects there and significant portions of private dwellings, including those of wealthy priests in the Herodian quarters.[24]

Rather than describing each of these important excavations, and cataloguing their most important finds, the rest of this essay will provide a summary interpretation of significant patterns in the archaeological record as a whole. The focus will be on first-century Galilee, and two significant ways in which the material culture's patterns relate to historical Jesus research: (1) the Jewish ethnicity of Galilee and (2) the impact of Herod Antipas's urbanization projects at Sepphoris and Tiberias.

Jesus and the Jewish Galilee

The identity of the Galileans in the first century underlies any study of the historical Jesus and reconstruction of Christian origins. Their religious and ethnic identity determines how Galilee-Jerusalem relations are envisioned at the time of Jesus, the significance of Jesus' visit to the Temple, and ultimately his death. The crucial question with regard to Galilean identity has been the significance of the Hasmonean annexation of Galilee at the end of the second century B.C.E. and its prior inhabitants. Whether or not Hasmonean rule from Jerusalem was enthusiastically received or bitterly resented turns on whether its inhabitants are construed as gentile, Jewish, or "Israelite," a question where the literary sources are silent or ambiguous but which the archaeological record can address.[25]

Archaeological surveys of Galilee and excavations at Galilean sites reveal a substantial gap in settlements after the eight century B.C.E., that is to say after the Assyrian conquest of the Northern Kingdom by Tiglathpileser III (2 Kings 15). Though a few way stations or small forts dotted the

Galilean landscape in the aftermath of the Assyrian invasion, there was no Galilean population to speak of for several centuries.[26] An inkling of repopulation began in Galilee during the Persian and Early Hellenistic Periods (fifth through second centuries B.C.E.), confined mostly to small hamlets along the larger valley. Several surveys and the results of stratigraphic excavations at Galilean sites conclusively demonstrate that Galilee was without an indigenous culture after the Assyrian conquest in the eighth century B.C.E., and was subsequently only marginally settled. Significant settlement began only with Hasmonean rule of Galilee in the first century B.C.E., with population growth continuing through the first century C.E.

That the increase in population was due to settlers from Judea is shown by the fact that four key aspects of Galilean material culture parallel that of Judea:

1. Accompanying the use of ceramic wares are several types of stone vessels, consisting of mugs, cups, and bowls that were carved from a distinct soft chalk limestone. Assemblages of such artifacts are unique to Jewish sites in the first century C.E., and stone vessels are frequently lauded for their imperviousness to ritual impurity in the later rabbinic literature.

2. Stepped plastered pools are found in most affluent private houses in Galilee and are present in public spaces of many of its villages. Likely *miqwaoth* that the rabbinic literature associates with ritual bathing, these structures are ubiquitous at sites around Jerusalem and wherever Jews lived. No similar structures are found elsewhere in the Levant.

3. The absence of pork bones in the faunal remains characterizes Galilean sites as well. Wherever in Galilee zooarchaeological remains have been analyzed, they point to the traditional Levitical prohibition against pork.

4. The practice of secondary burial in *kokhim*-style shaft tombs was likewise common in Galilee during the Roman Period. This typically Jewish burial practice consisted of shafts extending from chambers cut into the hillsides, often with bones stored in ossuaries.[27]

This characteristically Jewish profile in the material culture pervades the first-century strata at sites excavated in Galilee, including those sites most closely associated with Jesus. Ancient Nazareth, his hometown, was encircled by *kokhim*-style tombs and had several stone vessels excavated and *miqwaoth* excavated in its midst. At Capernaum, his base of operations, hundreds of stone vessels were found, distributed throughout each domestic unit, and though *miqwaoth* are absent, this was likely due to its proximity with the lake, a suitable means of washing, and its low socioeconomic status.

This archaeological profile of Galilean sites contrasts with those of the surrounding regions, accentuating its distinct Jewish character. The lack of stone vessels and *miqwaoth*, the presence of pork, and differences in burial practices characterize the material culture of the regions surrounding Galilee at this time. To the east and north, the Syro-Phoenicians along the coast

Table 1. Strata from Excavated Sites in Galilee

	Iron I	Iron II	Iron III	Pers.	Hell. I	Hell. II	ER	MR-LR
Sasa	•						?	?
Tell el-Wawiyat	•							
Tel Ein Zippori	•	•						
Tel Qarne-Hittin		•						
Tel Mador		•						
H. Rosh Zayit		•						
Tel Chinnereth	•	•	•	?	?			
Ayelet ha-Shahar			?	?				
Tel Harashim	•	•		?	?			
Hazor	•	•		?	?			
Bethsaida	•	•		?	?			
Gush Halav	•	•	•	•	•	•	•	•
Capernaum	•			?		•	•	•
Nazareth	•	?				?	•	•
Sepphoris		?	•		•	•	•	•
Tel Anafa				?	•	•	•	
Gamla						•	•	
Yodefat						•	•	
Khirbet Shema‘						•	?	•
Hammath Tiberias						•	•	•
Meiron						•	•	•
Qatzrin		?				•	•	•
Horvat Arbel						•	•	•
Nabratein							•	•
Beth She‘arim							•	•
Chorazin							•	•
Tiberias							•	•

and in the Huleh Valley had a completely different ceramic profile, and imported much more from the wider Mediterranean world.[28] To the north, the Itureans around Mount Hermon had coarser ceramic wares and lived in completely different houses more suitable to a pastoral lifestyle.[29] The inhabitants of the Decapolis to the east and south had many more imported fine wares and a taste for imported wines and other luxury items, all of which stand in stark contrast with Galilee.[30] Furthermore, in each of the areas surrounding Galilee, pagan-style temples have been excavated, which are entirely absent in Galilee.

Because the indicators of Jewish ethnicity—stone vessels, *miqwaoth*, avoidance of pork, and secondary burial—were in all areas of life controlled by the people themselves, and not part of the public realm dictated by rulers, Hasmonean rule in Galilee should not be construed as a political-economic or administrative veneer over non-Jewish indigenous Galilean population. Either the few Galilean inhabitants prior to Hasmonean rule—and their number was small regardless of who they were—readily adopted Judaism and flourished as they adopted it or, more likely, they were themselves Judeans who colonized the Galilee. Though the latter case is more likely, the fact that Galilee's population adhered to patterns of behavior in private space that existed in Jerusalem and Judea means that the Galileans were Jewish.[31]

What Kind of Judaism Existed in Galilee?

While Galilee's material culture shared a Jewish character with Judea, the basic attitudes of the Galileans and their differences with Judean Jews are not readily resolved from the archaeological record. One can only presume that the stone vessels and stepped plastered pools were in some way connected to purity concerns, but whether this was in the same way as envisioned by the later rabbinic texts cannot be determined from the archaeological record. Indeed, the fact that many of these pools do not fit precisely the later rabbinic prescriptions shows how questionable it is to assume adherence to or even awareness of rabbinic regulations.[32] One suspects, nevertheless, that since much of the overlap in material culture consists of implements possibly relating to ritual purity, they had some connection with the Temple and priests, and that the Temple took an important symbolic role in the minds of the Galileans.[33] The extent of pilgrimage to Jerusalem and what element of nostalgia or sincere devotion to the Temple Galileans held in general are elusive in the archaeological record. Notable, however, is that there is virtually no evidence in the first century for synagogue buildings, so that there are no apparent social structures that could transmit and consolidate such traditions. There is only one synagogue, at Gamla, which dates to the first century; two other possible synagogues, one from the first century at Masada and one on the Herodion, were meeting rooms built into previously existing structures by the Zealots in the First Jewish War. The synagogue structures most familiar to us do not become widespread in Galilee until the Late Roman and Byzantine Periods.[34]

How Hellenized Was Galilee?

Much has been made of the presence of two presumably Hellenistic cities in Galilee, Sepphoris and Tiberias. Herod Antipas rebuilt the former as his capital in Lower Galilee early in his reign, and then built the latter on the

Sea of Galilee. Whether these two cities were Hellenistic *poleis* isolated from the rest of rural Galilee or the very conduits that hellenized the entire Galilee has been debated for some time.[35] Significantly, these two cities, which one expects to be the most exposed to Hellenistic and Roman influences, were just as thoroughly Jewish as far as the archaeological patterns in domestic space are concerned. At Sepphoris, which has been extensively excavated, stone vessels and *miqwaoth* are present in each house, pork is entirely absent until the Byzantine Period, and burial in its necropolis was typically Jewish.[36]

As Antipas's urban capital, Sepphoris certainly had a Greco-Roman architectural veneer. Much of the city was laid out on an orthogonal grid, with two main thoroughfares, a *cardo* and *decumanus* meeting at a central location. Use was made of typical Roman building materials and styles: facades were plastered and frescoed, floors covered with mosaics and pavers in herringbone fashion, and planning accentuated columnated vistas. In the first century, however, only selective features of the Hellenistic polis or Roman urban parlance were present in Antipas's Galilee, presumably so as not to offend Jewish sensibilities. At Sepphoris and Tiberias, no temples have been found, nor statues or any imagery in public space whatsoever, and at this early date there were no public Roman-style baths, potentially offensive to Jewish views about nudity. The theater at Sepphoris, incidentally, was built very late in the first century, after both Antipas and Jesus. Antipas's coins were likewise aniconic, unlike those of his brother Philip and coins from the surrounding cities.[37]

With regard to the languages of Galilee, what is most notable is the meager epigraphic evidence from the first century or prior. Though dedicatory and other public inscriptions were a commonplace of civic life in the rest of the Roman world, they are absent in Galilee at this time, including the cities of Sepphoris and Tiberias. In the latter city, two epigraphic items, an ostracon and an inscribed weight from the Early Roman Period, shed some light on the epigraphic profile. The ostracon from a storage jar reads אפמליש painted in red Hebrew block letters, a translation of the Greek ἐπιμελητής, "manager, overseer, or treasurer."[38] The official wrote in Hebrew letters but had adopted a Greek administrative title.[39] The lead market weight was written in Greek, contained a Latin weight (HMI-ΛΙΤΡΙΝ), and including the two distinctly Jewish names as the *agoronomoi*, or market inspectors. The weight thus combines a Roman/Latin measure, in Greek script, testifying to Jews controlling important administrative matters, a pattern for which there is also epigraphic evidence from Tiberias.[40] At the administrative level, Greek seems to have been adopted as the language of choice, though the extent to which this choice permeated the rest of Galilean society is suspect.[41]

This epigraphic evidence points to the use of Jewish officials in the municipal apparatus in the Early Roman Period, and there is otherwise no indication that Gentiles served in such capacity at Sepphoris or Tiberias, whether Romans, Greeks, or Syro-Phoenicians. Such did eventually make their mark there, clearly visible in the well-known Dionysos mosaic from Sepphoris or in the faunal remains with pork from the Byzantine Period, much later than the first century, when Roman Legions were permanently stationed in Galilee.[42]

The general lack of imported items from the broader Mediterranean world in Galilee during the late Second Temple Period, especially when compared to the cities of the coast and the Decapolis, indicates that it was not as well integrated into the international economy and its major trade networks. Describing Galilee as isolated is too strong, but it can be characterized as provincial and with a limited regional economy. In this regard suggestions that it was bisected by the well-traveled *via maris* are inaccurate—the major branches of this route bypassed Galilee, going south through Scythopolis, or north through Caesarea Philippi. Galilee was, archaeologically speaking, a definable and somewhat secluded region, distinct from its immediate neighbors, but with close parallels to the material culture of Judea due to its Jewish heritage.

Implications for the Historical Jesus

The fact that the Gospels place Jesus' ministry almost entirely in Galilee, and that he and his named disciples were all Galileans, puts him in a Jewish context. The absence of Sepphoris or Tiberias in the Gospels, perhaps coincidental, cannot be construed as his avoidance of Gentiles, paganism, or Hellenism. If he did avoid these two administrative centers, it might have been for political reasons, namely to avoid the same fate as the Baptist did at the hands of Antipas. In fact, the Gospels portray him as flirting along border regions, whether in making his apparent home-base Capernaum on the periphery of Antipas's Galilee, or in his frequent incursions outside Antipas's jurisdiction into the regions (though never a city) of the Decapolis east of Galilee or Caesarea Philippi north of Galilee (Mark 6:53; 7:24, 31; 8:27). The border region around the more humble Jewish village of Capernaum put him in closer proximity to Gentiles and pagan cities. Still within a Jewish orbit among the Jewish villages on the northwestern shore of the Sea of Galilee, the Gospels portray Jesus' ministry as taking place on the geographical and cultural fringe. He was very close to Greek-speaking Gentiles living in the Decapolis region, as well as to Syro-Phoenicians in the Huleh Valley and around Caesarea Philippi. This setting fits rather well one of the key themes of the Jesus tradition, the use of Gentiles as positive models to shame a Jewish audience into accepting the community's message (e.g., Q 7:1–10; 11:29–32). However, while the situation reflected in the early Gospel traditions anticipates the possibility of a gentile mission, this had not yet been carried out. The crucial problems associated therewith, such as diet and circumcision, issues that permeate the Pauline corpus and Acts where the inclusion of Jews and Gentiles into a single community was at issue, are never addressed by the historical Jesus.

With Jesus' trip to Jerusalem, he and his Galilean followers crossed a different kind of barrier, from the geographical margins of Judaism in Galilee to its center, to the Temple in Jerusalem. That he reacted to the Temple cult and priestly hierarchy with a sense of alienation and protest is clear; the extent to which this represented the popular Galilean attitude is not.

Finally, it should be stressed that since Galilee lacked a substantial gentile component, had only two cities that were Jewish and in their infancy of hellenization, and lacked much evidence for interregional contacts via trade or otherwise, notions of Cynic itinerants influencing Jesus or his first followers seem improbable. Though the scholarly comparison of Jesus' teaching with that of Cynicism, or of his stance to society and theirs, merits attention as an analogy, any genealogical relationship between Jesus and Cynics is highly unlikely.[43]

Jesus in Antipas's Urbanized Galilee

The possible hellenizing role of Sepphoris and Tiberias has been much debated, but less attention has been paid their socioeconomic impact on Galilee. Patterns in the material remains, however, suggest that some of the most significant factors shaping first-century Galilee were the socioeconomic changes wrought by Herod Antipas's urbanization projects at Sepphoris and Tiberias.[44] Herod the Great's immense construction projects, consuming immense energy and resources, concentrated on Jerusalem, Caesarea, and palaces scattered around Judea. Herod the Great, however, by and large ignored Galilee in terms of construction projects. Not until his son Antipas inherited Galilee was it subjected to significant architectural projects, and urbanized for the first time with the rebuilding and construction of Sepphoris and Tiberias. Urbanization in antiquity introduced a power relationship into a region in which categorically larger settlements centered agriculture, trade, and manufacturing onto themselves, wherein the ruling and social elites lived, who constructed and maintained civic buildings primarily through rents and taxes from the countryside.[45] This phenomenon is apparent in Galilee with the building of Sepphoris and Tiberias, whose population growth during this period can be traced in their settlement size and estimates of population density.[46] These two cities' populations grew to between 8,000 and 12,000 under Antipas's reign, which had an immediate impact on the surrounding countryside. They were at the center of a major shift in Galilean demographics over the course of a single generation. This population growth—experienced across the entire Galilee and concentrated in Sepphoris and Tiberias—affected the countryside in profound ways. Prior to the Roman Period and the refounding of Sepphoris and founding of Tiberias, not all arable land was farmed in Galilee, and a biennial fallow could be practiced to reduce the chances of crop failure. Terraces and strip lynchets were yet to level many Galilean slopes into land suitable for plowing.[47] Archaeological surveys and some papyri from else-where indicate that families typically parceled out their land into smaller plots, the result of inheritance and dowry practices.[48] Dispersing a family's plots over wide areas, aiding self-sufficiency, and diversification of products or polycropping minimized the consequences of crop failure, and spread the required labor more evenly over time.[49] Taxes were mostly paid in kind, reciprocity among families was a primary means of exchange, and in times of crisis one relied on clan relations and fellow villagers.[50]

This situation changed with Herod Antipas's rule in Galilee. The rise in Galilee's population that accompanied the building of Sepphoris and Tiberias necessitated more intensive agricultural practices, whether by cultivating more land, letting less lie fallow, or otherwise farming it for higher yields. Economic structures were also changed: instead of farming their own necessities and trading for a few items in which they were deficient, peasant families became responsible for higher taxes to support the growing administrative apparatus, manufacturing sector, construction crews, and materials for the urban architectural projects. Polycropping inevitably waned, as increased taxation demanded monocropping to create economies of scale for higher yields. Cash crops were sold for coinage with which peasants purchased many of their necessities, so that an asymmetrical exchange of goods was introduced. At best, peasant farmers banded together fragmented holdings into larger fields of grain, the most desirable produce, or, more often, they were forced together into larger tracts by rulers or wealthy elites.[51] The Herodians monetized the local economy in part to facilitate paying Roman taxes in currency—the sources consistently refer to Herod the Great and Antipas's income and tributes only in terms of precious metals, and the numismatic evidence for this period drastically increases over the former, particularly in the larger denominations.[52] This accelerated the trend of peasants' selling their land to pay off their taxes in cash and then staying on their land as tenants or indentured servants paying rent, or simply leaving their land to ply an artisan trade and eke out an existence.[53] In the process of increased tenancy and larger estates, a substantial number of rural peasants moved to the cities, where they remained involved in agricultural production as tenant farmers or day laborers.[54]

How Poor Was Galilee?

Herod Antipas's urbanization and construction projects at Sepphoris and Tiberias introduced substantial socioeconomic change in Galilee. Though the extent of poverty is difficult to measure in any absolute sense, that these changes introduced a state that was viewed as worse by most Galileans seems very likely. Urbanization accelerated and also accentuated social stratification among the classes in Galilee. This is particularly apparent in domestic architecture. Many of the houses at the urban sites of Sepphoris and Tiberias were built in styles that set them apart visually from village or rural houses in Galilee. Those of the urban elites adopted materials from the broader Mediterranean style, with plastered and at times mosaic floors, frescoed walls inside, and sturdy walls on the outside built with well-fitting hewn stones, which were at times stuccoed and whitewashed, and with roofs covered with tiles. Such techniques and materials were infrequent in houses of Galilean villagers. At Capernaum, for example, most walls were made of unhewn stones, packed with mud, were covered with thatched roofs, and had beaten earth floors. This pronounced social stratification was also visible in the kinds of materials found inside houses, with the wealthy able to afford some small imported items like lamps or items of personal adornment, as well as their local imitations.

Social stratification is also apparent in artifacts that were essentially religious in nature, such as the style and type of burial in ossuaries, the size and shape of stone vessels, or the presence of *miqwaoth* in private houses. Ritual bathing by the majority of the population seems to have been done in the lake or streams or in the Jordan, in public sites such as synagogues, or in industrial sites such as olive presses, but the wealthier could perform this act in their own homes in private *miqwaoth*. While most households could afford the smaller hand-held stone vessels, the massive stone jars (such as are mentioned in John 2) were luxury items only afforded by the wealthy.

Such status differentiation not only bespeaks increased production and wealth, but also indicates that the resources and wealth were being managed and redistributed in different ways. The strain on agricultural production benefited the wealthy urban dwellers and some rural elites. But it was borne on the backs of the peasants, whose poverty in absolute terms is difficult to gauge, but whose poverty relative to the elites was apparent in first-century Galilee and to archaeologists today.

This picture of Galilee fits the world portrayed in the sayings tradition, where concern for sustenance, poverty, and landlessness are dominant. Though the cities are not in any explicit way targeted for criticism, the wealthy are deemed arrogant or idolatrous (Q 12:13–21), their judicial system suspected (Q 12:57–59), and wealth in general scorned as transitory and ephemeral (Q 12:33–34). Related to these themes are the many sayings apparently deriding the family (e.g., Q 9:59–60; 14:26; 12:51–53; Mark 3:31–35). In Antipas's new urbanized economy, the family or clan provided less of a safety net in case of crop failure or ill health. As the exchange of goods became increasingly asymmetrical between landowners and peasants, reciprocity at the local level and among the extended family no longer offered adequate protection for many Galileans. The call to exchange healing for food and the plea for hospitality toward itinerant members of the movement appear as a substitute or replacement for the protection of family ties (Q 10; Mark 6).

The Kingdom of God in Galilee

The archaeological record helps one imagine Jesus' message of the Kingdom of God and his first followers' attitudes in Galilee by reconstructing the milieu in which they lived. Antipas's building of Sepphoris and Tiberias and the accentuation of social stratification and asymmetrical exchange created considerable stress on the population. It is not surprising that Jesus' proclamation of the Kingdom of God alluded to and directly addressed some of these concerns created by Antipas's kingdom building. True wealth's elusiveness and the false security of earthly possessions undermined the new Galilean economy, and much of Jesus' message resonates with prophetic critique in the Hebrew Bible. Given Galilee's essentially Jewish character, that Jesus' vision of the Kingdom drew on this aspect of the Jewish heritage is not surprising. Similar to portions of the prophets, security was not to be found in the acquisition of objects or human-made structures, but in the divine and the new community's shared vision. Reliance on siblings, parents, or the extended family, including the entire kin of Abraham, was no longer adequate. Like the ancient Hebrew prophets, the new vision necessitated a radical response to the divine, which eventually led to a critique of most contemporary religious expressions within Judaism, including the Temple in Jerusalem and quite likely the priestly apparatus, which seems to have benefited from the Herodian economy under Roman rule. That this critique was "in-house" and represented some attempt at reform or revival resulting from a sense of alienation or resentment rather than hostility or opposition is clear from the Jewish character of Galilee. This critique, aimed at the end of Jesus' life towards the Temple and its extravagant architectural structure, seems natural from a Galilean Jew, whose own region had most recently been subject to construction projects and their consequences.

Notes

1. Common still in such standard works as John McRay, *Archaeology and the New Testament* (Grand Rapids, Mich.: Baker Book House, 1991); James F. Strange, "Has the House Where Jesus Stayed in Capernaum Been Found?" *BAR* 8 (1982) 26–39.

2. Evident in the 1870 foundational document of the Palestine Exploration Society, which states: "whatever goes to verify the Bible history as real, in time, place and circumstances, is a refutation of unbelief." Cited in R. de Vaux, "On Right and Wrong Uses of Archaeology," in *Near Eastern Archaeology in the Twentieth Century: Festschrift for Nelson Glueck*, ed. James Sanders (Garden City, N.Y.: Doubleday, 1970) 67.

3. Still seen in many Bible handbooks that feature excavations and finds that lend historical credence to the biblical record; see James Moyers and Victor Matthews, "The Use and Abuse of Archaeology in Current Bible Handbooks," *BA* 48 (1985) 149–59.

4. To some extent, this was in reaction to a misunderstanding of Bultmann's de-mythologizing program, which had rejected attempts to prove the Gospels' historicity as *theologically* illegitimate because they avoided the demand for an existential decision.

5. See, e.g., Jack Finegan, *The Archaeology of the New Testament: The Life of Jesus and the Beginning of the Early Church*, rev. ed. (Princeton: Princeton University Press, 1992).

6. See the fine excavation report by Shelly Wachsmann et al., "The Excavations of an Ancient Boat in the Sea of Galilee," *'Atiqot*, English Series 19 (Jerusalem: Israel Antiquities Authority, 1990); and, more popularly, Shelly Wachsmann, "The Galilee Boat: 2,000-Year-Old Hull Recovered Intact," *BAR* 14, no. 5 (September–October 1988) 18–33.

7. On the discovery of the theater at Sepphoris, see Leroy Waterman, *Preliminary Report of the University of Michigan Excavations at Sepphoris, Palestine in 1931* (Ann Arbor: University of Michigan Press, 1937); on the implications for Jesus, see Benedict Schwank, "Das Theater von Sepphoris und die Jugendjahre Jesu," *Erbe und Auftrag* 52 (1976) 199–206; and Richard Batey, "Jesus and the Theater," *NTS* 30 (1984) 563–74.

8. See, e.g., James H. Charlesworth, *Jesus Within Judaism: New Light from Exciting Archaeological Discoveries* (New York: Doubleday, 1988).

9. Valuable topographical and ethnographic studies were compiled by Gustaf Dalman, *Orte und Wege Jesu*, BFCT 2.1 (Gütersloh: Bertelsmann, 1919); *Arbeit und Sitte in Palästina* (Gütersloh: Bertelsmann, 1928–42); and Joachim Jeremias, *Jerusalem zur Zeit Jesu: Eine kulturgeschichtliche Untersuchung zur neutestamentlichen Zeitgeschichte*, 2 vols. (Göttingen: Vandenhoeck & Ruprecht, 1923–37).

10. This was also the result of developments in the discipline of archaeology as a whole; see the summary by William Dever, "The Impact of the New Archaeology," *Benchmarks in Time and Culture. An Introduction to Palestinian Archaeology. Dedicated to Joseph A. Callaway,* edited by Joel Drinkard et al. (Atlanta: Scholars Press, 1988) 337–52.

11. As has been argued for some time by Eric Meyers and James F. Strange, *Archaeology, the Rabbis and Early Christianity* (Nashville: Abingdon, 1983); and more recently, Meyers, "Jesus und seine galiläische Lebenswelt," *Zeitschrift für Neues Testament* 1 (1998) 27–39; and Strange, "Some Implications of Archaeology for New Testament Studies," in *What Has Archaeology to Do with Faith?* ed. James Charlesworth and Walter Weaver (Valley Forge, Pa.: Trinity Press International, 1992) 23–59; and Strange, "The Sayings of Jesus and Archaeology," in *Hillel and Jesus: Comparative Studies of Two Major Religious Leaders*, ed. James Charlesworth (Minneapolis: Fortress, 1998) 291–305.

12. See particularly the work of Sean Freyne, *Galilee, Jesus, and the Gospels: Literary Approaches and Historical Investigations* (Philadelphia: Fortress, 1988); "The Geography, Politics, and Economics of Galilee and the Quest for the Historical Jesus," in *Studying the Historical Jesus: Evaluations of the State of Current Research*, ed. Bruce Chilton and Craig Evans, NTTS 19 (Leiden: E. J. Brill, 1994) 75–121; and "Jesus and the Urban Culture of Galilee" in *Texts and Contexts: Biblical Texts and Their Textual and Situational Contexts*, ed. Tord Fornberg and David Hellholm (Oslo: Scandinavian University Press, 1995) 596–622.

13. See the articles in *New Encyclopedia of Archaeological Excavations in the Holy Land,* vols. 1–4, ed. Ephraim Stern (Jerusalem: Israel Exploration Society, 1993).

14. Eric Meyers et al., "The Meiron Excavation Project: Archaeological Survey in Galilee and Golan, 1976," *BASOR* 230 (1978) 1–24; *Ancient Synagogue Excavations at Khirbet Shema', Upper Galilee, Israel 1970–1972,* AASOR 42 (Durham, N.C.: ASOR, 1976); *Excavations at Ancient Meiron, Upper Galilee, Israel 1971–72, 1974–75, 1977* (Cambridge, Mass.: American Schools of Oriental Research, 1981); "Preliminary Report on the 1980 Excavations at en-Nabratein, Israel," *BASOR* 244 (1981) 1–26; "Second Preliminary Report on the 1980 Excavations at en-Nabratein, Israel," *BASOR* 246 (1982) 35–54; and *Excavations at the Ancient Synagogue of Gush Halav. Meiron Excavation Project Volume V* (Winona Lake, Ind.: Eisenbrauns, 1990).

15. David Adan-Bayewitz and Isadore Pearlman, "The Local Trade of Sepphoris in the Roman Period," *IEJ* 40 (1990) 153–72; and David Adan-Bayewitz, *Common Pottery in Roman Galilee: A Study of Local Trade* (Ramat-Gan, Israel: Bar-Ilan University Press, 1993).

16. David Adan-Bayewitz and Mordechai Aviam, "Iotapata, Josephus, and the Siege of 67: Preliminary Report on the 1992–94 Seasons," *JRS* 10 (1997) 131–65.

17. Danny Syon, "Gamla: Portrait of a Rebellion," *BAR* 18 (January–February 1992) 23–24.

18. See the articles and bibliography in Rebecca Nagy, *Sepphoris in Galilee: Crosscurrents of Culture* (Raleigh, N.C.: North Carolina Museum of Art, 1996); and Yizhar Hirshfeld, "Tiberias: Preview of Coming Attractions," *BAR* 17, no. 2 (March–April 1991) 44–55. Cana is now being dug by an expedition led by Douglas Edwards.

19. Gideon Foerster and Yoram Tsafrir, "Bet Shean Project," in *ESI 1987/1988* (Jerusalem: Israel Antiquities Authority, 1988) 6:10–43.

20. John Wilson and Vassilios Tzaferis, "Banias Dig Reveals King's Palace," *BAR* 24, no. 1 (January–February 1998) 54–61; and Rami Arav and Richard Freund, *Bethsaida: A City by the Northern Shore of the Sea of Galilee,* Bethsaida Excavations Project 1 (Kirkesville, Mo.: Thomas Jefferson University Press, 1995).

21. Sharon Herbert, *Tel Anafa I: Final Report on Ten Years of Excavation at a Hellenistic and Roman Settlement in Northern Israel,* Journal of Roman Archeology Supplementary Series 10.1 (Ann Arbor, Mich.: Kelsey Museum of Archaeology, 1994) Kedesh is currently being excavated by Sharon Herbert and Andrea Berlin, and Umm Reit by J. Andrew Overman.

22. Shimon Dar, "The History of the Hermon Settlements," *PEQ* 120 (1988) 26–44; *Settlements and Cult Sites on Mount Hermon, Israel: Ituraean Culture in the Hellenistic and Roman Periods,* BAR International Series 589 (London: Biblical Archaeology Review, 1993); and M. Hartel, "Khirbet Zemel 1985–6," *IEJ* 37 (1987) 270–72.

23. Kenneth Holum, *King Herod's Dream: Caesarea by the Sea* (New York: Norton, 1988); Avner Raban and Kenneth Holum, eds., *Caesarea Maritima: A Retrospective after Two Millennia* (Leiden: E. J. Brill, 1996); and Ehud Netzer, *Die Paläste der Hasmonaer und Herodes des Grossen* (Mainz: P. von Zabern, 1999).

24. Nahman Avigad, *Discovering Jerusalem* (Nashville: Nelson, 1980); and the articles in Hillel Geva, ed., *Ancient Jerusalem Revealed* (Jerusalem: Israel Exploration Society, 1994).

128 • Jonathan L. Reed

25. See most recently Richard Horsley, *Archaeology, History, and Society in Galilee: The Social Context of Jesus and the Rabbis* (Valley Forge, Pa.: Trinity Press International, 1996).

26. Contra Horsley's argument of a surviving Israelite village culture in *Archaeology, History, and Society in Galilee*; see Zvi Gal, *The Lower Galilee during the Iron Age*, ASOR Dissertation Series 8 (Winona Lake, Ind.: Eisenbrauns, 1992).

27. Jonathan L. Reed, *Archaeology and the Galilean Jesus: A Re-examination of the Evidence* (Harrisburg, Pa.: Trinity Press International, 2000) 43–51.

28. Andrea Berlin, "From Monarchy to Markets: The Phoenicians in Hellenistic Palestine," *BASOR* 306 (1997) 75–88.

29. Dar, "The History of the Hermon Settlements" and *Settlements and Cult Sites on Mount Hermon, Israel.*

30. Andrea Berlin, "Between Large Forces: Palestine in the Hellenistic Period," *BA* 60 (1997) 2–51.

31. Reed, *Archaeology and the Galilean Jesus*, 23–61.

32. Contra Hanan Eshel, "A Note on Miqvaot at Sepphoris" in *Archaeology and the Galilee: Texts and Contexts in the Graeco-Roman and Byzantine Periods*, South Florida Studies in the History of Judaism 143 (Atlanta: Scholars Press, 1997) 131–34. On purity and the archaeological record, see Eyal Regev, "Pure Individualism: The Idea of Non-Priestly Purity in Ancient Judaism," *JSJ* 21 (2000): 176–202.

33. E. P. Sanders, *Judaism: Practice and Belief 63 B.C.E.–66 C.E.* (Philadelphia: Trinity Press International, 1992).

34. Marilyn Chiat, "First-Century Synagogue Architecture: Methodological Problems" in *Ancient Synagogues: The State of Research*, ed. Joseph Gutman, Brown Judaic Studies 22 (Chico, Calif.: Scholars Press, 1981) 50–58.

35. The various options as to whether Jesus visited Sepphoris are also laid out by Wilibald Bösen, *Galiläa als Lebensraum und Wirkungsfeld Jesu* (Freiburg: Herder, 1985) 69–75. See earlier the debate between Shirley-Jackson Case ("Jesus and Sepphoris," *JBL* 45 (1926) 14–22) and Albrecht Alt ("Die Stätten des Wirkens Jesu in Galiläa territorialgeschichtlich betrachtet," reprint of 1949 original in *Kleine Schriften zur Geschichte des Volkes Israels II* [Munich: C. H. Beck'sche, 1959] 441–47). Summarized in Reed, *Archaeology and the Galilean Jesus*, 100–38.

36. See Mark Chancey and Eric Meyers, "How Jewish Was Sepphoris in Jesus' Time?" *BAR* 26, no. 4 (July–August 2000): 18–33.

37. Work in coinage here and iconography from Yaakov Meshorer, "Preliminary Report: The Lead Weight," *BA* 49 (1986) 16–17.

38. Ibid.

39. See the helpful comments by Eric Meyers, "Sepphoris on the Eve of the Great Revolt (67–68 C.E.): Archaeology and Josephus," in *Galilee Through the Centuries*, ed. Eric Meyers (Winona Lake, Ind.: Eisenbrauns, 1999) 112–13.

40. S. Qedar, "Two Lead Weights of Herod Antipas and Agrippa II and the Early History of Tiberias," *Israel Numismatic Journal* 9 (1986–87): 29–35.

41. On Galilee's linguistic profiles, see Horsley, *Archaeology, History, and Society in Galilee*, 154–75. On the use of Greek as a barometer for Hellenism, see further Glen Bowerstock, *Hellenism in Late Antiquity* (Ann Arbor: University of Michigan Press, 1990).

42. Zeev Safrai, "The Roman Army in the Galilee," *The Galilee in Late Antiquity*, ed. Lee Levine (New York: Jewish Theological Seminary, 1992) 103–11; and Eric Meyers, "Roman Sepphoris in the Light of New Archaeological Evidence and Research," in Levine, *The Galilee in Late Antiquity*, 321–38.

43. Note the comments by John Kloppenborg Verbin, *Excavating Q: The History and Setting of the Sayings Gospel* (Minneapolis: Fortress, 2000) 420–32.

44. Reed, *Archaeology and the Galilean Jesus*, 62–99; Douglas Edwards, "The Socio-Economic and Cultural Ethos of Lower Galilee in the First Century: Implications for the Nascent Jesus Movement," in Levine, *The Galilee in Late Antiquity*, 53–73; and Freyne, "Jesus and the Urban Culture of Galilee," 596–622.

45. See the valuable essays edited by John Rich and Andrew Wallace-Hadrill, *City and Country in the Ancient World*, Leichester-Nottingham Studies in Ancient Society 2 (London: Routledge, 1991); and Zeev Safrai, *The Economy of Roman Palestine* (London and New York: Routledge, 1994).

46. Reed, *Archaeology and the Galilean Jesus*, 62–99.

47. B. Golomb and Y. Kedar, "Ancient Agriculture in the Galilee Mountains," *IEJ* 21 (1971) 136–40.

48. Golomb and Kedar, "Ancient Agriculture in the Galilee Mountains" 136–40; Gildas Hamel, *Poverty and Charity in Roman Palestine, First Three Centuries* C.E., Near Eastern Studies 23 (Berkeley: University of California Press, 1990) 134–37; Magen Broshi, "Agriculture and Economy in Roman Palestine: Seven Notes on the Babatha Archive," *IEJ* 42 (1992) 230–40; Safrai, *The Economy of Roman Palestine*, 355–70; and Freyne, "Jesus and the Urban Culture of Galilee," 608–9.

49. Peter Garnsey, *Famine and Food Supply in the Graeco-Roman World* (Cambridge: Cambridge University Press, 1988) 43–55; Safrai, *The Economy of Roman Palestine*, 366.

50. See the comprehensive study by Douglas Oakman, *Jesus and the Economic Questions of His Day*, Studies in the Bible and Early Christianity 8 (Lewiston, N.Y.: Edwin Mellen, 1986).

51. David Fiensy, *The Social History of Palestine in the Herodian Period. The Land is Mine*, Studies in the Bible and Early Christianity 20 (Lewiston, N.Y.: Edwin Mellen, 1991).

52. Menahem Stern, "The Reign of Herod," *The World History of the Jewish People*, First Series, vol. 7, ed. Michael Avi-Yonah (Jerusalem: Massada, 1975) 92–97 [75–132]; and Oakman, *Jesus and the Economic Questions*, 69–72.

53. Keith Hopkins describes monetization introduced by Roman taxation in "Economic Growth in Towns in Classical Antiquity," in *Towns in Societies: Essays in Economic History and Historical Sociology*, ed. Philip Abrams and E. A. Wigley (Cambridge: University Press, 1978) 35–77; and "Taxes and Trade in the Roman Empire," *JRS* 70 (1980) 101–25. See also J. R. Patterson, "Settlement, City and Elite in Samnium and Lycia," in Rich and Wallace-Hadrill, *City and Country in the Ancient World*, 147–68, and Garnsey, *Famine and Food Supply*, 44–45.

54. See the helpful comments on the confusion of the term "peasants" among biblical scholars, John Dominic Crossan, *The Birth of Christianity: Discovering What Happened in the Years Immediately After the Execution of Jesus* (San Francisco: HarperSanFrancisco, 1998) 216–18.

· 7 ·

The Jesus Seminar and the Quest

Robert Funk

In the Jesus Seminar and the Westar Institute, we have attempted to identify issues in the sphere of Bible and religion that matter. Then we endeavored to enlist serious scholars who would devote the time and effort to address these issues. Finally, we agreed at the outset to do our work in full public view and to report in terms that any reasonably literate reader could understand.

As our first topic we elected to investigate the historical Jesus. Americans have a perennial interest in Jesus, but as the century drew to a close that interest intensified. The result was the organization of the Jesus Seminar in 1985.

The Jesus Seminar is made up of Fellows and Associates. Fellows are scholars with an advanced degree in biblical or religious studies. Associates are interested non-specialists. Westar has about thirty-five hundred members and another thirty-five hundred observers. About two hundred of these are scholars of the Bible or theologians. More than seventy-five Fellows have signed each of the two major reports published thus far.

Protocols

The first steps we took in organizing the Jesus Seminar back in 1985 turned out to be crucial. We agreed from the outset to form an agenda of issues on which we would come to decision, no matter how provisional or tentative. That in itself is uncharacteristic of humanists who prefer to hold all questions in perpetual abeyance pending further review. We adopted collaboration as our group process in order to expand the basis of decision making. We agreed to make our work cumulative, which meant that we built on consensus judgments as we pursued our agenda; we identified what we had in common rather than concentrate on our differences. Academic critics of scholarly essays tend to make the worst case they can for the publications of their colleagues, whereas the friendly critics of great literary works attempt to make the best case they can for their authors. We have behaved against academic type in striving to make the best case for our texts and each other, without blunting our critical acumen. This, I judge, has been our sharpest

130

departure from academic protocol that has resulted in our most significant achievement: the production of knowledge that makes a difference.

It may have been fortuitous that we assembled outside the university. We gathered beyond the confines but still within earshot of the churches, even beyond the demands of the seminaries training clergy. By dint of historical circumstance, we formed the Seminar outside the boundaries of the professional guilds. That made it possible for us to establish different protocols. We did all of this at some risk to ourselves.

We insisted on holding our sessions in public and making reports in non-technical language that any literate person could understand. Voting with colored beads and reporting with color-coded texts were ingredient to those aims. We took some additional risk in talking to reporters and appearing on talk shows. This aspect of our work has generated the most controversy.

We recognized at the outset that we are all facing an information glut in the electronic age. We are being bombarded with unsorted and undigested information from every quarter. On the subject of religion, the common view is that one opinion is as good as another. This conviction is a recipe for chaos, and that is just about what we have. By banding together and keeping our eye on a common goal, we had hoped to reduce confusion by a small fraction in *The Five Gospels* and *The Acts of Jesus*.

The Premises of the Quest

We have identified four premises of the quest.

1. The quest of the historical Jesus is the pursuit of the discrepancy between the historical figure and the portraits of him in the gospels.

The naïve view is that Jesus did and said everything that is reported of him in the four New Testament gospels. After more than two centuries of critical work we know that is not true. The New Testament gospels are a mixture of folk memories and creative storytelling; there is very little hard history. In addition, almost all critical scholars doubt that the New Testament gospels were composed by eyewitnesses. Furthermore, we now have the text, in whole or in fragment, of eighteen additional gospels to consider. Like the New Testament gospels, they, too, must be evaluated critically.

We know there is a discrepancy between the historical figure and the portraits of him in the gospels because the Jesus of the Gospel of John differs markedly from the Jesus of the Synoptics—Mark, Matthew, Luke. And the Jesus of Mark differs from the Jesus portrayed in Matthew and Luke. Further, the Jesus of the Gospel of Thomas is not always the same Jesus as we find in the Synoptics. And the Jesus of the Sayings Gospel Q, used by Matthew and Luke in creating their gospels, presents a picture of Jesus that differs markedly from all the others.

In addition, the Jesus of the apostle Paul has features unknown to the gospel writers. The Jesus of the Apostles' Creed is known by his miraculous birth, death under Pontius Pilate, bodily resurrection, and anticipated return, but absolutely nothing is said about how he lived or what he taught. And the Jesus of the Nicene Creed of 325 c.e. is the second person of the trinity who existed as part of the godhead from the beginning.

All but the most conservative scholars of the Bible agree that the historical figure who lived in Galilee during the first quarter of the first century differs in at least some important respects from the way he is remembered and pictured in early Christian texts. There is a quest for the historical Jesus because most scholars believe the Galilean sage has been obscured at least in part by the authors of ancient Christian documents. We would not be looking for something that has not been lost.

2. The problem, accordingly, is to distinguish fact from fiction in the 22 ancient gospels that contain reports about what he said and did. Many scholars hold the view that the ancient gospels contain virtually no reliable information about the historical figure. For them a quest of the historical Jesus is futile. But for those of us who think the gospels preserve some scattered information about him, even if only incidentally or accidentally, the quest is essentially a search for reliable data. Our job is to sort through all the information contained in the ancient gospels and other related texts and attempt to distinguish fictive elements from the facts. The first task of the quest is to establish a firm database from which to reconstruct features of the historical figure of Jesus.

3. Those who undertake the quest do so because they believe they can isolate at least a small fund of reliable historical data. The Fellows of the Jesus Seminar are questers because we hold the view that we can identify traces of the figure that has been obscured to one extent or another by Christian hope and piety. The question is whether we can develop criteria that will enable us to discriminate fact from fiction in all the ancient gospels.

4. If we succeed in assembling a significant database of reliable information, of what value are those data? Does knowledge of the historical Jesus carry any significance for Christian faith? That is the final question we put on our agenda.

The picture of Jesus found in the New Testament gospels and transmitted by the church through the centuries is a varied one. There are almost as many pictures of Jesus as there are churches and sects in Christendom. Nevertheless, the church has insisted, by and large, that not just any picture of Jesus will do as the basis of faith: the Jesus who is confessed as Lord must be Jesus of Nazareth. And, because of this conviction, the churches have countenanced the investigation of their traditions in an effort to disclose the historical figure at the base of those traditions, the Jesus that undergirds faith insofar as that faith identifies its Lord with Jesus of Nazareth. For that reason, the Seminar assumes that the quest has real, perhaps even critical, significance for faith.

The basic propositions underlying the quest, then, are these:

- The quest of the historical Jesus is the pursuit of the discrepancy between the historical figure and the representations of him in the gospels.

- The quest of the historical Jesus is the search for reliable data.

- The quest of the historical Jesus assumes that some reliable historical data are recoverable.

- Knowledge of the historical Jesus matters for faith.

The Jesus Seminar adopted these four propositions as the basis of its work. In so doing, it has acted in concert with the vast majority of critical scholars the world over.

The Agenda of the Jesus Seminar

The initial task of the Seminar was to inventory the data—all the data. We did not limit ourselves to the four New Testament gospels; we avoided canonical bias by including all 22 gospels (collected with fresh translations in *The Complete Gospels,* edited by Robert J. Miller, 1994 [see Bibliography for full bibliographic information]).

We then sorted the data into the actions reported of Jesus and the words attributed to Jesus. We further classified the materials by organizing the data into types of sayings and types of stories in accordance with the canons of form criticism.

The big job, which took us the first ten years, was to evaluate each item in the inventory. Papers were prepared and circulated in advance of each of our meetings (now amounting to 28 sessions). Each item on the agenda was debated and discussed until the Fellows were ready to indicate their judgments by voting. The object of voting was to determine whether there was a consensus among us and, if so, to discover its extent. The simple test was this: would you include this item—word or deed—in the database to determine who Jesus was and what he said?

In the first two phases of the Seminar we sorted through approximately 1,500 versions of 500 sayings attributed to Jesus, and identified those words that, in the judgment of the Fellows, most probably originated with him or were spoken by him in some proximate form. We wound up after six years of deliberations with a compendium of 90 aphorisms and parables that we think echo the voice of the historical Jesus.

When we had completed that task, we turned to 387 reports of 176 events and deeds and carried out a similar evaluative process. Twenty-nine of the 176 events were deemed to contain some historical information. In addition, we formulated and adopted 42 narrative statements based on information derived from stray data scattered across the gospels.

The result was the creation of a twin database: The first, on the words of Jesus, was published as *The Five Gospels* (1993), the second, covering the deeds of Jesus, as *The Acts of Jesus* (1998). (See Bibliography for complete information.)

Pursuing the Puzzle

It is common academic wisdom to beware of the scholar who can account for all the data. One can be sure he or she is manipulating the evidence. Research ought to begin with what your predecessors have left unexplained. The beginning is the puzzle others have not been able to solve. The puzzle the Jesus Seminar began with was why the parables and aphorisms, and the metaphorical language of Jesus, which play such a large role in the gospels, found so little place in earlier quests.

In pursuing this puzzle, we adopted the broad scholarly consensus on the history and relationships of the gospels. We affirmed with most scholars that Matthew and Luke were essentially revisions of Mark. We did not permit ourselves to make use of their revisions of Mark without powerful corroborating evidence. We assumed that Matthew and Luke also made use of the sayings gospel Q in supplementing Mark. We struggled with the difficulties in reconstructing the original text of Q. We acknowledged that some stray oral traditions may have been captured by Matthew and Luke. And we even conceded that the Fourth Gospel may have preserved some incidental historical data, in spite of the fact that many scholars dismiss John as of no real historical value. For example, we took seriously the observation that the first followers of Jesus were probably recruited from disciples of John in the Jordan Valley, reported only by John. We agreed that the Gospel of Thomas was useful in reconstructing the history of some individual traditions, as were other fragments of gospels. But nothing in our profiles of Jesus depends solely on data taken from Thomas or other extracanonical sources.

In our deliberations we held ourselves to the strict observance of this consensus. We did not permit each other to fudge. Out of dozens of individual decisions about particular sayings and parables, in retrospect we formulated "rules of evidence." Those rules reflect actual practice rather the theory of how the tradition grew and developed. It was on the basis of this complex method that we arrived at a shared database, which in turn functioned as the basis for individual profiles of the historical Jesus that bear some remarkable affinities. Those profiles are not monolithic, to be sure. But they do converge at many points.

Reporting

Our intention in creating a color-coded report was to make its contents immediately evident to the general reader without the necessity of reading hundreds of pages of commentary. We took as our model the red-letter editions of the New Testament widely known to students of the Bible. The original proposal was to print everything either in red or black: Jesus did or did not say or do it. We finally settled for four options:

Red meant that Jesus very probably said or did this.

Pink meant that Jesus probably said or did this.

Gray meant that Jesus probably did not say or do this (although in practice gray often meant that the data were ambiguous and no firm judgment was possible)

Black of course meant that Jesus very probably did not say or do this.

A final gray or pink designation in our reports will often reflect a mixed bag of colored beads, since we employed the weighted method of determining the final result.

Response

To our great surprise, *The Five Gospels* made it on to the religion best-seller list for nine months. Our Associate members, many of whom attend our sessions, have been enthusiastic in their support of our work. We are now producing two-day Seminar programs in churches across North America, New Zealand, Australia, and the United Kingdom at the rate of about two a month. Media interest has grown and matured. Some of our Fellows are regular contributors to television documentaries. We celebrated the consummation of the first phase of our work with a four-day celebration in October of 1999. The Once and Future Jesus conference took a look at the future of Jesus and Christianity for the third millennium. A conference on The Once and Future Faith is scheduled for March of 2001.

In spite of this encouraging public reception, the response we have elicited from some colleagues who did not participate has been nothing short of uncivil. We have been the butt of rancor, vituperation, name calling, and scathing satire. Rather than enter into critical dialogue about the emerging database, some scholars have felt it appropriate to attack members of the Seminar personally. In many cases, these responses have violated the canons of professional behavior.

There are three reasons, in my estimation, that we have gotten the kind of response we have.

First, we caught our colleagues by surprise in exposing widely held academic views to public scrutiny, perhaps for the first time in this century. The fact that the parish minister and priest have withheld this common information from their parishioners contributed to the surprise. The revelation of a closely guarded secret deepened the chagrin felt by many colleagues. An angry rebuttal is often the defense needed to buy time for thought.

In the second place, *The Five Gospels* intervened directly in the way Scripture is read and interpreted. The quest began to destabilize the canon—the authority of the New Testament gospels—and to introduce strange new documents into the discussion. Scholars and lay persons alike are not inclined to welcome change, especially change that demands utter candor and complete honesty. Suddenly, scholars who had been dissembling for years were forced out into the open on questions they preferred to leave unanswered.

Thirdly, the reports of the Seminar represented an attack on the previous consensus dating back to the popular book of Albert Schweitzer, *The Quest of the Historical Jesus* (see Bibliography). Schweitzer adopted the view of Johannes Weiss that Jesus was an apocalyptic prophet who believed the final days were at hand in his own time. The Seminar, in contrast, came to the view that Jesus was not an apocalyptic prophet, but a sage in the tradition of Israelite wisdom. His parables and aphorisms had been overlaid with apocalyptic views at the behest of his first followers, who had come from the circle of John the Baptist. They brought John's views with them into the Jesus movement, and when Jesus was gone, those older views simply displaced Jesus' own views of the Kingdom of God. The loss of a vulnerable Jesus, who was thought to be a failed prophet, meant that scholars and theologians had to rethink everything. Above all, it meant that the creation of the creeds as representations of Jesus might have to be reconsidered. That prospect provoked heated response.

Our critics continued to insist that Jesus was an average Jew who, according to them, believed and advocated what every average Jew believed and advocated—that the end of the age was at hand. If he did not share that view, and if he did not express that view in Aramaic, then we had robbed him of his Jewishness. Few of our critics have recognized what a monolithic and denigrating view of Second-Temple Judaism that is. And, of course, that view ignores the dozens of Jews who spoke and wrote in Greek during the period.

By looking for a single voice in a Galilean crowd the Seminar launched its quest as a discovery venture. Our critics responded by turning their so-called third quest into an apologetic for the orthodox view based, for the most part, on the three synoptic Gospels.

In the Seminar we took as our primary problem how the Jesus tradition got from around 30 C.E. to the first narrative gospel, Mark, in the 70s. Our critics adopt the synoptic Gospels as their starting point and roam around in those gospels indiscriminately as though the authors were eyewitnesses of the original events. They see little need to reckon with the forms of anecdotes that served as vehicles for the memories of Jesus, and they take even less notice of the formal structure of sayings that were likely to have survived twenty to fifty years or more of oral transmission. With the exception of the extremely conservative scholars, most do agree, however, that the Gospel of John is virtually without value as a source of information about Jesus.

It is worth taking note of the steady canonical bias in the protests of our critics. They use the Synoptics as though they were virtually reliable history, but reject all extracanonical sources as secondary and devoid of any historical merit. They deride our use of Q and Thomas and the other fragmentary gospels.

In spite of the fact that the parables appear in their canonical sources, our critics refuse to make use of them as distinctive traces of Jesus' voice because, they argue, who can say what the parables mean? The aphorisms, too, come in for short shrift because they blend in with the wisdom tradition of Israel. These deft moves permit them to ignore the primary database we have identified, using both form and content as clues, as essential to the rediscovery of the historical figure.

The alternative view our critics propose is to begin with the deeds of Jesus. Yet they have trouble isolating any particular deed as the bedrock of the tradition, beyond Jesus' baptism at the hands of John and the crucifixion—events no one contests who thinks Jesus was a historical person. They do not recognize the fundamental methodological problem put so pointedly by Julian Hills: the deeds of Jesus are *reported,* while the sayings of Jesus are *repeated.* In other words, deeds are narrated from a third person perspective, while the authentic words of Jesus betray his own perspective. In any case, the deeds of Jesus are literary artifacts apart from some interpretive assessment, and it is only Jesus who can really tell us what his acts were all about. For this his sayings are essential.

In clinging to the apocalyptic hypothesis, our critics are disposed to be literal-minded: the apocalyptic tradition is relentlessly literal and humorless. It is difficult to crack a joke if you think the world is about to end. And, of course, having a celebration just before Armageddon seems inappropriate. The Seminar, on the other hand, by paying close attention to the parables and witticisms of Jesus, finds them filled with metaphor, hyperbole, parody, paradox, and ambiguity. The contrast between Jesus' authentic words and the apocalyptic tradition could not be stronger.

It is striking that none of our critics, so far as I can see, ever takes note of the collapse of the mythic universe or the information revolution through which we are passing. They seem to think the old symbols are still in place and functional. But then I can see why they do so: the credibility of the apocalyptic worldview requires it.

The Quest and Faith

Why did we undertake this particular task? The legacy of the scientific age is scientism, which falls out as literalism in the general population: truth in the popular mind refers only to what is literally true, which nearly always means empirically verifiable. That same mind in naïve believers assumes that everything reported in the Bible is literally true or the Bible is not true in any respect. Yet historians and theologians know that faith cannot guarantee a single fact—believing does not make anything so. In this atmosphere, we decided to submit everything to a rigorous historical test in order to frustrate the believer's fantasy while satisfying the appetite for the factual.

Yet a second, more profound effect was our ultimate goal: we wanted to clear away the literalistic obstructions that burden the Christian and other religious traditions and allow myths and rituals to emerge for what they truly are: expressions of the needs and aspirations of the human spirit.

Nevertheless, learning who Jesus was historically apart from any faith claims may also have direct salutary effects. The question for us is whether Jesus himself has any input into the conception and practice of the thing we call Christian faith. For the orthodox Christian community, faith was faith in the faith of the first disciples. They believed because the first disciples believed. And they allegedly believed what those disciples believed. That set of relationships has tended to dominate the entire course of Christian history.

At the beginning, on the other hand, during the time Jesus went in and out among them, whatever faith Peter and others in the circle around Jesus had was inspired by Jesus himself. Their faith was not mediated by someone else. The question then arises: can we know enough of the historical Jesus for him to be the inspiration of our faith, an unmediated faith, so to speak?

The issue is even more complicated than that. For some in that first circle, Jesus himself may have become the object of faith. Some of his followers may have concluded, after Easter, that Jesus was the Messiah, or the son of man, by adoption. On this view, Jesus had become the object of faith.

For others, faith in Jesus meant to trust what he trusted. On that view, it was not Jesus who was the object of faith; on the contrary, his Father, God, was the true object of faith. Better yet, the Kingdom of God was the real object of faith. And faith was not belief; it was trust. Jesus did not call on people to believe in God; he called on them to trust in God's presence among them, to trust the creation, including other human beings. As he viewed it, the world is God's Kingdom or God's domain. God's domain was his perception of how the world is meant to thrive under the direct aegis of the Father.

In terms of the parties involved in the quest, the Jesus Party suggests that Jesus points to the Kingdom of God. The Apostolic Party thinks that Peter points to Jesus as the object of faith. The Bible Party believes that the New Testament points to the apostles as the foundation of the faith.

It would appear that faith in the New Testament is a derivative faith, twice removed from the Kingdom of God. Faith in Jesus is not the same thing as faith in God's imperial rule. Even faith in the faith of Peter and the apostles is secondhand faith. The question then becomes: Did Jesus call on his followers to believe that he was the Messiah, the apocalyptic son of Adam, or a miraculously begotten son of God? If he did not, were his followers justified in calling on subsequent believers to do so?

Jesus seems to have called on his followers to trust what he trusted, to believe that the world was God's domain, and to act accordingly. That dramatic shift in understanding could trail a radical reformation in its wake.

As the Jesus movement aged, an institution and an ideological orthodoxy began to emerge. As they did, the role of the words and deeds of Jesus began to diminish. What he did and said was gradually eclipsed by what was done to him—birth, crucifixion, resurrection—interpreted in the mythical framework of a dying/rising lord. By the time we come to the Apostles' Creed (possibly the mid-second century), the acts and words of Jesus are no longer central. Indeed, the creed itself has an empty center—it lacks any reference to what Jesus said and did, but includes only what was done to him.

The historical figure has been so overlaid with the Christian myth that the historical figure is overshadowed by the adoration of him as the Christ. In the course of this development, the iconoclast became an icon.

If the Christian movement readmits Jesus into its counsels, he will be a powerful critic of sedimented institutions and orthodoxies. That is what happened in the waves of reformation that swept through Europe in the sixteenth and following centuries. The rediscovery of the historical Jesus could again provoke a revision of Christian practice and belief.

Even a partial recovery of Jesus of Nazareth will serve to purge the clogged arteries of the institutional churches, arteries blocked with self-perpetuating bureaucracies and theological litmus tests designed to maintain the status quo. His voice will redefine the nature and parameters of the Christian life.

The recovery of the historical figure of Jesus may well serve as the catalyst of a new beginning for the Christian movement as it enters the third millennium. The words and deeds of Jesus were the catalyst of the original movement. There was an organized cluster of activities before there was an institution—a religion without dogma. The rediscovery of the historical Jesus may prompt the creation of a twenty-first century version of that early stage.

Bibliography

Funk, Robert W. and Roy W. Hoover. *The Five Gospels: The Search for the Authentic Words of Jesus.* San Francisco: HarperSanFrancisco, 1993.

Funk, Robert W., and the Jesus Seminar. *The Acts of Jesus: The Search for the Authentic Deeds of Jesus.* San Francisco: HarperSanFrancisco, 1998.

———. *The Gospel of Jesus.* Santa Rosa, Calif.: Polebridge Press, 1999.

Miller, Robert J., ed. *The Complete Gospels: Annotated Scholars Version.* Revised and expanded version. Santa Rosa, Calif.: Polebridge Press, 1994.

Schweitzer, Albert. *The Quest of the Historical Jesus: A Critical Study of Its Progress from Reimarus to Wrede.* New York: Macmillan, 1961. (Originally published in German in 1906.)

Julian Hills's couplet "Sayings are repeated, deeds are reported" is quoted by Lane C. McGaughy in "The Search for the Historical Jesus: Why Start with the Sayings?" *The Fourth R 9*, 5/6 (September–December 1996) 17–26.

Part Two

Images of Jesus
in Christology

• 8 •

Literal and Metaphorical Christologies

John Hick

Metaphor and Myth

The distinction between the literal and metaphorical uses of language is clear, and I want to apply it to Christologies. In particular, I shall look at Chalcedonian-type Christologies, meaning those that assert two natures or, in a new contemporary version, two minds, one human and the other divine. I shall try to show that these run into an insuperable difficulty over the freedom of the human nature or mind. I shall then argue that a Christology based on the metaphorical character of the concept of divine incarnation can be both logically viable and religiously attractive.

The literal/metaphorical distinction, as I am using it, is very simple. A literal statement uses words in their ordinary standard dictionary sense, and a metaphorical statement does not. Metaphors apply a term's meaning in its ordinary standard context to a different context in which the literal meaning does not apply, the point being to illuminate in some way that second context. For example, "Knowledge is the mirror of nature." Knowledge does not literally mirror anything—no literal mirrors are involved—but nevertheless the metaphor expresses vividly a correspondence theory of truth.

There are various categories of literal statements and metaphorical statements in religious and theological language. There are statements that most of us will agree are metaphorical, such as "God is our rock," "The church is the body of Christ," "God is the Father of all humanity," and such phrases as "Holy Mother Church." There are others that we will all agree are literal, such as "Jesus lived in the first third of the first century C.E.," "Jesus was crucified," "St. Paul died in Rome." And there are yet others that some of us use literally and others use metaphorically—for example, "This bread is Christ's body," "This wine is Christ's blood," "Jesus was the Son of God." It is these latter Christological statements that concern us here.

Let me dispose at this point of a mistake that some people make when they say that the distinction between literal and metaphorical language should be rejected because *all* our language is metaphorical. This is clearly a mistake because "metaphorical" only has meaning in distinction from "non-metaphorical," and if there were no nonmetaphorical language, it would be meaningless to say of any language that it is metaphorical.

Let me now make the connection between metaphor and myth. In the sense in which I shall use "myth" there can be true as well as false myths. By a true myth I mean a story, description, or statement that is not literally true but that nevertheless expresses and/or tends to evoke an appropriate dispositional attitude to the subject matter of the myth. That is to say, in asserting that a myth is mythologically true one is asserting that the attitude that it expresses and/or evokes is appropriate. As a small example, suppose a ten-year-old boy is caught viciously kicking the cat. His angry mother might say, "The devil's got into him." Assuming that she does not believe that there are in fact such beings as devils, the statement is metaphorical, transferring meaning from devil discourse to her description of the boy's behavior. And the connection with metaphor is that a myth is an expanded metaphor. Thus one could describe the behavior of the boy kicking the cat as devilish. This metaphorical description is expanded into a myth in the brief story that the devil got into him. In due course I shall be suggesting that the metaphor of divine incarnation is expanded into the mythological story of the Son of God coming down from heaven to earth to be born in Bethlehem as the child of a virgin mother and dying on the cross as an atonement for the sins of the world.

One further point: it is sometimes said that there are deep truths that can only be expressed mythologically, and this is particularly likely to be said of religious myths. There is indeed a sense in which myths do communicate something that cannot be otherwise expressed. For myths are expanded metaphors, and metaphors depend on the cloud of associations attached to the literal use, a cloud that is not fixed and definable and in which different elements may resonate with different people. For example, I might speak of the journey of life. This may connect with such notions as movement, change, progress, continual newness. These themes may well be positive for some who like change, adventure, progress; but negative for others who prefer stability, certainty, lack of surprises. The metaphorical statement can activate either set of associations, and probably others as well. And it is this openness of the web of associations that ensures that metaphors can never be definitively translated into literal terms. Likewise myths, as expanded metaphors, lack fixed semantic boundaries and so cannot be definitively substituted by literal statements. In other words, they have a range of possible meanings, each of which, however, taken by itself, can be translated literally, so that there is no untranslatable meaning. But because different people take different meanings from the myth, there can be no one single definitive translation; and it is this fact that gives rise to the idea of some deep mystery hidden within it. But there is in fact no such residual mystery. So why use myths? Because as a form of communication a myth is so often much more powerful than a bare literal statement, in spite of the fact that it does not carry any further inexpressible content.

The "Virgin Birth" of Jesus

Turning now to Christology, I have already mentioned the virgin birth story because it became at some stage part of the Christian myth, though I doubt if many of us today would want the incarnation doctrine to stand or fall by it.

The virgin birth, or more precisely, virginal conception, doctrine is only an issue today for theologically rather conservative Christians. But for their benefit let us pursue it a little. It entails that Jesus had no human father. Such miraculous conception stories were fairly common in the ancient world. There was such a story, for example, about the Buddha and there was also one about Zarathustra in Zoroastrianism. There were ancient Egyptian and also Aztec virgin birth stories. Closer to the New Testament world, the Roman emperor Augustus Caesar, born in 66 B.C.E. and, like Jesus, deified after his death, was supposed to have been divinely conceived.[1] Richard Swinburne, whose divided mind theory I shall be discussing presently, says in *The Christian God*[2] that the virgin birth doctrine is secondary and suggests that it would have been better if it had not been enshrined in the creeds. I agree with him, and I applaud his willingness to edit the creeds on the basis of rational considerations, trusting that he will extend the same freedom to others who may want to edit them differently. But although the virgin birth is not, in his view, properly of credal status, Swinburne says that he is nevertheless "inclined to believe that the virgin birth did occur."[3] He holds that the requirements of Jesus' genuine humanity would be "fulfilled sufficiently by genes being derived from one parent rather than two."[4] He asks, "if . . . an individual's genes come only from his mother (parthenogenesis), can that individual still be human? I would have thought," he says, "that the use of the word 'human' by most of us is such as to yield the answer 'Yes' to the latter question."[5] Without making a judgment about that, I would like to point out another aspect of the matter, available to us today through the modern science of genetics but unknown in the ancient world. The human genetic complement consists of forty-six chromosomes, which are the carriers of the genes that determine specific characteristics, twenty-three chromosomes being provided by each parent. If only the mother's were available, as Swinburne suggests, they would have to be doubled to produce the forty-six chromosomes required to produce a viable embryo, and that embryo would then have two X chromosomes and so would be female. So the virgin Mary's child would be a girl, a result that might well be welcomed by feminist theologians, but probably not by most of those who uphold the virgin birth doctrine.

So if we are determined to retain that doctrine we now have to launch on a series of ad hoc stipulations. Having jettisoned reliance on Mary's genes only, we shall have to postulate an additional set of genes that include the Y chromosome necessary for a male child. These chromosomes would have to be miraculously created by God and miraculously inserted into Mary. They would not be part of the human gene pool, the genetically continuous stream of life constituting the human species. However, since orthodoxy does not countenance the idea of Jesus being genetically half human and half divine, we must now make the further dogmatic stipulation that the twenty-three divinely created chromosomes are nevertheless to be regarded as authentically human. What characteristics would they carry? Presumably whatever characteristics God chose. But this provokes further questions. Would the divinely created chromosomes carry perfect characteristics? But does the notion of perfect human characteristics have any meaning? And would they be free from the inherited original sin affirmed by traditional Christian doctrine? If so, would Jesus now really be one of us, a member of the human race, sharing the weaknesses and temptations to which humanity is subject? Or would his genuine humanity be sufficiently ensured by his mother's genetic inheritance? But this was ruled out by another ad hoc stipulation, added later, namely the Immaculate Conception of the Blessed Virgin Mary. By now Jesus' humanity has become highly problematic.

The Chalcedonian Christology

The fact is that some elements of the theological tradition were introduced to preserve Jesus' divinity, and others to preserve his humanity; and it does not seem possible to satisfy both concerns. For the more we stress his sinless perfection, bypassing the taint of original sin that is said to be at the root of all our problems, the less authentically human he seems, while the more we stress his genuine humanity, subject to the weaknesses and temptations of human flesh, the less he seems to be God. So this brings us back to Chalcedon. Leaving aside its archaic substance language, the central Chalcedonian doctrine is that Jesus was God incarnate, in the trinitarian sense of being the second person of the divine Trinity incarnate, and was also at the same time fully human. That is to say, he had two complete natures, in one of which he was God and in the other a human male.

The basic question that this has always provoked, and which has been a central problem for Christology, is whether this complex idea is logically coherent. How could a historical individual have at the same time all the essential attributes of God, those attributes without which a being would not be God, and also all the essential attributes of humanity? The essential divine attributes, according to traditional Christian belief, include being infinite and eternal, being the sole creator of everything other than God, and being omnipotent, omniscient, omnipresent, and perfectly good. Within Christian theology the essential attributes of humanity are harder to specify, and more open to debate, because they are not listed in any of the traditional dogmas. But surely they must include being a finite creature, and therefore not the infinite creator of everything other than oneself, and not eternal, at any rate into the past, nor omnipotent, omniscient, omnipresent, or untemptable; and also being part of the human species as this has emerged within the process of biological evolution. How, then, can a historical individual be both divinely creator of everything and humanly not creator of everything, divinely infinite and humanly finite, divinely omnipresent and humanly located only in a particular part of space, divinely omnipotent and humanly limited in power, divinely omniscient and humanly limited in knowledge, divinely perfect and humanly fallible?

In response to this conundrum some have argued that not all of these human attributes are essential to being human.[6] It has been said, for example, that there could in principle be omnipotent and omniscient humans, and even, as the mystery of the virgin birth suggests, that there could be miraculously created humans who have not come to be within the evolving stream of biological life. Indeed, the tradition says that Adam was such. However, fortunately it is not necessary for our present purpose to reach agreement on these abstruse matters. It is enough that a human being is clearly and definitively not the sole creator of everything other than itself, whereas God is.

The Divided Mind Theory

Various solutions to the problem have been proposed. I am only going to discuss here the one that is most favored today among many Christian philosophers, namely the two minds, or divided mind, theory. This has been most fully presented by Thomas Morris in *The Logic of God Incarnate*[7] and is strongly defended by Richard Swinburne in another version in *The Christian God*, and it is to be found in the writings of several contemporary theologians, including David Brown,[8] Gerald O'Collins,[9] Richard Sturch,[10] and a number of others.

In approaching his theory Swinburne invokes Freud's account of a mother whose son has tragically died and who seems to have two partially different belief systems, insisting consciously that her son is alive, and usually acting on that belief, but having also a suppressed awareness that he is dead, and sometimes acting on that. Such a case, says Swinburne, "helps us to see the logical possibility of an individual for good reason with conscious intention keeping a lesser belief system separate from his main belief system, and simultaneously doing different actions guided by different sets of beliefs of which he consciously aware."[11] Building on this, he develops the idea of the divine mind of God the Son internally dividing itself so as to include within it the human mind of Jesus of Nazareth.

Although I don't want to make much of this here, it seems to me that Morris's idea of two complete minds, the human mind of Jesus of Nazareth and the divine mind of God the Son, with the latter enclosing but transcending the former, is clearer and more defensible than the idea, suggested by

Freud, of a single mind that is divided within itself. It also seems more faithful to Chalcedon, which insisted on there being two complete natures, not one divided nature. However, I have argued elsewhere that even Morris's stronger version, as it seems to me, fails.[12]

But I am discussing here Swinburne's version. He says, "What in effect the 'divided mind' view is claiming is that the divine and human natures are to some extent separated, and that allows the human nature of Christ to be not a nature as perfect as a human nature could be (e.g. in Heaven), but a nature more like our human nature on Earth, subject to ignorance and disordered desire, yet one connected enough with the divine nature so that Christ does no wrong."[13] It is this inability of Jesus to do wrong that we need to focus upon. "[A]n incarnate God," says Swinburne, "could not do wrong.... The 'subjection' of the human will to the divine must then be read only as a subjection which ensured no wrongdoing...."[14] He allows that Jesus might sometimes choose to do a lesser good, but insists that he could never do anything that is positively wrong, that is, morally forbidden. Here, in my view, is the Achilles' heel of the theory.

The proposed picture seems to be this. The human mind and will of Jesus, left to himself, might have acted wrongly, both objectively and subjectively. But this could never in fact happen because, if and when the human will chose wrongly, or was in the process of choosing wrongly, the divine mind and will of God the Son would always overrule the choice to ensure that in fact Jesus never actually did wrong, or perhaps even never got to the point of having clearly chosen wrong. Clearly, in this scenario, the divine mind of God the Son is free. But is the human mind of Jesus free? Surely not. He will think that he is free, so long as he is not aware of the divine mind that encloses and controls him, but he is not in fact a genuinely free moral agent. For although he is free to act rightly, he is not free to act wrongly. Curiously, in a footnote criticizing an aspect of Thomas Morris's two minds theory, Swinburne says, "If you do not really have such a choice [i.e., a choice to act wrongly], then you have the mere illusion of temptation."[15] This is surely correct; but does it not apply as much to his own theory as to Morris's?

The extent to which this matters depends on what the incarnation is for. According to Swinburne, the main reason for the incarnation is to effect atonement for the sins of the world. This is done by "[1] a life of perfect goodness, [2] offered as an atonement, [3] a life showing love for humanity, and [4] teaching them on authority important truths otherwise unknowable."[16] I have inserted the numbers to help us keep track. We can if we wish stipulate, as Swinburne does, that (1) Jesus lived a life of perfect goodness, since on his theory the enfolding mind of God the Son must have ensured this. This can, however, only be an a priori dogma, since we cannot possibly claim to know, as a matter of history, that Jesus always lived a life of perfect goodness. We simply do not have enough information about either his actions or his inner thoughts for this to be a historical judgment. And indeed Swinburne himself acknowledges at one point that "Even if the evidence suggests that much of the public life of Jesus was perfectly good, how do we know that he did not have secret malicious thoughts?"[17] That he never had any secret malicious or otherwise wrong thoughts can only be a deduction from the Chalcedonian dogma.

But (2), it is highly debatable whether, as a matter of history, Jesus thought of his death as an atonement for human sin. E. P. Sanders, having carefully discussed all the relevant texts, rejects "the whole line of thought that has Jesus intending to die for others, rather than just accepting his death and trusting that God would redeem the situation and vindicate him."[18] In that case the atonement doctrine, instead of providing evidence for the incarnation doctrine, is itself another equally a priori dogma. The two hang together within the same dogmatic system, and the system as a whole is a human theory. And the view that it is divinely revealed is simply another human theory.

On the other hand, we can all agree that, as Swinburne says, (3) Jesus showed love for humanity, although this was of course in no way unique to him. But the further idea that Jesus taught "on authority important truths otherwise unknowable" (4) has long been rejected even by conservative New Testament scholars. It is widely agreed that there is nothing in Jesus' teaching about God or about the living of human life that was not already present within Judaism.

So I cannot agree that there is any of what Swinburne calls "evidence" of divine incarnation. The Chalcedonian two-natures theory has to stand on its own legs without external support. And I suggest that the divided mind version of it fails because it insists upon the two incompatible conditions, (a) that to be human involves being genuinely free to make right and wrong moral decisions, and (b) that if Jesus had begun to make a morally wrong decision this would have been blocked by the divine mind of God the Son. Under these circumstances the human Jesus could have had the illusion but not the reality of genuine libertarian free will. Swinburne's Jesus thus would not be a fellow human being who faced and overcame our human problems and whom we can take as our ideal of humanity, as many contemporary Christians believe. To put it dramatically, he would be a semi-autonomous puppet whose strings are pulled whenever necessary by God the Son.

The Chalcedonian fathers believed, as their Definition states, that the two-natures dogma was "as the Lord Jesus Christ taught us." But the modern historical study of the New Testament has shown that he taught no such thing. Both the deification of Jesus and the two-natures doctrine were the work of the church. It is now agreed even among conservative biblical scholars that such Fourth Gospel sayings as "I and the Father are one" (John 10:30 RSV), "He that hath seen me hath seen the Father" (14:9), and "No one cometh to the Father, but by me" (14:6) cannot be attributed to the historical Jesus. They are words put into his mouth by a Christian writer, some sixty to seventy years after Jesus' death, expressing the faith as it had developed toward the end of the first century in his part of the church. There is general agreement that Jesus, the historical individual, did not claim to be God, or God the Son, second person of a divine Trinity, incarnate.[19]

And so the belief of virtually all Christians down to within not much more than the last hundred years, that Jesus claimed deity, has been abandoned. The fallback position that has emerged is that although Jesus himself did not claim this, nevertheless his deity was implicit in some of his words and deeds. But James Dunn says, "Just when our questioning reaches the 'crunch' issue (Was Jesus conscious of being the divine Son of God?) we find that it is unable to give a clear historical answer."[20] Jesus' implied deity is a matter of debate, and ultimately of faith, not an assured fact.

The big development, which culminated at Chalcedon in the mid-fifth century, was from Jesus as a metaphorical son of God to Christ as the metaphysical God the Son. I am not going to try to trace this development here. But clearly it was a gradual process. I have already suggested that no satisfactory literal meaning has been given to the two-natures dogma that was its conclusion. For every meaning that was suggested during the fierce christological controversies preceding and succeeding Chalcedon was rejected by the church as heretical. Today we do not brand failed theories as heretical, but fifteen hundred years ago the two-minds or divided mind theory might well have been rejected as heresy by those who insisted on the genuine humanity as well as divinity of Jesus as a morally free human agent. The heresy of which Thomas Morris and Richard Swinburne are guilty is that of falling to the philosopher's temptation to try to spell everything out as an intelligible theory. But the church has wisely treated the Incarnation as a holy mystery, a mystery which we cannot understand but which we accept because it is divinely revealed. This is the position, is it not, of most ordinary believers today?

This assumption that Jesus' combined deity and humanity is a literal truth, but one that is beyond human comprehension, will satisfy many good Christian people. It will not, however, satisfy any who realize that the fully God, fully man mystery is a philosophical proposal. It is not a divine revelation but a human creation. And its mysteriousness simply consists in the fact that it is a form of words with no intelligible meaning.

Incarnation as Metaphor

The two minds, or divided mind, theory is of course only one attempt to make the traditional two-natures dogma viable today. Alternatives, which however depart further from the two-natures marker, are the family of kenotic theories, and the much vaguer Christ-event theory. I am not going to discuss these here, though I have done so elsewhere.[21] Instead, let me proceed to the radically different conception of divine incarnation as a metaphorical rather than a literal idea.

As a first approach, consider the title Son of God. It is not today a matter of dispute that many figures in the ancient world were referred to as son of God or were otherwise accorded a divine status—some Egyptian Pharaohs, Roman Emperors, great philosophers, legendary heroes. Indeed, until the end of the Second World War the Japanese emperors, refusing to enter the modern world, were officially regarded as divinely descended. But it is not easy for us today, when the Christian term "Son of God" has long been filled with such stupendous meaning as the bearer of an absolute claim, to realize that in the world in which Jesus lived the idea of divinity was much broader and more elastic than it later became in Christian discourse.

It is particularly relevant to remember that the son of God title had long been familiar within Judaism. In Luke's Gospel (3:38), Adam is called the son of God as also, in the Hebrew scriptures, are angelic beings, and Israel as a whole, and also some of the ancient Hebrew kings, who were anointed as son of God—"Thou art my son, this day I have begotten thee" (Ps. 2:7) being probably part of the enthronement ritual. Indeed, any truly pious Jew could be called a son of God. In terms of our modern distinction between the literal and the metaphorical it is clear that all these uses were metaphorical. No one thought that the king was literally, i.e. physically, God's son. "Son of" meant "in the spirit of," or "specially favored by," or "divinely appointed to a special task." And quite likely Jesus, as a notable preacher and healer, was talked about during his lifetime as a son of God in this familiar metaphorical sense. As E. P. Sanders says, "the first followers of Jesus . . . when they started calling him 'Son of God,' would have meant . . . a person standing in a special relationship to God, who chose him to accomplish a task of great importance."[22] But the developed dogma that Jesus was fully God as well as fully man in virtue of having two natures came several centuries later and cannot possibly be attributed to Jesus himself.

The language of incarnation or embodiment or personification works unproblematically when we are speaking of an idea, an ideal, a principle, a value being incarnated in a person or in a work of art. We all know what we mean when we say that "Great men incarnate the spirit of their age," or "George Washington incarnated the spirit of American independence," or "Nelson Mandela incarnates the spirit of the new South Africa," or again that "The Voortrekker monument at Pretoria embodies the pioneering spirit of the Boers." These are all cases of something abstract being embodied in something concrete, whether a person or a stone monument. Whether or not we want to call these metaphorical is optional. It could be argued that they are cases of a metaphorical use having developed into a literal use. But when that which is said to be incarnated in a person's life is not an abstraction but a being, the living God, the situation is different. Here a literal understanding of the language is in principle possible, but would have to be given meaning in one or another of the various ways in which theologians have tried to spell it out in the course of Christian history, in terms of two natures, or two minds, or of some other metaphysical theory. But when all these have been seen to fail it becomes clear that the incarnation doctrine must be understood metaphorically.

How, then, does the metaphor of incarnation apply to Jesus? Jesus lived out—i.e., "incarnated"—the ideal of human life lived in full openness to God; and he lived out—i.e., "incarnated"—the ideal of *agape,* self-giving love; and in so far as he was doing God's will on earth, God was "incarnate" in his life. These are all intelligible Christian claims about the significance of Jesus.

But is such a metaphorical understanding of divine incarnation religiously viable? I think it is. For instead of seeing Jesus as God walking the earth, one whom we cannot possibly hope to emulate, we can see him as a fellow human who challenges us in an extraordinarily powerful way. Whenever anyone freely and unselfishly does God's will, in that action and in that moment we can say that God becomes in some degree "incarnate" on earth. In this sense we are all called to incarnate God's love. As the writer of the *Theologia Germanica* says, we are to be to God as one's hand is to oneself.[23] With this theology the church becomes a servant to humanity, committed to trying to express the divine love in the changing circumstances of our human history. The very practical challenge of Jesus' teaching comes alive as a call to embody his ideals in our own actions.

So, to conclude, I recommend that we abandon Chalcedon and the modern attempts to restate it, and move to a metaphorical conception of divine incarnation in human life. This is truer to the earliest Jesus traditions, more believable in our modern world, more morally challenging to ourselves, and also more open to a recognition of other great religious founders and prophets in an age when it is no longer realistically possible to think of Christianity as the one and only valid way to God.

Notes

1. For further details see, e.g., John Dominic Crossan, *The Birth of Christianity* (San Francisco: HarperSanFrancisco, 1999) 28–29.

2. Richard Swinburne, *The Christian God* (Oxford: Clarendon Press, 1994).

3. Ibid., 235.

4. Ibid., 196.

5. Ibid., 29.

6. For example, Thomas Morris says that "It is not true that an individual must be a contingent being, non-eternal, and non-omnipotent in order to exemplify human nature," in *Trinity, Incarnation, and Atonement,* ed. Ronald Feenstra and Cornelius Plantinga, Jr. (Notre Dame: University of Notre Dame Press, 1989) 116–17.

7. Thomas V. Morris, *The Logic of God Incarnate* (Ithaca and London: Cornell University Press, 1986).

8. David Brown, *The Divine Trinity* (London: Duckworth; LaSalle, Ill.: Open Court, 1985).

9. Gerald O'Collins, *Interpreting Jesus* (London: Geoffrey Chapman; Ramsey, N.J.: Paulist Press, 1983).

10. Richard Sturch, *The Word and the Christ* (Oxford: Clarendon Press, 1991).

11. Swinburne, *The Christian God,* 201.

12. John Hick, *Disputed Questions in Theology and the Philosophy of Religion* (London: Macmillan and New Haven: Yale University Press, 1993), ch. 4.

13. Swinburne, *The Christian God,* 208.

14. Ibid., 208.

15. Ibid., 205, n. 14.

16. Ibid., 221.

17. Ibid.

18. E. P. Sanders, *Jesus and Judaism* (London: SCM, 1985) 332.

19. I am not a biblical scholar myself, and so I shall cite three highly respected scholars, choosing English ones because they tend to be more conservative than their American colleagues. These are all people who personally believe wholeheartedly that Jesus was in fact God the Son incarnate, but as honest scholars they freely acknowledge that he did not himself teach this. Charles Moule, who is a great pillar of traditional orthodoxy, says, "Any case for a 'high' Christology that depended on the authenticity of the alleged claims of Jesus about himself, especially in the Fourth Gospel, would indeed be precarious," in *The Origin of Christology* (Cambridge: Cambridge University Press, 1977). The late Archbishop Michael Ramsey, who was a New Testament professor before becoming a bishop, said bluntly, "Jesus did not claim deity for himself," in *Jesus and the Living Past* (Oxford: Oxford University Press, 1980) 39. James Dunn concludes from his exhaustive study of Christian origins that "there was no real evidence in the earliest Jesus tradition of what could fairly be called a consciousness of divinity," in *Christology in the Making* (London: SCM, 1980). And I will add the Dutch Catholic scholar, Edward Schillebeeckx, who writes, "The distinctive relation of Jesus to God was expressed in the primitive Christian churches . . . by use of the honorific title 'Son of God' and 'the Son.' These were Christian identifications of Jesus of Nazareth after his death. Jesus never spoke of himself as 'the Son' or 'Son of God'; there is no passage in the synoptics pointing in that direction," in *Jesus: An Experiment in Christology,* trans. Hubert Hoskins (London: Collins, 1979) 258.

20. Dunn, *Christology in the Making,* 29.

21. John Hick, *The Metaphor of God Incarnate* (London: SCM Press; Louisville: Westminster John Knox Press, 1993).

22. E. P. Sanders, *The Historical Figure of Jesus* (London: Penguin, 1993) 245.

23. Susanna Winkworth, trans., *Theologica Germanica* (London: Macmillan, 1837) 32.

9

Pluralism, Inclusivism, and Christology

Charles T. Hughes

Introduction

The Christian tradition came into existence and imparted its gospel message within a religiously diverse context. Indeed, religious diversity has formed the normal state of affairs for developing Christian communities at many times and in many places, including today. Thus, the problems raised by different and competing religious traditions have been a part of the standard set of difficulties with which many Christians have had to struggle.

Recently, however, John Hick has posed an important contemporary challenge to traditional Christianity based upon his theory of Christian religious pluralism.[1] On Hick's view, it makes sense to deny the truth of many of the defining doctrines of orthodox Christianity and to affirm that all of the major religions provide equally valid contexts for both moral transformation and salvific or liberative transport. However, Christian inclusivists disagree with Hick's pluralism. They believe instead that the atoning work of the crucified and risen Jesus is the divinely ordained way to redemption. But they also hold that God nevertheless saves all those who do not know about Jesus if they respond to the light God gives to them both here and in the afterlife. This means that God's universal redemptive love is providentially operative throughout the created order, which includes both human cultures and religions.[2]

In my view, the first response John Hick merits for his striking efforts in developing a pluralist account of religion should be one of gratitude. Hick's fascinating and provocative work has motivated many philosophers, theologians, and scholars of religion to rethink how they ought to understand the world's religions from within the context of their own traditions, and in dialogue with the pluralist proposal. For having stimulated so much interest and renewed thinking about the theology of the world's religions, Hick deserves our sincere thanks.

However, even though Hick has convinced nearly everyone that they need to rethink their theology of religion, he has not yet convinced inclusivists and others that pluralism is the right view to adopt. So, it is my task in this essay to clarify briefly a few of the reasons why inclusivists in particular disagree with Hick's pluralism. In order to accomplish that task, I will first argue that two particular objections to traditional Christology are based upon questionable assumptions. Secondly, I will briefly summarize pluralism and inclusivism and then assess which of those two hypotheses provides us with the simpler and more adequate explanation of the data that they attempt to explain. I will conclude that inclusivism, as I define it, provides a simpler and more adequate explanation of the data than does Hick's pluralism.[3] However, it will soon become clear that my conclusion is based in part on my acceptance of several premises that Hick rejects. The same, of course, is true in reverse. Important conclusions that Hick accepts are based in part on his acceptance of premises that I reject. I admit this here to make the point that any analysis of the merits and demerits of theologies of religion is vexed due to the nature and quantity of the disagreements the disputants have with each other. These points of disagreement include questions about worldview, epistemology, special revelation, and providential guidance, to name only a few.

One unfortunate consequence of the parameters of this investigation is that I must exclude as dialogue partners other important Christian theologies of religion, like restrictivism[4] and universalism.[5] I intend no disrespect by not considering those positions, as well as others. But, given the ambitious goal of my essay, I will barely be able to do justice to the two positions I am comparing.

Objections to Orthodox Christology

Before I identify and discuss two objections to orthodox Christology, I had better define briefly what is meant by Christology. The two Christological models that are employed in orthodox Christianity include the Chalcedonian two-nature Christology and, at least since the nineteenth century, Kenotic models of Christology. Both models affirm literally that "Jesus is true God, and true man," and that "God was in Christ, reconciling the world to himself," but they posit different understandings of how God the Son became incarnate in Jesus. A Chalcedonian two-nature Christology is the view that God the Son assumed human nature as Jesus and thus that both the divine and human natures are united in his person. On this view, Jesus is literally the God-man.[6] In contrast to the two-nature model, the Kenotic model of Christology is one in which God the Son literally abandons his divine properties by a process of "kenosis" or self-emptying, and becomes man. On this view, Christ is literally the God who becomes man.[7]

So, what kinds of objections have been lodged against orthodox Christology? According to its critics, such a Christology is meaningless, unnecessary, anachronistic, arbitrary, restrictive, parochial, lopsided, arrogant, a justification for historical evils, and an intolerant *a priori* dogma, to recount only a few of its many alleged deficiencies.[8] Perhaps an efficient summary of or-thodox Christology thus understood would be simply that it is a "dangerous falsehood." And, of course, if orthodox Christology is false, and the additional charges against it are true, then it should be abandoned immediately in favor of a more ethical and evidentially acceptable position. However, some orthodox Christians have explicitly rejected the previously cited list of charges as either unsound or unproven.[9] In that spirit, I will briefly address the charges that the doctrine of the divinity of Jesus is the product of arrogance and that it has been used to justify historical evils.

First, what can be said in response to the charge that Christians who believe in orthodox Christology are arrogant? For, traditional Christians believe that they have been vouchsafed with revealed knowledge of God in Christ. They further believe that such revealed knowledge helps them to identify God's redemptive efforts in the world and carries with it implications for understanding the very being of God. Do such beliefs entail arrogance on the part of those who hold them? I think not. Instead, the mature response to such a gracious revelation should be one of awe, humility, thanksgiving, and even puzzlement about why God has granted such and so great a gift. And to show that this is not a case of special pleading, I will recast my point in two different religious contexts. First, if God graciously gave the Jews the opportunity to be his unique people and the Jews so chose, then does that special relationship with God need to result in arrogance on their part? I don't see why it would. In fact, the "mature response" I outlined above would be a more appropriate response to such grace than one of arrogance. The same "mature response" would also seem to be most appropriate for Muslims who believe that Muhammad is the messenger of God and the human instrument through whom the Qur'an, the very word of God, has been made available to humanity. Thus, if orthodox Christians are charged with arrogance because they believe that God was in Christ, then it follows that the charge of arrogance may be equally applicable to any who make truth claims about their religion or even their theory of religion. After all, even a pluralist can fail to be modest and can adopt an attitude of arrogance toward those who disagree with pluralism in favor of the basic truth of their own tradition.

But what about the charge that the doctrine of the divinity of Jesus has been used to justify some historical evils? Sadly, this criticism is based on historical facts. But what follows from this admission? Certainly not the conclusion that the divinity of Jesus is a false doctrine. For, to affirm that the doctrine is false because it has been used to justify evil, we would have to give credence to what I call the Invulnerable Purity Principle or IPP. The IPP is this: No doctrine is true if it can be or has been used as a justification or inspiration for evil actions or policies. But the IPP is clearly false. For, if we affirmed it, much that we know to be true would have to be abandoned. That is so because human beings are sinners and have proven themselves to be capable of abusing truths by employing them to justify evil actions or goals. For example, it is both possible and acceptable to affirm the existence of God even though belief in God has been employed to motivate people to perform wicked acts. Also, disbelief in the existence of God during this century has formed part of the basis for the rise of totalitarian regimes as well as atrocities committed on national and even global scales.[10] However, that both theism and atheism are capable of being abused by humans is not necessarily evidence against their respective truth claims. Furthermore, if pluralism were to be abused in this way, such abuse would not entail that pluralism was false, unless we were to affirm the IPP. But the IPP is clearly false.

I can linger no longer on Christological issues. So, the question I will now seek to answer is this: What are pluralism and inclusivism and how do they compare to each other with respect to their simplicity and explanatory adequacy?

Summaries of Pluralism and Inclusivism

Pluralism

John Hick believes that his version of religious pluralism provides a simpler and more adequate explanation of the data of religion than does any alternative hypothesis. One guiding principle he employs is to seek a hypothesis that takes account of all of the major traditions and not simply his own tradition. Accordingly, Hick interprets the particular doctrines of religious belief systems as arising out of culturally conditioned responses to ultimate reality, or "the Real," which function ideally to turn devotees from self-centered lives to reality-centered lives. So, even though religious belief systems lack much literal truth about the Real, they can nevertheless function as "mythologically" true of it. What this means is that religions can be equally valid moral transformers and salvific transports to the Real. And Hick believes that such an assumption is warranted due to the apparently equal level of moral transformation and spiritual maturity that is found in each major religious tradition.

Hick's argument for the truth of those claims may be summarized as follows.

1. If one world religion has a true conception of God, or the Real, then it follows that it would constitute a more obvious context for moral growth and spiritual salvation or liberation than the other traditions.

2. But the world religions are roughly equal as contexts of moral growth and spiritual salvation or liberation.

3. Therefore, if we take this moral and spiritual parity seriously, then it is very implausible that only one of the religious traditions has a true conception of God, or the Real. In fact, it seems to follow from this par-

ity that the different traditions all have an equally valid understanding and experience of God or the Real.[11]

But even if that argument is accepted, how does Hick account for the apparently contradictory conceptions of the nature of ultimate reality that are found in theistic and nontheistic religions? For some traditions posit a supreme, personal divine being, like Adonai, the Holy Trinity, Allah, and Vishnu, while other traditions posit a supreme, impersonal ultimate reality, like the Tao, Brahman, the Dharma, and Sunyata. To begin to answer this question, Hick incorporates insights from Kantian epistemology that he describes as "critical realism." He writes that

> there is a world around us but we can only know it as it appears to beings with our particular perceptual and conceptual resources. Thus critical realism takes account of the difference made by the act of perception itself. And applied to religion, it holds that there is a transcendent reality all around and within and above and below us, but that we can only know it in our own limited human ways.[12]

And what is the nature of this ultimate transcendent reality? Hick refers to it as "the Real" and claims that it makes sense to suppose there is only one Real due to the

> striking similarity of the transformed human state described within the different traditions as saved, redeemed, enlightened, wise, awakened, liberated. This similarity strongly suggests a common source of salvific transformation. So it seems . . . that the most reasonable hypothesis is that of a single ultimate ground of all human salvific transformation, rather than a plurality of such grounds.[13]

But the Real cannot be positively described with human terms because, Hick says, it "remains beyond our human conceptuality, including the concept of number."[14]

So, Hick distinguishes between the Real as it is in itself, and human descriptions of the Real based upon contextualized human experiences of the Real. In itself, the Real is ineffable. By "ineffable," Hick means that the Real has a nature to which we may attribute only formal qualities and that it is otherwise "beyond the scope of our network of human concepts."[15] However, at the phenomenal level of human experience and conceptual categories, the Real is experienced in some traditions as personal and in other traditions as impersonal. Thus, the sociocultural context in which the religious traditions are embedded affects the ways in which the Real is experienced and described by humans. In this way, the apparently conflicting descriptions of the Real are shown to be motivated by phenomenal categories and so do not apply to the Real as it is in itself. Instead, these varied phenomenal descriptions of the Real apply to it only mythologically, as instrumental means to evoke in us an appropriate response to the Real.

For example, speaking of the Christian "myth," of incarnation, Hick says that

> the story that God (i.e., God the Son) came down from heaven to earth to be born as a human baby and to die on the cross to atone for the sins of the world is not literally true, because it cannot be given an acceptable literal meaning, but is on the other hand mythologically true in that it tends to evoke in us an appropriate attitude to the Divine, the Real, as the ultimate source of all salvific transformation, and thus [is] benign from our human point of view.[16]

Thus understood, the orthodox doctrine of divine incarnation is reinterpreted as a model of grace in Hick's pluralist scheme. So, incarnation takes place "whenever and wherever God's will is freely done."[17]

Hick therefore believes that as the Christian Church increasingly absorbs and reflects the tenets of pluralism, Christianity will become "undogmatic" and the teachings of Jesus will be heard anew and aright alongside of the teachings of Judaism, Islam, Buddhism, Hinduism, and the other traditions. Thus, if Christians adopt religious pluralism, it will result in a new appreciation of their own tradition and a new and more tolerant appreciation of other traditions.

Inclusivism

There are three key beliefs that motivate orthodox Christian inclusivism. The first is that the triune God of universal redemptive love and mercy desires the salvation of all human beings. The second is that the incarnation of God in Christ has provided the means by which that salvation is accomplished as well as the foundation for a Christian understanding of God. Thus, the salvific victory of God, accomplished in and through the life, teachings, atoning death, and resurrection of Jesus, is the sole vehicle of salvation. The third idea is that the God of love graciously and actively makes this salvation freely available to all. Now the mechanism that explains how this occurs depends on the kind of inclusivist one is. But one version sees the Holy Spirit as working in and through every sphere of life, including the religions, in order to redeem sinful human beings. So, the Spirit may use those elements of the religious traditions that can effect moral and spiritual growth. In that way, the Spirit may impart to people the salvific work of Jesus even if he does not reveal it to them at that time.

It is the Spirit's work to convict the world of sin, righteousness, and judgment (John 16:8). And it is the Spirit's efforts in the lives of people that account for their moral transformation, understood as their exhibiting the fruit of the Spirit (Gal. 5:22–26). Beyond that, it is the work of the

Spirit that accounts for the salvation of people as they respond to the light he gives to them. So, it should come as no surprise that the creative and redemptive work of the missionary Spirit is evident in the lives of those who are formally outside of the Christian church. This also means that Christians do not have a monopoly on or control of the Spirit and that the fruit of the Spirit in the lives of those outside of the church should be both expected and celebrated.[18]

So, an orthodox inclusivist holds that an essential element of Christian belief is that the divinely ordained instrument of salvation is both revealed in and accomplished through the salvific work of Jesus. Thus, when God uses culture and religion as instruments to transform and save people outside of the Christian tradition, these are not divinely ordained means for salvation but rather contingent instruments of divine salvific opportunity. This idea is illustrated in a volume within C. S. Lewis's Chronicles of Narnia series entitled *The Last Battle*.[19] In it, Lewis describes the story of Emeth, a Calormene nobleman, whose good deeds and sincere devotion to the evil deity Tash are accepted by Aslan (God) as sufficient to give him entrance into heaven. Why? Because Emeth was faithful to the light Aslan had given him, Aslan accepted his good deeds and devotion to Tash as service and devotion to himself. There is an important moral to this story. If it is possible for God to transform and accept even those who are rightly devoted to an evil deity, then generally benevolent religious traditions may offer much more in the way of opportunities for God to transform and redeem the practitioners of those religions.

But the core of the orthodox inclusivist position is found in its Trinitarian foundations. Clark Pinnock, a well-known proponent of inclusivism, writes that

> The centerpiece of . . . inclusivism is belief in the Spirit as everywhere active, even in the context of the religious life, in advance of mission, preparing the way of the Lord. This belief is based on the doctrine of the omnipresence of one loving and personal God, whose Spirit is present everywhere in the world as the Spirit of the Father and the Son. Logically, if the breath of the gracious God is present, it follows that the Spirit is striving for life and wholeness in every sphere, including the religious. To affirm that the Spirit is prevenient and then deny that he wants to minister grace is tantamount to saying there are two Spirits—a God of creation and a God of redemption.[20]

In trinitarian terms, the universal salvific will of God the Father is carried out through the redemptive incarnation of the Son, and the ongoing empowerment and missionary efforts of the Holy Spirit. It is thus the Spirit who implements the salvific will of God even where Christ is unknown or not fully appreciated. In this way, the Spirit's ministry is what it has always been to premessianic people. That is, the Spirit speaks to premessianic people through creation and every other sphere of life that provides him with salvific opportunities. Thus, while Christ is the designated Savior of all people, not all those who come to him will acknowledge him explicitly in this phase of human existence.[21]

If the view I have been outlining is correct, then the Spirit of God has been active from the beginning in saving human beings both before Christ and then inside and outside of the Christian church. He did so before Jesus was born and does so now where Jesus is unknown or not truly under-stood. In support of that thesis, there are reports in the Old Testament of several "pagan" saints, including Melchizedek (Gen. 14:17–24), and Job, for example. In the New Testament, there are the examples of the Roman Centurion (Luke 7:2–10) and of Cornelius (Acts 11:1–48).

If this is right, then it means that inclusivism implies a new relationship with other religions. That is, it calls for an admission that the Holy Spirit may well be at work in the context of the world's religions. Thus, Christians should engage in a more respectful and dialogical relationship with other religious traditions and perspectives. In that way, even though orthodox Christians hold that Jesus is the criterion of truth in religion, they may be able to use that criterion to discern the fruit of the Spirit in the lives of people outside of the Christian tradition. That would indeed be cause for celebration.

Very well then, how might pluralists and inclusivists evaluate each other with respect to their comparative simplicity and explanatory adequacy?

The Comparative Simplicity and Explanatory Adequacy of Pluralism and Inclusivism

I propose to begin this brief analysis by assuming that Hick's conception of the Real, and orthodox Christian doctrines of the Trinity and Incarna-tion, are coherent. These are, of course, controversial assumptions. Some believe that the Trinity and Incarnation doctrines cannot be given a coher-ent formulation[22] or, even if coherent, cannot be given a religiously relevant formulation.[23] Others believe that Hick's notion of the Real in itself is or may be an incoherent concept.[24] But Hick and a number of orthodox Chris-tians believe in and have argued for the coherence of their ideas about the Real, the Trinity, and the Incarnation.[25] So, with a nod to the principle of charity, I shall accept the coherence of the pluralist concept of the Real, and of the inclusivist doctrines of the Trinity and the Incarnation.

It should come as no surprise to discover that pluralists believe that their theology of religion is true and thus identifies the core of the moral and redemptive mythological truth operative in each religion. Therefore, plural-ists believe generally that the unique doctrines of the world's religions are false because they are the products of sociocultural conceptions formed and developed in response to the Real. For that reason, traditional religious believers of every stripe qualify as prepluralist in their comprehension of the truth value of their own religious traditions and the nature of the moral and salvific means they supply.

Inclusivists, on the other hand, believe that orthodox Christianity is true and that the Spirit's universal redemptive efforts form the basis for God's moral transformation and redemption of everyone who responds positively to the light they are given. Inclusivists believe that Jesus is the criterion of truth in religion and thus that the world's religions have incomplete and even false conceptions where they conflict with what Jesus implies for God, salvation, and morality. Thus, devoted non-Christians have the status of premessianic believers whose full comprehension of the truth value of their own religious traditions is incomplete and at some points even false. Of course, discerning inclusivists do not claim to possess a fully integrated and infallible understanding of every aspect of their own religion.

So, for the reasons I have identified, it seems that pluralists and inclusivists are both committed to sets of beliefs that are bound to elicit strong reactions from inside as well as outside the circle of religious faith. But it should come as no surprise that one's theology of religion commits one to basic truth claims about the world's religions that are inherently controversial. For that reason, both pluralists and inclusivists of good will should grant that making a controversial truth claim about the world's religions does not necessarily entail either triumphalism or intolerance on the part of the pluralist or the inclusivist.

What about the comparative simplicity and explanatory adequacy of pluralism and inclusivism with respect to the data of religion? As we have seen, Hick claims that each significant religious tradition is an equally valid context of moral transformation and salvific efficacy. To account for that, he distinguishes between culturally conditioned responses to the Real and the Real in itself. The Real in itself has only negative qualities and no positive qualities beyond the merely formal. By formal properties Hick means that statements like "We can refer to the Real," "The Real has properties," or "The Real is itself and not another thing," may be genuinely predicated of the Real. By negative properties it is meant that statements like "The Real is not a ship," "The Real is not perfectly morally good and holy," and "The Real is not the creator and sustainer of the universe," may be legitimately said about the Real. In that way, Hick can avoid affirming the view that the logically incompatible collection of qualities attributed to the phenomenal Real apply to the Real in itself. But Hick's conception of the Real in itself may diminish its simplicity and explanatory adequacy by reducing its capacity to explain the data of religion that it is supposed to explain. In what way would it do that?

The answer to that question raises the first set of problems that inclusivists and others can raise for Hick's pluralism. That set of problems relates to Hick's conception of the Real in itself as an ineffable being about which nothing positive can be affirmed except purely formal categories. For if the Real is encountered in the religious experiences of humans and influences them, then it must be causally connected to them in something like the way Kant's noumenal realm provided the basis for the "raw material" of empirical experience. But in this case, the Real must possess the nonformal, positive qualities of having causal relations with humans and of exercising causal powers. This is in tension with Hick's view that the Real has only formal qualities.[26] But that understanding may not be fatal because it would remain open for Hick to agree to some positive, nonformal claims about the Real. But if he were to revise his conception of the Real, then the Real would begin to lose its status as an ineffable being. And such an admission on Hick's part could open the door to a line of reasoning that would conclude that the simplest and most plausible way to connect the Real to the data of religion it is supposed to explain is to admit that the Real is the theistic God.[27] Such an admission from Hick would have significant and problematic ramifications for his version of pluralism. That is so because theists affirm that God is personal, omnipotent, omniscient, and perfectly good and holy. That conception of divine reality means that religions that do not affirm the existence and primal importance of God are false or incomplete at that level of their belief systems. The fallout from that point would function to criticize the simplicity, explanatory adequacy, and truth of Hick's pluralism at a variety of points.

Inclusivists claim that the universal redemptive love of God explains more simply and adequately why a divine being would be involved in the moral and salvific transformations of all humans than does the pluralist alternative. That becomes clear once it is understood how much more difficult a prospect it is to try to connect an ineffable and virtually formless being to the moral and salvific transformations of humans. And, as I mentioned above, if a pluralist either assumed or invoked the universal redemptive love of the Real to explain why it is involved with humans, then the Real in itself would no longer be an ineffable being. In fact, the Real, thus conceived, would begin to take on the qualities of a personal theistic divine agent of gracious love and redemption. And any need to use such "borrowed capital" from the Christian tradition would expose an explanatory inadequacy in the hypothesis about the Real. So, from a comparative viewpoint, inclusivists maintain that the framework and categories required to explain human moral and spiritual growth are to be found by appealing to the plans, purposes, and actions of a loving, redemptive God rather than by appealing to the ineffable Real. Thus, the motivation to love God and others and so to grow and develop morally and spiritually is summed up in Christianity in 1 John 4:19: "We love because he first loved us."

But, as I have already claimed, if Hick does not permit any substantial, positive qualities to be predicated of the Real, then the Real itself may be so distant and remote from human experience and knowledge that its status as a simple and adequate explanation of religious data will diminish.

Of course, Hick may have a more "deistic" or absentee conception of the Real as one who structured the world in such a way that preprogrammed experiences of the Real are "triggered" in humans under certain religiously relevant circumstances. But even that understanding implies that the Real has redemptive purposes, plans, and goals, all of which are qualities of personal agency. And, furthermore, a deistic model may be vulnerable to a naturalist reduction of religious experience to merely psychological reactions to the environment, since naturalists too believe that religious experience is triggered in humans by their environment.[28] Thus, the problem of connecting the Real to the data to be explained exposes the lack of simplicity and the explanatory inadequacy of pluralism. For, if the Real is literally "beyond the scope of our network of human concepts"[29] then its power to explain data adequately is severely reduced since explanatory hypotheses depend for their credibility on concepts that fall within the scope of our network of human concepts.

In short, inclusivists believe that if the Real has only negative qualities and no positive qualities, apart from formal ones,[30] then this makes the Real both unknown and unknowable. Accordingly, the ineffable Real does not appear to be able to offer a simple or adequate explanation of moral transformation and redemption because the determinate qualities that are required to connect the Real to that data literally do not apply. That is, if the Real wants humans to move from a vice like self-centeredness to a virtue like reality-centeredness, then the Real must care for humans, intend their moral transformations, and be trying to influence them to do so by making its will clear to them in some way. But we cannot ascribe intentions, purposes, communication, or any other categories of personal agency to the Real. And it is considerations like these that have led some thinkers to wonder why it should be believed that the Real is benign as opposed to being evil, or otherwise interested in or involved with humans at all. Furthermore, such points tend to call into question how we would determine what an "appropriate" response to the Real would be, as opposed to an "inappropriate" response.

But there are difficulties for inclusivists to face as well. For example, Hick believes that an explanatory problem for inclusivism is exposed when it is claimed that Christ, or the Spirit, is invisibly active in religious traditions. Hick sharpens this charge when he writes that

> The problem is to spell this out more precisely. It needs to be shown by what kind of invisible causality the saving death of Jesus around 30 c.e. has operated to make the other great religious traditions effective contexts of salvation/liberation, apparently to much the same extent as Christianity.[31]

How can inclusivists respond to this objection? The first point to make is that inclusivists do not accept the premise that non-Christian religions are equally effective contexts of salvation. They believe instead that the Holy

Spirit is the missionary source of redemptive love and transformation to everyone, both inside and outside the Christian tradition. That is, since the Spirit is active in every sphere of life, it seems that elements of different religious traditions can be used as contingent instruments of divine salvific opportunity. And, in this context, it should also be pointed out that the Real is likewise posited as invisibly active in the religious traditions. Hence, if invisible causality is a problem for inclusivism, it is also a problem for pluralism. In fact, if what I argued earlier about the simplicity and explanatory adequacy of the pluralist hypothesis is right, then such causality would appear to be a bigger problem for pluralism than for inclusivism. That is so because the epistemic distance between humans and the ineffable Real has not been bridged adequately with relevant connecting qualities, or any special revelation to humans about the Real's plans. But, of course, problems raised for Hick's view do not necessarily exonerate inclusivism. So, how does inclusivism fare with respect to the alleged difficulty Hick raises for it?

Inclusivists affirm that the triune God of love has been actively engaged with humans both where they are and in ways that are relevant to their situations. Thus, they claim, the Spirit has been actively convicting the world of sin, righteousness, and judgment in order to procure the redemption of all those who respond to the light they are given, whether that is before or after Christ. Recall the story of Emeth the Calormene nobleman whose sincere devotion to Tash was accepted by Aslan (God) as sufficient for his redemption. But beyond that, inclusivists are not necessarily committed to the position that the religious traditions themselves are the major focus of God's redemptive efforts. Instead, these traditions may serve as only one dimension of life among others that are equally useful, like general revelation and morality.

To be sure, the answer that I have offered to deal with Hick's criticism of inclusivism is general and lacks specific details. Indeed, such a level of generality should be expected, given the subject matter. For I suspect that everyone must admit to considerable ignorance about the details regarding how God works in each life. This point may become more credible when we reflect on the fact that we cannot provide a detailed account of all of the ways God works in our own lives from the standpoint of our own tradition and experiences. And if that is true, then how can we be expected to grasp the details of how God works outside of our tradition, beyond providing a general speculative account?

Explanatory Problems for Pluralism
Exposed by Evil and Suffering

I will end my essay by identifying one final explanatory difference between pluralism and inclusivism. My point of comparison will be with respect to how each position deals with the problems raised for religious belief by the evil and suffering in the world. Theistic and nontheistic religions have versions of "the problem of evil" that are understood and answered by applying the relevant ideas that they each affirm. But what form does the problem of evil take for Hick's pluralism and what is his answer to it? Is this problem exposed as a "pseudo-problem" when we discover that the moral categories of good and bad, right and wrong, that generate the problem, do not apply to the Real in itself? No. Hick takes seriously the objections that evil and suffering raise for the credibility of religious belief and he offers in response an Irenaean type of Christian theodicy.[32] That theodicy posits two stages in the person-making process: a beginning as a creature created in the image of God and a freely chosen growth and development into the likeness of God as a rational, moral, and religiously mature being. Hick develops the implications of this theodicy from a pluralist perspective where he writes:

> How does this theodicy—or indeed any alternative Christian theodicy—fare when we think of the God of Christian faith as one among a plurality of personae and impersonae of the Real? . . . Such a theodicy is mythological in the sense that the language in which it speaks about the Real, as a personal being carrying out intentions through time, cannot apply to the ultimate transcendent Reality in itself. But such a theodicy nevertheless constitutes a true myth in so far as the practical attitudes which it tends to evoke amid the evils of human life are appropriate to our present existence in relation to the Real. The practical message of the myth is both that good can be brought out of evil and that, in Lady Julian's famous phrase, in the end "all shall be well, and all shall be well, and all manner of thing shall be well."[33]

In this passage, Hick admits that his proffered theodicy is literally false, i.e., "mythological" in his sense of the term. That is, it does not offer a real theoretical solution to the problem of evil that called it into existence as an answer. Instead, his theodicy has as its chief value its instrumental efficacy to evoke in believers an appropriate response to evil and to the Real.

But several difficulties exist for this way of dealing with the problems that evil and suffering raise for the theoretical and the practical credibility of religious belief. First, there is the difficulty of connecting the Real in any determinate way to the problems raised by evil and suffering, or to their proposed solutions. That is, the categories that make Hick's Irenaean theodicy a plausible theoretical response to problems of evil are related to the determinate qualities in God and in humans. These include an omnipotent, omniscient, and perfectly good and holy God who creates free, rational, and moral creatures in a world that operates according to natural regularities. But, as Hick has clearly recognized, once the ineffable Real is introduced, the connections between that ultimate and the world evaporate and the theodicy then fails to resolve theoretical difficulties raised by problems of evil. So, one consequence of Hick's pluralist approach here is that it adds evidential force to the arguments raised against religious belief by evil and suffering. And this may well have deleterious effects for the rational credibility of religion and religious life.

Furthermore, when naturalists call the theoretical integrity of religious belief into question with problems raised by evil and suffering, will the pluralist response salvage that credibility with the admission that its theodicy is false but nevertheless instrumentally valuable? I can see no reason to believe that such a response would be taken seriously. And the loss of explanatory adequacy for pluralism here would tend to undercut the view that the practical implications of that theodicy nevertheless represent an appropriate response to the Real. For example, if I determine that a position is false, I am obligated to reject it. I would not seek to use it simply because it helps me to achieve some end that I consider to be a good end. That is so because I do not want to endorse the immoral principle that the end justifies the means. This point further exposes the difficulty of determining what is supposed to count as an appropriate or inappropriate response to the Real.

On the other hand, and there is irony here, I believe that Hick's Irenaean type of Christian theodicy is theoretically credible as a literal response to the difficult theoretical problems raised for religious belief by evil and suffering.[34] In my view, then, the comparative explanatory advantage that this affords Irenaean inclusivism over Irenaean pluralism, in relation to the problems of evil, seems clear. That is, when taken literally, an Irenaean Christian theodicy is able to address credibly the theoretical difficulties posed by arguments based on evil and suffering. But the mythological account of that theodicy offered by pluralism cannot deflate the theoretical problems of evil or adequately commend practical responses.

If my comparative analysis has been correct, then Hick's pluralism offers a more complex and much less adequate explanation of the data of religion than does inclusivism. That is so because pluralism fails to connect the Real to the data of religion that require explanation, including evil and suffering. On the other hand, inclusivism affirms that God possesses the relevant connecting qualities that make it possible to explain simply and plausibly the important phenomena of religion, including the problem raised by evil and suffering. For all of these reasons, I conclude that inclusivism delivers a simpler and more adequate explanation of the data of religion than does Hick's pluralism.[35]

Notes

1. See, for example, John Hick, *A Christian Theology of Religions* (Louisville: Westminster John Knox Press, 1995); and *An Interpretation of Religion: Human Responses to the Transcendent* (London: Macmillan Press, 1989).

2. From this point onward, I will refer to Hick's Christian pluralism simply as "pluralism," and Christian inclusivism simply as "inclusivism."

3. I am arguing for the simplicity and superior explanatory adequacy of inclusivism over pluralism. I am not arguing for the truth of either hypothesis even

though I am comparing both theories with some of the indexes that are relevant for determining the truth of a hypothesis.

4. Christian restrictivism is the position that God will not save those people who never hear about Jesus and consequently do not come to faith in him prior to their death. Ronald Nash defends a restrictivist view in John Sanders, ed., *What About Those Who Have Never Heard? Three Views on the Destiny of the Unevangelized* (Downers Grove, Ill.: InterVarsity Press, 1995).

5. Christian universalism is the position that all people will ultimately be saved by Jesus. Or, put negatively, no one will be eternally separated from God in Christ. John A. T. Robinson defended universalism in his book, *In the End God* (New York: Harper & Row, 1968).

6. See Thomas Morris, *The Logic of God Incarnate* (Ithaca: Cornell University Press, 1986); and Richard Swinburne, *The Christian God* (Oxford: Clarendon Press, 1994).

7. See, Stephen Davis, ed., *Encountering Jesus: A Debate on Christology* (Atlanta: John Knox Press, 1988) ch. 2; and Brian Hebblethwaite, *The Incarnation: Collected Essays in Christology* (Cambridge: Cambridge University Press, 1987).

8. John Hick has used many of these labels to describe orthodox Christology. See especially *A Christian Theology of Religions*, ch. 4.

9. Refer to the relevant sections in Morris, *The Logic of God Incarnate*; Swinburne, *The Christian God*; Davis, ed., *Encountering Jesus*; and David Brown, *The Divine Trinity* (London: Duckworth, 1985).

10. For a breathtaking, guided tour of the Communist totalitarian horrors wrought during the twentieth century, and the ideas and ideals that fueled them, I recommend the following books: Robert Conquest, *Reflections on a Ravaged Century* (New York: W. W. Norton & Company, 2000); Stephane Courtois et al., *The Black Book of Communism: Crimes, Terror, Repression*, trans. Jonathan Murphy and Mark Kramer (Cambridge: Harvard University Press, 1999); and François Furet, *The Passing of an Illusion: The Idea of Communism in the Twentieth Century*, trans. Deborah Furet (Chicago: University of Chicago Press, 1999).

11. Hick, *A Christian Theology of Religions*, 68.

12. Ibid.

13. Ibid., 69.

14. Ibid., 71.

15. Ibid., 27.

16. Ibid., 101–2.

17. Ibid., 136.

18. Clark H. Pinnock, "An Inclusivist View," in *Four Views on Salvation in a Pluralistic World*, ed. Dennis L. Okholm and Timothy R. Phillips (Grand Rapids, Mich.: Zondervan Publishing House, 1996) 106. For more on inclusivism see also Pinnock, *A Wideness in God's Mercy* (Grand Rapids, Mich.: Zondervan Publishing House, 1992); and John Sanders, *No Other Name* (Grand Rapids, Mich.: Eerdmans, 1992).

19. C. S. Lewis, *The Last Battle* (New York: Macmillan Publishing Company, 1956) 153–57.

20. Pinnock, "An Inclusivist View," in *Four Views on Salvation*, 102.

21. Everyone will stand before the judgment seat of God in a postmortem stage of existence. Those who have been faithful to the light God has given them will meet Christ, recognize him as the truth they have both sought and served, and appreciate him for having provided the true meaning and purpose of their lives and their sal- ·vation. This realization will evoke from them a confession of Jesus as Lord. So, if that confession is a necessary condition for salvation (Rom. 10:9–10), then it will be formally fulfilled in a postmortem stage of existence (1 Pet. 3:18–4:6). On that understanding of the conditions both necessary and sufficient for salvation, a per- son's faithfulness to the light God gives them is a sufficient condition for salvation and is completed with the necessary formal confession of Jesus as Lord.

22. On the alleged incoherence of the Trinity doctrine, see William J. Wain- wright, "Monotheism," in *Rationality, Religious Belief, and Moral Commitment: New Essays in the Philosophy of Religion,* ed. Robert Audi and William J. Wain- wright (Ithaca: Cornell University Press, 1986) 289–314. On the alleged incoherence of the Incarnation doctrine, see, Michael Martin, *The Case Against Christianity* (Philadelphia: Temple University Press, 1991) 125–46.

23. John Hick, *The Metaphor of God Incarnate: Christology in a Pluralistic Age* (Louisville: Westminster John Knox Press, 1993).

24. Alvin Plantinga, *Warranted Christian Belief* (New York: Oxford University Press, 2000) 43–63.

25. Concerning the coherence of the concept of the Real, see Hick, *A Christian Theology of Religions,* ch. 3. Concerning the coherence of the Incarnation and Trinity doctrines, see, Morris, *The Logic of God Incarnate;* and Swinburne, *The Christian God,* chs. 8 and 9.

26. See Philip L. Quinn and Kevin Meeker, eds., *The Philosophical Challenge of Religious Diversity* (New York: Oxford University Press, 2000) 11.

27. Ibid.; see especially the articles by Keith Ward, Paul R. Eddy, and Philip Quinn, who all criticize Hick for his attempted appropriation of Anselmian perfect- being theology to discuss the Real in itself.

28. See the fine and detailed argument to that conclusion in Brown, *The Divine Trinity,* ch. 1.

29. Hick, *A Christian Theology of Religions,* 27.

30. Ibid., 59.

31. Ibid., 22.

32. In fact, Hick has been offering an Irenaean type of Christian theodicy since his prepluralist days. See John Hick, *Evil and the God of Love* (London: Macmillan and Company Limited, 1966).

33. Hick, *An Interpretation of Religion,* 359–60.

34. See Richard Swinburne, *Providence and the Problem of Evil* (Oxford: Clarendon Press, 1998); and Charles T. Hughes, "Embodied Human Agents In- habiting a Material World?" *The Thomist* 58 (July 1994) 389–413, and "Theism, Natural Evil, and Superior Possible Worlds," *International Journal for Philosophy of Religion* 31 (1992) 45–61.

35. I would like to thank Alan Padgett, Robert Prevost, and Christian Kettler for their remarks on an earlier draft of this essay.

10

Evidence for the Incarnation

Richard Swinburne

What reason do we have for supposing that Jesus Christ was God Incarnate, God in human flesh? Before I begin my answer to that question, let me say that my essay is an extremely wide-ranging essay; it touches on innumerable issues of philosophy, church history, and detailed New Testament scholarship, on each of which there is a prolific and contentious literature. The aim of the essay is not to solve these issues, but to show just how one's view on each of these is crucially relevant to reaching a justified conclusion about whether Jesus was God Incarnate. I shall, however, sometimes also give extremely brief arguments for my views on particular issues, in order to give some initial plausibility to those views.

"Incarnation" Defined

What I am concerned to assess is the truth of the official Christian doctrine of the Incarnation, put forward by the Council of Chalcedon in 451 C.E., given the way that doctrine has been understood subsequently in the vast majority of churches that accepted that definition. Chalcedon taught that Jesus Christ was and is essentially God, the Son, the second person of the Holy Trinity, his divine nature being his always, but that from his earthly conception he acquired also a human nature. Now a "nature" is not a thing, a substance; it is a collection of properties possessed by a substance. In virtue of his divine nature, Jesus had essentially all the properties essential to divinity—omnipotence, omniscience, perfect freedom, perfect goodness and so on.[1] A divine individual is not merely one who has these properties, but one who has them essentially, that is, is such that it is not logically possible that it could exist without these properties. In a literal sense, no one can become divine or give up his divinity. Such is the traditional understanding of divinity. But a human nature, unlike a divine nature, seems to me (as it seemed to Chalcedon) not essential to the identity of humans. I, for example, currently human, could, it is logically possible, cease to be human and become a crocodile instead. I could continue to have thoughts and feelings, but crocodile-type ones instead of human ones, and express them through a crocodilian body instead of a human one. And so a human nature, as a way of thinking and feeling, and its natural but not inevitable accompaniment, a human body, can be acquired by one who already exists but does not initially have them.

Chalcedon affirmed that in acquiring a full human nature, God the Son acquired a human body and a "rational soul," which I shall understand, I think plausibly, as a human way of thinking and feeling. To have a body is to operate on the world through that body, and to learn about the world through that body. A divine individual would, of course, be able to operate on and learn about the world without needing a body, but Chalcedon is telling us that in the Incarnation God the Son acquired an additional way of operating on and learning about the world. The two natures, Chalcedon affirmed, were to some extent separate. I shall understand that as claiming that in Jesus, God the Son did his human actions and acquired his human beliefs, to some extent unaware of all the beliefs and all the power which he had as God. But the natures, Chalcedon affirmed, were only to some extent separate; there was as it were a permeable membrane between the two, fully permeable from the divine side, only partly permeable from the human side. Two modern examples can help us to make sense of the notion that one individual can have two separate ways of thinking and feeling. First, there is the Freudian-type example of the person who claims with apparent honesty to have certain beliefs and desires and often acts in the light of them, but also acts often in the light of contrary beliefs and desires, which she denies having. The mother says that she has no doubt that her son is dead, but nevertheless does not seek to close his bank account or dispose of his possessions. The Freudian, and to my mind correct, way of interpreting this sort of case is to say that the mother has two contrary beliefs that guide different actions. Consider now the man who seems capable of pursuing two totally separate trains of thought and acting in the light of both at the same time; he holds a difficult telephone conversation, at the same time as writing a complicated letter about something quite different. These two examples soften us up for the suggestion that Christ, while being essentially divine, and so always omnipotent, omniscient, and perfectly free, allows himself when embodied to act with limited powers in the light of limited knowledge.

The Need for Background and Historical Evidence

What positive reason do we have to believe that Jesus of Nazareth was in this sense God incarnate? The claim that he was so is the hypothesis that a certain historical event occurred; at a certain time, between roughly 4 B.C.E. and 30 C.E., and at a certain place, in Palestine, God walked and talked, incarnate in Jesus Christ. It would not of course have been a very ordinary historical event, but a datable and placeable event nevertheless; and one that, if it occurred, had, as we shall see, lots of very ordinary historical components—Jesus saying and doing certain things, and certain things happening to him.

Now in assessing any historical hypothesis we have to take into account both detailed historical evidence and general background evidence. By the former I mean the testimony of witnesses about and the physical data caused by what happened at the time and place in question. If it is suggested that John robbed a certain safe, then our detailed historical evidence is what witnesses said (about who was at the place at the time in question, and where John was at the time in question), and physical data such as fingerprints and money found in John's garage. Insofar as the detailed evidence is such as you would expect to find if the hypothesis at stake is true, but not otherwise, that is evidence that the hypothesis is true. But we also have to take into account general background evidence of how likely the hypothesis is to be true (relative to rival hypotheses), independently of the detailed historical evidence. This evidence will be evidence of John's past behavior and the past behavior of other suspects, which might for example support strongly a theory that John is not the sort of person to rob a safe, whereas George is just that sort of person. In that case even if the detailed historical evidence is exactly what we would expect if John robbed the safe, but not quite what we would expect if George had robbed the safe, nevertheless, we may rightly conclude that George is the most probable culprit.

In this humble example, the background evidence was fairly narrow: the suspects' past behavior. But the joint influence of background evidence and detailed historical evidence operates also where the background evidence is far more general. Suppose the astronomer observes through his telescope a certain pattern of bright dots that is exactly what you would find if these dots were the debris of a supernova explosion. It is right so to interpret them if your theory of physics, best supported by all the other evidence available to the physicist—that is, the background evidence—allows that supernovae can explode. But if your theory of physics says that supernovae cannot explode, and that theory is supported far better than other theories, then the hypothesis that a supernova did explode on this occasion will need an enormous amount of detailed historical evidence (vastly improbable on any rival hypothesis) before we can regard that as probable—and if we do so regard it, we will have to regard the whole theory of physics that rules it out as itself improbable, given our new detailed historical evidence.

The claim that Jesus Christ was God Incarnate is a claim of cosmic significance; and in consequence the threads of evidence will stretch to the ends of the cosmos. We need to investigate whether our general background evidence about the world supports the claim that there is a God likely to become incarnate in human history in the kind of way Chalcedon said that he did, and then whether the detailed historical evidence is such as you would expect if he had become incarnate in Christ. The stronger your evidence of one kind for your view that Jesus was or was not God incarnate, the less you need to support your view by way of evidence of the other kind.

The Kind of Background Evidence Needed

Jesus could only have been God Incarnate if there is a God. Any evidence supporting the existence of God is therefore evidence in favor of that theory. Any evidence against the existence of God is evidence against the view that Jesus is God Incarnate. I have argued at considerable length over many years[2] in favor of the view that the existence of a universe, its almost total conformity to natural laws, and those laws being such as to lead to the evolution of human beings, those human beings having souls (a continuing mental life whose continuity is separate from the continuity of their physical life), the occurrence of various events in history, and millions of humans having experiences that seem to them to be of God are evidence that makes probable the existence of God. Others have argued that my evidence, together with other evidence, such as the fact of pain and suffering, makes the existence of God improbable. This needs to be argued out, and that cannot be done here. But the relevance is obvious; if the background evidence taken together suggests that there is no God, one would need an enormous amount of historical evidence to support the claim that Jesus was God Incarnate and to overturn the evidence that there is no God. So let us suppose that I am right about the force of the evidence. The kind of God it shows to exist, I have argued, is one defined by the divine properties listed earlier.

Being omnipotent, God could become incarnate in the way I have described, but, being perfectly good, he will only do so if he has good reasons to do so. I believe that he does have good reasons, and I shall so argue. But what I wish most to argue is the crucial relevance of the issue. If we have no good grounds to suppose that God has good reason to become incarnate, then we have a lot less good reason to believe that Jesus was God incarnate than we would have otherwise. When I give my reasons for supposing that God would become incarnate and live a certain sort of life, you will be right to feel that I would not have given these reasons, had I not derived them from the Christian tradition. I do not suppose that anyone, Jews of the first century C.E. or highly secularized Westerners today, would have been clever enough to think up these reasons for themselves. We need the Christian tradition to make us aware of a particular theory of the divine nature, and what a being with that nature might be expected to do (e.g., as worked out in St. Athanasius's *De Incarnatione* and St. Anselm's *Cur Deus Homo*). We need the tradition before we can judge whether or not, by objective standards, background evidence and historical evidence together supports that theory well. Most physicists could never have invented the general theory of relativity for themselves, but once it has been proposed for discussion, they can then assess whether in fact the evidence supports it.

So how should a God of perfect goodness and total power relate to the human race? What needs to be explained is not why God should occasionally intervene in human history, but why he is not in constant manifest loving interaction with all humans all the time; why he did not take all of us to heaven straightaway. And there can I think only be one answer to that, that he wanted us to choose over a significant period of time to find out for ourselves which actions and states of affairs are good or bad and, in the light of that knowledge, to choose the kind of people we are to be (to form our own characters) and to choose how to influence the kind of other people there are to be (to help them to form their own characters) and the kind of world in which we are to live. Therefore he gives to us our reason, experience of different kinds of possible states, free will, and much responsibility. He gives us this responsibility by making a world governed, almost totally, by regular laws of nature, so that our actions have predictable effects.

However, if humans do not adequately discover right and wrong and or if they have some knowledge thereof, but they nevertheless lie and break their promises, hurt and enslave each other, then God has reason to intervene, as any parent does when things get totally out of hand in the nursery.

Our Need for Atonement

The first such reason is to make atonement for the past. The primary reason that Christians have almost always given for the Incarnation of God in Jesus Christ and all that flowed from it was in some sense to reconcile us to God by making atonement for our sins. All humans have wronged God, directly and indirectly. They wrong him directly when they fail to pay him proper worship. Deep reverence and gratitude is owed to the holy source of their existence. They wrong him indirectly when they wrong any of his creatures. For thereby they abuse the free will and responsibility they have been given by God, and to misuse a gift is to wrong the giver. And in wronging God's creatures, they wrong God also in virtue of the fact that he created these creatures. If I hit your child, I wrong you, for I damage what you have exercised your loving care upon.

There are different accounts in the Christian tradition of how the life and death of Jesus could atone for the sins of the world, and they are in general compatible with each other. My account is basically that of Anselm, which I shall argue does not rule out some of the others from also being true.

When a person wrongs someone, he becomes a wrongdoer and acquires guilt. Guilt has to be dealt with. I shall call what needs to be done "making atonement." Atonement has four parts—repentance, apology, reparation, and penance—though all four elements are not needed in all cases. If I wrong you, I must make reparation for the effects of my wrongdoing. If I have stolen your watch, I must return it and compensate you for the inconvenience and trauma resulting from my thieving. If the watch has been destroyed, I must give you something of equivalent value. When I have deprived you of a service I owe you, I must perform the service and compensate you for the delay. But what needs to be dealt with is not merely the effects of wrongdoing; there is also the fact of wrongdoing, that I have sought to hurt you. I must distance myself from that as far as can be done. I do this by sincere apology, that is, by an apology deriving from repentance. But for serious wrongdoing, mere words of apology may sound empty. I can make the apology sincere by doing something extra for you—doing for you more than is needed to compensate for the effects of my wrongdoing. It is this "something extra" that I shall call penance. The process is completed when the wronged person agrees to treat the wrongdoer, in so far as he can, as one who has not wronged him, and to do that is to forgive. It is not necessary, in order for the wronged person to forgive the wrongdoer that the latter should make a full atonement. But, forgiveness, in my view, as opposed to condoning, is only possible if the wrongdoer repents and apologizes, and makes some small attempt at reparation. But how much of this is needed is for the wronged person to determine.

"No one can atone for the sins of another." Not fully, no. But, as Aquinas writes, although confession has to be made and contrition shown by the sinner himself, "satisfaction has to do with the exterior act and here one can make use of instruments"[3]—i.e., one can make use of reparation and penance provided by others. If my child has broken your window and does not have the money to pay for it to be repaired, I can give him the money but it is he who has to give it to you and make the apology. And what would be a suitable reparation and penance for humans to offer to God who owns the universe? An obvious answer might be just one perfect human life, more perfect even than it needs to be, which we others can offer as our reparation instead of the life we ought to have led. We ordinary humans are in no position to offer such a life; we owe so much anyway to God, and are too inclined to wrongdoing. God has no right to send some angel to do such work. He has abundant reason if he wants us to take our wrongdoing seriously enough to make reparation for it, to provide that reparation by himself taking a human nature and leading a perfect human life; and that means a human nature as much like ours as possible in its limitations and temptations, for only so will it be a substitute for our lives.[4]

Other Reasons for God to Become Incarnate

We need not merely atonement for the past, but better information about how to lead good lives in the future, and encouragement and help to do so. Humans can, and to some extent in the centuries B.C.E. did, find out for themselves what is right and wrong. But although the outlines may be discernible, the details are not easy to discover. Are abortion and euthanasia always wrong, or only wrong under certain conditions? Is divorce sometimes permissible? And in all these matters, humans are prone not to face the deliverances of their consciences. They need information. True, this could be provided through a revelation to some prophet without any need for incarnation. But moral information needs to be filled out by moral example;

we need to be shown what a perfect life consists of, and that God has no right to tell anyone else to do for him. It would be good for the information to include encouraging information, e.g., that God will take us to heaven if we trust him and fulfill his commandments. And it would be good if God gave us some extra help in leading the moral life, a community of encouragement, for example.

Then there are reasons why it would have been good anyway that God should become incarnate, even if things had not gone wrong in the human nursery. The most powerful of these reasons to my mind is this: God made humans subject to pain and suffering of various kinds caused both by other humans and by natural processes. God, being perfectly good, would only have permitted this subjection if it served some greater goods. Theodicy seeks to explain what are the relevant greater goods[5]—for example, the great good of humans having significant free choice that involves the possibility of their doing considerable harm to each other. We humans sometimes rightly subject our own children to suffering for the sake of some greater good (to themselves or others)—for instance, make them eat a plain diet or take some special exercise for the sake of their health, or make them attend a "difficult" neighborhood school for the sake of good community relations. Under these circumstances we judge it a good thing to manifest solidarity with our children by putting ourselves in somewhat the same situation— share their diet or their exercise, or become involved in the parent/teacher organization of the neighborhood school. Indeed, if we subject our children to serious suffering for the sake of a greater good to others, there comes a point at which it is not merely good but obligatory to identify with the sufferer. A perfectly good God would judge it a good thing to share the pain and suffering to which he subjects us for the sake of greater goods by becoming incarnate.

There are also a number of other reasons why, even if all had gone well with the human race, it would be good for God to become incarnate. Aquinas lists ten such reasons,[6] giving for each a supporting quotation from Augustine. There is no space to consider most of these, but I will mention just one. This is the reason that by becoming incarnate, God shows us how much he loves us.[7] He manifests his love by getting as close to us in our condition as possible. Recall Kierkegaard's parable of the King and the Maiden. The King seeks to win the love of the humble maiden, but if he appeared to her as a king, he might elicit her love for the wrong reason. So he comes as a servant—but not in disguise, for that would be deception, but really becomes a servant.[8]

But if God did become incarnate, led a perfect human life and gave us example and teaching, we would need both reason to suppose that he had done so in a particular human life, and a means whereby all the benefits of that life could be available to future generations. For if we do not know that a particular human individual led a perfect life, we cannot plead it in atonement for our sins; and if we do not know that the teaching of this prophet rather than that one is the revelation of God, it will be of no use to us. The prophet's teaching should therefore include teaching that this particular prophet was God incarnate and that his life was available as an atonement for our sins; and we would need that life to bear a signature that could come only from God himself. The divine signature can be made by a large violation of natural laws—for only God, who keeps the laws of nature operative, can set them aside. The life of God's prophet, then, needs to be signed by a supermiracle. And the incarnate one needs to provide a means through which God would ensure that the benefits of his life and teaching would be available to future generations and distant cultures; teaching that will include the teaching that the prophet was God incarnate and that his life was an atonement.

So, I conclude, if the background evidence suggests that there is a God of the traditional kind, then not merely does he have the power but good reason to become incarnate—but incarnate in a certain way, not in any prophet but in a certain kind of prophet. This prophet's life would be a perfect human life, providing deep moral teaching, which he announces is a divine life that is available as an atonement for our sins, and is culminated by a supermiracle, and provides a means that makes available that teaching and atonement to future and distant generations. It is in the light of this background evidence that we should look at any detailed historical evidence to see if we have got a good candidate for being God incarnate, for example, Jesus Christ. That is, we should seek detailed historical evidence in the sense of evidence to be expected if the hypothesis that Jesus was God incarnate is true, but not to be expected otherwise.

The Kind of Historical Evidence Needed

The first requirement on a candidate for being God incarnate is that he or she should have led a perfect life and provided deep moral teaching. That Jesus "preached and healed" is in the list of what E. P. Sanders regards as the "almost indisputable facts" about the life of Jesus.[9] That he had table fellowship with "publicans and sinners" as well as with Pharisees, and that he prayed much are also surely fairly uncontroversial. That life ended with him allowing others to do to him their paradigmatic worst—he was "crucified" (another of Sanders's almost indisputable facts). The historical evidence about so many other aspects of the public ministry of Jesus is of course, as New Testament experts have emphasized, scanty and controversial. But to the extent to which a picture does emerge, it is, I suggest, one that, with our limited moral sensitivities, we can recognize as a very good life. There are no blots of the sort which have disfigured many another purported Messiah. The moral teaching is deep, and clearly includes the availability of life after death in heaven to those who try to conform to it. Our limited evidence is that the first requirement is well satisfied for Jesus. But of course he is not alone among the world's prophets in this.

The second requirement is that the candidate should state publicly that his life, culminating in his death, was a sacrifice for sin which we could offer. That Jesus did this is of course controversial. My own view is that Jesus' threat to destroy the Temple and provide a substitute for it in three days has a historical basis,[10] and constitutes an undertaking to provide an alternative means of sacrifice to that of the Temple. Also, the words of institution of the eucharist ("This is my body," "This is my blood") reaffirm that, and provide a means whereby others could offer his sacrifice and obtain its benefits. And it was so much a part of the earliest Christian understanding of Jesus that he "died for our sins"[11] that it is natural to seek a common source for this in his own teaching.

Third, the teaching should also include teaching that the candidate was God incarnate. Now I don't think that Jesus said to anyone before the Crucifixion, "I am God"; it would have been almost impossible for any of the disciples to take that in, together with the fact that he also had a human nature and planned to allow himself to be killed. But I do think that he did and said many things before his Crucifixion from which after the event they could reasonably infer that he was making a claim to divinity. And a major reason why I think that they could reasonably infer this is that the Jewish authorities seemed to have inferred that he made a claim not far off this when they sentenced him to death on the charge of blasphemy[12]—which could hardly mean cursing God but rather belittling God by claiming divine prerogatives (such as the prerogative to forgive sins, praying to God as "Abba" etc.[13]). And again there is a great deal in different strands of the New Testament implying his divinity, so that it is not unreasonable to trace it back to a common source in his teaching, of word or deed.[14] But I acknowledge that the evidence for supposing that Jesus claimed divinity is distinctly weaker than the evidence that he claimed that his life provided atonement.

My fourth requirement is that the candidate should provide a means for subsequent humans to offer that sacrifice, learn the teaching, and be encouraged to follow it; in other words a church, and that that church should teach the doctrines of atonement and incarnation. That "Jesus called disciples and spoke of there being twelve" is one of Sanders's almost indisputable facts. To form a community based on twelve leaders could hardly be understood in first century Palestine other than as a foundation of a new Israel (whether the plan was that it should absorb the old Israel or become separate from it). Sanders writes that the use by Jesus "of the conception 'twelve' points towards his understanding of his own mission. He was engaged in a task which would include the restoration of Israel."[15] Although the gospels are not always in agreement as to who those twelve were, and which of them participated in which subsequent events, they mostly comment that all participated in the Last Supper, with its repeatable (and clearly very early repeated) ceremony, including the sacrificial words. This was a ceremony in which, St. Paul wrote, the participants "proclaim the Lord's death until he come";[16] and, of course, the church that originated from the twelve did teach the doctrines of Atonement and Incarnation.

And, finally, we need a supermiracle. And of course if indeed a corpse dead for thirty-six hours was brought to life again (as the traditional account of the first Easter maintains), we have the kind of violation of natural laws that God alone can bring about. In raising to life again him who had been sacrificed, it indicated the divine acceptance of that sacrifice. And in raising to life again him who had been condemned for certain teaching, it inevitably gave divine approval to that teaching. Since the main access to that teaching for subsequent generations must be through the subsequent witness of the Church which Jesus founded, God must be giving his signature of approval to that also. My view is that we do have quite good evidence for the Resurrection in the form of well-authenticated appearances, the absence of the body from the tomb, and the universal tradition of the Sunday Eucharist.[17]

I conclude that of my five requirements for being God incarnate, some are fulfilled by Jesus very well—some perhaps, let me concede, not so well; for example, maybe the evidence that he claimed divinity is not too strong. What is, however, surely incontrovertible is that there has not been so far in human history another remotely plausible candidate for satisfying my five requirements. There are to start with no other known humans who both led good lives, intended them as a sacrifice we could offer, claimed divinity, and founded a church which successfully taught these things. And what is even more incontrovertible is that there is no other religion at all (let alone one claiming an incarnation), for which there is evidence of the quality associated with Jesus' resurrection, for the occurrence of a supermiraculous foundation event. Muhammad claimed to perform no miracles except the writing of the Qur'an; and however great a work that is, there is little reason to suppose that for an uneducated prophet to write it constitutes violating a law of nature. And although the Israelite religion may have been founded on a miracle, such as the crossing of the Red Sea, the detailed historical evidence for it is simply not in the same league as the evidence of the Resurrection, whatever particular value one gives to the strength of the latter evidence.

But perhaps the one true incarnation is yet to come? If I am right about the reasons for incarnation, then that future incarnation would have to be in character much like that which the Christian tradition teaches that of Jesus to have been. And in that case in allowing the Jesus-phenomenon, God would have allowed a wicked and vastly influential plausible deception to be practiced on the human race for no obvious good purpose. In the light of that, I conclude that on the evidence before us, as I have assessed it, if God has good reason to become incarnate in the way which I outlined, it was in Jesus that he became incarnate.

The Formal Structure
of the Evidence for the Incarnation

Now let me give a little formal structure to the considerations that I have presented so far in fairly informal sentences. Let T be the theory that there is a God of the traditional kind. Let J be the hypothesis that he became incarnate in the kind of way analyzed in this essay (with the five requirements being satisfied), and let H be the hypothesis that he became incarnate in Christ. Let k be our general background evidence of the nature of the world (its orderliness, the existence of humans, and the occurrence of suffering), and let e be the detailed historical evidence—of what is written in the New Testament and other early writings, any relevant physical remains—or rather, more precisely, that there is this kind and quality of evidence in connection with one and only one prophet. Now what we are interested in at the end of the day is how probable it is, on all our evidence (e & k) that God became incarnate in Christ, which the probability calculus formalizes as $P(H/e \ \& \ k)$. And the value we give to that will be determined by the value we give to certain other probabilities. Let $P(T/k)$ be the probability that there is a God on that background evidence, which I shall call the prior probability that there is a God. Let $P(J/T \ \& \ k)$ be the probability, given the background evidence and that there is a God, that he would become incarnate in the specified way. $P(J/k)$ is a crucial term; this is the probability on our background evidence that God would become incarnate in the specified way; it is equal to $P(T/k) \ x \ P(J/T \ \& \ k)$. Now it would be absurd to think that we often give exact numerical values to probabilities of theories on evidence, be they scientific, historical, or metaphysical theories. But if we are to be able to assess the probabilities of theories, and all science and history suppose that we can, we must be able to give some sort of very rough value to such probabilities, e.g., "close to 1," "as probable as not" (that is, ½), or "very low." I am going to show the consequences for some probabilities of giving certain precise values to other probabilities; but it will be seen that even if you assign only approximate values to the latter, approximate values will also result for the former. But, since it is simpler to operate with precise values, let's suppose for purposes of illustration that $P(T/k)=½$ and $P(J/T \ \& \ k)=¼$; then $P(J/k)=⅛$.

Now there is a famous theorem of the calculus called Bayes' Theorem[18] that states, when J, e, and k represent any propositions whatever, including those which we have abbreviated by these letters, & means "and," and ~ means "not" then

$$P(J/e \ \& \ k) = \frac{P(e/J \ \& \ k) \ x \ P(J/k)}{P(e/k)}$$

$P(e/J \ \& \ k)$ is the probability, if God did become incarnate in the specified way, that (given the background evidence) you would find the kind and quality of historical evidence in connection with some prophet that New Testament scholars have considered in connection with Jesus. $P(e/k)$ is the probability that you would find that sort of evidence at all. It is equal to $P(e/J \ \& \ k) \ x \ P(J/k) + P(e/{\sim}J \ \& \ k) \ x \ P({\sim}J/k)$. The first conjunct simply repeats the higher line; it is the probability on k that God becomes incarnate and you find e. The second conjunct is the probability that on k God doesn't become incarnate and you still find that evidence. So whether $P(J/e \ \& \ k)$ is greater or less than ½ will depend on whether $P(e/J \ \& \ k) \ x \ P(J/k)$ is greater than $P(e/{\sim}J \ \& \ k) \ x \ P({\sim}J/k)$. Now if we say, as earlier suggested, for example, that $P(J/k)={⅛}$, then $P({\sim}J/k)={⅞}$ (for the probability of a proposition and its negation on any evidence always sum to 1). In that case it has to be more than seven times more probable that you'd find e if J is true than if J is false, for $P(J/e \ \& \ k)$ to exceed ½. Everything turns on the likelihood of finding e if God becomes incarnate, relative to its likelihood if he does not. As regards $P(e/J \ \& \ k)$, the evidence is plausibly of the kind and quality which you'd expect to find if the first, second, and fourth requirements for an incarnation were satisfied—such as you'd expect to find if there were a good prophet who taught that his life was an atoning sacrifice and who founded a church that taught the doctrines of his incarnation and atoning sacrifice. Whether it is such as you'd expect to find if the third requirement were fulfilled is more disputable; maybe there's not as much of his claiming by word or deed a divine nature recorded in the New Testament as you'd expect if he did really claim that. Is the Resurrection evidence such as you'd expect if he really rose? If there are too many discrepancies in the Gospel accounts of the Resurrection, maybe it isn't. But taking all the evidence e together, in my view it's not too improbable that if Jesus really was God Incarnate, you would find the kind and quality of evidence that you do. Let's give $P(e/J \ \& \ k)$ a provisional value[19] of ½. $P(e/{\sim}J \ \& \ k)$ measures how likely it is (given the background evidence) that you would find e if J is false. The issue is how likely it is that you would find Resurrection-type evidence in connection with the life of a prophet about whom there was all the other evidence. Now it's fairly unlikely, barring an Incarnation, that there would be even the nonmiraculous evidence in connection with the life of any prophet, evidence of the sort of strength there is in connection with the life of Jesus, that the prophet lived a holy life, taught that he was God Incarnate who would provide atonement for sin, and founded a church that taught these things. My reason for saying that this is fairly unlikely is that there has only been one prophet in human history about the requisite features of whose life there is evidence of that strength. It is also very unlikely that there should be Resurrection-type evidence of the strength in question in connection with any prophet, as again is evidenced by the fact that such evidence is connected with only one such prophet in human history. But that the two groups of evidence should coincide on the same individual is to my mind very improbable indeed if there is no Incarnation, whereas if there is an Incarnation you would expect the connection. Otherwise the coincidence is quite extraordinary. And, given the probabilities we have allocated so far, for purposes of illustration—that P(J/k)=⅛, P(e/J & k)=¼, P(e/~J & k) would have to be greater than ¹⁄₂₈ if the Resurrection is to have a probability of less than ½ on the total evidence.

What these artificial numbers bring out in more qualitative terms is that so long as (1) you think there's quite a probability on background evidence that there is a God, I've suggested ½; and (2) it's not too improbable that if there is a God, he would become incarnate in the specified way, I've suggested ¼. In other words, it's three times more likely that he would not become thus incarnate than that he would. And so long as (3) you think that if he did become thus incarnate there's a probability of at least ¼ that you'd find evidence of the kind and quality you find in the New Testament, then you'd have to allocate a probability of at least ¹⁄₂₈ to what I've suggested would be an extraordinary coincidence of significant evidence for a Resurrection (itself wildly more significant than that associated with any other prophet) connected with a prophet about whom there is substantial historical evidence that he satisfied all the other requirements for Incarnation, occurring if there is no God who becomes incarnate. I regard ¹⁄₂₈ as a wild overestimate of this. The only way you can save the hypothesis of Incarnation from being probable overall is to downgrade the provisional values I've given to the other probabilities. You may think that there are no good grounds for supposing there is a God—that the fact of suffering gives it a very low probability; I've had no space to discuss this. Or you may think that there's no good reason at all to suppose that if there is a God, he would become incarnate in the specified way—and that would mean a probability of less than ¼ for this. Or you'd have to claim that if God did become incarnate in the specified way it would be very improbable, the probability would be less than ¼, that you would find the kind of evidence you do in the New Testament, because it contains too many facets not to be expected if the hypothesis were true. But if you accept anything like my figures, or indeed, I would say, any figures of the same order of magnitude, P(J/e & k)>½. In that case, since apart from Jesus there is no other candidate for an incarnation of this kind P(H/e & k)=P(J/e & k), the probability that Jesus was God Incarnate will be greater than ½. The overall evidence will show that Chalcedon was right.

Now I have given no more than a few sentences in defense of my views of the force of the detailed historical evidence relevant to whether Jesus satisfied each of my requirements for the specified kind of incarnation, and vast volumes have been written on each of these issues. But what I hope you will accept is my account of the relevance of the force of this evidence to the claim that Jesus was God Incarnate. There are two crucial points. The first is you cannot reach any justified conclusion on this matter without assessing arguments for the existence and nature of God. And the second is that to reject the doctrine of the Incarnation you will have to give a significant value to the probability that there should be as much evidence as there is that all the requirements for incarnation are conjointly fulfilled in the life of one prophet, Jesus, and no other prophet, if Jesus was not God incarnate.

Notes

1. For my account of these properties and how they fit together, see *The Coherence of Theism* (Oxford: Clarendon Press, 1977); and *The Christian God* (Oxford: Clarendon Press, 1994) chs. 6 and 7.

2. See my book *The Existence of God*, 2d ed. (Oxford: Clarendon Press, 1991); and the short version *Is there a God?* (Oxford: Oxford University Press, 1996).

3. *Summa Theologiae* 3. 48. 2 ad 1.

4. My account of how Christ's life and death can serve as an atonement for our sins that we can plead is developed at full length in my *Responsibility and Atonement* (Oxford: Clarendon Press, 1989).

5. For my theodicy, see *Providence and the Problem of Evil* (Oxford: Clarendon Press, 1998).

6. *Summa Theologiae* 3.1.2.

7. Aquinas cites Augustine, *De Trinitate* 13:10—"nothing is so needful for us to build up our hope than for us to be shown how much God loves us."

8. S. Kierkegaard, *Philosophical Fragments*, trans. D. F. Swanson (Princeton: Princeton University Press, 1962), ch. 2.

9. E. P. Sanders, *Jesus and Judaism* (London: SCM, 1985) 11.

10. Sanders remarks that "it is hard to imagine a purely fictional origin for the accusation that [Jesus] threatened to destroy the Temple" (*Jesus and Judaism*, 72).

11. 1 Cor. 15:3.

12. Mark 14:64.

13. See the list of actions of Jesus that might reasonably be interpreted as claiming divine prerogatives in R. E. Brown, *The Death of The Messiah* (New York: Doubleday, 1994) 545–47.

14. If Jesus was to proclaim to the apostles his divine nature, the time when they would be most receptive to that claim would be after his Resurrection. Both Matthew and John claim that after the Resurrection disciples recognized the divine nature of Jesus, a recognition that Jesus did not reject. John records that the formerly doubting, now convinced Thomas confessed, "My Lord and my God" (John 20:28). St. Matthew's Gospel ends with the disciples "worshiping" (*prosekunesan*) Jesus, and with the command to baptize "in the name of the Father, and of the Son, and of the Holy Spirit" (Matt. 28:17–19). Critics, rightly ever on the watch for later interpolations, have of course cast grave doubt on the authenticity of this verse; but the manuscript tradition is unanimous and thus early. In the rest of the New Testament we have the explicit claims of Christ's divinity by the authors of St. John's Gospel (especially John 1:1), Revelation (e.g., 1:17–18), Hebrews (1:8–9), and—to my mind—Phil. 2.6 (a pre-Pauline hymn). Possible explicit claims are also Rom. 9.5 and Titus 2.13. And there are other New Testament passages where the authors attribute pre-existence in God the Father to Jesus. See R. E. Brown, *An Introduction to New Testament Christology* (London: Geoffrey Chapman, 1994).

15. Sanders, *Jesus and Judaism*, 106.

16. 1 Cor. 11:26.

17. I draw attention again to this very important and much-neglected piece of relevant evidence—the fact that all known Christian communities without exception, some of which were founded away from Jerusalem within two or three years of the death of Christ, celebrated the eucharist on a Sunday. See the "Additional Note" to my "Evidence for the Resurrection" in *The Resurrection,* ed. S. T. Davis et al. (Oxford: Oxford University Press, 1997). There are other days on which it might have been more natural for Christians to celebrate the Eucharist (e.g., on the day of the original Last Supper—probably a Thursday and certainly not a Sunday, or annually rather than weekly). No such different celebration days are known. There is no plausible origin of the sacredness of Sunday from outside Christianity (see W. Rordorf, *Sunday,* [London: SCM, 1968] 180–93 for this). There is only one simple explanation—the eucharist was celebrated on a Sunday from the first years of Christianity because Christians believed that the central Christian event of the Resurrection occurred on a Sunday. Yet such early practice would have included that of the eleven themselves, and so could only go with a belief of theirs that Christians had seen either the empty tomb or the risen Jesus on a particular Sunday. This shows that the visit to the tomb on the Easter Sunday was not a late invention read back into history to make sense of the appearances, but a separately authenticated incident.

One reason why people have believed the "third day" tradition to be late is that they have reasonably supposed that the early Christians searched the Old Testament to find possible predictions of the Resurrection and, finding the version of Hos. 6:2 in the Hebrew Masoretic Text that read, "After two days he will revive us: on the third day he will raise us up, and we shall live before him," they attributed the Resurrection to the third day. (If they knew only the Septuagint, they would not have known such a version, for it reads, "on the third day we shall be raised up" [*exanastesometha*]). The evidence of early Sunday eucharistic celebration counts massively against the suggestion that the "third day" prediction is late. Certainly early Christians searched the Old Testament for all they could find by way of types or possible predictions of New Testament events, and they had much success. Both 1 Cor. 15:4 and Luke 24:46 claim that "on the third day" was a scriptural prediction, and it is probably the case that these writers have Hos. 6:2 in mind here. However, it is quoted nowhere in the New Testament as a prediction of the Resurrection. (Indeed, the first text we have in which Hos. 6:2 is applied to the Resurrection is by Tertullian [*Adversus Iudaeos* 13].) Nevertheless it does seem the most likely source of the claim in Luke and 1 Corinthians that "on the third day" was a scriptural prediction. However, in the three predictions of the Passion in Mark (8:32, 9:31, and 10:34), the prediction is that Jesus will rise "after (*meta*) three days"; and in the saying about the Temple in Mark 14:58, repeated by Matthew, the prediction is that Jesus will build it again "in (*dia*) three days." So Mark does not quote the Hosea phrase. Matthew and Luke both replace the "after three days" of the Markan Passion prediction where they write it by "on the third day." (Luke does not contain a detailed second prediction.) This could be either because it fitted the known facts better or because it fitted Hos. 6:2 better. But Matthew gives elsewhere a quite different Old Testament text (the one text actually quoted for this purpose in the New Testament) in order to justify the claim of Resurrection as the third day—Jon. 1:17: "...Jonah was in the belly of the fish three days and three nights." Matt. 12:40 has Jesus say, "As Jonah was three days and three nights in the belly of the whale, so shall the Son of Man be three days and three nights in the heart of the earth." It would have fitted the one text we do know that Matthew had in mind as a prediction of the Resurrection better, to leave the Markan expression ("after") as it stood. So even if Matthew thought of Hos. 6:2 as a prediction of the Resurrection (of which we have no direct evidence), he had rival texts suggesting different days for the Resurrection, and there is no reason why he should change "after three days" merely to fit Hosea. He must have made the change in order to fit (what he believed to be) the facts. For applying Jon. 1:17 literally would mean that Jesus was raised on the Monday (after three days *and* three nights). Yet, of course, Matthew thought that Jesus was raised on the Sunday morning (Matt. 28:1), after only two nights in the heart of the earth. And indeed his quoting the Jonah text, an extremely inaccurate prediction of what he believed to be the day of the Resurrection, casts considerable doubt on whether he even thought of the Hosea text as a prediction of the Resurrection. I conclude that neither Mark nor Matthew can be accused of claiming that the Resurrection occurred on the third day merely in order to fit Hos. 6:2. Of course earlier Christians might have made the claim in order to fit Hos. 6:2. But 1 Cor. 15:4 appears to be part of an early creed cited by Paul; and one that he cited, having discussed what happened with Peter and James within a very few years indeed, of the events in question. And all of that makes it likely that even if "on the third day" is an (unacknowledged) citation of Hos. 6:2, it was cited because if fitted the facts believed to be such for other reasons.

Many Rabbinic passages of the third century C.E. associate Hos. 6:2 with the resurrection of the dead and with the idea that God will not allow the righteous to remain in distress for more than three days. (See H. K. MacArthur, "On the Third Day," *New Testament Studies* 18 (1971–72), 81–86.) But note that this association might be due to Christian influence (it is made in a general context where exact prediction is not at stake) and that the Jonah text is also quoted in several of these passages. So if this association was already there early in the first century, this general idea could have been extrapolated as easily to yield a Monday resurrection as a Sunday resurrection. But in all four Gospels, that the tomb was discovered to be empty on the first day of the week is central to those stories. I conclude that there is no reason to suppose that the "third day" tradition was derived from Old Testament texts, rather than the latter being found as (somewhat weak, in the case of Jonah) predictions of what was believed on other grounds.

18. For a good guide to the use of the probability calculus in assessing the worth of hypotheses, see C. Howson and P. Urbach, *Scientific Reasoning*, 2d ed. (Chicago: Open Court, 1993); or see my somewhat simpler *Epistemic Justification* (Oxford: Oxford University Press, 2001), chs. 3 and 4.

19. "Kind and quality of evidence" can be understood in various ways, ranging from the very rough to the very precise. In suggesting for $P(e/J \& k)$ the figure of $\frac{1}{4}$, I am understanding e in a rough sense—i.e., it is the probability that given J & k, you would find roughly that quality of positive evidence overall for the five requirements (while there could be more evidence for one requirement and less for another), with roughly the amount of discrepancies overall that we find—in connection with one and only one prophet. If you understood "kind and quality of evidence" much more precisely, clearly $P(e/J \& k)$ would be much lower. But then $P(e/{\sim}J \& k)$ would also be correspondingly lower. And so, it will be seen, the value of $P(J/e \& k)$ and so the value of $P(H/e \& k)$ will be unaffected.

11

Wisdom, Christology, and Women Prophets

Karen Torjesen

"Christ came to me in the form of a woman and endowed me with wisdom." This is the declaration of a leader of the New Prophecy movement that flourished in the second and third centuries and survived persecution by Christian emperors in the fifth century.[1] Epiphanius, notorious as a heresy hunter, catalogued the women leaders of the New Prophecy movement among the deceived and the deranged and called the prophet herself "that deluded woman."[2] His antipathy was directed at their reliance upon revelations and their practice of appointing women to the clergy. With Epiphanius's characterization of "that deluded woman" it is important to remember that writing in the 370s he is giving a fourth-century assessment of what was for him an archaic and unsettling form of second-century Christianity, whose style of worship and models of leadership failed to reflect the new forms of authority emerging in the imperial church.

By Epiphanius's time Christianity had become the religion of the empire. The authority of prophets and teachers had been gradually eclipsed by centralizing teaching, administrative, and liturgical authority in the office of bishop. Epiphanius's hostility notwithstanding, it is due to his diligence in collecting "heretical" trivia for his massive catalogue of heresies, *Panarion*, that we have some documentation of the beliefs and practices of churches that reverenced prophecy and valued the leadership of women. What Epiphanius's odd collection of groups (Priscillians, Quintillians, Cataphrygians, and Pepuzans) have in common is the prominence of women leaders.

The few clues about the prophecy churches preserved in Epiphanius's collection raise intriguing questions about a possible relationship between wisdom, prophecy, and women's leadership.[3] The wisdom Christology of first-century Christianity and the wisdom theology of Second-Temple Judaism have proved valuable resources for contemporary feminist scholars, for in these theologies the divine was conceptualized in a female personification: Sophia, Wisdom.[4] Wisdom Christology seemed to offer an alternative to the heavily masculinized Nicene Christology. In addition, wisdom Christology has been a critical element in the reconstructions of early Christianity that highlight women's roles in the formation of Christianity.[5] Feminist theologians have built, on the foundations of early wisdom Christology, a Christian theology informed by an alternate vision of the divine. The importance of wisdom theology for contemporary feminists prompted the question, Was wisdom Christology important for the women leaders of the prophecy churches and, if so, how and why?

The vision Epiphanius cites came from a collection of oracles made by the New Prophecy churches.[6] He attributes it to a woman prophet, either to Priscilla, an early leader of the movement, or Quintilla, a later one, or possibly the leader of another cluster of prophecy churches:

> For these Quintillians or Priscillians say that in Pepuza either Quintilla or Priscilla, I cannot say precisely, but one of them as I said, slept in Pepuza and Christ came to her and slept beside her in this manner as that deluded woman said. "In the form of a woman," she says, "Christ came to me dressed in a bright robe and cast wisdom in me and revealed to me that this place is holy and that Jerusalem will descend from heaven here."[7]

The passage condensed in these few lines of the original oracle recounts a vision—an appearance of the living Christ—an endowment with wisdom, and a revelation. This fragment of an oracle, preserved in a hostile context, designed to label women prophets as heretics, nonetheless opens up some new perspectives on the interconnections between prophecy, wisdom, and women's leadership. Is there a connection between wisdom Christology and prophecy? Why does Christ, the revealer figure, appear in the form of a woman? Why does an endowment with wisdom establish the vocation of prophet? Does a wisdom Christology create a favorable climate for women's leadership? These questions hold no interest for Epiphanius, so we will have to pursue them with the aid of different sources. Only after thoroughly exploring these questions will we return once more to Epiphanius's denunciation of women prophets.

Wisdom Christology and Prophecy

From the beginning, the connection between Jesus and Sophia or Wisdom ran through prophecy. Gospel writers portray Jesus as the emissary of Sophia or Wisdom because he delivers her oracles. In Matthew he becomes the prophet of Sophia when he proclaims, "I will send them prophets and some they will kill and persecute."[8] When Jesus is presented as Wisdom's prophet, Wisdom is represented as the heavenly revealer whose revelations have the status of prophecy. Both Paul and Matthew appeal to Wisdom as a revealer figure who grants revelations and prophecies to her followers. Matthew's Sophia even chooses to reveal divine things to "babes."[9]

Through association with Wisdom Jesus himself becomes a teacher and a revealer. In Matthew's Christology Jesus is not only Wisdom's representative but incarnates Wisdom herself. Jack Suggs in his pioneering work on wisdom Christology explains, "Jesus as incarnate wisdom can speak Sophia's oracle and utters Sophia's lament."[10] This early christology sees Jesus "as Sophia's finest and final representative as the mediator of eschatological and divine revelation."[11] The role of Jesus as sent from Sophia positions him in a succession of prophets of Sophia, underlining again the close connection between Wisdom and prophecy. Even the executions of Jesus and John and other prophets of Sophia confirm the relationship of the prophets to Wisdom. Sophia laments that she is rejected by her children who kill her prophets.

This connection between Wisdom and prophecy in the first century goes back to the close association between Wisdom and spirit in Second Temple Judaism. Wisdom and spirit are linked in Isaiah through the cluster of concepts: the spirit of wisdom and understanding, the spirit of counsel and might, and the spirit of knowledge and fear of the Lord.[12] Here Spirit is understood as the source of divine wisdom, knowledge, and understanding and the fountain of prophecy.[13]

Wisdom and Spirit make their home with special individuals, prophets, sages, and holy men. The writer of the Wisdom of Solomon declares: "From generation to generation Wisdom enters pure souls equipping them to become friends of God and prophets."[14] David Aune in his *Prophecy and Early Christianity* discusses these "friends of God and prophets" under the category of sapiential prophecy. Sapiential prophecy or wisdom prophecy is the form of oracular wisdom associated with the holy men, sages, or philosophers such as Rabbi Yohanan ben Zakkai, the Essenes, and the Jewish philosopher Philo of Alexandria.[15]

Although the connection between Wisdom and prophecy was important for Rabbinic Judaism, it was Alexandrian Judaism, with Philo as its main exponent, which gave primacy to Wisdom.[16] In Alexandrian theology Wisdom is the source of prophecy. It is Wisdom "entering pure souls" that establishes the succession of prophets. Even Torah or Law was derived from preexistent Wisdom; Moses was foremost a prophet and secondarily a lawgiver. The status of the Law as revelation was more significant than its status as a divinely ordained law. Moses' authority as a leader rests squarely on his status as a prophet.

The Wisdom who dwells with individuals shares in and manifests the divine nature. The writer of the Wisdom of Solomon uses *pneuma* and Sophia interchangeably to express the effulgence of God. Wisdom and spirit are the reflection of the eternal light, the mirror of God's power, the image of God's goodness.[17] These connections between Wisdom and Spirit express the conviction that the source of Spirit-inspired knowing is Wisdom.

Wisdom and the Vocation of Prophet

We know little of the Christology of the New Prophecy movement and little of the place of wisdom in their theology. We do know that in the Hellenistic period the pursuit of wisdom was equivalent to the pursuit of the divine. The cultures of the Mediterranean recognized many mediators of the divine—sages, prophets, and philosophers—all of whom enjoyed a special commerce with the divine. Such mediators were considered friends of God, they had a recognized vocation as prophets or sages. Christian teachers placed the figure of Christ at the center of the divine and made him the goal of the quest for wisdom. They took the idea of cosmic wisdom dwelling in the soul and reinterpreted it as the divine Christ taking up residence in the human soul. Newly baptized Christians who had received this indwelling wisdom were called the illuminated ones, the enlightened ones, for now they possessed the knowledge of the divine.[18]

In general the theology and self-understanding of first- and second-century Christians is difficult to discern for those communities for whom prophecy was central to their mode of worship. The later polemic against prophecy churches has eradicated most of the sources from which one could reconstruct their Christology and anthropology. However, Antoinette Wire is able to glean valuable insights into the connections between wisdom and the vocation of prophecy in the first century by using a method of rhetorical analysis.[19] Wire reads Paul's first letter to the Corinthians as a literary source for a debate over prophecy between Paul and the Corinthian prophets. By doing a surgical kind of rhetorical analysis, she has been able to dissect Paul's admonitory letter to show the strands that represent the self-understanding and worldview of the Corinthian prophets. What is at stake in the differences between Paul and the Corinthian prophets is the threefold relationship among Christology, anthropology, and prophecy. The points of dispute between the two parties are the nature of Christian wisdom, the form of its mediation (prophecy), and the nature of Christian identity or theological anthropology.

When Paul names Christian wisdom as "the things prepared for those who love God," "the depths of God," "the things of God's Spirit," and "the mind of Christ," he is defining the common ground between them—a wisdom Christology.[20] "The things prepared for those who love God" define Christian identity as future and atemporal, hidden and glorious. "The things of God," "the depths of God's Spirit," and "the mind of Christ" are Christian ways of designating the highest reaches of the noetic cosmos, the domain of Wisdom. Christian prophets mediate this cosmic knowledge.

It is at this point that the differences between Paul and the Corinthian prophets surface. The two parties differ on their theological anthropology or the question of Christian identity. Anthropology and cosmology are inextricably linked. The Corinthian prophets understood their baptism into

Christ to be the entry into a single common identity. This new identity is understood as a new humanity deriving from the person of Christ. Because this new humanity is in God's image, it is capable of mediating the divine. Consequently, the Corinthian prophets understood themselves to "have all knowledge" and believed that "to them all things were authorized."[21]

The spirituality of the women prophets celebrates their identity with Christ, their oneness with Christ, their possessing the mind of Christ, and their representing Christ's glory, and accepts as a given their power and right to manifest the divine in the human world. They possessed the wisdom, "the mind of Christ" that was "ordained from the beginning for our glory." Through possessing God's wisdom the Corinthian prophets have become wise, powerful, and honored.[22] Their self-confidence, their authority, and their honor derived exclusively from their Christology in which the divine is revealed through the human. God's glory and God's honor are realized through the presence of the divine in the human rather than through a sharp demarcation of the human from the divine.

Their life was modeled on the glorified resurrected life of Christ. It is the cosmic identity of Christ that establishes their identity as Christians. "They take their new life as a full, independent, and self-confirming presence of the divine Spirit in them."[23] This affiliation with Christ and participation in the resurrected life, new birth, and new creation invested the Corinthian prophets with a heavenly status, one that placed them above the intermediary daimons in that, unlike the daimons, they shared the status of the cosmic Christ. The Corinthian prophets, like angels, "represented consummate knowing and speaking across a porous boundary between the human and the divine."[24] Two dramatic consequences flow from this: They no longer are subordinate to the intermediary cosmic powers and, because they have a status elevated above the daimonic realm, they possess authority over all.[25]

Paul contests the Corinthian prophets' claim to this heavenly status by insisting that his gospel preached a *crucified* Christ, meaning Christian identity should be modeled on the crucified Christ. For Paul, a genuine spirituality is a spirituality of self-deprecation based on a profound awareness of the distance between divine and human wisdom, goodness, and power. Similarly, Paul's Christology recapitulates his spirituality of self-deprecation based on loss of status. Christ also voluntarily submitted himself to a radical loss of status: "Christ, who though he was in the form of God...emptied himself and took on the form of a servant" (Phil. 2:6–7, RSV).[26] Paul's strongest attack is on their sense of identity. His concern is that they cultivate a self-identity of subordination. Paul critiques their triumphant celebration of their new heavenly identity, their cosmic identity, as mere human boastfulness. In tones rich with sarcasm, he declares their sense of heavenly identity of being "already filled," "already rich," and "already ruling" as decidedly premature (1 Cor. 4:8, RSV).

What Paul particularly challenges is their claim to mediate cosmic knowledge, Christian wisdom. He does this by acknowledging their powers of revelation, prophecy, and knowledge, but he dissociates prophecy, tongues, and knowledge from wisdom by labeling them immature and partial.[27] Although they claim to speak wisdom among those who are perfect, they are in fact babes in Christ, not ready for full spiritual wisdom.[28] Not only are the prophets immature, their knowledge is only partial. If the knowledge that the Christian prophets mediate is partial, fragmentary, dark, and inchoate, then their spiritual status as mediators is necessarily restricted and limited.[29] By dissociating prophecy from wisdom and distinguishing the former as immature and the latter as mature, he creates a difference in social identity. He creates for them a diminished spiritual identity.

The Corinthian women prophets understand Christ's resurrection to be a present and existential event, a temporality into which they enter through baptism and a new life, a resurrected life that presently transforms every element of their existence. "The Corinthian women prophets claimed direct access to resurrected life in Christ through God's Spirit. Being thus filled, rich and ruling, they take part in Christ's joyful meal and God's word goes forth from them to each other in ever widening circles."[30] The resurrection life of Christ is mediated by the presence of the Spirit given at baptism to all and operating through all in prophecy, speech for God, and prayer, ecstatic speech to God.

Antoinette Wire's reconstruction of the wisdom Christology and self-understanding of the Corinthian prophets still leaves open the question whether these views were characteristic of other prophecy churches, although it does lay the groundwork for such an investigation. Karen King, a scholar of Gnostic Christianities, has built on Wire's work by analyzing texts from four different prophecy churches: the Gospel of Mary, Perpetua's diary, Tertullian's *On the Soul*, and the oracles of the New Prophecy. She has identified four features common to these diverse groups that value prophetic leadership:

Theological reflection centered on the experience of the person of the Risen Christ more than the crucified Savior. Jesus was understood primarily as a teacher and mediator of wisdom rather than ruler or judge.

Unmediated access to God through the Spirit is available to all. The spiritually advanced encouraged the beginners but are not set apart as a clerical order. . . . An ethics of freedom and spiritual development is emphasized over ethics of order and control.

Identity as a Christian is constructed apart from gender roles, sex and childbearing. Gender is itself contested as a "natural" category in the face of the power of God's Spirit at work in the community and the world.

In Christian Community the unity, power and perfection of the
Spirit are present now, not just in some future time.[31]

Her analysis shows that a wisdom Christology is associated with unmediated access to the divine, freedom from cultural ideas of gender, and an
emphasis on spiritual development, rather than clerical order. The realized
eschatology of these prophecy churches translated the implications of a wisdom Christology into the everyday lives of Christians who prophesied and
taught the truths of the transcendent realm and understood themselves to
have transcended gender.

Female Revealer Figures

Divine female revealer figures were not uncommon among these groups that
valued the role of the prophet and accepted the authority of revelations.
In Rome a female revealer figured prominently in another second-century
collection of vision and oracles, the Shepherd of Hermas.[32] A freedman,
Hermas, describes an encounter with a heavenly female figure who has the
appearance of the lady who had been his mistress. The first vision is a dialogue in which Hermas is exhorted and corrected by this familiar figure. In
succeeding visions she appears as an ancient woman and commissions him
to write down her revelations. At this point she is revealed to be the church,
"the first of all created things, for her sake the world was established," the
preexistent and eternal church who has chosen him as her messenger.[33]

Further north in the churches of Lyon and Vienne, prophets were
also honored and their revelations accepted.[34] The ethos of the prophecy
churches that saw in their women powerful mediators of the divine is
captured in the account of the martyrdom of their sister Blandina:

> But Blandina was hung on a post and exposed as food for the wild
> beasts let loose in the arena. She looked as if she was hanging in the
> form of a cross, and through her ardent prayers she stimulated great
> enthusiasm in those undergoing their ordeal, who in their agony saw
> with the outward eyes in the person of the sister, the One who was
> crucified for them.[35]

In the figure of Blandina, the martyred slave and leader of the small band of
Christians, arrested, imprisoned, and slated to be executed, the writer saw
the gynemorphic Christ, Christ in the form of a woman.

One collection of oracles did make it into the New Testament canon,
that of John the Seer, titled appropriately, Revelation. His revelation also
features heavenly female figures as central actors in his apocalyptic drama.
John's visions include "a woman clothed with the sun, with the moon under
her feet," the church, the bride, and the New Jerusalem clothed also in white
as a bride for the Lamb.[36]

In another first-century text, Joseph and Asenath, a female revealer figure, the angel Repentance, appears to Asenath upon her conversion from the pagan worship of the Egyptians to Judaism.[37] The storyteller describes the angel Repentance as beautiful and powerful, the sister to the chief of angels. Like Wisdom, the angel Repentance "renews all who repent and waits on them herself for ever and ever."[38] Through her encounter with this angel and her brother, "the ineffable mysteries of the most High" are revealed to her and Asenath gains the status of a prophetess.

While there are a variety of heavenly women, the female revealer figure par excellence is Sophia, divine Wisdom. In the theology of Second-Temple Judaism and early Christianity, divine Wisdom appears universally in the form of a woman and often in the role of a revealer.[39] The Wisdom who inspired the prophets and taught Moses the Law is Lady Wisdom. The same Lady Wisdom, pictured as descending and ascending, mediating between the human and the divine, imparts knowledge of the divine to prophets, sages, and holy men alike.

Sophia, Wisdom, appears regularly in Gnostic cosmologies as a female aeon, or hypostasis, a mediator between the divine and human realms.[40] In Gnostic Christianities Sophia is also a revealer figure, sometimes of partial knowledge, sometimes of full. It is her work as revealer and teacher that makes her a savior figure. Gail Corrington, in her fine study of female savior figures, has this to say of Wisdom: "She comes from the heavenly realm; she descends, in some form, to earth; and she is responsible for the ultimate salvation of humanity... imparting knowledge... calling her own out of the world and making them children of God."[41]

The Gynemorphic Christ

Returning again to the vision of Priscilla, we note that Christ as revealer appears in a female form to a woman prophet. What does the femaleness of this revealer Christ signify? The two scholars who have written extensively on women and Montanism, Anne Jensen and Christine Trevett, have offered different interpretations of this oracle. Jensen, who attributes the vision to Priscilla, locates it in the earliest stage of the New Prophecy movement.[42] For Jensen the vision of a gynemorphic Christ is unique: "the vision of Christ in the form of a woman is unusual and bold: there is no direct parallel in early Christian literature! The gnostic Sophia figure, the concept of the feminine nature of the Holy Spirit, and the personification of Jerusalem as a bride belong to other traditions."[43] Jensen sees no continuity between the gynemorphic Christ of Priscilla's vision and other female representations of the divine.

It is not exactly clear what Jensen means by other traditions. The cosmic Sophia of Gnostic Christianities, a female character in a cosmic drama, is also a revealer figure, and the female representation of the Holy Spirit in

Syrian Christianity also imparts wisdom. It may be safer to say that this is the strongest expression of the idea of a gynemorphic Christ.

Trevett assigns the vision to Quintilla, a later prophet and leader of the Quintillians. Trevett sees a continuity between Quintilla's vision of a female Christ and other literature of the same period, such as a conjunction of a vision of the New Jerusalem descending and a divine female figure.[44] She notes parallels between the New Prophecy churches and the community that produced 4 and 5 Ezra.[45] Both preserve visions of divine female figures in conjunction with a revelation of the descent of Jerusalem.[46]

Both Jensen and Trevett agree that the vision serves as a commissioning of the prophetess, although they disagree on who she is.[47] Trevett, who attributes the vision to Quintilla, sees in the female Christ a hypostasis of the church, though she acknowledges that the theme of Wisdom is clearly important: "the female Christ imparted Wisdom to Quintilla and Wisdom was itself female."[48] Jensen, who attributes the vision to Priscilla, identifies the gynemorphic Christ with Wisdom.

Priscilla's claim to be visited by Christ in female form may be unique, yet the gynemorphic Christ is surprisingly congruent with the theology and practices of the churches of the New Prophecy. A revealer figure who endows with wisdom correlates easily with a wisdom Christology that sees Christ as a revealer, a personification of Divine Wisdom. Trevett, in her discussion of the oracle, underlines the connection between Wisdom and the granting of a revelation, observing that also in the book of Revelation Wisdom is named "prior to the revelation of the hitherto hidden meaning." Paul himself speaks of the Spirit of wisdom and revelation as belonging together.[49]

Wisdom and Female Leadership

As with male leadership, it is Wisdom the revealer who speaks through the female prophet, female sage, or female teacher.[50] When the gynemorphic Christ appears to Priscilla in the form of a woman, the vision functions as a divine commissioning. The endowment with wisdom transforms her into a prophet and leader. So long as Wisdom resides with her, Wisdom is the source of the truth and of the authority of her teaching. It is the vision of a Christ who imparts wisdom to her and launches her career as a prophetess. However, the vision underlines her authority not so much as an ecstatic prophet but as a teacher of wisdom.[51] A prophet's authority as a teacher is not dependent on moments of divine inspiration; once wisdom has been imparted, she is a prophet, sage, and teacher for life.

The Gospel of Mary presents an even clearer example of a vision of the living Christ as a foundation for authority as a teacher and prophet. In the surviving fragments of the gospel, Mary narrates: "I saw the Lord in a vision and I said to him, 'Lord, I saw you today in a vision.' He answered and said to me, 'Blessed are you, that you did not waver at the sight of me. For where the mind is, there is the treasure.'"[52] Mary's role as it is represented in this gospel is to teach, guide, and instruct the disciples. The special revelation she has received becomes part of her teaching and the basis for her authority. Her authority did not go unchallenged. In the story told by this gospel, Peter questions the legitimacy of her revelation because it was secret and the legitimacy of her leadership because she was a woman. However, this challenge is successfully met, the other disciples confirm both her teaching and her leadership. Peter is finally rebuked.

The visions of Hermas, Asenath, and Mary Magdalene that serve to authorize their authority as prophets and teachers all imagine a dialogue between the prophet and the revealer. The process of revelation imagined here is not simple dictation, the recording of an oracle, but rather a process of teaching and learning in which the prophet plays an active part. The prophet as student questions, formulates an understanding, is corrected, gains a deeper understanding, and is finally recognized as having grasped the revelation. It is this dialogical character of revelation that establishes that the prophet is indeed a teacher, that she has grasped the mysteries and is capable in her own right of explaining them.

The revelation to Priscilla about Jerusalem and the endowment with wisdom presupposes an auditory experience as well as a vision and may have included a dialogue in its original form. In Tertullian's account of the experiences of the prophetess in his house church, she also holds conversations with the angels. A prophet who received revelation was one capable of "conversing with angels."[53] Not only was the process of receiving revelation dialogical, but the process of teaching was dialogical as well. Individuals who could mediate the divine were expected to be in constant communication with the divine, for Wisdom dwelled within them. Karen King summarizes her examination of women prophets in four different early Christian communities in this way: "Once a prophet's knowledge of God was acknowledged, her status as a teacher was ensured. Even where the role of teacher had become more formalized, it was still connected with prophetic inspiration."[54] An endowment with wisdom and the indwelling presence of Wisdom explained these unusual capabilities.

Gender and Leadership

Epiphanius concludes his synopsis of the prophecy churches with a diatribe against women's leadership:

> It is totally laughable among human beings to separate from the correct belief and turn to vanity and the variety of ecstasies and frenzies. Deranged minds follow those who do not hold fast to the anchor of truth and those who yield themselves to anyone who would lead them after any cause whatsoever. Even if women among them are ordained to episcopacy and presbyterate because of Eve, they hear the Lord saying:

"Your orientation will be toward your husband and he will rule over you." The apostolic saying escaped their notice, namely that: "I do not allow a woman to speak or have authority over a man." And again: "Man is not from woman but woman from man"; and "Adam was not deceived, but Eve was first deceived into transgression."[55]

Epiphanius expresses his outrage over women leaders by appealing to biblical supports for a gender hierarchy. Christians in the New Prophecy movement were, of course, familiar with these biblical passages but did not read them in the same way. Such divergence over scriptural meanings suggests that Epiphanius's own attitudes toward gender were conditioned more by cultural beliefs about gender than by a particular biblical hermeneutic. It is to these cultural beliefs that we now turn.

Notions of masculinity and femininity were interpreted through a single-sex theory of gender.[56] In this androcentric system humanity reached its fullest expression in maleness; femaleness was a diminished expression of humanity. Gender differences were simply relative positions on a single scale ranging from more perfect to less perfect. A man may be more or less masculine, a woman might become more or less feminine depending on how close or far they were from the single ideal of a perfected masculinity.

Ancient notions of gender were inextricably entangled in "the great chain of being" that stretched from inert matter through terrestrial life forms toward the highest reaches of the immaterial, abstract, or spiritual depending on the philosopher. This ontological scale was inextricably entangled in the ancient Greek notions of gender. Sexual differences were represented as degrees of differentiation along a single spectrum, locations along a single ontological gradient. Maleness stood higher on this ontological gradient than femaleness. Women's social subordination was reinforced by notions of her ontological inferiority.

This ontological deficiency of woman, her diminished maleness, is expressed culturally in the notion of female shame. At its core the concept of female shame signifies the recognition of this status of deficiency, the awareness of a lack, a consciousness of the kind of power and potency that a woman does not possess, and an acquiescence in that lack. This perspective on gender lies behind Epiphanius's attack on women leaders.

A different perspective on gender lies behind the gynemorphic Christ of Priscilla's vision. The appearance of Christ in a female form would create little dissonance among the congregations of the New Prophecy where women were appointed to the clergy and held the office of bishop and priest. The femaleness of Christ would not be read as a cipher for either social subordination or ontological inferiority. Their Christology recognized no hierarchy of gender. The formula "for in Christ there is neither male nor female" functioned like a charter for their church organization.[57]

The composite that Epiphanius creates out of the various groups associated with prophecy presents them as having their own theological anthropology, especially as it relates to ontological femaleness. These groups, explains Epiphanius, "attribute a special grace to Eve because she first ate of the tree of knowledge." Eve, the prototype of woman, also received a special endowment, a grace that endowed her with knowledge. The tree of which she ate imparted knowledge, not death. Eve is the prototype of the teacher rather than the prototype of the sinner.

According to Epiphanius's reading of the records of these groups, women are appointed to the clergy because they possess prophetic authority. Miriam, the sister of Moses, was a prophet, and the daughters of Moses were prophets. The women leaders of the prophetic churches stand within a lineage of female prophet/leaders. It is the leadership of women prophets that provides the precedent for women bishops and presbyters.

A Christology that understood Christ as divine Wisdom was important in the prophecy churches, not so much for the fact that the divine was gendered feminine, but because Wisdom mediated the divine in a way that transcended gender and indeed all social roles. Prophecy presupposed continuity between the human and divine realms. Prophets were presumed to share a kinship with the divine; they were even able to converse with angels. A prophet had not only access to the divine, but also the power to mediate the divine and the authority to represent it. The communion with the divine invested the prophet or revealer with wisdom and insight into the nature of things, into the reason for things, into the human heart, and into the future. On the basis of this authority women prophets became bishops and priests. As Wisdom was displaced by the rule of faith and prophecy by preaching, women leaders lost an important foundation for their authority.

Notes

1. Epiphanius, *Panarion* 49. Trans. from Ross Kraemer, *Maenads, Martyrs, Matrons, Monastics* (Philadelphia: Fortress Press, 1988) 226. The New Prophecy movement began in the late second century in Asia Minor. However, churches that embraced prophecy, whether or not they were associated with this movement, were located throughout the Mediterranean, in Spain, Gaul, and North Africa as well as in Asia Minor; the New Prophecy movement was especially strong in Phrygia. By the fifth century the New Prophecy movement was called by the name of the first prominent man in the movement, Montanus, hence Montanism. Older scholarship follows the nomenclature Montanism; recent scholarship uses the term New Prophecy.

2. Ibid. Epiphanius was Bishop at Salamis on the island of Cyprus from 367–403.

3. I have chosen the term "prophecy churches" to create a broader category than Montanism or the New Prophecy movement. Prophecy played a significant role in house churches from the first century forward. Not all churches that accepted prophecy were part of the New Prophecy movement that originated in Phrygia.

4. The importance of the Sophia traditions for Hellenistic Jewish thought and early Christian theology was already well established by male scholars such as

Jack Suggs and Burton Mack, but they made little of the gender of wisdom. See M. Jack Suggs, *Wisdom Christology and Law in Matthew's Gospel* (Cambridge: Harvard University Press, 1970) and Burton Mack, *Logos und Sophia: Untersuchungen zur Weisheits Theologie im Hellenistischen Judentum* (Göttingen: Vandenhoeck & Ruprecht, 1973).

5. Elisabeth Schüssler Fiorenza, *Jesus, Miriam's Child, Sophia's Prophet* (New York: Continuum, 1994); Elizabeth Johnson, *She Who Is: The Mystery of God in Feminist Theological Discourse* (New York: Crossroad, 1992); Ashphodel P. Long, *In a Chariot Drawn by Lions: The Search for the Female in Deity* (London: Women's Press, 1992).

6. Ronald Heine has collected the few surviving Montanist oracles in a volume, *Montanist Oracles and Testimonia*, ed. Ronald Heine, Patristic Monograph Series no. 14 (Macon, Ga.: Mercer University Press, 1989). William Tabbernee has added to these oracles and also published a rich collection of Montanist inscriptions, *Montanist Inscriptions and Testimonia* (Macon, Ga.: Mercer University Press, 1997).

7. Epiphanius, *Panarion* 49.

8. Matt. 23:34ff and Luke 11:49.

9. Matt. 11:25.

10. Suggs, *Wisdom Christology and Law,* 96.

11. Ibid., 97.

12. Isa. 11:2.

13. Suggs, *Wisdom Christology and Law,* 54. The fusion between Sophia and spirit is even more complete in Wisd. of Sol. 1:6–7, 7:22, and 9:17.

14. Wisd. of Sol. 7:27. R. W. Charles, *The Apocrypha and Pseudepigrapha of the Old Testament,* vol. 1 (Oxford: Clarendon Press, 1963).

15. David Aune, *Prophecy and Early Christianity in the Ancient Mediterranean World* (Grand Rapids, Mich.: Eerdmans, 1983) 244–52.

16. *Prophetes, Theological Dictionary of the New Testament,* ed. Gerhard Friedrich, vol. 6, CII.1.2. (Grand Rapids, Mich.: Eerdmans, 1976) 821. In Rabbinic Judaism the Law is the source of all and flows outward in the succession of prophets and sages. In Alexandrian Judaism, wisdom plays this role.

17. Wisd. of Sol. 7:26 in Charles, *The Apocrypha and Pseudepigrapha of the Old Testament.*

18. Justin, *Apology,* 61.

19. Antoinette Wire, *The Corinthian Women Prophets: A Reconstruction Through Paul's Rhetoric* (Minneapolis: Fortress Press, 1990). It should be noted that given the paucity of first century sources, most reconstructions of first century theologies rest on the same speculative basis. See also Thomas Gillespie, *The First Theologians* (Grand Rapids, Mich.: Eerdmans, 1994) 165–69 for the connections between prophecy and wisdom.

20. Wire, 48; 1 Cor. 2:6–16.

21. Wire, ch. 5.

22. Wire, 60–65.

23. Wire, 45; 1 Cor. 1:5–7.

24. Wire, 127.

25. Poimandres 1.15. Their heavenly nature means they have authority over all. It is only their mortal nature that is subordinate to the Fates. As superior to the heavenly bodies, they are impervious to Fate.

26. Wire, 63–65. Ann Wire suggests that the spirituality of self-deprecation has parallels in the Wisdom of Solomon, 4 Maccabees, and Philo's *Life of Moses*. Furthermore, Paul declared the preaching of Christ foolishness over against the wisdom claims of the Greeks. By implication the prophets are over against Christ as wisdom.

27. Wire, 48.

28. 1 Cor. 2:6; 1 Cor. 3:1; 1 Cor. 13:8–11.

29. 1 Cor. 13:8–11.

30. Wire, 185.

31. Karen King, "Prophetic Power and Women's Authority: The Case of the Gospel of Mary Magdalene," in *Women Preachers and Prophets through Two Millennia of Christianity,* ed. Beverly Mayne Kienzle and Pamela J. Walker (Berkeley: University of California Press, 1998) 33.

32. The Shepherd of Hermas is a collection of visions, mandates, and similitudes given as revelation to a freedman sometime in the mid-second century in the city of Rome.

33. Hermas, Vision ii.iv.

34. The account of the Martyrs of Vienne and Lyon executed in 177 is preserved in Eusebius, *The History of the Church,* trans. G. A. Williamson (London: Penguin Books, 1965) V.1.

35. Eusebius, *History of the Church,* 145.

36. Rev. 12:1; 21:2, 9.

37. Joseph and Asenath in *The Old Testament Pseudepigrapha,* ed. James H. Charlesworth (Garden City, N.Y.: Doubleday, 1985) 2:177ff. See also Ross Kraemer, *When Joseph Met Asenath: A Late Antique Tale of the Biblical Patriarch and Egyptian Wife, Revised* (New York: Oxford University Press, 1998).

38. Joseph and Asenath 16.14.

39. Celia Deutsch, *Lady Wisdom, Jesus and the Sages* (Valley Forge, Pa.: Trinity Press International, 1996).

40. Gail Patterson Corrington, *Her Image of Salvation: Female Savior and Formative Christianity* (Louisville: Westminster John Knox, 1992).

41. Corrington, 124–25.

42. Ann Jensen, *God's Self-Confident Daughters: Early Christianity and the Liberation of Women,* trans. O. C. Dean, Jr. (Knoxville: Westminster John Knox, 1996); Christine Trevett, *Montanism: Gender, Authority and the New Prophecy* (New York: Cambridge University Press, 1996).

43. Jensen argues persuasively that the vision was early and came to Priscilla and accounts for the importance of Pepuza as a "center for the new prophecy movement." See p. 166.

44. Trevett assigns the oracle that associates Pepuza and the descent of the New Jerusalem to Quintilla rather than Priscilla based on the absence of any reference to the connection to Pepuza and Jerusalem in Tertullian's writings (p. 98, also pp. 167ff.). The seer of the revelation had also prophesied that the church at Philadelphia would be the New Jerusalem (Rev. 3:12). Furthermore, Philadelphia

was also the home of the prophetess Amnia who was included in the prophetic line of the New Prophecy. See Trevett, *Montanism*, 23.

45. Ibid., 98.

46. The text of 5 Ezra describes the transfiguration of a mourning woman into a woman with a shining face and a countenance flashing like lightning, signifying her heavenly status and knowledge of the divine. 4 Ezra 9 and 10:25ff.

47. Trevett assumes Quintilla becomes the founder of a prophecy group known as the Quintillians.

48. Trevett, *Montanism*, 169. However, in a footnote she says that the female Christ is probably the personification of Wisdom (n. 75).

49. Eph. 1:17. Trevett, *Montanism*, 169.

50. Women prophets, revealers, and teachers were familiar features of second- and third-century Christianity. By name we know of Priscilla, Maximilla, and Quintilla of the New Prophecy movement, and of Amnia of Philadelphia (Eusebius, *History of the Church*, 5:17.3). The Acts of Paul mentions a Myrta in Corinth, Acts of Andrew 30 a Maximilla.

51. Jensen, *God's Self-Confident Daughter*, 164.

52. The Gospel of Mary in *The Nag Hammadi Library*, ed. James M. Robinson (San Francisco: HarperSanFrancisco, 1978) 525.

53. Tertullian, *On the Soul*, 9.

54. Karen L. King, "Prophetic Power," 23.

55. Epiphanius, *Panarion* 49.

56. Thomas Laqueur, *Making Sex: Body and Gender from the Greeks to Freud* (Cambridge, Mass.: Harvard University Press, 1990).

57. Epiphanius, *Panarion* 49.

• 12 •

Jesus in Process Christology

Ronald L. Farmer

Even before the appearance of the earliest canonical gospel, Christians were grappling with the difficult task of expressing the nature and significance of the Christ event. The apostle Paul, for example, juxtaposed three distinctly different metaphors in the space of a single sentence.[1] And the struggle to express what one believes, and does not believe, to be the nature and significance of that remarkable life has not diminished in the succeeding two millennia. Whether people engage in the creation of metaphorical images, credal formulae, or dogmatic doctrines or undertake scholarly historical reconstruction, one fact remains the same. All such activity is carried out against the backdrop of a worldview. Occasionally this is acknowledged, but usually it is not. This is, however, important to recognize, for christological reflections arising from one worldview may not be intelligible, let alone convincing, when viewed from the standpoint of a different worldview.

My remarks in this essay arise from that constructive postmodern worldview usually referred to as process thought, which is based on the seminal work of Alfred North Whitehead. Before I discuss what I feel are three significant contributions process theology can make to the field of Christology, it is incumbent upon me to attempt to sketch the process worldview. As anyone who has read Whitehead knows, the complexity of his thought, his many neologisms, and his weblike rather than linear writing style make this a formidable task.

In Whitehead's defense, I must make two remarks. First, "any given language orders the world in a particular way for those who use that language, and it conceals the aspects of the world that do not fit that order." Unfortunately, few people are aware of this subtle metaphysical operation of language. "The grammar of the Indo-European languages, which emphasizes nouns, encourages substance thinking."[2] Whitehead's neologisms and weblike writing style are deliberate attempts to overcome this obstacle inherent in the English language. Second, many standard philosophical terms are already loaded with connotations evoking substance thinking. In an effort to avoid the inevitable misunderstandings that would arise if he attempted to use these terms to express event thinking, he coined new words.

The Process Worldview[3]

The worldview developed by Whitehead is a process worldview. According to this view, what is real is what happens; that is, ultimate reality is composed of events. Viewing ultimate reality in terms of events or happenings rather than substances means that experiences, not tiny bits of matter, are the building blocks of the universe.[4] These energy-events or occasions of experience Whitehead labeled actual entities or actual occasions. Under certain circumstances, groups of actual entities, termed societies, can impinge upon the human sense organs as data in such a manner that they are perceived as the physical objects of ordinary human experience (e.g., rocks, trees, animals, and people). Individual actual entities are detectable only by means of scientific instruments or intense introspection; they are not observable through ordinary conscious human experience.

Although there are differences between actual entities, one thing that all entities have in common is that they transmit energy from preceding actual entities to succeeding actual entities. In some instances that which is inherited from preceding entities is transmitted to succeeding entities virtually unaltered; in other instances what is inherited is significantly modified before being transmitted. The former occurs in low-grade entities, which characterize phenomena typically labeled inorganic; the latter occurs in high-grade entities, which characterize phenomena associated with life and consciousness.

The process by which these brief occasions of experience come into being Whitehead labeled concrescence, a "growing together" of a diverse "many" into a unified "one." Each becoming occasion inherits, or appropriates as its own, energy or data from past actual occasions. This process of appropriating or "grasping" a datum from a past actual occasion is termed a prehension or feeling. Each prehension is clothed with a subjective form, which is "how" the becoming occasion feels that datum; examples in human occasions of experience include consciousness, joy, and anger. Clearly, then, the data of the past largely determine what the becoming occasion will be because the past requires of the becoming occasion that it somehow conform to or reenact the past. Yet this determination is never complete, for every actual occasion also exercises some degree of self-determination in its concrescence. What an occasion must prehend is determined, but how the occasion prehends it is not. In high-grade occasions such as animal or human experience this self-determination may properly be termed freedom; in low-grade occasions such as electronic or molecular experience one should speak rather of indeterminacy because this term does not imply consciousness and the "freedom" exercised by low-grade occasions is negligible. Thus, a becoming occasion selects, harmonizes, and supplements the data of the past, integrating and reintegrating the "many" feelings into "one" final, unified, complex feeling called the satisfaction of the actual occasion. This concrescence of feelings is guided by the occasion's subjective *aim*, which is a feeling of what the occasion may become. This subjective aim always takes into account (1) the givenness of past occasions, (2) the goal of achieving the greatest intensity of feeling in the becoming occasion, and (3) the goal of the becoming occasion contributing maximally to relevant future occasions.

In its moment of concrescence, every actual entity is a subject, though usually an unconscious one. As a subject, each actual entity presides over its own immediacy of becoming. But upon attaining satisfaction, this subjective immediacy passes over into objectivity in the sense of being a datum for prehension by succeeding entities. This aspect of being an object conditioning all concrescences beyond itself as something given is termed the entity's objective immortality; it "lives on" in the finite world through its effect on (or its prehension by) succeeding actual entities.[5] Thus, according to the process worldview, the "many" occasions of the past are unified in the "one" becoming occasion; but upon attaining satisfaction, the "one" becomes part of a new "many" that requires unification in a succeeding occasion. This dynamic rhythm of the many and the one is the continuing rhythm of process.

Thus far the discussion has focused on actual occasions as the microscopic building blocks of the universe—e.g., electronic and protonic occasions. However, the same is true on the macroscopic level of enduring objects[6] such as rocks, trees, animals, and people. As was noted above, large societies of actual occasions sometimes impinge upon the human sense organs in such a fashion that the perception of the physical objects of ordinary human experience occurs: that is, a common pattern of inheritance is perceived over a period of time among a group of actual occasions. Historically, the perception of many "things" as manifesting the same characteristic has been ascribed to the notion that the many things all correspond to the same idea or form or universal, as in Platonism. For example, all particular instances of gray are manifestations of the idea "gray." Although Whitehead agreed with many of the notions of these idealistic philosophies, he disagreed with others. For example, there is a tendency in such philosophies to consider these unchanging ideas or universals to be more real than the particular temporal manifestations. But for Whitehead, there is nothing more real, i.e., more actual, than the particular entities manifesting these ideas; consequently, he avoided the traditional terminology and referred to these ideas or universals as eternal objects. Eternal objects are defined as "pure possibilities," which indicate how something might be actual. As "potentialities of definiteness" they are capable of specifying the character of any actual entity, but in themselves they refer to no particular actual entity.

A becoming occasion prehends a past occasion by means of one of the past occasion's own prehensions. Ingredient in each component prehension of the past actual occasion is at least one eternal object. Thus, the becoming occasion's prehension of the past occasion by one of its own prehensions results in the two occasions sharing an eternal object. Although the same eternal object has ingression[7] in both actual occasions, "how" the eternal object is felt by the two occasions will not be identical; that is, the subjective forms of the two feelings will differ to some degree ranging from negligible to considerable. Because most actual entities transmit, without significant alteration, to succeeding entities the data they have inherited from past entities (i.e., the same eternal object has ingression throughout the series and is felt in quite similar ways by each entity in the series), there is order, repetition, and continuity in the universe. Large groups or societies of these low-grade occasions account for the enduring objects of ordinary human sense perception.

But if occasions become what they become simply by inheritance from the past, how is one to account for instances of genuine novelty instead of only slight variations within an endless pattern of repetition? Granted, most enduring objects exhibit change, and slight change at that, only over a long period of time (e.g., molecules and rocks), but in the case of animals and human beings change can be both rapid and dramatic. The occurrence of genuine novelty means that new possibilities have been actualized. Therefore, eternal objects that were not ingredient in any past occasion must somehow be available to new becoming occasions. One could attempt to explain this simply by asserting that the "realm" of eternal objects is available to becoming occasions. A problem immediately arises with this explanation, however. For a novel concrescence to occur, the infinite multiplicity of eternal objects must be ordered in such a manner that certain eternal objects which have not been realized in past actual occasions become relevant to the situation of the concrescing occasion.[8] The past actual world of the becoming occasion determines which pure possibilities are relevant, i.e., which pure possibilities are real possibilities for actualization given that situation. For example, one hundred years ago flying to Rio was a pure possibility; today it is a real possibility, at least for those who can afford to purchase an airline ticket. But how is the vast realm of eternal objects ordered or graded so that certain unrealized eternal objects become relevant to each new concrescing actual entity? As with many thinkers, Whitehead felt that only what is actual has agency.[9] Eternal objects in themselves are abstract not concrete, possibilities not actualities; consequently, agency cannot be attributed to eternal objects in themselves. The eternal objects realized in the past are available to becoming occasions through the agency of past actual occasions; in like manner, eternal objects unrealized in the past must be made available through the agency of some actuality. Thus, because novelty exists there must be an actual entity that so orders the realm of eternal objects with respect to each becoming occasion that certain unrealized eternal objects become relevant to each individual concrescence.

Obviously this entity must differ in certain respects from all other actual entities.

1. Whereas actual occasions in the mode of objective immortality are available only to those occasions that succeed them, this entity must be universally available to all becoming occasions. There can be no occasions that do not prehend it. Furthermore, whereas actual occasions have their moment of subjective immediacy and then perish, this entity must be an everlasting[10] entity (the justification for this statement will become evident below).

2. Although an actual occasion is the realization of only a limited number of eternal objects, this entity must envisage the entire realm of eternal objects, for apart from their envisagement in one actuality, eternal objects would not be available for ingression in other actual entities.

3. For particular, finite actualities to exist there must be some limitation on possibility; because it orders the realm of eternal objects with respect to each becoming occasion, this entity serves as the necessary "principle of limitation."

4. Moreover, the very existence of particular, finite actualities requires that this envisagement of the realm of eternal objects be primordial in nature. Unless this act were primordial, there could be no particular actualities, absolutely none. Thus, the ordered envisagement of the realm of eternal objects by this entity is prior to and presupposed by all other actual entities.

Whitehead named this entity God; the primordial envisagement of the realm of eternal objects he designated the primordial nature of God; and the ordering of possibilities offered to each becoming occasion he called the initial aim.[11] The initial aim God supplies each becoming occasion is the initial phase of the development of that occasion's subjective aim. Although the initial aim contains that possibility which is the optimum way to unify the many into a novel one—i.e., if adopted it will guide the concrescence in such a way as to result in the richest, most intense unification of feelings possible in light of the past and the relevant future—the occasion is not bound to implement that possibility. Because the initial aim offers a graded relevance of possibilities,[12] there is room for the becoming occasion to accept, modify, or reject the optimum possibility in the development of the subjective aim that will guide its concrescence. According to the process worldview, then, God's power is persuasive rather than coercive. God seeks to lure each occasion toward that ideal way of becoming which is in keeping with God's own subjective aim of promoting intensity of harmonious feeling in the world.

Although God's primordial nature is timeless and thus in this respect God can be described as a nontemporal actual entity, God is an actual entity and so must meet the basic requirements for actuality. In a manner similar to the way in which every occasion of experience influences succeeding occasions and is influenced by preceding occasions, God also both influences and is influenced by the temporal world. Thus, God cannot be described as nontemporal without qualification. Although the primordial envisagement of the realm of eternal objects was unconditioned by any preceding actualities and thus is timeless, every subsequent act of divine concrescence is influenced by whatever actualities have come into being. With respect to God, the rhythm of process may be summarized as follows. God supplies the initial aim to "begin" each new actual occasion. After the occasion achieves its satisfaction God prehends it in its totality, saving everlastingly what has been accomplished in the divine consequent nature.[13] What has been accomplished in the temporal world, preserved everlastingly in the consequent nature, is then integrated with the divine envisagement of eternal objects, the primordial nature, in such a way that the divine satisfaction results in relevant initial aims for prehension by the next generation of occasions. According to the process worldview, then, temporal actualities matter; they matter both to succeeding temporal occasions of experience and to the divine experience.

One final aspect of the process worldview remains to be introduced for the purpose of this essay: conscious human experience. A human being is composed of an immense number of societies, and societies of societies. Yet there is within human beings, and in most animals, for that matter, a single center of control and spontaneity typically spoken of as the self or soul. Although one experiences this self as continuously existing (i.e., as a "substantial" self), the self is actually composed of a series of individual occasions of experience.[14] This serially ordered society is the dominant or presiding society within a human being. At any given moment the dominant or presiding occasion within this society inherits from (1) all past occasions in that serially ordered society (the ability to inherit from occasions other than the one immediately preceding is nontechnically referred to as "memory"[15]), (2) all of the occasions composing the human body (primarily, though not exclusively, through the brain and nervous system), (3) all of the occasions of the past actual world of the human being (primarily, though not exclusively, through the sense organs), and (4) God (the initial aim).

The human self or soul is a remarkable type of society. Whereas the occasions composing most societies are unconscious, the occasions of the human self contain some prehensions whose subjective form includes consciousness. These dominant occasions are capable of such high-level experience due in large part to the complex organization of the human body (especially the central nervous system) that insures a constant flow of novelty from the various body parts to the brain. Thus, novelty rather than repetition characterizes the occasions forming this remarkable society.

With the contours of the process worldview in mind, I turn now to three contributions process thought can make to the field of Christology.

Metaphysical Consistency

As the preceding sketch demonstrates, a process worldview is thoroughly incarnational; God is incarnate in each actual occasion via the initial aim. For Christian theologians rooted in substance thinking, there has been no way to give a rational explanation of the two natures of Jesus affirmed in the church creeds. The only step they have been able to take beyond merely affirming the creeds—or to put it another way, beyond simply stating the problem—has been to voice what they do not mean by declaring certain attempted explanations to be heresy. But rather than posing an insoluble problem or being a source of intellectual embarrassment, the Christian doctrine of the incarnation in Jesus is rational and coherent to process thinkers. In fact, the task set before process theologians is not to explain how the divine and the human could combine in Jesus of Nazareth; rather, it is to explain how and to what extent Jesus is a unique manifestation of "God with us."

According to the process worldview, each actual occasion is unique. No two occasions share exactly the same past actual world, receive exactly the same initial aim, or prehend exactly the same eternal objects with exactly the same subject forms. Thus, each actual occasion is unique in its concreteness, no matter how similar it may be to other entities. But this understanding of uniqueness obviously is not what theologians have meant when they have affirmed the uniqueness of Jesus. In what way would a process theologian affirm that the incarnation in Jesus was theologically unique? In what way was he "God with us" in a unique sense?

Marjorie Suchocki has suggested that four conditions would have to exist for such a special revelatory event to occur.[16] First, past events would have to have prepared the way for such an incarnation. Earlier I noted that the initial aim God is able to give to a particular occasion is conditioned to a considerable extent by the past. It is an axiom of process thought that God works with what is to bring about what can be. Periodically in the creative advance of the world, *kairotic* moments arrive. Positive turning points in history occur when these rare opportunities are grasped by spiritually perceptive people. Such was the case in the time of Jesus. As the apostle Paul put it, Jesus was born "when the fullness of time had come."[17]

Second, the content of the initial aim must be a communication of the nature of God. Because initial aims serve to guide the concrescence of actual occasions, they are normally more reflective of the world than of God. The resulting hiddenness of God in the world is typically referred to as general revelation. For special revelation to occur—such as Christians affirm happened in the life and teachings of Jesus—the initial aims supplied at that *kairotic* moment would need to be for a revelation of God to the world.

Third, the initial aims would have to be adopted fully by the recipient. Usually initial aims are adapted to varying degrees by actual occasions. The initial aim forms the beginning of the subjective aim, but in the course of concrescence the subjective aim usually deviates to some degree from the initial aim. In Jesus' case, however, this adaptation would not occur. As a result, he would not perceive God's will and his will to be in opposition.

John Cobb and David Griffin explain Jesus' uniqueness in terms of this "co-constitution":

> In Jesus' authentic sayings an existence expresses itself which does not experience this otherness of the divine. Instead, his selfhood seems to be constituted as much by the divine agency within him as by his own personal past. We may think of Jesus' structure of existence in terms of an "I" that is co-constituted by its inheritance from its personal past and by the initial aims derived from God. There is not the normal tension between the initial aims and the purposes received from the past, in that those past purposes were themselves conformed to divine aims and thereby involved the basic disposition to be open to God's call in each future moment. Whereas Christ is incarnate in everyone, Jesus *is* Christ because the incarnation is constitutive of his very selfhood.[18]

Fourth, this co-constitution must be a continuous process rather than a once-for-all happening. The human self, it will be recalled, is a series of actual occasions. Each momentary self in the series would have to continue this co-constitution for the incarnation in Jesus to remain theologically unique, that is, to remain revelatory of God's nature.

The confluence of these four conditions resulting in the unique incarnation in Jesus did not do away with his humanity; on the contrary, it perfected it. Metaphysically speaking, the dynamics of the incarnation in Jesus were no different than the dynamics of the incarnation in all actual occasions. But theologically speaking there were differences, differences in the content of the initial aims (a revelation of God's nature) and differences in the quality of his response to those initial aims (co-constitution).

The preceding explication of a process understanding of the incarnation in Jesus raises three questions. (1) Could God give some other spiritual person the initial aim to reveal the nature of God? Yes. (2) Could the content of that revelation be the same? No. To some extent, the past actual world of another spiritual person would not be identical with the past actual world of Jesus; consequently, the initial aims supplied to each would have to differ. To the degree that the past actual worlds and initial aims differed, so too what would be revealed of God's nature would differ. (3) Could people other than Jesus experience co-constitution? Yes.

The preceding questions all begin with *could*; consequently, they are metaphysical and thus are easily answerable once one understands process thought. If, however, one were to begin the questions with *has* or *is,* one would be required to step outside the realm of the theoretical into the realm of the historical. If one were to do this, one would discover that other people claim to have experienced what process theologians call co-constitution. Likewise, other people claim to have received the imperative to reveal the divine nature. And as would be expected, there are differences, sometimes significant differences, in understandings as to the nature of the divine or ultimate reality or whatever term one might use. These historical observations bring us to the next section of the essay: the contributions of a process Christology to interfaith dialogue.

Interfaith Dialogue

Contemporary Christian attitudes toward people of other faiths can be summarized under three broad rubrics: exclusivism, inclusivism, and pluralism. According to the exclusivist perspective, there is salvation only for Christians. Conversion to the Christian faith is required of all people. Exclusivists engage in interfaith dialogue, if at all, with the goal of converting their dialogue partners.

Since at least the mid-twentieth century a widespread movement has existed among both Catholics and mainline Protestants toward inclusivism. According to this view, salvation is still Christian salvation, but it is available to all people whether they are Christian or not. Devout people of other faiths may be regarded as "anonymous Christians," for everyone is included within the universal scope of Christ's saving work. Inclusivists engage in interfaith dialogue to build healthy relationships and possibly to help their dialogue partners see that their religions find fulfillment in Christianity.

More controversial is the position known as pluralism. Pluralists view the various religions as valid spheres of salvation, each assuming a characteristically different form. Other religions are not secondary contexts of Christian redemption, but rather are independent pathways to salvation. This should not be understood to mean that all religions are the same— they are not—or that people will experience the various religions as equally salvific—they will not. Different religions appeal to different people because they have different spiritual needs. A Christian pluralist believes that God "bends to our condition, shaping redemption according to the uniqueness of every particular human situation."[19] Pluralists advocate interfaith dialogue based on the belief that an appreciation of spiritual diversity will lead to mutual enrichment of the various faiths.

The process worldview provides strong support for religious pluralism.[20] According to Whitehead, the ultimate principle is actually a triad: the "one," the "many," and "creativity." As was noted above, the many become one in a ceaseless dance of creativity. Now it is important to note that from any member of this triad, the other two members can be deduced. For example, the one implies the many and creativity; likewise the very process of creativity is the unification of the many into a new one. Thus, there is a balance or harmony within the triad, which can be attained no matter which of the triadic members serves at the starting point. It is also true that the harmony finally attained reflects the starting point. For example, starting with the one leads to seeing the many and creativity primarily in relation to one; that is, the resulting harmony will be viewed primarily in terms of its unity. If, however, we start with the many, the complexity of the final harmony will be stressed; and if we begin with creativity, what will stand out will be the process leading to the harmony.

What would happen if this basic understanding of reality were to be applied to religious experience? We would expect to find religions that stress the way of creativity. They would focus on that aspect of reality characterized by universal flux, rise and fall, being and becoming, centerless centers, and ceaseless flow. Although there are variations within it, Buddhism is something like that.

We would also expect to find ways of life that focus on the manifold nature of the world. Although these ways of life are frequently called secular, many of them are quite spiritual though not religious in the normal sense of the term. For these people, the concrete manyness of reality might well be seen as the focus of life, deserving of one's ultimate loyalty and commitment. Many humanists and environmentalists fit this description.

In contrast to those who follow the pathways of creativity or the many, Jews, Christians, and Muslims testify that the road toward well-being and harmony is tied up with the experience of God as the One. And for Christians, that One is revealed most clearly in Jesus of Nazareth.

As this brief analysis demonstrates, Whitehead's notion of the triadic "category of the ultimate" supports the position of religious pluralism. Some pluralists envision the emergence of a universal religion that will transcend and replace the existing particular religions. Process theologians neither anticipate nor desire such a development. As was noted earlier, although the other two members of the triad are implied by whichever member one begins with, the harmony finally attained always reflects the particular starting point. Interfaith dialogue may lead to appreciation of spiritual diversity and mutual enrichment of the various religions, but it will not lead to the development of a universal religion. The radical historicity of concrete human existence precludes it. "No finite manifestation of religion could be universal."[21]

Historical Jesus Research and the Nature of Religious Experience

Because it asserts the full humanity of Jesus, process Christology is interested in and dependent upon historical Jesus research. The worldview underlying process Christology requires that Jesus be fully human, but that worldview cannot know in advance what Jesus actually said and did. For this, process theology must rely upon the empirical results of biblical scholarship.

Modern biblical scholarship is a child of the Enlightenment; consequently, the assumptions of the modern worldview underlie and permeate both the development and application of the criteria and methodologies that have emerged over the past three hundred years. Most of these criteria and methodologies are thoroughly compatible with a process worldview.

For example, process-informed interpreters utilize the criteria of multiple attestation and dissimilarity, and the methodologies of form and redaction criticism. There are, however, notable differences between the modern worldview and the constructive postmodern worldview known as process thought. Because of these differences in assumptions and perceptions, process thought offers several significant contributions to the field of biblical scholarship. In this context, I must limit myself to one example. For additional contributions, I refer to my book, *Beyond the Impasse: The Promise of a Process Hermeneutic.*[22]

A process-informed interpreter would not reject a priori the miraculous dimension of the gospels. Actually, a process theologian would not use the word *miracle* for that is a term presupposing the modern worldview. For that matter, miracle is not a biblical concept either—or as I like to tell students, "the Bible doesn't believe in miracles." That arrests their attention. The New Testament writers did use words such as *mighty deeds, wonders,* and *signs* to describe certain deeds attributed to Jesus, but they did not use the word *miracle*. Such a concept was foreign to their worldview.

The word *miracle* presupposes the natural-supernatural split of the modern worldview. In the early modern period, people thought that the natural world follows "natural laws" established by God. God seldom intervenes in the natural word, but on those rare occasions when God does, a supernatural event called a miracle occurs. Over the years, problems inherent in this natural-supernatural model of reality became so great that scholars increasingly abandoned belief in a supernatural realm. In the late modern period, reality has come to be conceived purely in terms of a natural world following natural laws, a curious expression because it implies a lawgiver.

Developing against this background, biblical scholarship increasingly came to reject a priori those aspects of the gospels that were perceived as miraculous. At first, this meant a rejection of certain events and deeds such as the virgin birth, healings, walking on water, and the resurrection. Increasingly, however, the notion of the miraculous or supernatural came to include the whole notion of human religious experience. This later development assumed a variety of forms, on a spectrum ranging from Bultmann's existential theology in which "theology" is understood to be "anthropology" (although Bultmann did not deny the existence of God), to atheistic naturalism's explanation of religious experience entirely in terms of psychology or sociology.

If one subscribes to the modern worldview, this is not only logical but also inescapable if one strives to be consistent with modernity's presuppositions. But what if one subscribes to the constructive postmodern worldview known as process thought? How would an interpreter understand these unusual Jesus stories? And to view the matter from a more inclusive perspective, how would one understand the phenomenon of religious experience? Let me begin with the general and move to the specific.

The process worldview rejects the dualistic natural-supernatural understanding of reality associated with the modern worldview. For process thinkers, no aspect of reality is devoid of the activity of God. Indeed, each event arises from the gift of the initial aim. To distinguish it from both the "supernaturalistic theism" that characterized early modernism and the "atheistic naturalism" that characterizes later modernism, David Griffin refers to the process world view as "naturalistic theism" or "theistic naturalism."[23] Religious experience does not imply a supernatural incursion into the otherwise natural affairs of the world and human experience, nor is it reducible to psychological or sociological analysis. On the contrary, metaphysically speaking, human religious experience is no different from any other creaturely experience, for God's initial aim is present to every actual occasion. All that distinguishes religious experience from other creaturely experience is a heightened awareness—i.e., a raising to the level of human consciousness—of the activity of God in the experience. And sometimes these experiences are "wondrous" indeed, like that set of experiences we refer to as the collapse of the Berlin Wall. Numerous secular news accounts underscored the religious component of this contemporary "mighty deed." Process theologians are not perplexed when the unexpected occurs, because for them natural law does not denote a set of fixed physical laws governing the world. Rather, natural law is conceived of as the latest description of the way things normally happen. But because process thinkers understand God and the world in terms of change rather than permanence, of creativity rather than status quo, of becoming rather than being, they expect the unexpected to emerge in the creative advance of the world. Because of the evocative lure of God, that which today is a mighty deed, a wonder, might tomorrow be commonplace.

But is such God-talk legitimate? Indeed, deconstructionists move beyond existential theology and deny the referential dimension of language altogether: words only refer to other words in endless play! Obviously, a discussion of a Whiteheadian understanding of language is beyond the scope of this essay; for that I refer to chapter 4 of *Beyond the Impasse*.[24] Let me summarize that discussion by simply saying that we are not locked in a linguistic universe; there is a referential dimension to language. Contrary to the assertion of the deconstructionists, one can speak truly, though not exhaustively or without error, about concrete experience in the "real world." And this means that, contrary to Bultmann, one can speak truly, though not exhaustively or without error, about religious experience. Theology has the potential of actually being theology as well as anthropology.

In light of the preceding discussion, it is obvious that a process-informed interpreter would not reject a priori the so-called "miraculous" dimension of the gospels. This does not mean, however, that a process-informed interpreter is predisposed to accept such stories as historically accurate. On the contrary, precisely because they are unusual rather than common, the burden of proof lies with those who interpret these aspects of the Jesus tradition as historical. Such stories may well be mythical rather than historical, intended to convey some spiritual teaching rather than to portray a historical event (e.g., stories of the miraculous conception). And should a story have a historical kernel, discerning it beneath layers of embellishment (so common in ancient stories) is a difficult task, indeed (e.g., the postresurrection appearance stories). Nevertheless, by refusing to excise such stories a priori a process-informed interpreter may experience "creative transformation" through the very act of grappling with what is foreign to his or her immediate experience and sensibilities.

Conclusion

"Who do you say that I am?" the Markan Jesus asked his disciples.[25] For nearly two millennia people have wrestled with that question, and the answers have been quite diverse. I contend that process Christology has much to contribute to the ongoing discussion of the nature and significance of Jesus of Nazareth.

Notes

1. Rom. 3:24–25 draws from the courtroom ("justified"), the slave market ("redemption"), and the temple ("sacrifice of atonement").

2. Ronald L. Farmer, *Beyond the Impasse: The Promise of a Process Hermeneutic,* Studies in American Biblical Hermeneutics 13 (Macon, Ga.: Mercer University Press, 1997) 68.

3. An abridgment of ch. 3 in Farmer, *Beyond the Impasse.*

4. The term "experience" can be misleading. Although Whitehead derived the term from human experience, he did not mean that the building blocks of the universe were exactly like human experience. Most occasions of experience lack such things as sense perception, consciousness, and imagination ("experience" does not necessarily imply these things, however; for example, people do speak of unconscious experience).

5. One should note that Whitehead overcame one of the destructive dualisms of modern thought: the subject-object split. The subjective and the objective are not opposing realities, as in dualistic thought, nor is either of them unreal, as in materialism and idealism. On the contrary, both are alternating aspects of each actual occasion.

6. Although *enduring object* is a technical term for Whitehead, it is used here in a nontechnical sense. As a technical term, an enduring object is a series of occasions, only one of which exists at a time, and each of which inherits its data primarily, though not exclusively, from the immediately preceding occasion in the series (thus, an enduring object is a serially ordered society). In enduring objects repetition of the past, rather than novelty, predominates resulting in stability (e.g., an electron is a series of electronic occasions each of which largely repeats the experience of the preceding occasion). An enduring object in the nontechnical sense (e.g., a rock) is a collection of enduring objects in the technical sense. Whitehead called enduring

objects in the nontechnical sense *corpuscular societies* because they are composed of numerous "strands" of enduring objects.

7. Other equivalent expressions are *realization, participation, exemplification,* and *illustration.*

8. That is, a "graded relevance" must be established in which unrealized eternal objects are graded on a scale from very relevant to not relevant at all. See below on the initial aim, n. 12.

9. Whitehead labeled this the *ontological principle.* This principle can also be expressed, "everything must be somewhere; and here 'somewhere' means 'some actual entity....' It is a contradiction in terms to assume that some explanatory fact can float into the actual world out of nonentity. Nonentity is nothingness. Every explanatory fact refers to the decision and to the efficacy of an actual thing" (Alfred North Whitehead, *Process and Reality: An Essay in Cosmology,* corrected ed. Edited by David Ray Griffin and Donald W. Sherborne [New York: Free Press, 1978; New York: Macmillan, 1929] 46). Thus, unrealized eternal objects or new possibilities cannot come to a becoming occasion out of "nowhere."

10. *Everlasting,* not *eternal,* is the appropriate term to describe this entity, for if the entity were eternal it would be totally separate from time. As the following discussion reveals, this entity is related to all finite, temporal actual entities. Occasionally Whitehead referred to this entity as nontemporal, but this expression is misleading because it applies to only one aspect of this entity (see the discussion of the primordial nature below, n. 13).

11. One should note that Whitehead's introduction of God was not religiously motivated; he introduced God in order to give a philosophical explanation of the world.

12. The initial aim is the envisagement of a *set* of related, relevant possibilities for actualization; the becoming occasion "chooses" from among them.

13. Whitehead's description of God in terms of the primordial and consequent natures should not be understood as implying that God can be "divided" into two natures in the usual sense of the term. Rather, these expressions refer to two functions of one reality. The primordial nature is the aspect or dimension of God typically discussed in Western philosophies (God as eternal, unchanging, infinite, and so forth). It is to Whitehead's credit that he also emphasized the neglected dimension of God.

14. This dominant occasion is the occasion humans are aware of most directly through conscious introspection.

15. The prehension of these past, noncontiguous occasions is by means of *hybrid physical prehensions.* Not all of the past occasions in the series will be prehended consciously at any given time, but all are potentially available for "recall."

16. Marjorie Hewitt Suchocki, *God, Christ, Church: A Practical Guide to Process Theology,* rev. ed. (New York: Crossroad, 1989) 90–92.

17. Gal. 4:4.

18. John B. Cobb, Jr. and David Ray Griffin, *Process Theology: An Introductory Exposition* (Philadelphia: Westminster, 1976) 105.

19. Suchocki, *God, Christ, Church,* 170.

20. The following discussion is based largely on Suchocki, *God, Christ, Church,* 171–75.

21. Ibid., 171.

22. See n. 2 above.

23. David Ray Griffin, *God and Religion in the Postmodern World* (Albany: SUNY Press, 1989) 3.

24. See n. 2.

25. Mark 8:29.

Subverting Authoritarian Relation: Jesus' Power and Ours

Carter Heyward

It was so hard and sad, holding you as you lay dying, my body pressed against yours, my hands kneading your warm, thick fur.[1]

You, precious beast, were so fully present, vulnerable, unsure, trusting

You tucked your head beneath my stomach, your face into my left palm. I rubbed your nose.

Bones pressing bones: one body, you and i.

We breathed together in that awful moment, wanting so badly, both of us, to "go with," the way we'd always done it: the essence of your dogness, my humanness, our friendship.

O Teraph, slowly and so sadly, it was happening; I knew it (did you?): you were slipping away (or was I?)

Could you tell how much i wanted it to be a gentle passage for you, my beloved friend?

Aware that your breath was weakening, your body becoming still beneath me, i knew i could not go much further with you.

But did you know that something was pulling me into a place i had not been before in quite this way; that in my soul, the place we had grown together, i too gave up the ghost: an illusion that we can hold onto those whom we love?

—from my journal, after the death of my dog Teraph,
March 19, 1990

Why do I speak mostly of "Jesus," seldom of "Christ" or "Jesus Christ"?

Because "Christ" language, since the canonization of the Christian Bible, has been the language of Christian imperialism, exclusivism, and domination. "Christ" has been shorthand for the raising up of Jesus as the firstborn Son of God who was, eternally, God himself—God the Son, the second person of the Trinity. When "Christ" is named, seldom is there room for anyone else.

I use the name "Jesus" rather than his christic title because history shows that "Christ" language actually obscures the christic—redemptive—meanings of the Jesus story. In making Jesus *the* sole proprietor of the title "Christ," we Christians not only have wreaked violent havoc in the lives of those who are not Christians (Jews, Muslims, pagans, Buddhists, and others) but also have disempowered ourselves as Daughters, Sons, People, and Friends of the Sacred, bearers together of the same sacred, christic, power that Jesus experienced in relation to others.

To speak of "Christ" surely can be, and sometimes has been, a way of trying to speak of a Holy Spirit that we share, "The Body of Christ." Still, given our Western minds, which jerk dualistically into either/or thinking, it is hard for us not to get stuck in the fundamentally faulty assumption that Jesus was, and is, *The* Christ in a unique and singular way that applies to him alone. In others words, he, not anyone else with, before, or after him, was and is *The* Savior, whereby only Christians, not others, are "saved," and in fact only those Christians who hold this "right" view of Jesus Christ are "saved." Everyone else is "wrong" and "damned"—that is, condemned by our own faithlessness to float beyond the capacity of God himself to "save" us from the hellfires of eternal estrangement from God.

The problem with our getting stuck in this traditional ("He, not we") Christology that turns Jesus alone into Christ, or God, and Christianity alone into The Religion of Those Who Are Right, and Saved, is that it weakens our spiritual ability to experience ourselves in relation to others—including non-Christians, nonhumans, and everything radically "other"—as God-bearing in the world.

If we are to speak of "Christ" at all as a healing and liberating Spirit, "Christ" must be a synonym for the risen, ongoing, spiritual presence of Jesus with us as a fully creaturely brother, or sister, seeking to be in right—mutually empowering—relation, with all other creatures. If we are committed to "Christ" in this sense, then we realize that we, like Jesus, are lured by the Spirit of justice-love[2] into a shared commitment to be christic—liberating—God-bearing characters together in history.

the problem with authoritarian power

Authority, or the "power to authorize," can be held and given in just and unjust ways. It is a morally neutral concept, neither good nor evil in itself. By contrast, *authoritarianism,* the hoarding of power over others, is always spiritually problematic and morally bankrupt. In creating and submitting to authoritarian power, we literally abdicate our shared spiritual capacity and moral responsibility to live deeply human, creative and liberating, lives.

Authoritarian experiences and images of Jesus Christ, in which we set him above us and ourselves beneath him, are problematic because they distance us from the Spirit that is closer to us than our next breath, the One that is ever empowering us to live fully human lives. Looking beyond ourselves, beyond our humanness and the Spirit in our midst for right answers, we miss the wisdom here with us now.

When we ascribe all power to Jesus Christ, we step away from the friendship to which Jesus invited and, as we do, we step back from knowing and loving the Spirit of life the way Jesus himself did, intimately and immediately.[3]

Putting ourselves under the authority of a deity we have created in the image of kings and lords—men of the ruling tribe—we turn our backs on the brother who prays in the garden and, in turning away, we allow him to be taken away again to be crucified. Once more, then, we blame ourselves for not seeing what has been going on. And still, instead of seeing that we are failing to take our sacred power seriously enough, we imagine that we are failing to take Jesus' authority seriously enough. So we raise him up even higher and put ourselves down even lower, until we hardly can bear the shame. And he reigns on and we pray that he will forgive us. In this psychospiritual scenario, we are certain of very little, but one thing we know for sure: we are right that Jesus is Lord.

Many African-Americans have pointed out the significance, in the context of white racism, of Black people's affirmation that Jesus is Lord!—Jesus, not the slave owner; Jesus, not systems of chattel slavery or modern racism; Jesus, not the white man or white woman, is Lord and Master! This is the main reason I have continued to participate in worship from time to time that uses authoritarian images of christological power such as the Lordship of Jesus Christ. In singing or praying publicly to Jesus as Lord, I mean to be standing against white people as "lord" and against other oppressive structures, such as male supremacy, which function as false gods. I have serious misgivings, however, that the deification of any one human figure, even Jesus of Nazareth, is a reliable or longstanding spiritual solution to the ongoing politico-theological problem being generated by the exercise of authoritarian power—in the Black Church, among feminist Christians, or anywhere else.

Regardless of our tribe, gender, or particular social locations, we Christians who think that we, and we alone, are right about Jesus need an authoritarian Jesus Christ to assure us that we are. This he does by delivering us from the complexities and confusions that accompany all life rooted deeply in sacred Spirit. It may be true that we who give Jesus Christ all power and glory experience fewer misgivings about God and the world than those who know Jesus more as a sibling and a spiritual friend. But it also is likely that those who love Jesus as a brother, rather than worshiping him as a god, come to see more clearly who this Jesus really was and who the rest of us are as well.

Authoritarian power has three unmistakable qualities: (1) *Power is wielded over others.* Some dominant group or individual wields power over others. The power may be economic or political, psychological or physical, spiritual or intellectual. (2) *The power does not change hands.* It is a static, well-defined "possession" of those who have it. (3) In this relationship, while the dominant figure remains basically unchanged by the dynamic, *the subordinate character(s) are shaped according to the judgment and will of the dominant.* The Christian Right ascribes this kind of authoritarian power to Jesus Christ; he is Lord of all. His power is his and his alone and, whereas those who believe in him are affected and transformed, he himself is not.

Those Christians for whom Jesus is more a spiritual friend or an embodiment of love than a Lord and God are commonly dismissed by right-thinking Christians as simply wrong, misguided people. If we happen also to be feminists, womanists, gay, lesbian, or other queer folk, we are assumed to be worse than simply mistaken; we are seen as contemptuous of Jesus Christ, hostile toward him, and dangerous to his mission.

It is my thesis and a theme of much feminist and womanist theology that authoritarian relational dynamics are not morally neutral "conduits" through which either good or evil relationships can be fed. Authoritarianism is an evil politic, grounded in the hoarding of power over others and dependent upon the radical subordination of their freedom and imagination, creativity and desire. All authoritarian relationships are morally corrupt, regardless of who the authoritarian figure may be.

To be sure, from a liberation perspective, we cannot simply affirm "mutuality" or "mutual relation" as our interconnectedness in the cosmos, our state of being, irrespective of our ethics—what we are doing, how we act, what we value, and with whom we stand. It is never enough simply to notice that our lives are connected and that whatever affects any of us touches us all. But noticing, becoming aware of reality, is a critical step in the process of liberation.

"Relational theology" should be understood as metaphysics, built not merely on speculation but on *experiencing* one another (including the planet and all creatures) in the course of our daily lives, work, and love. At the same time, relational theology should be understood as a theo-ethics of liberation. It is about *noticing* what is real—our loveliness and pathos, our interconnectedness and fragmentation—and it is about changing the world.

relation

Whoever does the will of God is my brother and sister and mother.
(Mark 3:35)

Like Jesus, we begin in relation.
Relation is not merely a reciprocal dynamic. It is the ground of our being.
When Jesus prayed to God, he was acknowledging the ground of his own being.

When Jesus prayed, the Spirit of God spoke through him, opening more fully to its own purposes, and Jesus' also, as he went with God.

The Spirit yearns through us as well, opening through us more fully to itself.

We pray to be opened through, and with, God.

Christian theologians historically have worked on the basis of patriarchal assumptions about God and his relation to Man (gender reference intentional).

Patriarchy is the hierarchical ordering of the world on the basis of the (ruling class/tribe) fathers' rights to control the world and their responsibilities to care for those under their control.

In spite of this sexist, racist, classist theological framework—a major stumbling block to our doing what is good or learning what is true—certain of the earlier church "fathers" understood that God is a relation, not a person. I am thinking especially of such theologians as the fourth-century Cappadocians.

Still, even with this insight into the relational character of the divine, Christian theologians on the whole have not seen that neither God, nor Jesus, nor the rest of us can be known and loved on the terms of patriarchal theology.

As a system of social control, patriarchy is a system of nonmutual relation.

Love and patriarchy are incompatible. Love is mutual relation. Patriarchy is its antithesis and, as a system of control, cannot tolerate mutuality, except in matters deemed trivial and of no consequence—like women's work and children's play.

We cannot worship both the radically loving God that infused the life of Jesus and the deity constructed by ruling-class Christian men *in their patriarchal image*.

We cannot love both God and mammon.

God is, in the beginning and in the end, a relation.

God is not a self-contained entity or a self-absorbed being.

God is love—the immediate and intimate reaching, into and through every moment, toward the celebration of mutuality throughout the cosmos.

God is the intimate and immediate yearning for justice and compassion.

God is the Spirit celebrating mutuality, the Energy generating justice, the Root of compassion, the Power in the reaching and the yearning.

power

...Truly I tell you, there are some standing here who will not taste death until they see that the kingdom of God has come with power.

(Mark 9:1)

To think about Jesus is to think about power.

Like Jesus, we too are here to bear witness to the realm of God coming with power. This is as true today as ever and it is as confounding to most Christians today as it was to Jesus' closest friends.

Jesus was our human brother. One of us. This is not to say that he wasn't "divine." The Spirit of God was surely with him. The Sacred Wisdom whom Greek-speaking Christians called "Sophia" infused his life. The Source of all life and goodness, which people of the world know by many names and in many images, poured through Jesus' life and death and raised him into the future, where we who come later meet him, and God with him, in one another.

Jesus was divine in the same way we all are: together, in mutual relation with our sisters and brothers. No one of us alone is "God." God is the Holy Spirit connecting our lives, moving with us and through us.

God is our sacred power for healing and liberation. God was Jesus' sacred power as well.

We do not know what Jesus thought about his vocation, his "call," in relation to God and the world. Did he think of himself as "Messiah" (or "Christ"), the one anointed by God to play a special redemptive role in the history of Israel? In Mark, we meet an enigmatic figure who prefers that those closest to him "not tell anyone" about him. We do not know exactly what he, or they, thought was going on.

Whatever he might have thought about himself, Jesus seems to have been rooted deeply in a commitment to a Spirit that he experienced as radically available to everyone; a God who cared more about people's well-being than propriety, customs, or laws; a Source of social and personal transformation; a Wellspring of liberation and healing, judgment and forgiveness.

Jesus' historical significance, his christic—redemptive—meanings, originated in his faith in the power he experienced in relation to sisters and brothers.

Any discussion of Jesus is a discussion of power.

Power is ability, power is energy.

Who "has" power and who doesn't isn't as clear as most power analysts, including feminists, suggest.

No one is simply "with" or "without" power, as if "it" were a substance borne, like bottled water, according to one's race, class-location, gender-identity, age, or ability.

All creatures, because we have lived, participate in imaging and reimaging power of many kinds.

I may be able to use a chain saw to fell an oak, but the oak has a great deal more power than I to live in the forest amidst many generations of oaks with only soil, sun, and rain as its food.

I have no power to be an oak, and the tree has no power to be me. But we both have power to relate to one another and other creatures.

But what about "social power"—the economic, cultural, and customary power that certain groups of people have accrued historically, which they use to control—and often abuse and violate—those who have less, or none, of what they have?

Throughout human history, various particular groups of people—white people, Christians, men, wealthy folks, adults (who are not yet "old"), to name just a few—have wielded oppressive control over other people and creatures. Such "wielding" and "controlling" is an abusive use of social power.

Whenever people use whatever power they have—economic, racial, sexual, professional, age—to betray, lie, steal, beat, belittle, humiliate, or otherwise violate others, this is an abusive use of social, and often personal, power.

But it is also true that social power is generated and constructed historically. It never constitutes a static, total, or final advantage or privilege.

Social power, like the power of the oak to perpetuate its species and the power of a baby to laugh, is dynamic, a source of activity and movement. Social power is also specific and limited. A man may have the power to rule the New York mob. But, if imprisoned, he no longer has the power to walk down the street to buy an ice cream cone or to play with his children.

Social power, like all power, is subject to historical change and transformation. It is not simply a given. Male gender hegemony, white racism, advanced monopoly capitalism—none of these sources of social power is simply "the way it is." They are "constructed."

Whatever has been constructed can be "deconstructed." Whatever has been built can be tumbled. Whatever has power can be bumped against until it falls. Power is a dynamic relational movement against the very boundaries that move against it. It is the water pushing against the dam that is holding back the water.

To argue simply that men have "power over" women, that white people have "power over" people of color, or that doctors have "power over" patients, as if this were all that needed to be said in order to understand these historical systems of control, is not only a simplistic analysis of social power. It also disregards the immediate, ongoing possibilities for social transformation, for committing ourselves *together* to use power differently, to struggle to build different systems and, through processes of conversion, be "constructed" differently ourselves, as persons. This is constantly our possibility, neither mine nor yours alone, but ours, together.

Thus, it is misleading to speak of "power over," "power within," and "power with" as if these moments of power were set in stone in our lives, even in our social locations.

Faith is revolutionary spiritual struggle toward social change and personal transformation. We need not struggle, or believe in anything, if we have resigned ourselves to accept the world the way we found it.

It is misleading to think of Jesus as having "power over" anyone, then or now. If we "give" him our power, we diminish both his sacred power and our own, because this "divinity," sacred power, is what we generate together.

Sacred power is "sacred" only because it belongs to no *one*.

It is a mistake to imagine that Jesus had "power within" in a sense that his sisters and brothers do not. If we believe that he was a "better person" than any of us, we sell ourselves short and him as well.

It is also unimaginative to assume that Jesus' "power with" others, then or now, was an unchanging, smooth, and settled way of being in mutual relation.

Mutual relation is not easy. To struggle for mutuality, which is involved in all real loving, promises tension and turbulence.

Power is resource, like wind or sun, energy for life.

All kinds of power can be sacred. Whether economic or racial, sexual or religious, species-based or age-defined, whenever power is used to make justice-love, to struggle for mutuality, to celebrate right relation, to generate more "power with," it is Sacred Power.

The problem with patriarchal images of God, Jesus, and ourselves is that we so often are disempowered by them, made smaller than when we are most fully human selves, our selves in right relation to one another and to the Spirit who connects us.

Only when we are true to our common humanity and, more basically, our common creatureliness, are we empowered, like the wind or sun, energized for life.

"we"

We are empowered to god (verb). By myself, "I" am not empowered to god—but then I am never simply "by myself." In the beginning is our relation.

I am not speaking primarily of the sort of relational encounters we call "relationships" or "personal relationships" (one to one or small groups of friends). I am speaking of the holy ground on which we stand together, we people and other creatures. In the beginning is our relation. In this radically relational situation, I am never by myself—although I may *feel* alone, or be in solitude.

You and I, as individuals, are forged out of *us.*

We are the image of God—we women and rocks, we kids and kitties, we men and roses, we whales and waterfalls, we elephants and city streets.

Through *us,* the Spirit roars and spins and whispers!

Jesus was one of us. In the realm of Spirit, he still is.

truly human

Is this a ridiculously idealistic image of our selves, beyond our capacities to imagine, much less embody a day at a time?

It is our reality, who we are here on this planet—people and other creatures together. We need to live as sisters and brothers, in a spirit of mutual respect and shared responsibility for this earth and one another. It is that simple.

To be truly human is to live in what our Buddhist friends might call "codependent arising." This refers to a basic, valuable, liberating dimension of our common life, socially and economically, politically and spiritually. Psychologically—mentally and emotionally—we need to help one another learn to feel this in ways that enlarge, rather than diminish, our power in mutual relation. So much classical and pop psychology, like most popular Christianity, has got it backwards: as if the Self, its center and its growth, were the beginning of what it means to be fully human.

Neither divinity nor humanity, neither Creator nor creature, is "self-absorbed" when it is in right relation with all else.

Self-absorption and mutual relation are incompatible. The self-absorbed spirituality (and psychology) of advanced global capitalism and Western Christianity will not tolerate our power in mutual relation.

The self-absorbed spirituality of those who are right does not permit us to be fully human.

There is no room in most popular Christianity today to remember the fully human brother from Nazareth or to live as his brothers and sisters.

The popular deity of Christianity in today's world is the Golden Calf of Wall Street, the Lord of profits, an idol carved out of our self-absorption.

The Spirit that sparked the life of Jesus leaps among us, too, threatening to transform us, calling us to god.

godding

We Christians have for too long imagined that we have no sacred power, no divinity, nothing good, in and among our human selves. With devastating historical, social, and personal consequences, our patriarchal religious tradition has failed to convey to us the central, and most important, meaning of the Jesus story—*God is with us, in the flesh, embodied among us, in the beginning and in the end.*

Like Jesus, and in his Spirit, we too are created to god.

That is what it means to be human—to god.

That is what it means to be created, a creature of earth, water, sky—to god.

That is why we are here—to god.

Godding is loving—*justice-loving.*

To be fully human is for us, together, to make justice-love roll down like waters!

To be fully divine is for us, together, to share the earth and all resources vital to our survival and happiness as people and creatures.

To god is to know, deeply in our bodyselves, that the Spirit that creates and liberates the world is with us, incarnate among us, here and now.

Trinity

Participants together in this fully human life, we reflect the Trinity, which earlier Christian theologians presented as an image of God in relation to Jesus and themselves. Despite its patriarchal construction, the Trinity is rooted in an intuition of mutual relation, rather than self-absorption, as what is most fully divine and fully human. The Trinity is an image of dynamic movement, not of static unchanging being, as the very essence of God; of passion and yearning, not of dispassion or apathy, at the heart of the Sacred; of wholeness and holiness woven through diversity and multiplicity, not through sameness.

Those who shaped the doctrine of the Trinity intuited that "something" of God was *in Jesus;* that this "something" had been always, from the beginning; and that this same "something" connected subsequent generations to Jesus and God. What was startling and new about the Trinity was that here were Jews and Gentiles suggesting that this "something of God"—this ineffable mystery—was not only beyond human knowing and speaking but was also completely in our midst, "fully human and fully divine" and fully with us, able to be known and loved, in the flesh.

God is not merely *one* of us. God is with and among us *all*. We can glimpse the mystery, see the face of God, in *any* one of us, not just Jesus. The holy mystery that is our sacred power was in the beginning, it was in Jesus, and it is with us now.

In order to distinguish between these historical experiences of this power—the God of Israel to whom Jesus prayed; Jesus himself; and the way Jesus is connected to the rest of us—the early fathers, using patriarchal relational terms that reflected their own experiences, suggested that the One God of All is in "three persons"—Father, Son, and a Spirit not as "personal" as Father and Son, but rather a way of connecting them with the rest of us.

Of course, in a patriarchal social and ecclesial order, trinitarian thinking functions in primary ways to hold sexist power in place—"God is Father, so shall be his priests" has been the cry of frightened men and women against the ordination of women. In this way, the Trinitarian theology usually serves to constrict our images and experiences of God to those that contribute to the pedestalization of men and boys and the worship of God in their image.

This patriarchal interpretation is a dreadful misrepresentation of God, Jesus, and the rest of us. Its consequences and ongoing causes continue to be the sacrifice of women and girls on the altars of white male supremacy "in the name of the Father, and of the Son, and of the Holy Spirit." This blasphemy against the God of love—God of mutuality and justice—is a violation of the Spirit that touches all persons who love God and their neighbors as themselves. It is not worthy of the name of Jesus, nor of your name, nor of mine.

The Trinity, rightly understood, should expand our God images, not constrict them; it should stretch our capacities for wholeness and holiness, not shrink us; it should sharpen our religious imaginations, not dull our sensibilities. God as Trinity means that whatever is Sacred is relational, never self-absorbed, always moving beyond itself to meet the new, the other, the different, never set in its ways or stuck on itself as the only way. A Trinitarian faith rooted and grounded in the love of God would never require that people be Christian in order to be saved, that only males be priests, or that others be like us in order to be acceptable.

A strong Trinitarian faith, which most surely was the faith of Jesus—in God, in himself, and in others, all in relation to one another—is never acceptable to those who are right.

And how do we live a Trinitarian faith? In our struggles for mutual relation, we break free from the self-absorption that historically and existentially distorts the image of what is most fully human and divine.

hologram: whole and holy

Looping back to Teraph's death, we see a moment of loving, dying, and letting go that was mutual. That moment, and every such occasion of mutual relation in our lives, images who we are together. Ethically, such an image can help sharpen our commitments to building our life together in such a way that persons and other creatures are able to live and die more fully in mutually empowering ways. Let us look a little more closely.

It is an image of bonding and holding, touching and mutual knowing, between creatures who have grown together as friends—each helping the other to be as happy, proud, and healthy as possible, one day at a time.

It is an image of godding—in which the Sacred is not fastened to either creature but is sparking between, and generated by both. And not only by both as individual creatures but as embodiments of social, political, economic, and natural histories.

At Teraph's death, not only he, as one dog, and I, as one woman, came together in this letting go. We brought with us, into the moment, all who had made us who we were, as dog, woman, and friends.

How often do you experience similar relational "moments" as a representative, in some sense, of all who have ever loved, held, yearned, lost? This experience is not merely a "subjective," much less loony, kind of notion: it reflects our participation with one another in the whole of God's life, our experience of "holiness."

Such a moment is as real and transformative as anything that happened to Jesus or to those who touched him, like the woman who was hemorrhaging (Mark 5:28–34). Like others of us, this woman was healed *not* by Jesus' power but by power that moved between them, between Jesus and herself (and all others who were with them, in person or spirit).

Because they failed to grasp the radically mutual character of Jesus' life, death, and resurrection, the authors of the Christian Scripture do not tell us in what ways *Jesus* was moved and changed in relation to those whose lives he touched. How was Jesus healed, liberated, transformed by this woman? by John the Baptist? by his mother Mary? Peter? Mary Magdalene?

The Christian Scriptures and the vast majority of Christians who have taken the Bible to heart have not understood (because church teachers have not helped us realize it) that God was no more in Jesus than in us; and that truthfully—and wonderfully—God really is in, with, and among us— intimately and immediately, here and now, forever.

And so the lives and deaths of those we love—an animal companion, a partner, a beloved friend, a child, a parent, a spouse—are always occasions to go with God, again, into the gratitude and grief that come with all real loving, justice-making, godding.

When Teraph died, I entered with him into that mysterious and sacred realm beyond the boundaries of human intelligence in which i knew that both he and i were participants in the life of God, and would be forever. In him, in that sad moment, i met the Sacred, again, and saw that She was as really present in the dog as in Jesus or me, and that through any such experience in our lives, we can meet and know and love the One who is Trinity:

> She who, from the beginning, has been the source of all loving, dying, and letting go throughout and beyond the cosmos;
>
> He who—at the same time, in every moment—is embodied through us in our fur and paws, our hands and hearts;
>
> the same Spirit connecting our loves, celebrations, and griefs to those of persons and creatures in all times and places, strengthening us through the real presence of those who've gone before and who will come after us, too.

In any given moment of our lives, on the mountaintop, in the valleys, we can glimpse the whole. The entire life and purpose of God—to make justice-love—takes root in each moment of our lives and histories, our cultures and cosmos. Like a mustard seed—small and irrepressible—the holy needs only to be noticed and cultivated.

Notes

1. This essay is abridged and adapted from my book *Saving Jesus from Those Who Are Right: Rethinking What It Means to Be Christian* (Minneapolis: Fortress, 1999). See ch. 3, 55–76.

2. "Justice-love" is a term used in the document *Keeping Body and Soul Together: Sexuality, Spirituality, and Social Justice* (Louisville: The General Assembly Special Committee on Human Sexuality, 1991).

3. A number of these themes on "authority" and the "intimacy and immediacy" of sacred connection are raised and explored in greater detail in several other of my books, including especially *The Redemption of God: A Theology of Mutual Relation* (Lanham, Md.: University Press of America, 1982); *Touching Our Strength: The Erotic as Power and the Love of God* (San Francisco: Harper Collins, 1989); and the book from which this essay is taken (see n. 1).

• 14 •

Christology after Auschwitz: A Catholic Perspective

Didier Pollefeyt

It can be called an irony of history that Jesus, who symbolizes the bond of unity between Jews and Christians, has all too often become the sign and the origin of dissension and even violence between the two faith communities. Jesus of Nazareth embodies the paradox of uniting Jews with Christians and of separating Jews from Christians. What makes the encounter between Judaism and Christianity so important as well as difficult is the fact that the major differences between the two religions show up in their radically different interpretations of just those matters that unite them. None is more crucial than their understanding of Jesus of Nazareth. In short, between the church and the synagogue stands the crucified Christ. He divides Jews and Christians.

Jews, Christians, and the Crucified Christ

Historically speaking, Christians could only interpret the Jewish "No" to Jesus as an absolute mockery of their own Christian identity. In the on-going existence of Judaism as a living religion they saw and sometimes still see the threat of Christianity's exposure as a doubtful and perhaps even deceitful religion. Therefore, Christians could not tolerate the survival of Judaism alongside themselves. About this, Karl Barth writes: "The existence of the Synagogue side by side with the church is an ontological impossibility, a wound, a gaping hole in the body of Christ, something which is quite intolerable."[1]

Israel, the Church, and Theology of Substitution

In 1933, Cardinal Michael von Faulhaber gave a sermon in which he said that after the death of Christ, Israel was dismissed from the service of revelation. "She [Israel] did not know the time of her invitation. She had repudiated and rejected the Lord's Anointed, had driven Him to the Cross. The Daughters of Sion received the bill of divorce and from that time forth [the Jews] wander, forever restless, over the face of the earth."[2] According

229

to this perspective, the covenant with Judaism was abrogated with the appearance of Christ. In history, Christians have often inquired whether Israel was still the people of God, whether the church has replaced Israel. An affirmative answer to the latter inquiry is often described as the "theology of substitution," or "displacement theology," or "supersessionist theology."[3] Christians assumed that, thanks to their belief in Jesus as the Messiah, the election of the Jewish people had been transferred definitively and exclusively to them. The church had taken the place of Judaism for all time and completely. The implication of this theology is that there is no longer any place for Israel in God's plan of salvation. Israel no longer has a role to play in the history of revelation and redemption. The Jewish "No" to Jesus, the Messiah, meant the end of God's involvement with Israel. The new chosen people, the true, spiritual Israel, under the new covenant, now occupies center stage and assumes the rights and privileges of the nation that has been rejected.

Accordingly, Christian exegesis, Christian liturgy, and Christian catechesis represented the relationship between the first and the second testament in terms of "promise and fulfillment," "old and new," "temporary and definitive," "shadow and reality." The ultimate consequence of these supersessionist expressions is that, while Israel was the beloved of God at one time, after she missed her invitation, she lost her election and thus her right to existence—she is a cursed nation or, at best, an anachronistic one. Many Christians still share the view that the death and resurrection of Christ have rendered the "old" covenant obsolete.

This theology of substitution came to prominence so early in Christian thought that it is hardly surprising that it was for centuries an uncontested element of Christian faith and teaching in the churches of the West and the East. Already in the second century, Tertullian (c. 160–225) speaks about the "disinheritance of the Jewish covenant and the Jewish election in favor of the Christians."[4] This supersessionist construction was even grounded in the gospels, especially in the passion narratives, which portrayed the Jews as the enemies of Christ and responsible for his death, and so no longer the people of God. The events of Good Friday mark the end of Jewish history. The continuing existence of the Jews was primarily thought of in terms of divine rejection and retribution, because they are not only regarded as those who killed Christ, but also as those whose hearts were so hardened that they continued to reject him.

A consequence of this theology of substitution is a moralistic, apologetic and intolerant Christian attitude toward the Jewish people: if your understanding about the things concerning Jesus of Nazareth is not identical with ours, then you are the enemy of the truth and fit only to be cast aside. In this way, the theology that with the coming of the church of Christ the historical vocation of Israel is fulfilled, that her role in sacred history was ended at that time and place, became the cornerstone of theological anti-Judaism.

Judaism in itself is not accorded any continuing and definitive salvific value, but has value only insofar as it contributed to the history of Christianity.

Christologies of Discontinuity

Christology played a decisive role in the legitimation of the age-long history of calamity that was the result of this theological anti-Judaism. Ruether even calls anti-Judaism "the left hand of Christology."[5] With McGarry and Eckardt, we like to call these kinds of Christologies, in the light of the sub-stitutive relationship between Judaism and Christianity, "Christologies of discontinuity."[6] Christian protagonists of these Christologies of discontinuity declare the brokenness of original Israel's election. Christianity is the successor of Judaism, is the "faithful remnant" that truly carries forward the sacred role of Israel. Common among the Christologies of discontinuity is an emphasis on the unique and universal saving efficacy of Christ. Each of these Christologies understands Jesus of Nazareth as the perfect fulfillment of all Old Testament messianic prophecies. In Christ, Israel's election found its fulfillment and new embodiment—Christ is the new elect of God, and his church, his body, is the new people of God. The Christology of discontinuity thus stresses the uniqueness and finality of Christ; the universality of Christ as the sole mediator of salvation; Christ as the fulfillment of Jewish hopes and prophecies; Christ as the leader and embodiment of the New Israel, suc-cessor to Judaism; Christ as Messiah; and the necessity of preaching Christ to the Jewish people. The position of sharp discontinuity almost seems to say that Jesus was the Christ *in spite of* the fact he was a Jew rather than *because* he was a Jew. Theologians with this christological position are not interested in a Jewish-Christian dialogue. The Jews are not a special category of non-Christians in the universal mission of the church. The contemporary existence of the people Israel does not imply specific questions for their own theological position.

The Christology of discontinuity declares that evil was conquered once and for all by the Christ event. The history of humankind upon the com-ing of Christ is regarded as a period of unredeemedness. Belief in Jesus as the Christ allows humankind to enter the new messianic time. In her famous study, *Faith and Fratricide*,[7] Rosemary Ruether shows how Christians could have understood Jesus only as fulfilling the prophecies by a twofold process of historicizing the eschatological (primarily Luke, who, in the absence of Christ's return, interpreted the church as the beginning of the Kingdom's establishment, superseding the old chosen people) and spiritualizing the es-chatological (primarily John and Paul, who made the eschatological events of the messianic era a matter of internal, undetectable transformations rather than observable events in an undefined future). The consequence of this pro-cess has been a spiritual, political, and ecclesiastical triumphalism of the church and of Christians, which made them blind to concrete evil, espe-cially evil that is in and is caused by their own Christian story. For Paul Van

Buren, the irony of the classical christological tradition is that it made of the designation Son of God—a Jewish term of service, intimacy, fidelity and humility—a title of power, dominion, and assertion.[8]

Christologies of Discontinuity and Jesus. A specific exegetical consequence of these Christologies of discontinuity is that the Jews are considered to be blind to the deeper theological and spiritual meaning of their own Scriptures, whose only proper understanding is a christological one. Christologies of discontinuity will recommend "typology" as the exegetical method to approach the Hebrew Bible. Typology is a way of reading the Bible where events of the New Testament are presented as the fulfillment of events in the Hebrew Bible.[9] So, in Christian liturgies, the Hebrew Bible is often reduced to an allegorical significance. A typological approach allowed Christians to interpret Hebrew scriptural characters and events as "types" or "figures" that proleptically prefigured characters and events in the New Testament. Typology can best be summarized with the well-known adage of Augustine in *Quaestiones in Heptateuchum*: "The New Testament lies hidden in the Old and the Old Testament is unveiled in the New."

Typology in itself is not wrong. It can be a fruitful exegetical method that was, in fact, already applied in the Hebrew Bible and that also belongs to the New Testament, as I will indicate later. Historically speaking, though, the consequences of a typological exegesis are almost always negative and injurious toward Judaism. Typology became an instrument of Christologies of discontinuity. The covenant between God and Israel is often seen as only a preparatory phase in salvation history, without any intrinsic value, having a meaning only in relation to the coming of Christ. This kind of typology then becomes an apologetic instrument, which, as in the ancient church literature against the Jews (*Adversus judaeos*), is employed to challenge the intrinsic value of Judaism. In the hands of Christian interpreters, Cain is typologically the murderous elder brother (i.e., the Jews) who kills his younger brother (i.e., Christ). Cain is then forced to flee, the prototype of the "wandering Jew," and carries with him a mark distinguishing him from others (i.e., circumcision). Hence, typology allows Christians to read the "Old" Testament with Christian eyes. And because the Jews did not (do not) have this sight, they saw (see) only the literal meaning of the texts and were (are) blind to its deeper meaning.

In typology, the Old Testament becomes a temporary truth that can only be replaced with the coming of Christ, as a shadow replaced by the light, as the old replaced by the new. This way of presenting the coming of Christ makes the history that preceded him in itself empty and senseless. It leads to the opposition of two images of God (justice or love), of cult (ritualistic or spiritual), of salvation history (announcement or realization), of morality (imperfect or perfect), and of life (under the influence of fear or of love).

Christologies of Discontinuity and Religious Intolerance. Christologies of discontinuity do not automatically imply religious intolerance. Theologians who holds this christological position today will accompany their theories with exhortations to Christian respect for people of all religions. Israel is still the object of God's love but, with the coming of the Messiah, Israel has ceased to have positive meaning in salvation history.

The history of Christian anti-Judaism is dramatic proof, however, of the violent potential that is implicit in this Christian theology and Christology of substitution. When Cardinal von Faulhaber spoke in that symbolic year 1933, the year in which Hitler came into power in Germany, in his sermon about the "bill of divorce" the Jews had paid, he did not know that the Jewish people had yet to pay the biggest price for their being Jewish. Holocaust scholars often have recognized a parallel between the Nazi "final solution" (*Endlösung*) and much in the traditional attitude and practice of Christians and their churches. However fundamentally different Christian moral presuppositions may have been from those of the Nazis, the Hitler program can be seen as a radical application of the Christian world's age-old warning: "Beware of the Jews!" And a major reason why the Nazis could go as far as they did was that Western culture had been steeped so thoroughly in a very negative Christian dogmatic and theological understanding of the Jewish people.[10]

Gregory Baum is very sharp in his articulation of this insight: "The Holocaust acted out the church's fantasy that the Jews were a non-people, that they had no place before God and that they should have disappeared long ago by accepting Christ."[11] And Baum concludes: "The church is now summoned to a radical reformulation of its faith, free of ideological deformation, making God's act in Christ fully and without reserve a message for life rather than death."[12]

Auschwitz as the End of Christological Triumphalism

Auschwitz means the definitive end of christological salvation triumphalism. The Jewish philosopher Emil Fackenheim asks if Good Friday has not again overwhelmed Easter. "Is the Good News of the Overcoming [of evil in Christ] not itself overcome?"[13] For the Jew Fackenheim, after the Holocaust there can be no radical wonder or Good News that is not threatened by radical horror. It is for him not surprising that to protect the wonder most Christian theologians today ignore the horror of the Holocaust, minimize it, flatten it out into a universalized horror that is at the same time everything and nothing.

We can say, however, that Vatican II was a theological answer to the Holocaust and meant a new start in Jewish-Christian relationships, even if the overwhelming hermeneutical principle at work in the Vatican II Document in general with regard to the Old Testament is to see it still primarily as a preparation for the Christian belief in Christ as the fulfillment of prophecy and the finality of revelation.

234 • *Didier Pollefeyt*

The conciliar declaration regarding the Roman Catholic Church's attitude to the non-Christian religions, *Nostra Aetate* (1965), speaks another language, however. It dedicates its fourth paragraph completely to the relationship between the church and Judaism and contains the challenging statement that "the Jews should not be presented as repudiated or cursed by God, as if such views followed from the holy Scriptures."[14] Pope John Paul II has made the Jewish-Christian encounter one of the priorities of his pontificate. On October 31, 1998, the Holy Father received the scholars attending the Vatican symposium on "Roots of Anti-Judaism in the Christian Milieu." In a speech referring to Vatican II, he said that the Jewish people "perseveres in spite of everything because they are the people of the Covenant, and despite human infidelities, the Lord is faithful to his Covenant. To ignore this primary fact is to embark on the way of a Marcionism against which the church immediately and vigorously reacted." Further, John Paul II criticized theologians "who regard the fact that Jesus was a Jew and that his milieu was the Jewish world as mere cultural accidents, for which one could substitute another religious tradition from which the Lord's person could be separated without losing its identity," as "not only [ignoring] the meaning of salvation history, but more radically [challenging] the very truth of the Incarnation."[15]

Recognizing the continuing validity of Judaism and accepting the fact that Jesus was born a Jew is crucial to his identity and to the faith of the church and has important christological implications. In dialogue with the Jewish faith, and in acknowledging the abiding validity of the Jewish religion, one is challenged to describe his faith in Jesus differently. If Judaism is admitted to be a continuing, valid religious expression, can one still say that Christ has fulfilled the messianic promises contained in the Hebrew Scriptures, especially when Judaism's continued existence is the very evidence that it does not believe Christ to be the Messiah? Can a Christian admit the continuing validity of Judaism without compromising belief in the uniqueness and the finality of Jesus Christ? I would like to show how reflection on Israel affects the way the church understands and defines itself. A proper Christology for the church today should free the church to affirm God and itself in Christ without having to negate others.

Christologies of Continuity

Contemporary "Christologies of continuity" try to answer these challenges.[16] They argue that with the coming of Christ the election, chosenness and love of God for Israel were not transferred to the Christian church, leaving the Jewish people without a God, a mission, or validity. In other words, Christologies of continuity are decidedly nonsupersessionist. For Mc-Garry, Christologies of continuity stress Christianity as the continuation of Israel's covenant, which Christ does not abrogate, but which he opens up to the gentile world. These Christologies speak about the abiding validity of the covenant with Israel; the positive witness of the Jewish "No" to Jesus as a constructive contribution to the ultimate salvation of humankind, not as an act of unfaithfulness or haughty blindness; the positive Jewish witness to the unredeemed character of the world; Christ as *partial* fulfillment of Jewish messianic prophecies; and the eschatological unification of all God's people. Christologies of continuity underline that if there is a true sense in which God has manifested himself uniquely in Jesus of Nazareth, it must be said that the mystery of this divine act is in principle no greater than the sacred acts through which Israel was originally elected. The Resurrection and Christ experience function in a paradigmatic way for Christians in the same way as Exodus functions for hope for the Jewish people.

In these Christologies of continuity, the Christian exegesis as typology can have a specific meaning and positive value. The christological reading of the First Testament has then to be regarded as the discovery of a new layer of meaning in the texts, but not the only and certainly not the first or most original layer of meaning. In other words, Christian typology must leave room for other ways of reading the Hebrew Bible that are just as valuable. I can refer here to the extremely rich, diversified, classic and contemporary Jewish readings of the First Testament. Paul Ricoeur pointed out that the Hebrew Bible itself is filled with this sort of typological methodology.[17] We can find in it a succession of different covenants, where each covenant is a reinterpretation of the former one and where the idea of a "new covenant" can already be found in Ezekiel and Jeremiah.

Hence, the typological link between Judaism and Christianity has to be seen as a continuation of the constant reinterpretation of the covenant inherent to the Hebrew Bible. In other words, if typology is to be acceptable as an exegetical method in contemporary Christian theology, it has to be withdrawn from the apologetic and substitutional scheme, "imperfect-perfect," and it has to be interpreted anew as one method to use in the rich, complex, and continuous tradition of biblical explanation so typical of Christianity and Judaism, for the enrichment of the mutual belief of Jews and Christians in Yahweh. Christian typology always has to bear in mind that it is not exclusive, but that it is in fact situated inside the internal typological pluralism that is part of Judaism and of which it elaborates only one branch, namely the eschatological. Seen like this, typology can even become the expression of respect for the primordial, irreducible value and inextinguishable richness of the First Covenant, which is and remains open for a nonchristological hermeneutical reading.

One Covenant and Two Covenant Theories

John Pawlikowski's authoritative article "Ein Bund oder zwei Bünde?" divides the Christologies of continuity between those that see Judaism and

Christianity as two basically distinct religions despite their shared biblical patrimony and those that believe in the simultaneous and complementary participation of Judaism and Christianity in the same covenant.[18] These are respectively the double- and single-covenant theories.

The single-covenant theories tend to view the Christ event as the extension of the one basic covenant, originally made with the Jewish people and still in their possession, to the non-Jewish world. Judaism and Christianity participate in a simultaneous and complementary way in the same covenant. They belong finally to one covenantal tradition, which started at Mount Sinai. The Christ event is not so much the fulfillment of Messianic prophecies, but it presents the possibility for the Gentiles to become incorporated in the covenant of God with Abraham, Isaac, and Jacob. In the presence of original Israel, the gentile question is no longer "How can the Jew be saved," but becomes "How can I be included in the unbroken covenant of God with Israel?" A representative of this one-covenant theory is Franz Rosenzweig, who saw Judaism as "the star of Redemption," and Christianity as the rays of that star.[19]

The second, two-covenant school prefers to look at Judaism and Christianity as two distinct covenantal religions that are different, but complementary in an ultimate sense. The two-covenant theories recognize the enduring bond between Judaism and Christianity. But then they turn to the differences between both traditions and communities, and show how the service, the teaching, and the person of Jesus mediate an image of God that is surely new.

In my view, Pawlikowski is right in criticizing the one-covenant theories. In these theories, Christianity becomes Judaism for Gentiles. The one continuous covenant can be described as new after the Christ event only in the sense that now it embraces both Jews and Christians. The two-covenant theories are more adequate in representing the relation between Judaism and Christianity, historically as well as theologically. The Christ event is more than Judaism for Gentiles. Why, Pawlikowski asks, start a new community called the church, when Gentiles were already entering the Jewish community in some numbers at the time of Jesus? Why then not simply reintegrate the church in the synagogue—why bother with a separate faith community? The double-covenant theories are in need of answering the question whether the granting of the vision to the Gentiles through Jesus added anything to the vision. Unless Christianity is able to articulate some unique features in the revelation of Christ, then it should fold up as a major world religion.

In his study on Judaism, Hans Küng warns us that today we paint, out of fear of anti-Judaism, Jesus and Judaism to such a degree as grey on grey that it becomes very difficult to recognize Jesus' own distinctive profile, and even impossible to understand why a religion different from Judaism came into being, one that from the beginning took his name and not that of anyone else.[20] In this way the opposition between Jews and Christians is reduced to one long, two-thousand-year-old misunderstanding, and Jewish-Christian dialogue to shadow-boxing. For Küng, neither Jews nor Christians are helped by this kind of illusion. Paul Van Buren mentions that Israel's negative witness is to Christ novelty: the Jewish rejection says that Jesus Christ is something new and different.[21] What has happened with Jesus' coming and going is not simply part of Israel's story. Jesus has also caused a break in the continuity of the covenant. For Pawlikowski, without maintaining some uniqueness and centrality for the Christ event, there remains little reason to retain Christianity as a distinct religion.

A. Roy Eckardt mentions that his earlier and repeated insistence upon the membership of Christians in the Jewish family has been determined in considerable measure by the necessary warfare against Christian supersessionism. Supposing that this fantasy is at last overcome, he asks now, must the family stay together? "I am uncertain how to answer. I do know that loved ones part from one another and go their different ways—though they need not thereby cease their loving or their caring."[22] In the same line, for Paul Van Buren, it is essential to see that the task of Christology after Auschwitz is not to make it appealing to Jews. A Christology for the Jewish-Christian reality is not a Christology formulated by the church so that Jews might come to accept it or at least find it permissible for the church. On the contrary, a Christology for the Jewish-Christian reality will be a Christology for a church that acknowledges that the reality in which it lives is rightly definable only when Israel's continuing covenant with God is recognized and confessed as essential to it.

Continuity and Discontinuity

This means that we have to explain both continuity and discontinuity between the two faith communities. In one respect Christianity is totally grounded in Judaism. In another respect Christianity is a different religion from Judaism. It's a distinct religion based on salvation in Christ and in this way Christian. Küng is defending a Christology of continuity, but combined with a two-covenant theory. "There is now one way for Jews and one way for Christians. Christians are to respect and recognize the independent way of the Jews, for behind it stands the reality of the one God of Israel, who is also the God of the church."[23] For Eckardt, we have to set ourselves intellectually at times on the side of discontinuity and difference, and at times on the side of continuity and unity. We must seek to mediate between these two sides, to relate each to the other, and to go beyond both.[24]

The question now becomes whether there is a way to repudiate any supersessionist theology and Christology while trying to maintain the uniqueness of the singular grace of Jesus Christ. Is it possible to see Jesus in continuity with Judaism, to confess him as the Christ, and at the same time to hold onto the idea that the divine choice of original Israel retains a positive, constructive effect? For Christianity, this is a crucial question. Christianity does not, in comparison, constitute the same problem for Judaism that Judaism constitutes for Christianity. Christian faith is not dogmatically necessary to Jewish faith; had there been no Christianity, Judaism would probably still be alive. But had there been no Judaism, there would be no Christianity. The church has a theological and christological vested interest in Israel, as Eckardt rightly explains.[25]

Explaining what separates Christianity from Judaism and Jesus from Jewish tradition is a precarious enterprise. Most of the lines often drawn between the Jewish and Christian faith are false and supersessionist. Most familiar is the dichotomy according to which, in praise of either a schizophrenic Bible or a schizophrenic Lord, an "Old Testament God of wrath" is ranged against a "New Testament God of love." On an entirely different level, though still largely supersessionist, are the society-person, rituality-spirituality, law-grace, and fear-freedom dualities.

Moltmann's Christology

It is the Christology of Jürgen Moltmann that may help us enter into the true dialectic between Judaism and Christianity. As a German theologian, Moltmann is strongly convinced that it is impossible to formulate a meaningful contemporary Christology without reckoning seriously with the implications of Auschwitz. In *Der Weg Jesu Christi*, he formulates the fundamental question at the center of Christology as follows: "Is the Jewish 'no' [to Jesus] anti-Christian? Is the Christian 'yes' [to Jesus] anti-Jewish? Are the 'no' and 'yes' final or provisional? Are they exclusive, or can they also dialectically acquire a positive meaning for the people who feel compelled to utter them?"[26] The answer he gives to these questions can be seen as a strong and authentic example of a Christology of continuity, but one that shows respect for the different covenantal realities of Judaism and Christianity.

Moltmann stresses that, although Christians trust that the messianic times have definitively begun in Jesus and that the Kingdom of God is among us, they are also aware that not all biblical prophecies about the Messiah have been fulfilled yet. The messianic sign that embodies the end of all evil, and the end of oppression for all people, has not yet come. Moltmann indicates that this is the innermost reason for the Jewish "No" to Jesus. At this point, we can quote with Moltmann the famous statement of Martin Buber in which he explains why the Jews do not believe in Jesus as the Messiah: "The church rests on its faith that the Christ has come, and that this is the redemption which God has bestowed on mankind. We, Israel, *are not able* to believe this."[27] Moltmann mentions correctly that it is not a question of Jewish unwillingness or hard-hearted defiance. It is an "inability to accept." It is well known that Buber had a deep respect for Jesus; but his statement of the inability was grounded in a even deeper personal and collective Jewish experience: "We know more deeply, more truly, that world history has not been turned upside down to its very foundations—that the world is not yet redeemed. We *sense* its unredeemedness. We can perceive no *caesura* in history. We are aware of no centre in history—only its goal, the goal of the way taken by the God who does not linger on his way."[28]

Why So Much Evil in the World?

Based on their experience of the unredeemedness of the world, Jews are unable to believe in Jesus as the redeemer of the world. This is the Jewish question to Christian existence: "The Messiah has come, why is the world so evil?"[29] Christians answer this challenge by saying that they live in the tension between the "already" and the "not yet." In the Christ event God's full victory is assured, but not completely realized. Each messianic statement about Jesus must be spoken in the future tense, not as a contemporary reality. Jesus will become the Christ only at the end of times.

Moltmann sees here also the possibility for a positive Christian theological acceptance of the Jewish "No" to Jesus, not merely as an act of unfaithfulness or haughty blindness. "Even the raised Christ himself is 'not yet' the pantocrator. But he is already on the way to redeem the world. The Christian 'yes' to Jesus' Messiahship, which is based on believed and experienced reconciliation, will accept the Jewish 'no,' which is based on the experienced and suffered unredeemedness of the world. The Christian 'yes' to Jesus Christ is not in itself finished and complete. It is open for the messianic future of Jesus."[30] If Christians and Christian communities would have heard the meaning of this Jewish "No," they would have been better protected against all kinds of triumphalism and self-idolatries, as Eckardt remarks.[31]

Moltmann refers to St. Paul's Israel chapters (Rom. 9–11), where Paul saw God's will in Israel's "No."[32] "Their rejection means the reconciliation of the world" (Rom. 11:15 RSV). It is not the "No" of unbelievers, but a special "No" that must be respected. God imposes on the whole of Israel an inability to say the "Yes" of faith to Jesus, in order that the gospel may pass from Israel to the Gentiles. Had the Jewish people as a whole somehow come to acknowledge Jesus as the Christ, how could the covenant have been opened to the nations, Moltmann asks? The nonrecognition of the messiahship of Jesus by most of historic Israel falls within the sovereign purposes of God, for through this series of historical events his redeeming grace could be extended to the pagan realm. Without the Jewish "No," the Christian church would have remained a messianic revival movement within Judaism itself. Moltmann hopes that Israel, in spite of its own observance of the Jewish "No," can also view the Christian "Yes" to Jesus as a positive contribution to the ultimate salvation of humankind, as the *preparatio messianica* of the nations.[33]

In Jesus, the Kingdom of God has begun and Christians are challenged and encouraged to give the best of themselves on its behalf. At the same time, Christians know that they cannot realize this divine dream on their own. The ultimate accomplishment of humanity is also a gift, a divine talent, for which they hope in prayer. In other words, like the Jews, the Christians are waiting hopefully for the final coming of the Kingdom of God on earth. This is known in Christianity as the Second Coming of the Messiah. That is how Christians wait. But they are not alone. The unredeemed world is a problem for the Jew as well. This is a Christian question to Jewish existence: "If there is so much evil in the world, why is the Messiah not coming?" Moltmann is correct that the hard fact of the "unredeemed world" does not only speak against the Christians. It speaks against the Jews, too. Judaism also awaits the coming of the messianic age. For Christians and Jews wait together, in spite of their differences of belief, working for and dreaming of the same goal. Christians and Jews can meet in this common hope, founded on the same promise to Abraham (Gen. 12:1–3; Heb. 6:13–18). Hans Küng speaks here of a perspective on the future for whose consummation Jews and Christians wait together.[34] And J. B. Metz calls for a "Koalition des messianischen Vertrauens" ("a coalition of messianic trust") between Jews and Christians.[35]

Critique of Moltmann's Christology

From the Jewish side, the solution of Moltmann and others, to see Jesus as Christ in the fullest sense only at the end of times, and to understand his messiahship in a proleptic, anticipatory way, has been severely criticized. It is said that the original essence of Israel means something infinitely more than the nonacceptance of Jesus as the Christ, and for that matter, infinitely more than service as a corrective instrument vis-à-vis the Christian church. In Moltmann's solution, the synagogue is finally still subordinated to the church. And although this eschatological solution of the problem creates theological room for Judaism in the present, one asks the question whether this might only be putting the question one step back.[36] The Jewish thinker Manfred Vogel criticizes this modern trend to put the resolution of Jewish-Christian tensions in the end times:

> [This] deferment of the problem from the present to the future [en-ables] one to overcome the urgency of the present and accept the *status quo* for the time being. [This] means that the messianic claim of Jesus *vis-à-vis* the Jewish people is cancelled for the present. If the first coming of Jesus makes a messianic claim on the world, the Jews are exempt! Thus the Christian can overcome the disquietude caused by Jewish nonacceptance of Jesus only by surrendering for the time being the messianic claim.[37]

McGarry asks the question how different it is, substantially, to say (a) that the Jews are not called upon now to recognize Jesus as Messiah (either historically fulfilled or eschatologically proleptic), (b) that he is working in them unrecognized, or (c) that in the end time all will be reconciled in Christ.[38] Also, Eckardt argues that Christians might be doing nothing more than pushing the classic concept of Judaism's invalidation by the Christ event only one step back to the end of times.[39] The great Jewish philosopher Franz Rosenzweig, quoted by Küng, said: "whether Jesus was the messiah, will become evident for Jews when the messiah comes."[40] Küng interprets this remark as follows: "When the Messiah comes, then, as Christians are convinced, he will be none other than Jesus of Nazareth, the crucified and risen one."[41] The same critique can be uttered here. Anti-Judaism is merely tempered, not finally overcome in this theological stance. The final fulfillment is postponed to the end of times, but Jews still need Christ to reach the Kingdom.

We believe Moltmann's eschatological solution of the Jewish-Christian relations is not a step back. At least it neutralizes the potential violence between Jews and Christians by opening ways to mutual respect and collaboration for the Kingdom of God on earth in the present. Do the Jews then still need Christ to be saved? Elie Wiesel states that "Jews don't like to make the world more Jewish, but more human. Christians often think that the world can only become more human by becoming more Christian."[42]

Constitutive and Representative Understandings of Jesus as Savior

Here I would like to introduce the distinction Schubert Ogden made between a constitutive and a representative understanding of the saving character of Jesus.[43] In a constitutive interpretation of the saving nature of Jesus' life, Jesus is not simply representing salvation. His life and work constitute salvation. Traditional Christology has claimed some sort of efficacious quality to Jesus' life, whose life definitively revealed the Father and constituted salvation, and through whose life men and women have the possibility of resurrection, forgiveness, and life. In a constitutive Christology, the life and work of Jesus bring about salvation in a way that can never happen in any other way. In a representative interpretation of Jesus' saving life, the possibility remains open to recognize the potentiality of salvation earlier than, and after, the coming of Jesus, primarily given with the beginning of creation. This does not mean, of course, that Jesus is not confessionally constitutive for Christians, but it is to say that he is not ontologically constitutive.

While a constitutive Christology will inevitably end up in substitution, a representative Christology opens up the possibility of confessing Jesus as the Christ without repudiating the covenantal representation of salvation in the First Covenant with the Jews. It is only in such a representative Christology that the salvific meaning of Jesus can be described as a representation of the covenantal commitment of God expressed in creation and validated at Sinai. In the same representative way, the covenant of Sinai is an articulation of the covenant of God with humanity given from the beginning of creation. And this does not exclude the possibility of seeing Sinai as confessionally constitutive for the life of Israel, just as the Christophany of Easter is confessionally constitutive for Christian life. The resurrection and Christ experience function in a paradigmatic way for Christians in the same way as Exodus functions as hope for the Jewish people. In a representative interpretation, the confession of Jesus as Messiah does not have to lead to a theology of contempt and substitution. Jesus, seen in the perspective of Sinai, represents the covenant mediated there, too. Jesus is perceived by Christians as the one who generously represents this covenantal reality.

Christ Past and Present

Of course, this does not dissolve the difference between Jews and Christians, but at least it overcomes the destructive concentration on the question who is "with God" and who is not. Instead, it focuses on the way to honor and represent, as well as possible, in the present, the covenantal reality of God with humanity within each religion. Representative Christology can be a help to avoid two imbalances: to think of fulfillment first and foremost as past fulfillment in Jesus or in the church, or to think it only a thing to be accomplished in the future. The search for the novelty of Christ is mostly put in the past tense. Theologians ask what was different about him, what change took place with his coming and going. Putting the question in that way implies speaking of the Resurrection as a past event and asking what really happened. To be sure, these questions about the past play an important role in a living church, but they are not the most crucial ones. In the first place should always be Christ present. I quote here with approval Van Buren: "What was new about Christ in the past is what is new about him today or the church's faith is in vain. Living faith will begin in the present, look to the future, and then retell the past."[44] Or to say it in the words of Moltmann: "Every confession of Christ leads to the way, and along the way, and is not yet in itself the goal. 'I am the way,' says Jesus about himself according to one of the old Johannine sayings (John 14,6)."[45]

This means that Christians recognize the Christ-in-his-becoming, the Christ on the way, the Christ in the movement of God's eschatological history. We see here revelation in the first place as a mission in the present, more than as an accomplishment in the past or in the future. Christology should be open to a constant revision, because revelation stands before us as well as behind us. The story is not over. In different ways, each of the witnesses to Jesus as Lord made this clear. Paul is teaching in Rome "quite openly and unhindered" (Acts 28:31, RSV). Revelation in the present is also for us much more a quest than an accomplishment.[46]

Moltmann emphasizes the different stages in God's eschatological history with Jesus: the earthly, the crucified, the raised, the present, and the coming one.[47] A possible seduction in Moltmann's approach is that in Jewish-Christian dialogue we now become too preoccupied with the final end. When so much emphasis is placed on the christological end of the story, Van Buren argues, the intervening chapters we have to write today in the story of Christ are in danger of being taken with less seriousness. "To live in an unfinished story is to realize that one is contributing to its writing by that living. It is to realize that the story's development and its future course depend not only on God but also on God's partners."[48]

How Jesus Will Be the Messiah

This implies in my view that the way Jesus will be the Messiah will depend upon the way we represent him today. When the church or some of its members fail to represent Jesus' cause authentically, to that extent Jesus' cause is set back and will affect the way in which Jesus will or will not be the Messiah.

We must return here to the issue that lies in our view at the center of dialectic tension between the two faiths, but also points to their inner bond: the issue of the unredeemedness versus redeemedness of the world, as we pointed out already with Moltmann. The basic difference between Jews and Christians consists fundamentally in the experience of realized eschatology in the Christ event. Christians are linked to, are baptized into, this eschatological event, and they must extend its meaning and its historical dimensions to human history, in time and space. Jews are witnesses to the "not yet" of the entire messianic age. Schalom Ben-Chorin adopted this argument as follows:

> The Jew is profoundly aware of the unredeemed character of the world, and he perceives and recognizes no enclave of redemption in the midst of an unredeemed world. The concept of a redeemed soul in the midst of an unredeemed world is alien to the Jew, profoundly alien, inaccessible from the primal ground of his existence. This is the innermost reason for Israel's rejection of Jesus, not a merely external, merely national conception of messianism. In Jewish eyes, redemption means redemption from all evil. Evil of body and soul, evil in creation and civilization. So when we say redemption, we mean the whole of redemption. Between creation and redemption we know only one *caesura*: the revelation of God's will.[49]

Christians must agree with the Jew that the world is not yet redeemed and recognize the importance of Israel's continuing witness to this fact. They must also accept the critique that the Christian insistence upon redeemedness has occupied a central place in the church's ideological justification of its own social dominance. In the light of this historical Christian triumphalism, what could it possibly mean that Jesus is the Redeemer of Israel? In the opinion of Eckardt, the Jew is obliged to ask a painful question of his

Christian brother: "When you set out the cup of communion wine in remembrance of the sufferings of Jesus, what possible *specific* meaning or lesson is embodied in this symbolic act? Are you ready to suffer as Jesus did? Tell me, where were you when we Jews were living and dying in Auschwitz? In sum, just who are the witnesses of the Redeemer?"[50]

The fact that Christians historically did not always represent authentically the redemption in Jesus does not mean that Jesus is for Christians no longer the Redeemer. Also, after Auschwitz, Israel's vision centers in Israel's restoration and the church's eye is on the figure of Christ. Israel's vision of the way to the reign of God's peace and justice on earth turns around its own faithfulness to the commandments; the church sees trust in Christ as the way, as Van Buren puts it.[51] It is and remains a fact of Christian life that Christians experience mercy, or justice, or forgiveness, or love for the enemy in particular lives and communities, and when they experience this radical novelty in the present, they can trace it to the newness of Christ in their lives.

Redemption in the Present

Here we touch upon the unique quality of Jesus' life and message: redemption in the present, even for those who have wronged, as the strongest manifestation and anticipation of the messianic times here and now. In a recent and beautiful document of the French bishops, "Lire l'Ancien Testament. Réflexion du Comité épiscopal pour les Relations avec le Judaïsme," I read the following passage:

> Jesus radicalized the commandment of love by extending it to forgiveness for the enemies. Does this forgiveness not presuppose that the messianic age is anticipated and that even in Israel the difference between Jews and nations, between the oppressor and the victim, is overcome, although this difference is at the very heart of the Law? It is necessary to ask what right Jesus has to "transcend" the borders of the Law and Israel. Does he do that out of his own initiative as an apostate who renounced the belief of his religious community and in this way, at least implicitly, declared the erroneous character of this belief? Or is he doing this in the name of the very finality of the Law and in this way following messianic logic?[52]

The great Jewish scholar David Flusser also sees here an element of newness in Jesus' message, as John Pawlikowski clearly states. Jesus' message of love for the enemy stands in contrast to Pharisaic teaching, which only insisted that the person be free of hatred toward the enemy but never insisted in the same way on the need to show love toward him or her. I quote, with Pawlikowski, David Flusser: "According to the teachings of Jesus you have to love the sinners, while according to Judaism you have not to hate the wicked. It is important to note that the positive role even toward the enemies is Jesus' personal message. In Judaism hatred is practically forbidden. But love to the enemy is not prescribed."[53]

In this radicalization of the commandment of love in Jesus' message, we find the strongest sign that in his person and message, the redemption of the world becomes "yet" possible. However, this is not something Jesus constituted in the past through his life and death ontologically, but something Christians have to represent in the present, to open the messianic future of Jesus.

At this point, we have to mention that the relation between Judaism and Christianity cannot be reduced to a simplistic dialectic between law and grace. Eckardt shows that the relation between Judaism and Christianity holds a much deeper complexity. "*Relative to their Christian neighbors,* Jews tend to *talk* about unredeemedness, though not very much about sin, as meanwhile they *experience* the sin of the world as a brutal fact yet behave, nevertheless, in a more redeemed way. *Relative to their Jewish neighbors,* Christians tend to *talk* about the crying need of redemption while *behaving* more as though there were no such thing as redemption. There could be no more convincing evidence than this of both the barrier and a blurring of the lines between the two faiths."[54]

The Christian response to the message of Jesus must always have a certain strange sound to the Jew whose knowledge of the Christian cross is so vividly one of his own suffering at the hands of Christians, rather than one of the suffering of Christians for the sake of their faith. Jews know from experience that sometimes Christians are the last ones to love their neighbors as themselves. The dialectic between Jews and Christians is thus a strange one. While Jews suffer more, they show greater social responsibility and utopianism. While Christians suffer less, they show less social hope and more social irresponsibility. Christians like to whisper to themselves that were they to live the fullness of redemption in Christ here and now, the cost would be too great. And precisely this prompts the Jews to point to the unredeemedness of the world. And, on the other hand, the moral quality of life of the Jews is a partial refutation of their concentration on the unredeemedness of the world and shows what redemption could mean, even if it is not motivated by the power of Christ. We think here of the Jewish refusal to treat Christians the way Christians treat Jews.

Does this mean that Christians should give up their belief in Jesus as the Redeemer? On the contrary. The confrontation with Judaism asks Christians to be more authentically Christian. The sole goal of Jewish-Christian dialogue is, as Fischer puts it, that Jews may have the opportunity to become better Jews, and Christians may become more authentically founded in and representative of their Christianity.[55] Christians should thus not leave open the question of the messiahship of Jesus, but they should accept the fact that Jews are leaving this question open, as Dietrich Bonhoeffer said. Christians need to learn to live with the Jewish belief in the "No" to Jesus for the sake of their own Christology. The way Jesus will come as the Christ and the Redeemer of the world will depend on the way Christians represent him in the present. If Christians are not able to bring his redemption to the world today, especially in relationship with the Jewish people, I fear that at the end of times they will not meet a triumphalizing Messiah, but what I would like to call a "weeping Messiah," a Messiah weeping for the injuries and the unredeemedness Christians caused, especially to his own people. Then it could be that not the Christians, with their triumphalistic messianic perceptions, but the Jews will be able to recognize first the Messiah as the Savior of the world.

Notes

1. K. Barth, *Die Kirchliche Dogmatik* (Zürich: Theologischer Verlag, 1960–75) 4–1:671.

2. A. Davies, *Anti-Semitism and the Christian Mind: The Crisis of Conscience after Auschwitz* (New York: Herder and Herder, 1969) 70.

3. D. Pollefeyt, "In Search of an Alternative for the Theology of Substitution," in D. Pollefeyt, ed., *Jews and Christians: Rivals or Partners for the Kingdom of God? In Search of an Alternative for the Christian Theology of Substitution*, Louvain Theological and Pastoral Monographs (Leuven: Peeters, 1998) 1–9.

4. F. Gleiss, *Von der Göttesmordlüge zum Völkermord, von der Feindschaft zur Versöhnung: kirchliche Antijudaismus durch Zwei Jahrtausende und seine Überwinding* (Horb am Neckar: Geiger, 1995) 17–19.

5. R. R. Ruether, *Faith and Fratricide: The Theological Roots of Anti-Semitism* (New York: Seabury Press, 1979) 88.

6. M. B. McGarry, *Christology after Auschwitz* (New York: Paulist Press, 1977) 62–92; A. R. Eckardt, *Elder and Younger Brothers: The Encounter of Jews and Christians* (New York: Charles Scribner's Sons, 1967) 50–55.

7. Ruether, *Faith and Fratricide*, 65, 72, 112, 116, 160.

8. P. Van Buren, *A Theology of Jewish-Christian Reality. 3. Christ in Context* (Washington: University Press of America, 1995) 292.

9. *Catechism of the Catholic Church* (London: Chapman, 1994) 34.

10. D. Goldhagen, *Hitler's Willing Executioners: Ordinary Germans and the Holocaust* (New York: Knopf, 1996).

11. G. Baum, "Catholic Dogma after Auschwitz," in *Anti-Semitism and the Foundation of Christianity*, ed. A. T. Davies (New York: Paulist Press, 1979) 137–50, 142.

12. Ibid.

13. E. Fackenheim, *To Mend the World: Foundations of Future Jewish Thought* (New York: Schocken Books, 1982) 286.

14. "Declaration on the Relationships of the Church to Non-Christian Religions," in *The Documents of Vatican II*, with Notes and Comments by Catholic, Protestant, and Orthodox Authorities, ed. W. M. Abbott and J. Gallagher (New York: Guild, 1966) 666.

15. See *We Remember: A Reflection on the Shoah* (Commission for Religious Relations with the Jews) of March 16, 1998. This is the first Catholic Church document completely devoted to the problem of the Shoah. Three main critiques can be uttered vis-à-vis this document: (1) The distinction between Christian anti-Judaism and Nazi (racial) anti-Semitism is considered too radical and used rather apologetically. (2) The sharp distinction between the Church and the responsibility of individual Christians implies some serious ecclesiological questions. (3) The role of Pope Pius XII remains controversial in the light of the inaccessibility of the Vatican archives on that matter. It is remarkable that the introduction of *We Remember* by Pope John Paul II is much stronger than the corpus of the text by the commission.

16. See J. Parkes, J. T. Pawlikowski, E. Fleischner, A. R. Eckardt, and R. R. Ruether in McGarry, *Christology after Auschwitz*, 72–92.

17. P. Ricoeur, *La critique et la conviction. Entretien avec François Azouvi et Marc de Launay* (Paris: Calmann-Lévy, 1995) 248.

18. J. T. Pawlikowski, "Ein Bund oder zwei Bünde? Zeitgenössische Perspektiven," in *Theologische Quartalschrift* 176, no. 4 (1996) 325–40.

19. F. Rosenzweig, *Der Stern der Erlösung,* Bibliothek Suhrkamp 973 (Frankfurt a.M.: Suhrkamp, 1988).

20. H. Küng, *Judaism* (London: SCM, 1992) 318.

21. P. Van Buren, *Theology,* 199.

22. A. R. Eckardt, "A Response to Rabbi Olan," in *Religion in Life* 42 (1973) 409.

23. H. Küng, *Judaism,* 318.

24. A. R. Eckardt, *Elder and Younger Brothers,* 99.

25. Ibid., 143.

26. J. Moltmann, *Der Weg Jesu Christi. Christologie in messianischen Dimensionen* (Munich: Kaiser, 1989) 45.

27. M. Buber, *Der Jude und sein Judentum: gesammelte Aufsätze und Reden* (Colonia: Melzer, 1963) 562.

28. Ibid.

29. R. M. Brown, "The Coming of Messiah: From Divergence to Convergence?" in M. D. Ryan, ed., *Human Responses to the Holocaust: Perpetrators and Victims, Bystanders and Resisters* (New York: Edwin Mellen, 1981) 205–23, 210.

30. Moltmann, *Der Weg,* 32–33.

31. A. R. Eckardt, *Elder and Younger Brothers: The Encounter of Jews and Christians* (New York: Scribner, 1967).

32. Ibid., 51.

33. Ibid., 55.

34. H. Küng, *Judaism,* 344–45.

35. J. B. Metz, *Voorbij de burgerlijke religie. Over de toekomst van het christendom,* Oekumene 6 (Baarn: Ten Have, 1981) 44.

36. G. Baum, "Introduction," in R. R. Ruether, *Faith and Fratricide,* 15.

37. M. Vogel, "The Problem of Dialogue between Judaism and Christianity," in *Journal of Ecumenical Studies* 4 (1967) 684–99, 689, n. 2.

38. McGarry, *Christology after Auschwitz,* 83.

39. Eckardt, *Elder and Younger Brothers.*

40. Ibid., 345.

41. Küng, *Judaism*, 345.

42. Robert Brown, *Elie Wiesel: Messenger to All Humanity* (Notre Dame, Ind.: University of Notre Dame Press, 1983) 88.

43. S. M. Ogden, *Is There Only One True Religion or Are There Many?* (Dallas: Southern Methodist University Press, 1992) 97–104.

44. P. Van Buren, *Theology*, 204.

45. J. Moltmann, *Der Weg Jesu Christi*, 51.

46. See also R. Bieringer, "The Normativity of the Future. The Authority of the Bible for Theology," in *Bulletin E.T. Zeitschrift für Theologie in Europa* 8 (1997) 52–67.

47. J. Moltmann, *Der Weg*, 50.

48. Van Buren, *Theology*, 281–82.

49. S. Ben-Chorin, *Die Antwort des Jona. Zum Gestaltwandel Israels. Ein geschichts-theologischer Versuch* (Hamburg: Reich, 1956) 99.

50. Eckardt, *Elder and Younger Brothers*, 112.

51. Van Buren, *A Theology of Jewish-Christian Reality*, 198–99.

52. Comité épiscopal pour les relations avec le judaïsme, "Lire l'Ancien Testament. Réflection du Comité épiscopal pour les Relations avec le Judaïsme," in *La documentation catholique* 79(13) (1997) 626–32. Translated by Didier Pollefeyt.

53. J. T. Pawlikowski, *Christ in the Light of the Christian-Jewish Dialogue*, Studies in Judaism and Christianity (New York: Paulist Press, 1982) 106, in D. Flusser, "A New Sensitivity in Judaism and the Christian Message," in *Harvard Theological Review* 61, no. 2 (1968) 107–27, 126.

54. Eckardt, *Elder and Younger Brothers*, 113.

55. E. J. Fisher, *Faith Without Prejudice: Rebuilding Christian Attitudes toward Judaism*. Revised and expanded edition (New York: Crossroad, 1993) 82.

Part Three

Images of Jesus
in Judaism, Islam,
and the Future

• 15 •

Jewish Perspectives on Jesus

S. David Sperling

That a Jewish scholar is asked to provide Jewish perspectives on Jesus is itself a significant matter. First, it demonstrates how far Jews and Christians have progressed in interreligious scholarly dialogue. It is probably fair to say that for most of the past two millennia what little Jewish scholarly attention was directed toward Jesus had to do with countering Christian claims against Judaism.[1] It is probably equally fair to say that within the same period most of Christian scholarship on Jews and Judaism took little cognizance of the forms of Judaism that have developed since the first century, and contented itself with New Testament portrayals of first-century Jews.

Second, to speak of Jewish perspectives on Jesus is to emphasize the difference between our subject and other discussions in comparative religion. What I mean is that it would be odd in the late twentieth century to sponsor a lecture on Jewish perspectives on Buddha. It would sound odd even to speak about Jewish perspectives on Zoroaster, whose teachings influenced Judaism (and Christianity) far more than is generally acknowledged. After all, it is from Zoroastrianism that we received the notions of the last judgment and the resurrection of the body. But the relation between Judaism and Christianity is different from that between Judaism and Zoroastrianism and also different from the relation between Judaism and its daughter religion, Islam. Islam claims a new revelation, but Judaism and Christianity regard the same body of literature as sacred Scripture. The Jews may call it Hebrew Bible or Tanak and the Christians Old Testament, but it is the same collection of writings.[2] As a result, conflicting Jewish and Christian interpretation of Scripture has historically been a fight over the same turf.

For much of the last two millennia the question was not who had the right Scripture but who got Scripture right. Was the Old Testament properly fulfilled in the person of Jesus and in the New Testament writings of the early church, or was it more likely to find its fulfillment in the traditions and interpretative strategies of the rabbis, the founders of rabbinic Judaism? More important, Muhammad, the founder of Islam, came from the outside. In contrast, the central figure of Christianity, Jesus Christ, was born in Bethlehem and lived his life as the Jew Yeshua bar Yosef, which is the way the name Joshua son of Joseph would have been pronounced in first-century Palestine. As a result, the enmity between Jews and Christians often took the form of family infighting, and family infighting is often more acrimonious than fights outside of the family circle. I recall the frequent observation of Morton Smith that triumphant Christian Rome created far more Christian martyrs than pagan Rome ever had. Closer to our own day, the rival Jewish camps of Hassidim and Mitgnadim defamed each other in the eighteenth and nineteenth centuries in language that makes some of the examples to be cited shortly seem quite tame in comparison. If we keep in mind that what we are dealing with is infighting, we more easily understand the bitterness of the Jewish-Christian struggle in the centuries before it became dialogue. Once we realize that we are dealing with a family feud, we will understand how Jesus was the fair-haired boy in the eyes of some of the relatives and the prodigal son in the eyes of others.

Jews, Christians, and Polemics

In a brilliant article published in the *Journal of Biblical Literature*,[3] Luke Johnson demonstrated that the New Testament slander of the Jews was a product of its times. In polemics of Jesus' day Jews used the same kind of defamatory language to attack other Jews with whom they disagreed, while pagan philosophers did the same in their disputes. Unfortunately, for most of the past two millennia neither Christians nor Jews were aware of the historical circumstances that produced the slander. And so Johnson is completely correct when he writes: "The scurrilous language used about Jews in the earliest Christian writings is a hurdle neither Jew nor Christian can easily surmount. It is a source of shame (finally) to Christians, and a well-grounded fear to Jews."[4] As a Jewish scholar, I want to build on Johnson's remarks.

First, Jewish fear was indeed "well-grounded." Scurrilous language could easily be translated into economic and political oppression, forcible conversion, and sometimes into murderous force. Second, Jewish literature of the premodern period is itself not lacking in scurrilous language about Christianity, much of it directed against Jesus. But the Jesus against whom this material is directed has little to do with the Jesus of history. The images of Jesus represent him as the embodiment of the hostile Christian religion; the prodigal who betrayed his own family, the Jewish people, and the Jewish religion.

Here are some examples from the Babylonian Talmud, a product of late antiquity that became the major source of Jewish law and religion in the Middle Ages and in the premodern period. It is useful to observe that external and internal censors removed these selections.[5] Only in the recent decades have they become available in the standard editions. It must be emphasized that we have no (non-Christian) Jewish sources contemporary with Jesus from first-century Palestine.[6]

Jesus Burns His Cooking

The first talmudic selection[7] is an exposition of Psalm 134:14. The psalm verse reads: "There is no breach, there is none who leaves; there is no outcry in our streets" (author's translation).

> "There is no breach." That means: May our group not be like that of King David, which produced the wicked Ahitophel. "No one leaves." That means: May our group not be like that of Saul, which produced the wicked Doeg the Edomite. "There is no outcry." That means: May our group not be like that of Elisha, which produced the wicked Gehazi. "In our streets." That means: May our group not produce a son or a student[8] who burns his cooking in public like Jesus of Nazareth.

Ahitophel, the first of the examples, betrayed his master David by siding with Absalom,[9] David's rebellious son. Doeg the Edomite killed the very priests among whom he had sought purification.[10] Gehazi sullied the reputation of his master Elisha by soliciting gifts from Naaman, whom Elisha had healed, claiming that Elisha had authorized the solicitation.[11] Jesus is depicted as one "who burns his cooking," a euphemism covering various kinds of scandalous behavior.[12] In the above statement Jesus is an exemplar of the son or student[13] who goes bad and publicly disgraces his parents and teachers. For Jews, Christianity was a gross perversion of Judaism, a perversion personified in Jesus himself.

Jesus Is Hanged and Stoned

The same theme is elaborated in the next passage.[14] First there is a legal ruling:[15]

> When someone is to be executed a herald precedes him on the way to the execution. The herald proclaims: "So and So, son of So and So is being executed for committing such and such a crime, and So and So are the witnesses against him. Anyone aware of extenuating circumstances[16] must come forth and make these public."

Commenting on the ruling, an anonymous speaker deduces from the words "on the way to the execution" that it is only at that point that the herald is to make his proclamation, but no earlier. But if that is the case he cannot reconcile his deduction with the following anecdote:

> It was taught: On the eve of Passover they hanged Jesus of Nazareth. The herald preceded the execution of the sentence by forty days, proclaiming: "Jesus of Nazareth is being taken out to be stoned because he practiced sorcery and led Israel into worship of false gods. Anyone aware of extenuating circumstances must come forth and make them public." But no such circumstances were found and he was hanged on Passover eve. Ulla (a 4th century Babylonian scholar) said: "Why

should you think that we should seek extenuation? Jesus of Naza-reth led Israel into worship of false gods, and Scripture (Deut. 13:9) prohibits even seeking extenuation."

Ulla's objection is answered:

Jesus was different. He (merited special treatment) because he was related to the royal family.

This anecdote has some interesting features. For example, the date of Jesus' death follows John[17] and not the Synoptics.[18] Second, Jesus needs to be hanged[19] because that Christian tradition is well known to the Jew, and it fits the Roman technique of crucifixion as well. But he needs to be stoned because sorcery and leading Israel into illicit worship are Jewish crimes pun-ishable by stoning.[20] So, once more we have Jesus the Jewish criminal. What is particularly fascinating is that there is no accusation of blasphemy or of pretending to be Messiah or king of the Jews. Indeed his royal blood is acknowledged. This late Talmudic tradition views Christianity as *abodah zarah,* the worship of false gods. Jesus is not a sectarian Jew or a false mes-siah, but a Jew who advocated the worship of foreign gods in contravention of Deuteronomy 13:6–10:

If your brother, the son of your mother, or your son, or your daughter, or the wife of your bosom, or your friend who is like your very self, entices you secretly, saying, "Let us go serve other gods, which neither you nor your ancestors have known," ... you shall not consent to him, nor listen to him, neither shall your eye pity him, neither shall you spare or conceal him. But you shall surely kill him. Your hand shall be first upon him to put him to death, and afterwards the hand of all the people. You shall stone him to death, because he has sought to thrust you away from the Lord your God.

Jesus Boils in Feces

A third talmudic example is a bit more elaborate:[21]

Onqelos son of Kalonikus was the nephew of Titus (who destroyed the Jewish temple in 70 C.E.). But Onqelos wanted to convert to Judaism. So he raised the ghost of Titus out of hell and asked him: "Who is im-portant in this world?" Titus answered: "Israel." "Shall I join them?" asked the nephew. Titus answered: "They have many laws and you won't be able to observe them all.[22] Go oppress them and you will prosper." Onqelos then said: "What is your punishment?" He an-swered: "What I brought upon myself. Every day I am burned and my ashes are scattered on the seven seas." Onqelos then raised Bal-aam and asked him: "Who is important in this world?" He answered: "Israel." He asked: "Shall I join them?" He answered: "Seek not their good or welfare ever" (Deut. 23:7). Onqelos then said: "What is your punishment?" He answered: "I boil in semen." Onqelos then raised Jesus of Nazareth. He asked him: "Who is important in this world?" He answered: "Israel." He asked: "Shall I join them?" He answered: "Seek their welfare, not their punishment. Whoever strikes them might as well strike the apple of his own eye."[23] Onqelos then said: "What is your punishment?" He answered: "I boil in feces." For the master taught, "Whoever scoffs at the word of the sages is punished (in hell) by boiling in feces."

The story is followed by an anonymous observation:

See how much better is a Jewish sinner than a heathen prophet.

In other words, the heathen prophet can never be expected to seek Israel's good and welfare, but even a wicked Jewish sinner like Jesus might be so expected.

Scandalized as we might be by the image of Jesus' torture in hell, he comes off better than the other two perceived enemies of the Jews; according to the Bible it was Balaam who had advised the Moabites to seduce innocent Israelite males and then after they had had sex, to entice them into the worship of foreign gods,[24] hence the punishment in boiling semen. Titus, as we have seen, burned the Jewish temple and so was punished by being himself burned. He also erected an arch in Rome that depicted his troops looting the temple. The arch bears the inscription Judaea Capta. Compared to these archfiends, Jesus, who scoffed at the words of the sages, is relatively benign.

Jewish Poetry against Christian Persecution

In the Middle Ages the lot of the Jew in Christian Europe, although not the unmitigated disaster depicted in popular treatments of Jewish history, was often insecure. Some of medieval Jewish misfortune was inflicted in the name of Jesus and the Christian religion. The Jewish communities of the Rhineland in particular suffered much violence during the Crusades[25] despite the efforts of some high-ranking leaders of the church to protect the Jews. There was also the infamous blood libel according to which Jews were believed to kill Christian boys, much as they had killed Jesus, and to use the blood in Jewish ritual.[26] In many of the violent attacks upon the Jews, members of the Jewish communities were forced to convert to Christianity. Medieval Jewish liturgical poetry responds to these events by heaping scorn on Christian worship and on the figure of Jesus, often interweaving biblical verses ironically in order to heighten the effect. The following lines commemorate the massacres in Speyer. Written by Rabbi Judah bar Kalonymous, they urge the Jews to keep their faith and not to succumb to the false religion of Christianity. The following free translation attempts to capture the simple rhyme of the original.[27]

> I answered thus to my tormentor,
> I forsake not my defender.
> No bastard the congregation of the lord shall enter.[28]
>
> A molten image[29] in his grave is he,
> can a rotten corpse a symbol be?
> One cursed by God hung on a tree.[30]
>
> Cut off and hanged on the tree no less,
> one brought to the pit[31] shall I confess,
> and serve his strange ungodliness?
>
> Buried and sealed in a tomb defamed,
> "rotting bones" was this one named;
> if I worship him by God I'm shamed.
>
> My soul and heart and guts compel,
> my thought on God alone to dwell,
> my loyalty I shall not sell.
>
> Though you slay me it won't matter,
> though my body you may shatter,
> I serve the God of my father.
>
> In him I trust though I be slain,[32]
> his covenant with me will still remain.
> One God not two, my faith not vain.

There is much more to this poem that I am not citing. I am not citing Rabbi Judah's sense of tragedy nor his prayerful words in which he urges God to remember his fallen martyrs. I cite Rabbi Judah's attacks on Jesus and Christianity for another purpose. Rabbi Judah refers to the live Jesus as a "bastard" who "cannot enter the congregation of the Lord" But more important, the dead Jesus is really dead. Ironically echoing Paul's use of Deuteronomy, Rabbi Judah refers to Jesus cursed, and hanged on a tree. He is no more than rotting bones. He is not a god, for there is only one, and it is that God whose covenant with the Jews has not been superseded by Christianity.[33] Christian readers may find Rabbi Judah's words offensive, and indeed they are, but the following point must be made: The poem was written in Hebrew, not in the German vernacular spoken by both Jews and Christians. The poem is addressed to a Jewish audience, a Jewish audience that might be tempted to think that the success of the deadly mob was due to what the mobsters said, namely that it was a punishment for the Jewish rejection of Jesus. By denying the resurrection of Jesus and the divinity of Jesus, Rabbi Judah closes off a significant option. Yes, perhaps the God of the Jews had punished the Jews of Speyer for their sins, but the rejection of Jesus was not one of them.

Jesus in Jewish and Christian Scholarship

The phenomenon of Jews attempting to take Jesus seriously without converting to Christianity is one of the salutary elements of modernity. Sometimes the attempts have not lacked humor. Isaac Mayer Wise, the nineteenth-century Reform rabbi and founder of my home institution, Hebrew Union College,[34] was a man who believed in the spirit rather than the letter of Jewish law, and in the application of biblical tenets sought to promote social justice. His work on Jesus depicted him also as a man who believed in the spirit rather than the letter of the law and one who applied biblical tenets to promote social justice; in other words, Wise saw Jesus as a nineteenth-century American Reform rabbi.

Fortunately, neither Jews nor Christians are compelled any longer to portray Jesus in our own images. We are no longer limited to contrasting a static pharisaism or "normative" rabbinism with a static New Testament. Classical Christianity and Classical Judaism can now be studied as products of an extremely diverse religious situation in Roman Palestine and the Jewish diaspora. Thanks to such archaeological discoveries as the Dead Sea scrolls, the Nag Hammadi library, and the refined methods of scholarship in New Testament and rabbinic literature, we know more about the complex histories of formative Judaism and Christianity than we ever have.

Luke Johnson demonstrated in the essay with which we began that a significant desideratum of contemporary scholarship is to place the adversarial histories of Judaism and Christianity in historical context. When controversies and armed conflicts can be seen as products of their time, they no longer have to be eternal. If we can apply contextual historical scholarship to deepen our understanding of each other, and disseminate that knowledge on a popular but academically responsible level[35] within our respective faith communities, it can only be to the good.

Notes

1. Very few Jews read the New Testament, and certainly not systematically. For a notable exception see *Sefer Nitsahon Yashan: The Jewish Christian Debate in the High Middle Ages*, a critical edition of the Nizzahon Vetus with introduction, translation, and commentary by David Berger, text in Hebrew and English (Philadelphia: Jewish Publication Society, 1969). The Hebrew term *Nizzahon/Nitsahon Yashan*, means "old debate."

2. We omit the Apocrypha from consideration. We also leave discussion of those Christian groups who rejected the Old Testament for another occasion.

3. Luke T. Johnson, "The New Testament's Anti-Jewish Slander and the Conventions of Jewish Polemic," *JBL* 108 (1989) 419–41.

4. Ibid., 419.

5. The balance of power was such that Christians never felt compelled to censor homologous anti-Jewish material in Christian literature.

6. The famous "testimony" in Josephus *Antiquities* 18:3.3 (par. 63) can hardly be completely genuine, and is, in any case, over a half century later than the crucifixion.

7. Babylonian Talmud Berakot 17b.

8. The master-disciple relationship exhibited some of the features of the father-son relationship, replacing the relationships among members of the biological family. In certain cases, the obligation of the disciple to serve the master took precedence over the obligation of the same disciple to serve his own father. See, e.g., Mishnah Baba Mesia 2:11; Mishnah Keretot 6:9; cf. Matt. 12:46–50; Luke 14:25.

9. See 2 Samuel 15–17, especially 2 Sam. 15:31.

10. 1 Sam. 21:8; 22:18.

11. 2 Kings 5:20–27.

12. See Babylonian Talmud Sanhedrin 103a.

13. Traditions from the Talmudic period through the Middle Ages depict Jesus as a renegade student of Joshua b. Perahiah. See J. Naveh and S. Shaked, *Amulets and Magic Bowls: Aramaic Incantations of Late Antiquity* (Jerusalem: Magnes, 1985) 162. This anachronistic connection between Jesus and Joshua b. Perahiah was probably due to their identical names, and to the association of both men with magical healing and exorcism.

14. Babylonian Talmud Sanhedrin 43a.

15. Mishnah Sanhedrin 6:3.

16. Literally: "anyone who can demonstrate merit for him."

17. John 19:14.

18. It is unlikely that many Jews in late antiquity read either John or the Synoptics. In all likelihood their information would have come from Christian preaching, dialogues with Christians, or from relatives and friends who had converted to Christianity.

19. The Hebrew verb employed here is *talah,* which in biblical Hebrew refers to hanging someone on a tree after he has been executed. See, e.g., Deut. 21:22. In Mishnaic Hebrew *talah* could be replaced by *salab,* "crucify." Cf. Paul's citation of this verse in Gal. 3:13. See further A. Bendavid, *Biblical Hebrew and Mishnaic Hebrew,* text in Hebrew (Tel-Aviv: Mahbarot le-Sifrut, 1967) 366.

20. Talmudic sources generally attributed much more jurisdiction to Jewish law than was actually the case during the Roman period. There is very little evidence, for example, for the Sanhedrin, the alleged supreme autonomous institution of the Jews of Palestine during the Roman and early Byzantine periods. See D. Goodblatt, "Sanhedrin," *Encyclopedia of Religion,* ed. Mircea Eliade (New York: Macmillan, 1987) 13:60–63 (with literature). The above talmudic source, although devoid of historical value, has no problem with Jewish participation in the execution of Jesus, unlike modern Jewish historiography. Two factors were operative: First, the rabbis believed that Jesus deserved his punishment. Second, whenever possible, the rabbis of late antiquity extended the theoretical applicability of Jewish law.

21. Babylonian Talmud Gittin 56b–57a.

22. Cf. Gal. 5:3.

23. See Zech. 2:12

24. Num. 31:16.

25. Perspective is important. Muslims recall how the Crusades were directed primarily against them. Jews recall, accurately, how they secondarily became a target in Europe. But aside from professional historians most people forget about the Fourth Crusade in 1204, which was directed successfully against the Christians of Byzantium; and perhaps about the "crusade" against the Albigensians of southern France (1209–29).

26. Despite the fact that the blood libel was vociferously denounced by Pope Gregory X (1271–76), it continued to be applied to Jews for centuries.

27. The translation is based on the text published by A. Habermann, *Gezerot Ashkenaz we-Sorfat* (Jerusalem: Rabbi Kook Institute, 1945).

28. Deut. 23:2.

29. And thus a forbidden object of worship according to the second commandment (Exod. 20:4–5).

30. Deut. 22:23, and see above.

31. Biblical Hebrew *bor,* "pit," regularly refers to the grave or the underworld. See, e.g., Ps. 30:3, 9; Isa. 38:18.

32. Job 13:15.

33. Contra Heb. 8:13.

34. The College is the first school in history for the training of rabbis to have a regular professorship in New Testament.

35. An excellent example is Samuel Sandmel, *We Jews and Jesus* (New York: Oxford University Press, 1973).

• 16 •

Jesus in Islam

F. E. Peters

To speak of Jesus in Islam is to plunge immediately into an enormous paradox. Jesus of Nazareth, the person regarded as the Son of God by the Christian church, reappears emphatically and often in the Qur'an as a prophet.[1] There are signs that some of Jesus' own contemporaries may also have thought of him as such (Matt. 16:14). But to regard Jesus as merely a prophet in the seventh century of the Christian era was clearly a degradation of status, and as such it has generated a polemical tension between Muslims and Christians over the centuries. There is no indication, let me stress, that Muhammad himself viewed Jesus with anything other than awe and respect; indeed, the Prophet of Islam invoked the Prophet of Nazareth to define and support his own call. But if Muhammad relied on the paradigms of Moses and Jesus in furthering his own mission, his followers had no need of such. In Muslim eyes Muhammad far outshines all those previous messengers. That is, Muhammad's prophetic paradigms have been replaced by Muhammad himself. Thus today there is no cult of Jesus among Muslims—Islam recognizes no intercession with God, not even Muhammad's—and the cult of saints, the "friends of God," as the Muslims call them, is officially condemned by the religious authorities, if not by the religious culture. Jesus is part of Islam's *Heilsgeschichte,* but he is not an effective element in Muslim religious sensibility.

Let me properly begin, then, by making a distinction between the Jesus we find in the Qur'an, which reflects how he appeared to, or was understood by, Muhammad, and Jesus in Islam, how Jesus of Nazareth has been regarded in the community of Muslims. These latter amount to somewhere in the vicinity of a billion souls, give or take a few, but a great many people nonetheless. If we add to this calculus the fact that the enterprise we reify as Islam has been in existence for some fourteen centuries, the folly of attempting to say what Muslims think, or thought, about Jesus becomes manifest. Let us settle then for something more modest, the original portrait of Jesus, a sketch really, of Jesus as it is presented in the Qur'an, and how the details of that portrait were painted in by the earliest generation of Muslims.

The Qur'an

A few words of orientation are needed to begin with. The Qur'an is the collection of Muhammad's pronouncements over the course of the twenty-two years of his prophetic calling. For Muslims these are no less than the words of God; for the non-Muslim historian they are an authentic record, the *ipsissima verba,* no less, constituting Muhammad's public discourse first at the shrine-center Mecca and then, from 622 until his death ten years later, at the oasis of Medina. Formally, however, these are all pronouncements, naked kerygma without benefit of covering narrative; the Qur'an is in fact not a German invention but a real, flesh and blood Q, unframed aphorisms that have been set out in 114 *sûras* or chapters. These latter divisions are not of Muhammad's own making, however, and many of the *sûras* are unmistakably composite, that is, one or more independent pronouncement pericopes have been assembled as a single *sûra.*

Nor are they presented in chronological order. The *sûras* in the standard Qur'an are arranged generally in order of their decreasing length and not in the order of their pronouncement or revelation. For the true scripturalist believer this probably makes little difference since the words of God are entirely and simultaneously true and so unfold like a Möbius strip or a continuously repeated fugue. But for the historian this reshuffling of the pronouncements, whose rationale is still unknown to us, presents a grave disability. The historian must inevitably regard the Qur'an, or any other Scripture, as a privileged view of the mind of the author or editor rather than as an unfolding of the thoughts of God. Thus, the loss of the original chronology inhibits our tracing the growth of an idea or of a concept, newer or fuller understandings, or, indeed, changes of mind or perspective on the part of Muhammad. The Qur'an is patently filled with widely differing attitudes toward everything from the use of force to the consumption of wine and the hours of prayer, as well it might be since it presents the thoughts of a man whose public ministry covered twenty-two years. During that time, Muhammad went from a hesitant prophet and fearful preacher in a one-horse shrine town to the thunderously successful head of a burgeoning empire in western Arabia. Muhammad knew something about Jesus and the Jews when he was a forty-year-old with two strikes on him in Mecca, but he knew much more when he was sixty and batting .400 at Medina.

Both Muslims and non-Muslims have addressed, albeit for different reasons, the question of the order of the *sûras* of the Qur'an, and they have come up with a provisional solution. It is possible, both groups agree, to assign the various *sûras* to distinct periods of Muhammad's career, to his early, middle, or late period at Mecca, for example, and even, somewhat more boldly and much less convincingly, to arrange the individual *sûras* in each group in a plausible chronological order. Thus, it is possible, in spite of the editors who assembled the *ne varietur* text of our present scrambled

Qur'an sometime about 650 C.E., some twenty-odd years after Muhammad's death, to trace Muhammad's thinking about the intriguing Isa ibn Maryam.

Why Jesus Is in the Qur'an

But before we examine the Qur'anic portrait, it may be worthwhile explaining why Jesus is in the Qur'an in the first place. The reason is rather straightforward. From the outset Muhammad seems to have understood his mission as the continuation and, as his confidence grew, as the fulfillment and culmination of God's providential plan for mankind. Man had been sinful from the beginning, and God in compassionate response dispatched to humankind a series of prophets to warn them of the eventual consequences of resisting his will. What God required was submission (in Arabic, *islâm*), an acknowledgment of God as creator and humankind as his creature. But humankind was stiff-necked and resistant; they persecuted God's envoys to their own eventual sorrow. Now God in his mercy had sent the last of his prophets, Muhammad, with the final version of his call to submission. But Muhammad's audience was resistant as well, and for their benefit the Qur'an often rehearses the history of the earlier prophets and the exemplary punishments visited upon those who resisted them.

Though the tales of a few of those prophets are drawn from Arabian lore, by far the majority of them are well-known biblical figures ranging from Adam and Abraham and Moses to David and Solomon; oddly, however, none of what we call the Major or Minor Prophets is mentioned in the Qur'an. But Jesus is, and so is John the Baptist. All of them were venerable and venerated figures for Muhammad, but three are signaled for special attention. Abraham is the prototype "submitter" (in Arabic, *muslim*), since he was the first of fallen mankind to acknowledge the One True God. Indeed, Muhammad came to insist that what he was preaching was nothing less than the "religion of Abraham," a pristine monotheism that antedated both Judaism, which began with Moses and the Torah (the *Tawrât*) and Christianity, which had its beginning with Jesus and the Gospel (*al-Injîl*).

We must pause over this *Injîl*, as the gospel is called in the Qur'an, using an Arabic transformation of *euangelion* that may have already been current in Muhammad's time. Muhammad is a convinced scripturalist; the Qur'an proceeding from his mouth, though the word itself means "recitation," he clearly understood was a Book, a Sacred Book like those possessed by the Jews and the Christians. Muhammad, who had probably seen such Books in a liturgical context in the hands of Jews and Christians, was perfectly incapable of reading so much as a line of them; on the face of it, he had certainly never read or even looked into the Bible or the New Testament, nor could he have since there was no Arabic translation of either until late in the eighth century. Indeed, the expression "New Testament" never occurs to Muhammad; Qur'anic references to Christian Scripture are always to an *Injîl*, are always in the singular, and they leave the unmistakable impression that Muhammad thought of the Christian Scripture as a book, a single book, given by God to Jesus, much as the Torah had been given to Moses and the Qur'an "sent down" to Muhammad.

Some Christians did in fact have a single "gospel," the harmonized Syrian text called the *Diatessaron* that is attributed to the second-century Tatian. It is not impossible that Muhammad had that in mind. But, since he seems not to have known that the Gospels were *about* Jesus and not something revealed *to* him, it is equally plausible that in referring to a singular *Injîl*, he was merely inferring that the "gospel" had to be like the Jews' Torah, a copy of which he had almost certainly seen in the possession of the Jews of Medina. His inference may have stretched somewhat farther, however. Muhammad must have been aware of the Christian claim that Jesus' coming had been foretold in the Jewish Bible; surely that was the reason why the Qur'an asserts more than once that Muhammad's own prophetic mission was foretold in both the *Tawrât* and the *Injîl*.

Nobody questioned that assertion in Muhammad's own day, when knowledge of such matters was thin indeed, but later Muslims had to answer importunate questions of Christians on the exact location of the gospels' prediction of a coming "Ahmad" (Sûra 61:6), as well as an explanation for the Qur'an's understanding that there was only a single gospel. The answers were various, including an attempt to find a predictive text in the gospels—John 15:23, with its reference to a coming Paraclete, was a popular candidate—but there was at hand a far simpler retort that would answer both objections, namely, that the Christians, like the Jews (Sûra 3:72), had tampered with their Scriptures; they had corrupted the single *Injîl* into four Gospels and they had of course removed all references to the prophet to come.

The Style of the Qur'an

Before we look at what the Qur'an actually says about Jesus, it is important to have some sense of Qur'anic discourse. The style of the Qur'an is extraordinarily difficult. As already remarked, its pronouncements are often put forward as part of a flow of ideas that more often than not appear to be linked only by free association, and whose stops and starts are signaled by nothing more than an abrupt shift in the rhythm or rhyme scheme; they do not, in any event, come framed within a narrative that might help us in parsing them. There are no markers of time, place, or even personality to help us understand what is being said, to whom, and why. Beyond that, the shapes of the utterances themselves are sometimes vatic, often apophatic, and they expect the listeners—the Qur'an was, after all, delivered orally in the first instance—to grasp what now strike us as extremely fugitive allusions. Pronouns float through the discourse without antecedent. God is often the apparent speaker (sometimes in the singular, sometimes in the plural, sometimes in the first person, sometimes in the third); but there are

sudden shifts of subject and the frequent introduction of "They say...,"
which we know must refer to an individual or a group that is talking back
to Muhammad, but unfortunately off-mike.

The Story of Jesus in the Qur'an

The story of Jesus is not, then, told in any consecutive form, but he is referred
to often and sometimes in detail, particularly in the later *sûras* from Medina.
There is a quite particular reference to his mother Maryam, who is not
only the only female referred to by name in the Qur'an, but is mentioned
more often here than in the entire New Testament. Before her birth, Mary's
own mother, who is identified merely as the wife of 'Imran—this latter is
also given as the name of Moses' father; there is some reason to believe
that Muhammad may have confused Miryam, Moses' sister and Maryam,
Jesus' mother—vowed that her child would be a consecrated offering to
God. There was disappointment when that child turned out to be a girl, but
her mother nonetheless asked for God's protection from Satan for her and
her offspring.

When Mary had grown to maturity, the priest Zechariah was chosen
by lot to be her guardian. Mary was raised in the Temple, and whenever
Zechariah went into the sanctuary, he found that she had food that she
claimed had been supplied by God (Sûra 3:33–7:44). Zechariah's own role is
enhanced when he asks God to provide him with an heir. He is incredulous—
he is struck dumb for his disbelief—when he is told that despite his advanced
age and his wife's barrenness, he would have a son (Sûra 3:38–41 and 19:2–
15). That son is John the Baptist. Yahya, as he is called in the Qur'an, is
eulogized, but there is little about his life or mission.

The story of the Annunciation is told twice in the Qur'an (Sûra 19:16–
22; 3:42–47). In one account it is said to have occurred through "angels"
when Mary had withdrawn toward the east and was concealed by a curtain
or screen. Mary was told that God had chosen her and made her pure and
preferred her above all the women of creation. She was given good tidings
of a word from God whose name was the Messiah, Jesus Son of Mary; he
would be illustrious in the world and in the hereafter. In the other version
the news is said to have been announced by God's Spirit "who took the form
of a perfect man" and who reassured the frightened Mary that he was only
a messenger sent from her Lord in order to bestow on her a pure boy. Mary
asked how she could have a son since she had not been unchaste. According
to one version, she received the reply that God creates what he wills by
simply decreeing it. According to the other, she was told that it was easy
for God and that her son would be made a sign for mankind, a mercy from
God, and a thing ordained. In neither of these accounts of the Annunciation
are we told how the conception itself took place, but elsewhere there are two
brief allusions to God's breathing into Mary of his Spirit (Sûra 21:9; 66:12).

The Muslim commentators accepted, in any event, a virginal conception and birth.

When Mary had conceived, she withdrew to a distant place, perhaps a reference to Bethlehem, as it was later thought. There she was driven by the pangs of childbirth to the trunk of a palm tree and she wished that she were dead and forgotten. A voice "from beneath her"—the allusion is obscure—told her not to grieve but to drink from the rivulet that her Lord had placed there and to eat the ripe dates that would fall upon her when she shook the tree (Sûra 19:22–25; cf. 23:50). Mary was instructed not to speak to anyone. She then brought the child to her own folk who expressed their stunned amazement at what must have seemed her immorality, addressing her as "sister of Aaron" and reproving her by pointing out that her father had not been a wicked man nor had her mother been a whore. She pointed to her newborn and the infant Jesus spoke to them in her defense, asserting that he was God's servant, that God had given him the Scripture and had appointed him a prophet. He said that God had made him blessed wheresoever he was and had enjoined upon him prayer and almsgiving for the duration of his life. Finally he declared that peace was upon him on the day of his birth, the day of his death, and the day of his being raised to life (Sûra 19:26–33).

The Qur'an has little to say about Jesus' teaching, although at the Annunciation Mary was told that he was destined to speak to mankind in the cradle and also when he was of mature age (Sûra 3:46). To perform his task he was strengthened by the Holy Spirit and given signs (Sûra 5:110; 2:87) and God taught him the Scripture and wisdom and the Torah and the gospel (Sûra 3:48; 5:110). Jesus attested the truth of what was in the Torah (Sûra 3:50; 5:46; 61:6), though he also made lawful some of the things that were forbidden to the Children of Israel in his day (3:50; cf. 3:93). He came to them with wisdom and made plain to them some of the things about which they were in disagreement (Sûra 43:63). He enjoined on them fear of God and obedience to himself. The main thrust of his message was that God was his Lord and their Lord and that to worship God was the straight path (Sûra 3:50-52; cf. 5:72, 117; 19:36; 43:64). Jesus warned the Jews that paradise was forbidden to those who ascribe partners to God (Sûra 5:72), and he cursed those of the Children of Israel who went astray (Sûra 5:78). The religion that he was sent to establish was that of Noah, Abraham, Moses, and, subsequently, of Muhammad himself (Sûra 33:7; 42:13). The gospel that was bestowed upon him contained guidance, light, and admonition (Sûra 5:46). Like the Torah, which it confirmed, and the Qur'an, which was revealed after it, the *Injîl* contained God's promise of paradise to those who gave their lives fighting in God's cause (Sûra 9:111). And as already noted, the *Injîl* also mentioned the coming of an unlettered prophet (Sûra 7:157), and Jesus himself brought good tidings of one whose name would be Ahmad (or "more highly praised," Sûra 61:6). He summoned his own disciples to be "helpers" in God's cause and they described themselves as those who were "submitted" and who "bore witness" (Sûra 3:52ff.; 5:111; 6:14).

According to the Qur'an, Muhammad was called upon to produce miracles or signs (*âyât*) but he determinedly refused to do so, maintaining that the Qur'an will be his prophetic miracle. But the other prophets produced signs aplenty, and the Qur'an knows of Jesus' miracles, which are summarily listed twice. First, at the Annunciation, Mary was told (Sûra 3:49) that he would be a messenger to the Children of Israel. As a sign for them from their Lord, he would fashion a bird from clay that would become a real bird when he breathed into it; he would heal the blind from birth and the leper; he would raise the dead and he would announce to them what they ate and what they stored in their houses. The second list (Sûra 5:109–10) is given in retrospect when God reminds Jesus of his past favors towards him and his mother. The list is very similar to the first one, but it lacks the reference to Jesus' clairvoyance. Moreover, in reminding Jesus of his favor, God adds that he restrained the Children of Israel from him when the unbelievers among them reacted to his coming to them with clear proofs by accusing him of sorcery, the same charge that is alleged in a contemporary Jewish account of Jesus' death, the *Babylonian Talmud*.

Let us pause here and reflect on matters. The account of Jesus' miracles, like the account of the Annunciation, pulls back, however so little, the veil that covers the religious landscape of Muhammad's world. We can attempt to write the historical Jesus firmly against the Jewish Palestinian background provided by Josephus, Qumran, and the biblical apocrypha. With Muhammad we have only a blank screen onto which to project the accounts of his life, and the Josephus of pre-Islamic Mecca is, in fact, a Belgian Jesuit whose 1924 account of Mecca on the eve of Islam has provided the canvas upon which every subsequent critical study of Muhammad has been inscribed.[2] Lammens's work was based on a close reading of the pre-Islamic poets, but what we hear in the Qur'an of Jesus' miracles, the story of his turning childish clay modelings into live birds, for example (Sûra 3:49), tells us that we are now deep within the world of the New Testament apocrypha, the Eastern Christian world that produced the Infancy Gospels of James and of Thomas, where the same story occurs. The Infancy Thomas in fact spawned out of its Syriac version an only slightly later Arabic version of the same, and though the illiterate Muhammad never read those or similar works, their contents were clearly in circulation even in the religious outback of western Arabia in the seventh century, though in what precise form we cannot say.

But the veil goes back only so far. The account of Jesus' miracles in Sûra 5 ends with a story of the disciples asking Jesus whether his Lord was able to send down a table spread with food for them to eat so that they might know for certain that he had spoken the truth. Jesus asked God to send it down as a feast, more properly a feast-day (*'îd*), for them and those who would come after. God responded that he would send it down but that thereafter he would severely punish any who disbelieved (Sûra 5:112–15). It is an absolutely opaque story. Some Muslim commentators thought it might refer to the Last Supper—"as a feast-day for them" is suggestive—but others thought it must reflect the story of the miraculous feeding of the five thousand. The apocrypha here offer no help. Was Muhammad drawing upon some Christian tradition unknown to us or had he or someone earlier simply garbled a remote evangelical memory? The Qur'an is too far off the beaten literary track for even a guess.

The Qur'an's remarks about the death of Jesus—there is nothing there that even approaches an "account"—is the most problematic of all its views of Jesus. The event is noted in passing on a number of occasions, for instance, when Jesus is blessed "on the day of his birth, the day of his death and the day of his being raised up alive" (Sûra 19:33). This might appear to be a reference to Jesus' execution and resurrection as described in the gospels, but the same is said of John the Baptist earlier in the same *sûra*, and so it seems far more likely to us, as it did to the Muslim exegetical tradition, that the resurrection in question was that of all the dead on the Last Day. By that calculus the mortal Jesus has either already died or will at some future point. But on the Qur'anic witness, it seems quite certain that he was not executed by crucifixion, as the gospels claim.

Muhammad was not interested in disproving the gospel story. Rather, it is the Jews he has in his sights in Sûra 4 of the Qur'an:

... they [the Jews] violated their covenant and disbelieved in the signs [*âyât*] of God, and killed the prophets unjustly.... They denied the truth and uttered a mighty slander against Mary. And they said: "We have killed the Messiah, Jesus son of Mary, the messenger of God." They did not kill him and they did not crucify him, but he was made to resemble another for them.... They did not kill him for certain. But God raised him into his presence.... (Sûra 4:155–59)

The translation "he was made to resemble another for them," or "he was counterfeited for them," which suggests that the Jews mistakenly crucified a substitute, someone who resembled Jesus, is by no means certain. The same Arabic words might equally well yield "but they thought they did." The Muslim tradition has generally preferred the substitution reading and has as usual produced a number of stories to fill in the details, how all his disciples were made, or volunteered, to look like him and the wrong man was chosen, or how Judas was made to resemble Jesus and so got his just deserts. Jesus meanwhile was assumed live into heaven, whence he will return at the End Time to suffer the fate of all mortals.

Our earliest preserved commentary on these extraordinary verses of the Qur'an comes not from a Muslim but from the Christian theologian and heresiographer John of Damascus (d. ca. 750), whose family had served in the Muslim administration and who knew a good deal about the Qur'an and its exegesis. He chides the Muslims for saying that the Jews "crucified his shadow; but Christ himself, they say, was not crucified nor did he die; for God took him up to Himself into heaven because He loved him."[3] Ibn Sa'd, a Muslim exegete and historian who died in 845 C.E., completes the essential picture. "God raised him (to heaven) with his body. He is still alive and will return to this world and will be king of the whole earth. Then he will die like other living beings."[4] There is much more, of course: Jesus' return will signal the End Time and he will be pitted in combat against the Antichrist (in Arabic al-Dajjâl, " the Deceiver"), whom he slays.

This apocalyptic side of the Jesus story brings us to one characteristic of the Qur'anic Jesus that nicely resumes many of our problems in understanding the provenance and even the exact contours of Muhammad's thinking about Jesus. In the Qur'an Jesus is called not only by the matronymic "Ibn Maryam," but also by the title al-Masîh, "the Messiah." Unlike the case of Injîl, where the Qur'an, like the Syrian Christians, had available a transcription of the Greek euangelion, the Qur'an, either by ignorance or by choice, passes over the Greek Christos for the Semitic, and probably Syriac, Masîh for Jesus' christological title.

But if there is a title, what is Jesus' messianic function in the Qur'an? First, it must be remarked that, apart from the notion that Jesus confirmed the Torah that had been sent down before him, the Qur'an recognizes no organic connection between the Old Testament and the New and, as already noted, the very notion of New Testament is missing from the Qur'an. Al-Masîh looks very much like a name in the Qur'an since the Qur'anic Jesus is not the promised Messiah in any recognizable Jewish or Christian sense of that word. Though in his lifetime Jesus was only a prophet, like Muhammad, a warner, he does have, as we have just seen, what can be regarded as a messianic function in the eschaton, when he returns to earth to suffer his mortal death.

There is another eschatological figure on the Islamic landscape, the Mahdi or "Guided One," and it is not at all clear, from either the Qur'an or to the Muslim exegetes of that book, whether Jesus was the Mahdi or whether room would have to be found on that blasted apocalyptic landscape for two champions of righteousness and Islam.

This, then, is in some respects a very full portrait of Jesus, and generally speaking, it is a highly favorable one. In the main, it parallels the gospel accounts of Jesus, but in some respects there are significant departures, as already noted, in the matter of his death, for example, and all that it implied. On that larger issue of Jesus' significance, the Qur'an is firm; Jesus was a messenger and no more. Christians err grievously in calling him the Son of God (Sûra 4:171), and those who make God, Jesus, and Jesus' mother Mary into members of a divine Trinity suffer from grave disbelief (Sûra 5:72ff., 116).

Difficult and Provocative Questions
for the Historian

If we take the Qur'anic portrait of Jesus as a whole, it raises a whole series of difficult and provocative questions for the historian. When we ask, as invariably we must—just as the Muslim commentators must *not*—where this extraordinary portrait came from, there are very few convincing answers. It came from Muhammad's head, obviously, and perhaps we owe this particular combination of ingredients solely to him. It is a tempting hypothesis. Not only does it spare us the charge of reductionism; it also explains why, though we can find some of the concrete particulars in the canonical and apocryphal gospels, there is no version or brand of Christianity that held this particular set of *beliefs* about Jesus. For generations historians have been holding up to the Qur'an the profile now of Monophysite, now of Nestorian Christianity, in hopes of finding a match. Docetists, Tritheists, and Monothelites have all been marched into the lists without uncovering any convincing similarity to what Muhammad thought about Jesus. Many Christian keys seem to fit the Qur'anic lock, but loosely, and the bolts never quite turn. The Qur'an offers us a low Christology, but low Christologies, whether Ebionite or Nestorian, do not require a Docetist ending to Jesus' life, as Muhammad's Christology apparently did. And it is an ending, let me remind you once again, that is directed not against a redemptionist Christianity but at the Jews; the death of Jesus is denied precisely to counter the Jewish claim, presumably voiced by the Jews of Medina, that they had put Jesus to death

Thus we do not have, and probably never will have, a Christian template to "explain" the view of Jesus put forward in the Qur'an. We should not be surprised, perhaps. Our best attested Eastern Christianities are all of the Hellenic stripe, conciliar Christianity, as it has been called, with a profound interest in theology. The vernacular Syrian churches drank from different wells, however. For them, as for Muhammad, religion was a "way" rather than a system, practices rather than dogma. The Qur'an too, for its part, though it seems aware of the doctrine of the Trinity, shows little real interest in Christian theology or in the larger significance of Jesus for Christians. The Syrians professed a low Christology whereby Jesus was regarded as the "Servant of God," a position close to the Qur'an's own. For these same reasons, there are those who have professed to see behind the Qur'an's version of Jesus some sort of Judeo-Christian sect that not implausibly survived into the seventh century out on the Syro-Arabian steppe frontiers. There were Christian tribes all along those eastern *limites*, the vagrant flocks of Eastern monks who dwelled in many of those same remote places. Their vernacular was Arabic, but their *lingua sacra* was Syriac and so too was their religious culture, the beliefs held and exchanged in desert encampments. If Muhammad encountered Christians, as surely he must have, they were almost certainly those same illiterate nomads who have left behind no literary texts, churches, chapels, or shrines, but whose traces may still be preserved in the Qur'an, and through it, have found their way deep into Muslim consciousness.

To resume and conclude: neither Muhammad nor the Muslims after him knew much about Jesus of Nazareth, the man of Galilee of whom the gospels, whatever else they may have had in mind, profess to give a historical portrait. The reasons are simple and direct. Neither Muhammad nor the earliest generation of Muslims who fashioned the construct we call Islam had access to those gospels. And later, after the ninth century, when the gospels were available in Arabic, Muslims declined to read them. First, there is a matter of principle. The Qur'an was understood to complete and perfect the earlier Scriptures. Hence, there is no soteriological necessity of consulting them. This is an end-game position, however. Earlier in his career, when the scoffers had doubted his tales of the prophets, Muhammad urged his listeners to go and confirm his preaching by asking the "People of the Book," the Jews and Christians, whether what he said was so. From Muhammad's day to this, it has been a matter of dogma that the gospel has been tampered with, that the Scripture in the hands of the Christians, and of the Jew too for that matter, is not the authentic one sent down by God. And so they once again decline to read it. And continue to do so.

Notes

1. All translation is interpretation, and one reliable English translation of the Qur'an is M. Marmaduke Pickthall, *The Meaning of the Glorious Qur'an: An Explanatory Translation* (New York: Knopf, 1992).

2. Henri Lammens, *La Mecque à la Veille de l'Hégire* (Beyrouth: Imprimerie Catholique, 1924).

3. John of Damascus, *On Heresies*, ch. 100.

4. Ibn Sa'd, *Tabaqat* I 1:26.

The Global Future and Jesus

Lloyd Geering

The year 2000 formally marked two thousand years of the Christian era. This calendar, however, is a human convention projected upon the planet as a convenient way of measuring historical time. Moreover, it is a Christian convention arising from the conviction that the birth of Christ was a cosmic event cutting history into two—the years before Christ (B.C.) and the years of his lordship over the world (A.D.). Further, it rests on a miscalculation. We do not know what year Jesus was born. If we pay too much attention to the year 2000 we are in danger of being deceived by our own cultural creation, like a spider entangled in its own web.

The Christian calendar was a creation of Christian civilization. But what is the future of Christian civilization? There are many signs that all is not well. Just as the ancient Roman calendar disappeared with the decay of Roman civilization, the decline of Christian civilization may ultimately lead to the adoption of a new and non-Christian calendar for universal use. We could have come to the end, not only of the second millennium, but also of all Christian millennia.

Rapid Cultural Change

We are caught up in a process of cultural change more rapid, more deeply rooted and more widespread than ever before in human history. During the last 150 years our view of the world we live in, our knowledge of human history, and our understanding of the human condition have changed out of all recognition from what they were for all our earlier forbears. This knowledge means we are better placed than they ever were to take our bearings in relation to human history.

Until the last century our Christian forbears believed the universe was six thousand years old; now we are being told it is about fifteen billion years old. They believed all living species were created just as they now exist; we have found good reason to believe that life has been evolving on this planet for about three billion years. They believed that humans were separated from

---

This essay is adapted from my book *The World to Come: From Christian Past to Global Future* (Santa Rosa, Calif.: Polebridge; Wellington, New Zealand: Bridget Williams Books, 1999).

all other species by an unbridgeable gulf; we find that the human species evolved out of earlier prehuman species and it is only because of the quality of the language-based cultures that we humans have slowly created that we find ourselves to be so different from the other higher animals.

Phases of Cultural Evolution

To understand the nature of the process of cultural change we are currently experiencing it is illuminating to see it in the broadest possible context. To do this, it is useful to divide the complex evolution of human culture into three successive phases, which may be called the Ethnic, the Transethnic, and the Global.

Ethnic Cultures

The earliest cultures we know are the Ethnic cultures. They revolved around the welfare and survival of the tribe or ethnic unit. The tribe is held together largely by a commonality of blood and culture. Each such culture contains a common language, a shared view of reality, a shared set of values and goals, and common behavioral patterns, both moral and ritualistic. The strength of tribalism lies in the personal bonds of mutual loyalty which hold the tribe together, give it an identity, endow it with strength and courage to overcome threats, and enable it to survive from generation to generation. In the Ethnic Phase of human culture, tribal identity overshadowed individual identity. The tribal cultures focused their attention on the forces of nature; there was keen awareness of how dependent they were on nature for sustenance and survival. There is much that is commendable in tribalism. It has been essential to human survival, at least until the present, and it still remains at the base of all human cultures to this day.

Ethnic cultures were essentially conservative and found change threatening to their identity and their survival. It is all the more surprising, therefore, that about two and half thousand years ago a great wave of cultural change occurred more or less simultaneously in several different places. It was pioneered by people who began to ask questions about the traditional cultures. We know them as the Greek philosophers, the Israelite prophets, Zarathustra of Iran, the Buddha, the Hindu seers, and Confucius of China. Karl Jaspers judged this time to be a cultural axis that cut human history in two, and named it the Axial Period.

Transethnic Cultures

There was, of course, nothing like a complete break with the past at the Axial Period. Human history does not divide into neat segments. There is always some continuity. The transition taking place at the Axial Period had the effect of creating a new cultural layer over what remained from the past. This new layer transcended the preceding Ethnic traditions and can be appropriately termed Transethnic. It incorporated the Ethnic traditions.

Instead of destroying them, it subordinated them to a secondary place. This new cultural layer is found today in what are commonly called the "world religions," such as Zoroastrianism, Judaism, Christianity, and Islam from the Middle East, and Hinduism, Buddhism, Jainism, and Confucianism from East and Southeast Asia. They spread out from their point of origin and crossed over ethnic barriers.

The three Transethnic traditions that spread most successfully were Buddhism, Christianity, and Islam. By the beginning of the modern era they had carved up the world into the Christian West, the Islamic Middle East, and the Buddhist Far East. They had several features in common. They were no longer primarily concerned, as the Ethnic religions had been, with this world and its basic needs of food, survival, and reproduction. They often devalued the things of this world in favor of a transcendent realm of reality more lasting than this, to which they looked for the eternal destiny of the essential human being. Each developed a dualistic view of reality.

The dualistic worldview had both strengths and weaknesses. One great strength of the Christian dualism was that the otherworld provided an imagined standpoint from which to look critically at this world and to treat it objectively as something humans could manipulate for their own ends. They were free to do this since the sacred elements originally thought to be present in it had been transferred to the otherworld. The great strength of Christian dualism is that the otherworld provided the meaning of this world. It not only explained why this world is finite but it gave meaning to everything that occurs within this world, including human existence itself.

The weakness of Christian dualism was that it devalued this world, as people were encouraged to fasten attention more and more on the otherworld. This world was declared to be a fallen world, destined for final destruction. Humans were taught to see themselves as sinful, worthless creatures, who could achieve nothing of value without the grace of God. Nothing could be expected from this world or from the human species that dominated it. The only lasting reality was to be found in the otherworld.

Over the last five hundred years the reality of that otherworld has been fading from human consciousness, at least in the West. Copernicus, Galileo, and their successors have brought the heavens, the visible space occupied by the otherworld, into this world. The Protestant reformers in one fell swoop abolished purgatory, which in the late Middle Ages had become that section of the otherworld that was of central and urgent interest for personal human destiny. From the Enlightenment onwards the concept of God, around whose throne the otherworld had been devoutly visualized, was coming increasingly under question. The Holy Scriptures and ecclesiastical tradition, on whose authority the otherworld had long been proclaimed, were being increasingly recognized as human in origin and content.

The result of all this has been that Christendom no longer exists. We are nearing the end of the global supremacy of the Christian West. We are even seeing the collapse of conventional Christianity as we suffer the loss of what we long took to be the eternal Christian verities and certainties. We are now entering a post-Christian and uncertain global future. What does this mean, not only for the post-Christian West, but also for the world as a whole?

Global Culture

It means that we have entered a third cultural phase in the history of human-kind, involving a cultural transition just as radical as that of the Axial Period. It may be called the Global Phase, since it is global in its influence and horizon and is already creating aspects of human culture that are becoming universal to the planet. It may also be called the Secular Phase, in that it fastens attention on this world rather than on the otherworld. Global culture is already subordinating the Transethnic traditions in much the same way as they subordinated the Ethnic cultures that preceded them.

It is for this reason that we may see the year 2000 as a critical turning point in human history. It marks not only the end of the Christian Era but the end of the supremacy of Phase Two culture and the beginning of Global Culture. I have sketched our cultural past and its chief turning points to enable us to take our bearings as we now look ahead and try to plan for a worthwhile future.

In the Global Phase of culture we are coming to focus attention on the human species itself, as part of the planetary biosphere. We have become aware of what all humans have in common irrespective of class, race, religion, gender, or age. We have developed a growing concern for human rights. We have come to see that what were regarded in Phase Two as divine or transcendent absolutes are actually of human origin and, however valuable they may be judged, they are to be seen as relative to time and place.

But, just at the point where we are coming to acknowledge how much of the world in which we live has been created through the millennia by the human species itself, the frightening truth is beginning to surface in our collective consciousness that this human world is also a very fragile world. What has taken millennia for the human species to construct can also be destroyed in a very short time. The human species has within it both the capacity to create and the capacity to destroy. We can destroy quite deliberately and often do so, as in warfare. And we can also destroy through ignorance, by gross interference with the planetary ecology on which our life depends.

We now have to take stock of just where we are. It is only in the last 150 years that humans have become increasingly aware of the phenomenon of change as something that permeates the whole of reality. From geology we have come to understand that, in geological time, the earth is continually changing its surface and the physical environment within which life is to be lived. Hard on the heels of the idea of a slowly changing earth came the notion of biological evolution. We had barely enough time to become adjusted to the ideas of evolution and historical development in the distant past before the current process of cultural and religious change began to accelerate. Thus it seems that nothing in the world stays the same. The Buddhist idea of universal impermanence has largely been confirmed. So radical is the current global change that many national and minority cultures are now threatened with extinction and are beginning to take desperate measures to try to preserve themselves.

We can, therefore, no longer take the future of the world for granted, as our forebears tended to do. But neither can we afford simply to ignore the future and stoically await what comes. If there are still different possible futures for planetary life in general, and for human existence in particular, those futures have come to depend increasingly on decisions now being made by the human species. We now have to plan, not only for our personal future, but also for the future of the earth itself.

Globalization

First we must take account of the great new fact of our time, the process of globalization. Although the term originated in economics, it may be used for a much wider phenomenon. Globalization may be described as the process by which all human activity—cultural, religious, economic and scientific—is being integrated into one complex worldwide network. Humans of all ethnic groups, all nations, all cultures, and all religious traditions are being drawn together into one global community. Without our being able to exercise much individual choice, we are becoming part of a global interchange of news, knowledge and ideas; we are increasingly dependent on one global economy, and influenced by an emerging global culture. This is in spite of our diversity, our frequent mutual animosity, and our continuing tribalism.

To a large extent globalization is the product of the Christian West. First, it was in the Christian West that there evolved the enterprise of empirical science responsible for the rapid accumulation of reliable knowledge about the world and ourselves. The German physicist and philosopher C. F. von Weizsacker claimed, in his Gifford lectures on *The Relevance of Science*, that "modern science [is] a legacy of Christianity."

Second, it is modern technology, made possible by that science, which has led to the speeding up of the transmission of information through the printing press, telegraph, telephone, radio, television, and the Internet, and to the speeding up of travel through railways, automobile, and airplane.

Third, it was the activity of Christian missionaries during the nineteenth and early twentieth centuries that spread the expectation of a global world. Of course they hoped to make the whole world Christian; but that is not what is taking place. The Christian mission to the rest of the world had the unintended effect of spreading the process of secularization, which was already occurring in Europe from the eighteenth century onwards. Someone once observed that the first Christians went out preaching the coming of the

Kingdom of God but what actually arrived was the Church. Similarly we may say that in modern times Christians went out to bring the nations of the world into a global Christendom but what has actually arrived is the global secular world.

This means that the global and secular world now coming to birth is evolving of its own accord. No one is planning it; it lacks any intrinsic design, meaning, or purpose. It has given us the freedom to make our own personal choice about what makes our life worthwhile, and to draw upon our traditional cultures just as we choose in order to find our own sense of personal fulfillment. But this has also allowed us collectively to blunder along blindly without any clear sense of global direction. This leaves us in a very vulnerable state.

The traditional cultures of the past, whether Ethnic or Transethnic, evolved to maturity as the collective human unconscious provided for each of them, respectively, an appropriate system of meaning that gave cohesion and a common view of reality. In the Transethnic cultures that system often originated with a founding prophet and was later developed by others, all motivated by the quest for meaning. That meaning was understood chiefly in terms of a spiritual destiny toward an otherworldly destiny. Today, however, we are concerned with the immediate destiny of the human species on this planet.

Prophets of the Emerging Global World

Already voices are being raised by people who may someday come to be acknowledged as the seers, prophets, and philosophers of the emerging global world. They tell us that human technology has been developing so rapidly during this century that it is now beginning to produce negative and destructive results. What we took to be the freedom to explore is now being judged as greedy exploitation. What we took to be the welcome expansion of human power and inventiveness is now seen to contain the seeds of our own destruction. Such voices warn us of a two-fold nemesis looming on the human horizon. First, we humans are becoming a danger to ourselves. Second, we are unknowingly destroying the natural forces of the planet on which all life depends.

We humans are becoming a danger to ourselves simply because of our natural capacity to multiply indefinitely in what we now realize is a finite planet. Globalization is being accompanied, and has been partly promoted by, the population explosion. Due to disease, epidemics, famine, and high mortality among infants and children, world population growth was relatively slow, so that by 1750 it had still only reached about 800 million. All that has been drastically changed by such otherwise beneficial developments as medical science, education in personal hygiene, better sanitation, and the improved economic conditions brought about by the industrial revolution.

Population growth began to accelerate from 1750 onwards. By 1800 the world population had reached one billion, and it had taken some two million years to do so. But by only 1930 it had doubled to two billion. A third billion was added by 1960, a fourth by 1974, the fifth before 1990, and the sixth by 1998. When artificial forms of contraception were coming into common use in the first half of the twentieth century, the debate that took place was pursued purely on the basis of personal morality. Now that global population is reaching the limits of the Earth's sustainability, contraception has become a widespread social concern even more than a purely personal one.

The population explosion also means an increase in human density in those areas of land that are suitable for normal human habitation. This is reflected in the increase in urbanization. In 1800, less than 3 percent of the world's population were living in cities of twenty thousand or more. In the year 2000 about half the world's population are living an urban existence.

The global city could provide exciting new possibilities for humankind, but it also presents challenges far exceeding any that the human species has had to face in the past. The various nations with their burgeoning populations and their diverse cultures are being pushed together rather like the continental plates on the Earth's surface. Just as the clash of these plates is the chief cause of our earthquakes, so we can expect massive cultural earthquakes as the great cultures are forced into closer contact.

Ambivalence in Globalization

There is a strange ambivalence present in globalization. On the one hand, it is drawing all nations and cultures into one complex state of global interdependence, which has the capacity to eliminate the wars of the past and establish a stable global society. On the other hand, it has stimulated a resurgence of both ethnic and religious tribalism, which is causing new pressures, tensions, and hostilities to emerge.

After a long period of dispersion over the whole earth the human race is now being pushed together, whether we are ready for it or not. We find that, with millennia of civilization behind us, there is much primitive tribalism still beneath that veneer. Either we learn how to live in harmony with one another or else the human species goes the way of the dinosaurs. Instead of finding our enemies in other ethnic groups, as in racial animosity, or in spiritual principalities and powers such as the Devil, we humans are just beginning to realize that we are becoming our own worst enemies. We are at war with ourselves.

One of the chief obstacles in the way of global harmony is fundamentalism; it exists in a variety of religious, ethnic, and economic forms. Global society calls for flexibility of thought and practice, for compromise in a spirit of good will; it requires mutual cooperation for the common good. Fundamentalism, by contrast, is socially divisive, calling for absolute blind loyalty to a holy book, a set of fundamentals, or a rigid ideology. Fundamentalists are not open to dialogue or human reasoning; they are so sure of the truth that they readily become fanatics.

We live in a global world and we have a common destiny on this planet, but our decisions are hampered by narrow-mindedness and shortsightedness. The majority of us are so immersed in our personal affairs in our own small part of the world that we are unaware of the sword of Damocles now suspended over our heads—a sword that hovers because of the continuing tribalism that keeps us in a state of war with other humans, and because the very earth on which we live is now issuing its own a set of warnings about the limitations on a human future.

During the last few decades an ever-increasing number of books have appeared, warning that a frightening nemesis now hovers on the horizon as a result of our changing relationship with the earth. They started with Rachel Carson's *Silent Spring* (1966); later came titles such as *The Fate of the Earth* by Jonathan Schell (1982), *The Dream of the Earth* by Thomas Berry (1988), *Earth in the Balance* by Al Gore (1993), and *The Sacred Balance* by David Suzuki (1997).

We are being awakened to the fact that our greatly increased technology, coupled with our rapidly expanding population, is causing great strains on the natural forces of the planet. We are polluting such basic commodities as clean air and water. We are causing rapid destruction of animal and plant species. We are rapidly consuming nonrenewable resources. Above all, we are interfering with the very delicate and complex ecology of the planet. Humankind is not only at war with itself; it is also at war with the planet.

Far from moving into the future in the confidence that the ever increasing economic growth will provide higher living standards for all within the context of a peaceful and harmonious world, we face the prospect of more major upsets and social catastrophes than were experienced in the twentieth century. That was bad enough, with two world wars, genocide on a massive scale, wholesale liquidation of certain classes of citizens, as in Russia, China, and Cambodia, and new diseases such as AIDS.

Salvation and Globalization

What should we prepare for? Humanity's threat to itself and the human threat to the planet that sustains its life suggest a number of possible scenarios of the future that may result. None of these is certain but all are possible; some are probable. They are not alternatives; rather, each can exacerbate the others, so that the cumulative effect could be worse than any one of them. Here are some of them: a thermonuclear holocaust, World War III, the rise of authoritarian dictatorships, mass starvation, pandemics, destruction of the ecological balance, collapse of the global economy, sliding into social chaos.

Can there be a scenario of saving ourselves and the planet? It is ironic that in this secular global age we should be once again speaking of salvation, for that has been a very religious word in the past. Indeed, there is much about the end times in which we live, which is reminiscent of the end times (*eschata*) in which Christianity came to birth. But whereas they looked to a metaphysical deity to save them "from the wrath to come," we know that we have caused our current problems and it is we who have to solve them. Of course there will need to be economic planning at all levels, local, national, and global. But it is not just, or even primarily, a matter of economics as commonly understood. A global society, harmonious both with itself and with the planet, will not be achieved by authoritative planning and direction from the top. It depends on the willing and spontaneous response from people as a whole. For that we shall need to develop a new form of consciousness, global consciousness, and a new form of spirituality to motivate us and draw us into a unity. That is what the religious dimension provided for both Ethnic and Transethnic cultures.

The spiritual dimension of global culture, if it comes at all, will be humanistic in form, because our humanity is what we all have in common and all human cultures have been humanly created. And second, it will be naturalistic in origin and character and not supernaturalistic. It will arise out of a conscious response to the natural forces that shape us and on which we depend.

Yet, as no new culture can start from scratch, the spiritual dimension of this global culture must evolve out of the religious dimension of the many cultures that have preceded it. Each culture must be free to draw from its own past, but always in such a way as to direct it toward the needs of an ecologically sensitive global society. In this regard the Christian heritage is likely to play a leading role, simply because the civilization of the Christian West indirectly contributed to the modern world's coming into being.

Globalization, Humanization, and Jesus

How much or how little of the traditional religious ritual and terminology is retained in transformed religious forms will depend on the readiness of the Christian West to reshape its spiritual inheritance to meet the needs of the new global age. There is no one verbal symbol or concept from the past, such as God or Christ, which it is essential to retain for the spirituality of the global society. All languages and all symbols are humanly created. They have no permanence.

The affirmation of the completely human Jesus in place of the mythical and divine Christ figure (a change which traditional Christians have found very threatening) is actually turning out to be a great gain. It is not the Jesus who was elevated into a mythical heaven who is of relevance to us, but the fully human Jesus who has been recovered in modern times by Reimarus, Strauss, Weiss, Schweitzer, Bultmann, and now the Jesus Seminar. Even though this human Jesus is still largely hidden behind the mythical dress with which he was so quickly clothed, it is he, and not the heavenly Christ, who shared the tensions, enigmas, and uncertainties that we experience concerning the present and the future.

It is the Jesus who could look both appreciatively and also critically at his cultural past, who can inspire us as we in turn look back to a receding Christian past and forward to an unknown global future. It is Jesus the teller of stories, which shocked people out of their traditional ways of thinking and behaving, who can free us from the mind-sets in which we become imprisoned. The Jesus most relevant to us is he who, far from providing ready-made answers, prompted people by his tantalizing parables, to work out their own most appropriate answers to the problems of life.

Modern Old Testament scholars have observed for some time that the Wisdom literature represented the deposit of Hebrew humanism. It was always on the margins of Israelite religion and hence placed in the Writings. It showed little interest in the great themes of the Torah and the Prophets. It was more universal to the human race; it was largely this worldly or secular. It is this stream that has become so relevant for the future of the human race in the modern global world. Now some scholars of the historical Jesus have been finding that Jesus, more than being a prophet, king, or personal savior, was one of the great sages of history. If this were so, it would mean that the modern secular world came into being, by an indirect route, from the long-term influence of the sage Jesus. The rediscovery of this secular sage can continue to shake us out of our complacency, as he did long ago. He can challenge us to think for ourselves and encourage us to face the unknown future with faith and hope.

The spirituality of the global future must be of such a kind that it will be able to motivate people of all religious and cultural backgrounds to stand in awe of this self-evolving universe, to marvel continually at the living ecosphere of this planet, to acknowledge the inestimable value of life, to show gratitude for our human past, to nurture the human potential to love and be loved, to show compassion and selfless sacrifice, to be engaged in the quest for what is true and meaningful, and to accept in a selfless fashion the burden of responsibility now laid upon us for the future of our world and all its planetary life.

In the world to come, we humans shall be dependent wholly on our own inner resources, yet not so much individually as corporately. Whether the global society will ever be fully realized, we cannot say. What we can do individually is to hope for it, try to visualize it, and do our utmost to bring it to pass. Unless we humans are strongly motivated to become a global society, we are likely in the imminent future to suffer horrendous catastrophes that will be of our own making. The realization of the global society will require from the whole of humanity creative thinking, self-sacrificing endeavor of the highest order, and all the mutual good will of which we are capable.

Bibliography

Berry, Thomas. *The Dream of the Earth*. San Francisco: Sierra Club Books, 1988.
Schell, Jonathan. *The Fate of the Earth*. New York: Avon Books, 1982.
Suzuki, David. *The Sacred Balance: Rediscovering Our Place in Nature*. Amherst, N.Y.: Prometheus Books, 1998.

Contributors

COLIN BROWN is Professor of Systematic Theology, Fuller Theological Seminary.

JOHN DOMINIC CROSSAN is Professor of Religious Studies, Emeritus, DePaul University.

RONALD L. FARMER is Dean of the Wallace All Faiths Chapel, Chapman University.

ROBERT FUNK is Director of Westar Institute and Founder of the Jesus Seminar.

LLOYD GEERING is Professor of Religious Studies, Emeritus, Victoria University, New Zealand.

CARTER HEYWARD is Howard Chandler Robbins Professor of Theology, Episcopal Divinity School.

JOHN HICK is Fellow of the Institute for Advanced Research in Arts and Social Sciences, University of Birmingham, England.

CHARLES T. HUGHES is Associate Professor of Philosophy and Religious Studies, Chapman University.

MARVIN MEYER is Professor of Religious Studies, Chapman University.

F. E. PETERS is Professor of Middle Eastern Studies, History, and Religion, New York University.

DIDIER POLLEFEYT is Professor of Theology, Katholieke Universiteit Leuven, Belgium.

JONATHAN L. REED is Associate Professor of Religion, University of La Verne.

JAMES M. ROBINSON is Professor of Religion, Emeritus, Claremont Graduate University.

S. DAVID SPERLING is Professor of Bible, Hebrew Union College, New York.

RICHARD SWINBURNE is Nolloth Professor of Philosophy of the Christian Religion, Oxford University, England.

KAREN TORJESEN is Dean of the School of Religion, Claremont Graduate University.

N. T. WRIGHT is Canon Theologian, Westminster Abbey, London, England.

Index